Going Private in China

GOING

PRIVATE

IN CHINA

The Politics of

Corporate Restructuring

and System Reform

Edited by Jean C. Oi

THE WALTER H. SHORENSTEIN
ASIA-PACIFIC RESEARCH CENTER

THE WALTER H. SHORENSTEIN ASIA-PACIFIC RESEARCH CENTER
(Shorenstein APARC) is a unique Stanford University institution focused on the
interdisciplinary study of contemporary Asia. Shorenstein APARC's mission is to
produce and publish outstanding interdisciplinary, Asia-Pacific–focused research;
to educate students, scholars, and corporate and governmental affiliates; to
promote constructive interaction to influence U.S. policy toward the Asia-Pacific;
and to guide Asian nations on key issues of societal transition, development,
U.S.-Asia relations, and regional cooperation.

The Walter H. Shorenstein Asia-Pacific Research Center
Freeman Spogli Institute for International Studies
Stanford University
Encina Hall
Stanford, CA 94305-6055
tel. 650-723-9741
fax 650-723-6530
http://APARC.stanford.edu

*Going Private in China: The Politics of Corporate Restructuring and System
Reform* may be ordered from:
The Brookings Institution
c/o DFS, P.O. Box 50370, Baltimore, MD, USA
tel. 1-800-537-5487 or 410-516-6956
fax 410-516-6998
http://www.brookings.edu/press

Walter H. Shorenstein Asia-Pacific Research Center Books, 2011.

First printing, 2011.
13-digit ISBN 978-1-931368-22-3

Typeset by Classic Typography in 10.5/13 Sabon MT Pro

To the Memory of Walter H. Shorenstein

Contents

Tables and Figures

Tables

Figures

Abbreviations

ABC	Agricultural Bank of China
AFC	Asian financial crisis
AMC	asset management company
APEC	Asia Pacific Economic Conference
BOC	Bank of China
CBRC	China Banking Regulatory Commission
CCER	China Center for Economic Research
CCP	Chinese Communist Party
CCPB	China Construction Bank
CEWC	Central Enterprise Work Committee
CPPCC	Chinese People's Political Consultative Conference
CSRC	China Securities Regulatory Commission
CWGC	China Worldbest Group Corporation
ETO	economic and trade office
FAW	First Automotive Works
FDI	foreign direct investment
FIE	foreign-invested enterprise
FSB	former Soviet bloc
GDB	Guangdong Development Bank
HP	Hewlett Packard
IC	institutional complementarity
ICBC	Industrial and Commercial Bank of China

IPO	initial public offering
JV	joint venture
MBO	manager buyout
MCS	modern company system
MOC	Ministry of Commerce
MOF	Ministry of Finance
MOFTEC	Ministry of Foreign Trade and Economic Cooperation
MoLSS	Ministry of Labor and Social Security
NAV	net asset value
NBS	National Bureau of Statistics
NDRC	National Development and Reform Commission
NPC	National People's Congress
NPL	non-performing loan
NSSF	National Social Security Fund
PBOC	People's Bank of China
PICC	People's Insurance Company of China
PO	Production Office
QFII	qualified foreign institutional investor
ROA	return on assets
RONA	return on net assets
SAFE	State Administration for Foreign Exchange
SAIC	Shanghai Automotive Industry Company
SAMB	State Asset Management Bureau
SASAC	State-owned Assets Supervision and Administration Commission
SDC	State Development Commission
SDPC	State Development and Planning Commission
SEC	State Economic Commission
SETC	State Economy and Trade Commission
SEZ	special economic zone
SOE	state-owned enterprise
SPC	State Planning Commission
TVE	township-village enterprise
VoC	varieties of capitalism
WFOE	wholly foreign-owned enterprise
WTO	World Trade Organization

Glossary

baozhuang   packaging

chanquan lingdao xiaozu   property rights leading group

danwei   work-unit
duijia   consideration

gaizhi   restructuring
gaizhi zhibiao   restructuring criteria
geren zhanghu   individual savings fund
getihu   individual business
gufenzhi gaizao   transformation of ownership to a joint-stock system
guifan yijian   standard opinion
guoqi gaige, zaiyu zhongshi   SOE reform requires attention
guoyougu jianchi   reduction in holdings
guquan fenzhi   share segmentation
guquan fenzhi gaige   share segmentation reform

hangye xiehui   sectoral industrial association
Houwang   Monkey King
Huoli Erba   Power28

jingmao xitong   economic and trade system
jituan   business group
ju   bureau level

kaohe zhibiao   performance criteria

kekongxing   controllability

kong zhanghu   empty individual account

kui 100 wan, wo qiu yinhang, zhengfu, kui 1000 wan, jiude yinhang qiuwo, zhengfu jiuwo   If the SOE loses only one million RMB, then I have to beg the bank and the government for help, but if the SOE loses ten million RMB, then the bank needs to beg me to repay the outstanding loans and the government will have to come to our rescue

lao, ruo, bing, can   the old, the weak, the sick, and the handicapped

lirun zhibiao   profit criteria

liushi   lost state assets

maidan   pick up the bill

meiyou nengli   incompetence

Neng bu? Buxing, huanren   "If not, then we will replace you with someone else"

quan liutong   100 percent float

renzhi   rule by persons

sannian tuokun   relieving difficulties in three years

sanxian   Third Front

Shanghai Dongli Jixie Zhizao Gongsi   Shanghai Automotive Machinery Manufacturing Company

shehui tongchou zijin   social pooling fund

shenfen   [worker] status

shenpi quan   project approval right

shidian   experimental point

shiye danwei   non-profit government-funded organization

shuzhi baogao   performance report

suoyouzhi gaizao   ownership transformation

xianbao zhiye, zaigan shiye   we need to ensure the security of our own jobs first before thinking about building grand careers

ying zhibiao   hard target

yipiao fojue   priority target with veto power

yong sannian shijian, shi daduoshu guoyou qiye zouchu kunjing   getting most
   SOEs out of difficulties within three years

yusuan nei   within-budgetary

zhengji   political credit

zhengzhi kongjian   political easing

zhongyang qiye   central-level enterprise

zhuada fangxiao   "grasp the large and let go of the small"

ziyuanxing chengshi   city where industry depends on natural resources

zonghe peitao gaige   comprehensive coordinated reform

Contributors

Editor

JEAN C. OI is William Haas Professor in Chinese Politics in the Department of Political Science and Senior Fellow at the Freeman Spogli Institute for International Studies at Stanford University. In 2007 she became the founding director of the Stanford China Program at the Walter H. Shorenstein Asia-Pacific Research Center. Her work focuses on comparative politics, with special expertise on Chinese political economy. Her books include *Growing Pains: Tensions and Opportunity in China's Transformation* (2010), co-edited with Scott Rozelle and Xueguang Zhou; *Rural China Takes Off: Institutional Foundations of Economic Reform* (1999); *Property Rights and Economic Reform in China* (1999), co-edited with Andrew Walder; and *State and Peasant in Contemporary China: The Political Economy of Village Government* (1989). Currently, Professor Oi continues her research on rural finance and local governance in China and has started a new project on the logic of administrative redistricting in the Chinese countryside.

Contributors

YONGSHUN CAI is Associate Professor, Division of Social Sciences, Hong Kong University of Science and Technology. Professor Cai is the author *of Collective Resistance in China: Why Popular Protests Succeed or Fail* (2010).

MARY E. GALLAGHER is Associate Professor, Department of Political Science, and Director, Center for Chinese Studies, University of Michigan.

HAN CHAOHUA is Senior Research Fellow, Department of Economics, Chinese Academy of Social Sciences (CASS). A graduate of the graduate school of

CASS in 1987, Han worked as a research fellow at the Institute of Economics of CASS from 1987 through 2008, and has served as academic secretary in the Department of Economics of CASS since 2009.

SEBASTIAN HEILMANN is Professor for Comparative Government and the Political Economy of China and Director of the Center for East Asian and Pacific Studies, Trier University, Germany. He is a Board Member of the German Association of Asian Studies and Editor of the Internet publication China Analysis (www.chinapolitik.de), which has become a major platform in Europe for disseminating up-to-date research on China's political economy. Professor Heilmann has published extensively on China's political economy, with a special focus on economic policy-making and regulation. Together with Elizabeth Perry of Harvard University, he is Co-editor of *Mao's Invisible Hand: The Political Foundations of Adaptive Governance in China* (2011).

JOO-YOUN JUNG is Assistant Professor of Political Science, Korea University (Seoul). After receiving her Ph.D. in Political Science from Stanford University, Dr. Jung worked as a Postdoctoral Fellow at the Weatherhead East Asian Institute (WEAI) of Columbia University and Assistant Professor in the Department of Political Science of the University of Alberta. Dr. Jung's major field is comparative political economy, focusing on China and South Korea. Her research interests include the economic role of the state, the state bureaucracy, and the politics of institutional reform.

BYUNG-SOO KIM is Assistant Professor of Sociology, Hanyang University (South Korea). After receiving his Ph.D. in Sociology from Stanford University and before returning to South Korea, Kim served as Assistant Professor of Sociology at the University of Missouri. His academic interests include the Sociology of Organizations, Economic Sociology, Social Networks, and Family and Marriage. He has published in *American Sociological Review, Sociological Inquiry,* and *Research in Political Sociology.*

YUE MA is Risk Analyst, Structured Trade and Political Risk Division, QBE Americas. He is responsible for analyzing political and corporate credit risks in emerging market countries. A graduate from the University of Michigan in 2006 with a BA (Honors) in Economics and Political Science, he is currently studying for an MBA at New York University Stern School of Business.

WORAWUT SMUTHKALIN currently works in the Department of East Asian Affairs, Thailand Ministry of Foreign Affairs. He received his Ph.D. in the Department of Political Science, Stanford University.

KELLEE TSAI is Vice Dean of Humanities, Social Sciences, and Graduate Programs, and Professor of Political Science and Director of East Asian Studies, Johns Hopkins University. She is author of *Capitalism without Democracy: The Private Sector in Contemporary China* (2007), *Back-Alley Banking: Private Entrepreneurs in China* (2002), and various other publications.

CARL WALTER is Managing Director and Chief Executive Officer of China Business, J.P. Morgan Chase Bank (China) Co. Ltd. Prior to joining J.P. Morgan, Dr. Walter was Managing Director and Member of the Management Committee of China International Capital Corporation, China's premier investment bank. During his twenty years of working in China, Dr. Walter participated in a number of landmark equity and debt offerings as well as efforts to further open the country's financial markets to foreign investment. He holds a Ph.D. from Stanford University and is the co-author of *Privatizing China: Inside China's Stock Markets* (2006).

JIN (JULIE) ZENG is Assistant Professor, Department of Politics and International Relations, Florida International University. Her research interests include Chinese politics, privatization in transitional economies, international political economy, and international relations in East Asia. She is currently revising her dissertation on privatization in China into a book manuscript.

LU ZHENG is Assistant Professor, Department of Sociology, Texas A&M University. His research focuses on institutional and corporate change in China in general and public firms and China's stock market in particular. He also conducts research on employment practices in the American workplace and on pollution emissions of large American corporations. His recent publications have appeared in the *China Quarterly*, *Research in Political Sociology*, and *Social Science Research*.

Preface

In summer 2006, Jennifer Amyx, Byung-Kook Kim, and I brought a group of leading young scholars to the Walter H. Shorenstein Asia-Pacific Research Center (Shorenstein APARC) at Stanford University. We had in mind an ambitious project to understand corporate restructuring in China, Japan, and Korea, with the goal of analyzing the constraints on corporate restructuring in a way that maximizes comparability. At the same time, we recognized that the set of institutions required to move corporate structuring forward would likely differ in each country. Thus, rather than insist on addressing an identical set of issues, we sought to identify the critical institutions necessary for corporate reform in the three respective countries.

The explicit assumption that frames our investigation and subsequent writings is that successful corporate restructuring requires "system restructuring." Following the lead of the Varieties of Capitalism literature, we focus on institutional complementarities in the reform process. The depth of institutional interdependence varies significantly across each political economy.

Our goal was to produce a collection that brings together cutting-edge research. We sought papers that offer tightly focused theoretical discussions backed up by rich empirical evidence to remedy the existing literature on the political economy of reform in the three cases. This literature often fails to explain variations in the political dynamics of reform over time, and consequently depicts system restructuring as a static process. We asked each author, in telling his or her story, to explain change over time and to address the evolution and sequencing of reform. The papers benefited from insightful comments from invited commentators David Kang, Hong Yung Lee, Alicia Ogawa, Daniel Okimoto, Steven Vogel, and Anthony Zaloom. Thanks also go to Stanislav Markus for comparative insights on Russia.

The participants produced a rich collection of papers, which have gone through many revisions and updates since they were initially drafted for the conference. Our dilemma was whether to produce one massive volume that would include all three cases or separate country volumes based on similar frameworks and organized in parallel fashion around the same core questions. In the end, we elected to publish separate volumes so that they can be used individually to teach in single-country courses or together in comparative courses. This book is the first of the three volumes on the politics of corporate restructuring and system reform in East Asia. Forthcoming in our series are the companion volumes: *Adapt, Fragment, Transform: The Politics of Corporate Restructuring and System Reform in South Korea* and *Syncretization: The Politics of Corporate Restructuring and System Reform in Japan*.

It would have been impossible to complete these volumes without the assistance of a number of people and institutions. Jennifer Amyx was instrumental in organizing and spearheading the conference and in providing the initial set of comments on all the papers for the three volumes. Unfortunately, shortly after she provided her insightful comments, serious health problems forced her to withdraw from active participation in the final stages of the project. We greatly appreciate all of her input and support, and wish her a speedy recovery. We are grateful that Kay Shimizu and Kenji Kushida agreed to step-in for Jennifer and handle the bulk of the editing for the Japan volume. A very special thank you to Eun Mee Kim for graciously agreeing also at a late date to do the yeoman's share of the editing and compilation for the Korea volume, after co-editor Byung-Kook Kim was called away to government service. We are grateful to Nancy Hearst and Jennifer Jung-Kim, who meticulously edited the China and Korea volumes, respectively. Victoria Tomkinson managed the entire editorial process. We also wish to thank rapporteurs Yuen Yuen Ang and Charlotte Lee for providing us with a useful record of the proceedings.

A special note of thanks goes to Byung-Kook Kim and the East Asia Institute (EAI) based in Seoul, which co-sponsored the conference and provided the able administrative support of Hajeong Kim throughout the project. We thank Chairman of the EAI Board of Trustees, Dr. Hong Koo Lee, for his generous support. We are also grateful to our co-sponsor, Shorenstein APARC, and its director Gi-Wook Shin and staff, for generous support during the conference and completion of the volumes. Sadly, we mourn the recent loss of Walter H. Shorenstein and dedicate this China volume to his memory. His enthusiasm and support for a better understanding of Asia will be greatly missed.

Jean C. Oi
Stanford, CA
January 2011

Going Private in China

1 Politics in China's Corporate Restructuring

Jean C. Oi

The problems facing China's state-owned enterprises (SOEs) at the beginning of the reform period in the 1980s seemed almost insurmountable.[1] Naughton notes that at the lowest point "industrial SOEs were losing almost as much money as they were making."[2] As a result, as the Chinese Communist party-state tried to reform its centrally planned economy, one of the most challenging policy questions was how to reform its SOEs. The difficulty was rooted in an ideological conundrum of whether the Chinese Communist Party (CCP) should support a move from public to private ownership of the means of production. If so, what would be the political fallout? Worker unrest and resistance? Loss of regime legitimacy? In the rural reforms China sidestepped the property rights issue by adopting the household responsibility system whereby land ownership remained collective. In the countryside China reformed around the collective ownership of the means of production to "grow out of the plan."[3] Land was distributed relatively equitably and consequently no one was displaced, leading some to dub this "reform without losers."[4]

Reforming China's urban industrial sector has been much more problematic precisely because successful change required the regime to ultimately alter

---

1 See, for example, Edward S. Steinfeld, *Forging Reform in China: The Fate of State-Owned Industry* (New York: Cambridge University Press, 1998).

2 Barry Naughton, "SOE Policy: Profiting the SASAC Way," *China Economic Quarterly* 12, no. 2 (June 2008): 19–26.

3 Barry Naughton, *Growing Out of the Plan: Chinese Economic Reform, 1978-1993* (New York: Cambridge University Press, 1996).

4 Lawrence J. Lau, Yingyi Qian, and Gérard Roland, "Reform Without Losers: An Interpretation of China's Dual-Track Approach to Transition," *Journal of Political Economy* 108, no. 1 (February 2001): 120-43.

the property rights to the means of production, i.e., the state-owned facto-ries. After various attempts to tinker with incentives for managers and workers without making any structural changes, it was clear that the state needed to modify the property rights to its state-owned enterprises and to cut the work-force. Earlier studies had stressed that the localities had an interest in privatiz-ing their SOEs, many of which were mired in losses.[5] Later studies made it clear that although this may be the case, a distinction must be made between incentives to privatize and the ability to act on such incentives.[6] Politics con-strained those who wanted to change the system. If privatization were to be allowed, could the regime survive the fallout from the millions who would be-come the "losers from reform"? As surprising as it may be, when the reforms began, China, long known for providing workers with an "iron rice bowl," had no national social security system and did not have the resources to fund such an institution. Moving from public to private ownership challenged the core el-ements of the socialist ideology and the legitimacy of the Chinese Communist Party that claimed adherence to socialism. Corporate restructuring was a pol-icy nightmare fraught with economic as well as political consequences.

China's Surprising SOE Turnaround

It is well known that China took the less risky political road and es-chewed full privatization. It adopted a series of halfway measures to restruc-ture publicly owned firms so as to minimize layoffs. During the 1980s and into the early 1990s relatively few workers lost their jobs, but firms remained mired in red ink. Little progress seemed to ensue. Many analysts noted problems of corruption[7] and some dismissed China's piecemeal reforms as a recipe for failure.[8]

5 Yuanzheng Cao, Yingyi Qian, and Barry R. Weingast, "From Federalism, Chinese Style to Privatization, Chinese Style," *Economics of Transition* 7, no. 1 (1999): 103–31.

6 See, for example, Guy S. Liu, Pei Sun, and Wing Thye Woo, "The Political Econ-omy of Chinese-Style Privatization: Motives and Constraints," *World Development* 34, no. 12 (2006): 2016–33. Also see Jean C. Oi, "Patterns of Corporate Restructuring in Chi-na: Political Constraints on Privatization," *China Journal*, no. 53 (January 2005): 115–36.

7 On corruption and asset-stripping, see, for example, works by Melanie Manion, *Corruption by Design: Building Clean Government in Mainland China and Hong Kong* (Cambridge, MA: Harvard University Press, 2004); Andrew Wedeman, "The Intensifica-tion of Corruption in China," *China Quarterly*, no. 180 (December 2004): 895–921; and X.L. Ding, "The Illicit Asset Stripping of Chinese State Firms," *China Journal*, no. 43 (January 2000): 1–28.

8 See, for example, Wing Thye Woo, "The Real Reasons for China's Growth," *China Journal*, no. 41 (January 1999): 115–37; Jeffrey D. Sachs and Wing Thye Woo, "Under-standing China's Economic Performance," NBER Working Paper, no. 5935 (February 1997); also Steinfeld, *Forging Reform*.

At the same time that the SOE reforms seemed to be going nowhere, China achieved a record-breaking rate of economic growth. Over the last two decades, unlike the other Leninist systems that undertook reform, China's economy has remained strong and is indeed becoming stronger.[9] This is in spite of the well-known problems such as the high rates of non-performing loans (NPLs) and an ever-troubled banking sector. Much of the growth, especially during the 1980s and into the 1990s, was due to the growth of township-village enterprises (TVEs) and to the rise of a private sector. What is most surprising is that after a very slow start, during the last several years China's SOEs have become stronger.

Not all SOE problems have been solved, but an economic turnaround in China's SOE sector has been achieved.[10] Since the mid-2000s the largest and most important state-owned enterprises—those under central control[11]—have reported large increases in production, profits, and taxes paid to the state.[12] Enough change had occurred that by the mid-2000s China announced that its corporate restructuring had come to a successful end. Many of the worst-performing SOEs no longer exist; they have either been closed or sold. There has been a significant culling of thousands of SOEs, and there are now fewer than 150 wholly state-owned central-level enterprises controlled by the State-owned Assets Supervision and Administration Commission (SASAC) in Beijing. These are mostly the top performers in strategic sectors. Other top performers are owned by local-level SASACs. Privatization, although delayed, has occurred, with millions of workers laid off during the process.

Those who know China well will immediately point out that the change is still limited. Despite the restructuring, the state is still a shareholder, and often the controlling owner, in some of the largest and most important firms. However, the state is no longer the sole owner. This may appear to be a very limited change, but it has relieved the state of significant responsibility with regard to firm funding and problem-solving.

The fact that the Chinese state has managed to solve the thorny economic and political obstacles to corporate restructuring, and in the process

9 As of August 2010, China passed Japan as the world's second-largest economy.

10 See, for example, the special issue of *China Economic Quarterly* 12, no. 2 (June 2008), especially the article by Naughton, "SOE Policy."

11 These are the enterprises under the control of the State-owned Assets Supervision and Administration Commission (SASAC) of the State Council, which is responsible for investment in state-owned assets.

12 News release from a press conference held by the Information Office of the State Council on General Information on Reform and Development of Central SOEs and Development of State-owned Assets Management System Reform, SASAC, December 19, 2006, at http://www.sasac.gov.cn/n2963340/n2964712/3059894.html, accessed September 4, 2010; also Naughton, "SOE Policy."

radically improve performance, raises many questions that challenge existing theories about the requisites for development and reform, i.e., the importance of private ownership.

Although those SOEs that remain centrally owned are in strategic sectors, some would argue that they constitute monopolies and, comparatively speaking, are the better performers. Moreover, the greatly improved economic returns are fairly recent phenomena. Explanations offered so far, often by economists,[13] point to the reduced costs of credit; the profitability of the sectors that remained state-owned; the strict performance criteria applied to managers and the lucrative incentives for good performance; the competition that has been injected within certain sectors; and, of course, the continued preferential treatment of SOEs by the state. Although these provide useful insights into SOE restructuring,[14] many questions remain unanswered. Specifically, how did the CCP manage to cull so many of its original SOEs and undertake extensive property-rights change resulting in so many job losses even though the reforms were politically sensitive and contentious? Why were some firms changed from being completely owned by the state to shareholding cooperatives, whereas others became either listed companies or something in between? Some were completely sold and others were closed down and declared bankrupt. What explains the variation in the forms of China's corporate restructuring? What were the triggers for effective reform? By examining the processes and incentives that shaped the actions of the key actors who determined the outcome of China's corporate restructuring, this volume attempts to answer these questions. This will further our theoretical understanding of the requisites for development and will offer rich insights for policymakers interested in how reform is possible despite limited resources and numerous constraints.

We begin by examining the policy context, identifying what is different about China's corporate restructuring and how China's experience suggests modifications to existing frameworks for understanding corporate restructuring.

Varieties of Corporate Restructuring

In the market economies, corporate restructuring often means restructuring debt and repaying loans. Corporate restructuring is also commonly

13 See, for example, the special issue of *China Economic Quarterly* 12, no. 2 (June 2008).

14 One of the most useful recent works is Stephen Green and Guy S. Liu, eds., *Exit the Dragon? Privatization and State Control in China* (London: Blackwell, 2005).

associated with privatization, which was the most common form of property-rights reform in the former Soviet bloc (FSB) countries.[15] Privatization is usually understood as a one-step restructuring to change the property-rights regime. The assumption is that ownership of the means of production is immediately directly transferred from the state to private hands. State-owned enterprises are presumed to become fully privately owned. However, corporate restructuring does not have to be a single-step process.

Corporate restructuring in China has been carried out as a multi-step process. Forms of restructuring have changed over time and have varied by region and sector. Different ownership forms were accepted according to the economic and political conditions. This may explain the seemingly lack of change in the SOEs until recently. State-owned firms seldom were privatized immediately. Many that eventually were privatized were first restructured into some form of diversified ownership, most commonly shareholding, with the state still holding control. Management of other firms was simply leased, with the state retaining ownership. The fluidity and variation in the degrees of privatization are essential aspects of China's restructuring process. Privatization was only one end of the spectrum of restructuring possibilities.

China's overall goal of corporate restructuring was to diversify ownership, not to privatize. The state sought to divest from being the sole owner of firms, but it did not necessarily want to give up ownership of all firms. This distinction is important because the changes in a number of state-owned firms that are provided in various statistical compilations are misleading. The number of wholly state-owned firms has dropped dramatically. However, not all non-state-owned firms are private. Many are still state-controlled, or at least have sizable state-owned shares. Restructuring in China thus includes more than privatization. To separate privatization from other forms of restructuring, we use the term "corporatization."

In corporatization, there is a partial change of property rights whereby a firm's assets are assessed and denominated into shares. As Walter stresses in this volume, this process, sometimes unprecedentedly, clarified the total assets of the enterprise. Corporatization provided the necessary basis for clarifying and dividing the property rights, but whether the restructuring then moved on to the final step of privatization is a separate matter.

Corporatization travels only part of the way toward privatization by exhibiting some of the characteristics of private firms, but it also is distinct from privatization. In shareholding, a common form of corporatization,

15 See Stephen Green, "Privatization in the Former Soviet Bloc: Has China Learned the Lessons?" in Green and Liu, eds., *Exit the Dragon*, 42–59.

for example, some shares are sold to workers or managers within the firm. These shares then become privately owned by the workers and managers. However, the state often retains the controlling stakes, especially in the larger firms. In a firm that the state decides should remain state-owned, a portion of the firm is allowed to be spun-off as a new firm. Again, some of the owners of the new firm may be private, especially if the firm is listed. However, the parent firm, which is still state-owned, will continue to hold shares, most likely controlling shares. This is an example whereby China allows a mixture of property rights to exist within a single economic entity. There is a state-owned parent with a "privately" held spun-off child. Although corporatization is taking place in all these instances, privatization, in the sense that the firms are completely owned by non-state entities, is not. Corporate restructuring in China includes but cannot be defined as simply privatization.

Market versus State-Led Restructuring

There is a rich comparative literature on corporate restructuring. One of the most influential is the varieties of capitalism (VoC) literature, especially the work edited by Hall and Soskice.[16] The analytical framework in the VoC literature is firm-based. The most important actors are the firms, even though it is acknowledged that actors may include "individuals, firms, producer groups, or governments."[17] In this framework, restructuring is a firm-level decision. These are reasonable assumptions about the market economies that the VoC literature considers—both "centrally managed economies," such as Germany, and "liberal market economies," such as the United States. However, such assumptions fail to hold for firms in countries like China, where the state was the sole owner of most of the firms when the restructuring began. Consequently, different levels of the state—the owners, not individual firms—decided the question of restructuring. As Oi and Han's chapter in this volume documents, state initiation of restructuring has remained constant throughout the reform process. Restructuring is a policy issue for the central state and its agents at the local levels.

Because restructuring is state-led in China, we need to address a set of questions that do not exist in the VoC literature. What are the incentives for the state, especially a one party-state, to restructure, i.e., to give up ownership of assets that were created by and serve as a basis of state power?

16 Peter A. Hall and David Soskice, eds., *Varieties of Capitalism: The Institutional Foundations of Comparative Advantage* (Oxford: Oxford University Press, 2001).

17 Hall and Soskice, eds., *Varieties of Capitalism*, 60.

Earlier studies stressed economic incentives, but profitability may not be the utmost concern to Chinese policymakers as it is to policymakers in the market economies. Might political incentives be stronger in a still state-led economy like China? Do political pressures and targeted campaigns explain the variations in speed and timing across localities?

Transitional Systems and the Lack of Institutional Complementarities

Insights from the VoC literature underscore the need to consider the context and the supporting institutions in which the firms operate. Hall and Soskice's pioneering work argues that each type of political economy has its own set of institutions that are designed to work together—institutional complementarity (IC).[18] Political actors operate in the specific context of the respective country's political economy. The degree to which there are institutional complementarities affects a firm's competitive advantage, and the absence of one or two institutions may prevent a firm from achieving its goals. As a result, the success or failure of a firm hinges on a host of institutions and actors.

The IC framework implies that institutions in differing political economies are likely to be incompatible. Piecemeal institutional change may create contradictions and hinder firm performance. Thus, change is best accomplished simultaneously, with complementary institutions being adopted in tandem. Few would argue with the premise of institutional complementarity; obviously, any institution will perform better when there are strong complementarities. But for policymakers, the political and economic realities often do not allow such wide-sweeping changes to occur all at once.

The problems of change are even greater when a country is in transition from one economic system to another. Should entire systems be imported? Those who advocate the "big-bang" approach in the transition from a planned to a market economy respond in the affirmative. But what if a country does not have the option or want to import entire systems? What institutions should be adopted and how should they be adapted, if at all, to the home country's realities and constraints? Under what conditions does the *inability* to create complementarities still allow reform? By exploring these questions, this volume suggests that we need to change some of the assumptions and broaden the questions that guide research and policy-making regarding restructuring.

18 Hall and Soskice, eds., *Varieties of Capitalism*, 60.

The China case suggests that when the state is in a position to determine the sequence of corporate restructuring, it can mediate the lack of supporting institutions. Among the many puzzles associated with China's successful heterodox model of development is how it has managed to move the reforms forward in the absence of many of the institutions presumed to be necessary to transition to a market economy. The key example is China's lack of a national social security system. How should policymakers handle the millions who will lose their jobs from restructuring?

When China began its restructuring process, fear of worker reaction due to the lack of a unified social security system was a major obstacle that shaped the course of the restructuring and property-rights reform. Nonetheless, reform was eventually achieved. Earlier studies suggest that China moved forward with "imperfect institutions" by taking a series of small steps.[19] In this volume, we flesh out this logic and examine both the sequence and consequences of China's multi-step corporate restructuring. The various chapters examine how the state was able to break the equilibrium and establish a new political economy even though institutions were either lacking or "imperfect."

In some cases, when China lacked the institutions to move forward in its market reforms, it simply imported them. For example, when the reforms began in the 1980s, China lacked equity markets that were needed to raise capital. Thus, China subsequently established stock markets in the 1990s.[20] A common assumption is that listings on stock markets will improve corporate governance and transparency, but this was not the case in China. Institutions require time to be crafted, funded, and implemented, and institutions may also be altered during the process of implementation.

The fate of China's stock markets brings into sharp relief a phenomenon that has existed since China began its reforms – the mixing of institutions from different political and economic systems. The dual-track price system is one of the earliest and clearest examples of how institutions from different political economies could operate side by side, resulting in market prices as well as state-set prices for the same items. China retained the institutions that were part of its centrally planned economy, but it also adopted new institutions imported from market systems. This mixed-economy strategy allowed China to proceed through the transitional stages of reform.

19 Yingyi Qian, "How Reform Worked in China," in Dani Rodrik, ed., *In Search of Prosperity: Analytic Narratives on Economic Growth* (Princeton, NJ: Princeton University Press, 2003), 297–333.

20 Carl E. Walter and Fraser J.T. Howie, *Privatizing China: The Stock Markets and Their Role in Corporate Reform* (Singapore: Wiley, 2003).

However, this did not occur without costs. Much has been written about the opportunities for corruption when there are both market and state prices. The imported institutions were also affected. The chapters in this volume will describe the adaptation of imported institutions to China's political economy and the resultant problems. The state attempts to intervene to either attenuate the problems or to pay the costs of the inefficiencies created by the lack of institutional complementarities. These are some of the many questions addressed in the chapters that follow.

Rethinking Institutional Complementarities: Contributions to This Volume

China's reform process, to the degree that it has been successful, stems largely from the willingness of the regime to be flexible and its ability to create ad-hoc, temporary solutions to accommodate the existing political and economic constraints. This strategy has been well documented with regard to the decision to develop the collectively owned TVEs that proved so successful in the 1980s. Although collectively owned enterprises were not the most efficient, they were the most economically and politically feasible during the late 1970s and the early 1980s when the rural reforms were first taking hold.[21] The chapters in this volume will reveal that a similar political pragmatism was at work during the SOE restructuring, as politics shaped the policies that could be adopted.

The first part of the volume lays out the patterns of change and provides insights into what allowed such changes to take place. Oi and Han show how the major changes in the pattern of corporate restructuring reflect the ability of the state to end its social contract with state workers. The process has been slow and deliberate, but ultimately it has been effective. The forms of corporate restructuring were sequenced in accordance with the local political and economic constraints during various periods. The strategies adopted during the early period were radically different from those adopted in the later periods. Early forms of restructuring were purposely chosen because they were less threatening to the social contract and the socialist ideology. The Fifteenth Chinese Communist Party Congress in 1997 officially marked the beginning of the second and more radical phase of corporate restructuring. Many of the barriers to privatization were eliminated. SOE restructuring is now more rapid, with widespread change in ownership form, but also with increased layoffs. Private enterprise is now officially recognized

21 See Jean C. Oi, *Rural China Takes Off: Institutional Foundations of Economic Reform* (Berkeley: University of California Press, 1999).

as an important component of the economy. As dramatic as these changes are, it remains an open question, especially with regard to the large firms in which the state still holds the controlling shares, whether the firms that are now called "private," including those that are listed, are in fact private. Oi and Han argue that corporatization rather than privatization is a better description of the change from sole state ownership to a more diversified ownership.

Although restructuring in China has been a state-led process, it has also been a decentralized process, with considerable local variation depending on the local political and economic contexts. The central state has allowed local-level government officials to implement the restructuring, resulting in variations in both the pace and the patterns of change across localities. Local officials calculated their strategies based on local resources and political interests. The VoC literature stresses the distinctiveness of political economies, and our findings suggest that there are multiple political economies across China's regions. Prosperous areas, such as Shanghai and Hangzhou, had many more options than poor county seats in the hinterland to deal with the major constraint facing corporate restructuring—how to deal with those workers who would lose their jobs as a consequence of the reform.

Zeng and Tsai probe corporate restructuring in the three municipalities of Wenzhou, Xiamen, and Shenyang to tease out the determinants of the patterns, timing, and speed of corporate restructuring, especially privatization. Their study provides new insights into the triggers of reform, a variable that the IC literature does not consider. Unlike earlier studies that focus almost exclusively on economic incentives, Zeng and Tsai argue that the incentives of local officials for privatization are affected by a combination of the local economic structure and the criteria by which the local officials are evaluated. This is but one example where the political incentives outweigh the economic incentives.

Zeng and Tsai's study also yields counter-intuitive findings about how the availability of alternative sources of employment, namely private enterprises, affects incentives to restructure. One might think that the existence of a large private sector would accelerate corporate restructuring because of an alternative and ready-made source of jobs for those who are displaced from state firms. If a major stumbling block to restructuring is job losses, then restructuring might be facilitated when those who lose jobs in the state sector can find new work in the large developed private sector. Contrary to expectation, however, Zeng and Tsai find that "... a booming private sector actually delayed much-needed SOE restructuring in some localities." This divergent finding sheds light on the risk-adverse nature of workers who have long enjoyed employment in the *danwei* (work-unit) system and it fleshes out the more complex political calculus of local-level officials who must determine the priorities of the various types of reforms. Although a booming private sector facilitated *implementation* of local restructuring by providing laid-off workers with alternative jobs, ". . . it negatively affected local officials' incentives for privatization by making the *initiation* of restructuring a low priority." Zeng and Tsai conclude that when the political mandate from above was strong, even with a lack of supporting institutions for privatization, "local officials made up for this deficiency by innovatively devising many ad-hoc practices or measures to cope with the restructuring of a large number of SOEs, including measures to maintain social stability by assisting laid-off workers."

The limited ability of the state to provide for all those dislocated by restructuring posed a tremendous problem for the state. Oi and Han show how sequencing the forms of restructuring helped mediate the number of those who were laid off, but over time the number of those affected increased. How did the state decide how and to whom to give its limited resources? The answer to this question requires an understanding that in China there has always been a hierarchy of workers, with those working in the state sector above those working in the collective sector. Both state and collective firms were considered publicly owned firms, but the state-sector workers were privileged over the collective-sector workers due to their ability to eat their fill from the "iron rice bowl."[22] Yongshun Cai provides insights into how this hierarchy was handled in China's rust-belt area in the Northeast. Cai describes the distinction the government made among those workers who lost their jobs, either through layoffs or unemployment. Policies implemented for long-term regular workers in state-owned enterprises were different from policies for those who worked in less prestigious and smaller collectively owned firms. The notion of a social contract between workers and the state applied to those in the state-owned sector, but not to those who worked in the collectively owned firms. For the latter, the relationship with the state was less binding and the state had less of a moral obligation to provide for them during the restructuring. This hierarchy of workers was institutionalized into different treatments during the restructuring. Cai argues that the government used its limited resources strategically to accommodate the most powerful groups of workers while ignoring the weaker ones.

22 Even within the state sector, as Walder notes, there was tremendous variation in what was provided. See Andrew G. Walder, *Communist Neo-traditionalism: Work and Authority in Chinese Industry* (Berkeley: University of California Press, 1986).

Although the differences between collective and state workers have long existed, Cai's chapter reconciles radically different views in the existing literature regarding treatment of laid-off workers.[23] There are rich and convincing accounts of the plight of laid-off workers that show that SOEs and local governments have taken great pains to care for these workers. Cai reveals there are differences in the treatment of workers, however, depending on their status in the hierarchy. He shows that although "laid-off workers from urban collective enterprises accounted for a significant portion of the total number of laid-off workers, they were almost entirely ignored by the central and local governments during the initial years of the reform." The government calculated that workers from collective enterprises were "politically weak." Cai's chapter underscores the point that "... reform policy is shaped by both the state power and the power of the victims or losers of the reform."

After laying out the strategies and patterns of change, this volume turns to the policy-making process that allowed China the flexibility to adopt and adapt during corporate restructuring. On the one hand, China's one party-state obviates policy debates such as those plaguing health reform in the United States. However, the decision-making process is not as top-down or smooth as one might imagine. Heilmann shows that although China is still a one-party authoritarian regime, the top leaders cannot routinely push through their will in terms of policy-making. Contrary to what one might expect, "decision-making at the apex of China's political system is hampered by informal consensus rules. Controversial policy proposals are rarely pushed through by a lone decision of the Communist Party's general secretary or by a majority vote in the Politburo but rather postponed until a consensus among the major policymakers can be reached." The overarching theme in all the chapters of this volume is how those who wanted reform managed to overcome the political and economic constraints. Heilmann highlights the particular feature of China's policy-making process whereby policies are tried out before they are actually put into law— "experimentation first, laws later." "Experimentation served as a crucial means for avoiding policy deadlock and reducing the frictions and delays characteristic of top-level consensus-building and inter-agency accommodation. Experimental points (*shidian*) allowed innovation into 'a rigidly organized polity.'" This highly unusual degree of policy flexibility allowed those who wanted change to "smuggle in reform." It opened the door for much

---

23 For a recent work on laid-off workers, see Thomas B. Gold et al., eds., *Laid-Off Workers in a Workers' State: Unemployment with Chinese Characteristics* (New York: Palgrave Macmillan, 2009).

more tolerance for different types of solutions to be tried out without first being subject to close scrutiny and debate.

Heilmann's chapter highlights a crucial difference in the ability of different political regimes to implement reform. Unlike Korea, for example, China was able to try out policies before they were brought before any political debate. Unlike pluralist democracies, policies were not shaped and in some cases gutted by the need to engage in electoral party politics. This is not to say that China's reforms are not subject to political constraints—the political backlash from the "new left" continues to this day.[24] But that type of constraint is fundamentally different from the legislative politics one finds in Japan and Korea. This insight highlights the need for further comparative work across regimes types.

In examining China's corporate restructuring, we also see that CCP leaders, not unlike politicians elsewhere, use external threats to push through politically sensitive reforms. Reformers, like all policymakers, need to justify implementation of painful policies. By the late 1990s China's desire to enter the World Trade Organization (WTO) provided just such an excuse. On the one hand, this required that firms become more internationally competitive in anticipation of the entry of foreign firms into the Chinese market. But, on the other hand, as Jung's chapter argues, the need to be ready for the WTO created an ideal excuse for Zhu Rongji to push through more radical and more politically sensitive SOE reforms than were previously possible. Jung's chapter argues that a political leader can " . . . utilize the crisis to pursue his own reform agenda and produce specific institutional outcomes."

Jung also stresses that we need to distinguish between politics and institutional change. She cautions that we should distinguish between the dismantling of pilot institutions of the former central planning system from the retreat of the state. This is an essential distinction that underscores the fact that China's corporate restructuring was and remains a state-led effort. State direction of the economy has evolved without necessarily receding over time. The new institutions that have been established may be nothing more than new entities created to represent the state. In the case of corporate restructuring, the SASAC falls into such a category. Jung argues that the Chinese central state "is now pursuing a more focused and efficient mode of intervention especially for SOEs in key priority issue areas. The discrepancy between the façade of state withdrawal and the actual reinvention of

---

24 Jean C. Oi, "Political Crosscurrents in China's Corporate Restructuring," in Jean C. Oi, Scott Rozelle, Xueguang Zhou, eds., *Growing Pains: Tensions and Opportunity in China's Transformation* (Stanford: Walter H. Shorenstein Asia-Pacific Research Center, Stanford University, 2010), 5–25.

the central state intervention suggests . . . the Chinese central state strongly retains its dominant role in the entire national economic system."

Gallagher and Ma provide a further piece of the puzzle regarding how change came to China's SOEs. They argue that the foreign factor, specifically foreign direct investment (FDI), played both an indirect and direct role in advancing SOE reform. They show that cooperation, copying, and competition were three mechanisms of change emanating from the inflows of FDI. Different forms of FDI playing different roles have evolved over time. Gallagher and Ma posit that competition is the main mechanism for change during the most recent period of reform. FDI provided "a remedy to discipline and improve the health of the state sector, but large inflows of FDI . . . have also led to the transformation of many state firms into FIEs (foreign-invested enterprises). . . ." Although some might fear the crowding out effect of FDI, Gallagher and Ma reveal that the numbers indicate that in the long run the weeding out of the less competitive firms may have been beneficial.

The third part of the volume examines the new Chinese institutions required for corporate restructuring. Corporate restructuring was not possible without broader systemic reform. However, the problem is what does a regime do when it does not have such institutions? China was able to move forward in corporate restructuring without many of the assumed requisite institutions because it adopted ad-hoc measures that served political and economic needs at different stages of the reform. Implicit in this observation is the idea that the reformers knew what was required but could not implement the needed institutional changes. Here we examine the ad-hoc strategies that allowed the reforms to move forward as well as the efforts to build more sustainable supporting institutions. One of the most important of these institutions is a social security system.

Since the late 1990s the state has tried to create a unified welfare system. But this process was fraught with political tensions. The result, as Smuthkalin's chapter shows, is that China's social security system is still a work in progress. Although social security reform is a state-led process, i.e., planned and regulated by the central government, it must be implemented by the local authorities. The complex negotiations and compromises are reflected in the limited policies that China has been able to implement to date. Despite the intentions of the center to facilitate the corporate restructuring of SOEs, political, fiscal, and administrative constraints have limited the optimal utilization of social security reform to accommodate the corporate restructuring. The tremendous variation in the burden and wealth of different localities has created obstacles to an integrated national system of welfare, such as the pooling problem that also exists in many other countries. China's leaders, like those in other political regimes, including electoral systems, face the problem of how to fund public goods. The localities are unwilling to pay for the welfare of their poorer neighbors. In the case of China, policymakers chose to compromise in order to move the reform process forward, even if the solutions are not ideal.

A separate but intimately related problem in China's corporate restructuring is financing. NPLs plague China's banks because of the need to maintain high levels of employment, and banks are yet to be fully reformed. The various attempts to use economic incentives, including interest rates, to encourage firms to be more efficient in the use of funds only resulted in more NPLs. Prior to these reforms, the funds received by the SOEs were grants rather than loans. As Walter's chapter shows, it was the development of capital markets and the decision to allow firms to engage in self-financing that eventually led to the establishment of stock markets, which in turn successfully forced firms to embark upon corporate restructuring. For the first time firms evaluated their assets to clarify ownership and to sell shares so as to raise funds. Walter examines what happens when a market institution is imported into a transitional system. Unlike the social security system where ad-hoc measures could mediate the lack of supporting institutions, in the case of the stock markets the state was less able to make up for the lack of institutional complementarity in the financial sector. Walter analyzes how China's stock markets ended up being perverted, adapted, and hijacked by the different political actors and interests. He sees the stock markets as a Pandora's Box that once opened resulted in unforeseen consequences as the reforms continued. We see how bureaucratic in-fighting and attempts to capture the wealth contained in stock-market opportunities distorted other policy objectives, including funding for the much-needed social security system, and corrupted stock market operations. Walter's chapter is a vivid accounting of the price China has paid for trying to mix institutions from different political economies.

The insights in Walter's work resonate with and are further developed by Zheng and Kim, whose chapter examines the informal and often opaque relationship between listed firms and their parent company. Whereas Walter makes clear that the role of the state continues as an owner in a so-called privatized firm, Zheng and Kim delve into a micro-level analysis of the fiscal flows between spun-off and parent firms. They argue that what differentiates China is not the concentration of shares, but the identity of the controlling shareholders. They show how the dominant role of state ownership in Chinese public firms has compromised corporate governance. Zheng and Kim's chapter further elaborates on what happens when institutions from two different political economies operate side by side. Again, the result is distortion and/or adaptation of the institutions. Zheng and Kim use the example of the operations of the boards of directors, which on paper are central to good corporate governance. They show what happens when additional players, in this case the CCP, are introduced into the operating context. We see that, despite an identical form, the actual roles of the players are very different.

The core of Zheng and Kim's chapter is about the spin-offs from the SOEs, which are only briefly mentioned in earlier chapters. They explore the impact of a SOE parent and the state as a major shareholder and describe what happens when top managers are simultaneously in charge of both the parent group and the listed company, often both in the same industry. The resultant related-party transactions open the door to a world of murky business transactions where "[A] substantial part of the related-party transactions are actually used by the parent group to transfer capital or profits out of the listed firm." We see how spin-offs are used to support a still unreformed and ailing parent firm. In the process of examining these related-party transactions and the relationship between parent SOEs and their spin-offs, Zheng and Kim suggest that we need to expand our questions and frameworks to include norms and cultures within institutions, arguing that it is difficult for managers to adopt new norms of behavior due to previous social ties and expectations. This work presents an additional variable in our understanding of institutional creation and change.

Institutional Catch-Up and the Role of the State in Corporate Restructuring

All of the chapters in this volume address theoretical as well as policy-relevant questions about reform programs in China in particular, and in East Asia more broadly, where corporate restructuring has been a key issue since the 1990s, especially after the Asian financial crisis. Although all three cases—China, Japan, and Korea—have been criticized for not implementing certain reforms or for not implementing them quickly enough, by delving into the context in which these decisions were made, this volume provides an understanding of what may be the deeper, underlying reasons why certain institutional choices were made over others. The chapters bear out the premise that the fate of corporate restructuring is deeply affected by many other types of reform. In that sense, the VoC literature, and its emphasis on context and what is termed institutional complementarities, provides useful insights. Our study commences from the idea of institutional complementarities in that we assume that firms exist within a specific political-economic context. However, the findings in this volume suggest that we need to rethink the assumptions of the VoC literature if the framework is to be effectively extended to understand state-led economies like China and other countries where the state also plays a key role.

First, and perhaps most important, instead of putting firms at the center of the analysis of corporate restructuring, as the VoC literature does, our findings on China underscore the possibility that it is the state that is the key political actor. This change does not detract from the idea of institutional complementarities. It simply allows for the state to play an explicit and determining role in corporate restructuring. What this means is that the state may have the ability to mediate problems by adding or modifying institutions in the larger process of reform. There is a high degree of interdependence between the success of corporate restructuring and systemic reforms, not only in China but perhaps in the other East Asian countries as well where there have been other types of state-led development.

Our focus on the state, however, is not simply a return to the state development model. This volume is not about the role of the state; it is about the institutions, which may or may not be created by the state, and their impact on corporate restructuring. Our focus is on institutional change and the effects that interactions among institutions have on the ability of both firms and the state to move forward in the corporate reform process.

The relevant question is not who decides on the institutions, which likely varies by institution and regime. The more interesting question is what happens when a regime and its firms attempt to effect change but cannot. China's corporate restructuring experience suggests that reform can proceed in the absence of key institutions, including a social security system. China adopted ad-hoc measures to mediate the lack of such institutions. These key structural changes thus were achieved without fundamentally altering the underpinning of the political system and the basis for the legitimacy of the ruling party. China has shown impressive flexibility in experimenting with solutions, but it has the luxury of not having to worry about the messy and often debilitating impact of party politics.

This volume also shows that when market institutions, such as stock markets, are adopted, they are subject to capture. The stock market was adapted to China's transitional system and essentially turned into an institution that plays a role different from that in the Western market economies. The problems of China's stock markets suggest that we need to examine how institutions are adapted and changed by new contexts.

Although the chapters in this volume focus on China, similar questions apply to other cases of state-led development. We hope that readers will use the insights from China to consider more broadly the impact of various institutions, or their absence, on corporate restructuring in other political economies. A comparative effort will allow a better understanding of the most critical constraints on corporate restructuring in each country. The aim is to examine the extent to which the constraints differ across countries. There are a number of striking similarities in the nature of the problems that are plaguing firms in very different political economies. The pervasiveness of NPLs is perhaps the best known. When one delves into the reasons for NPLs in Japan and Korea, a surprising similarity is a hesitancy to cut the workforce. It is obvious why this is the case in China, a country with a socialist centrally planned economy where workers occupy a privileged position. But why do Korea and Japan face a similar problem? A closer examination of these systems may reveal that these seemingly radically different political economies share some surprising institutional similarities. We hope that this volume not only will shed new light on the case of China's corporate restructuring, but also will raise new questions about how we think about the process of institutional change in different political and economic contexts.

2 China's Corporate Restructuring

A MULTI-STEP PROCESS

Jean C. Oi and Han Chaohua

In the 1980s and into the 1990s the prospects for successful state-owned enterprise (SOE) restructuring in China were dim. Debts, non-performing loans, inefficiencies, and surplus workers were synonymous with China's SOEs. Although some argued that it was a lack of political will or threats to the power of the one party-state that hindered reform, China faced a fundamental problem—it lacked institutions to provide for the workers who would be laid off by the restructuring. As surprising as it may be, China, which has long been known for its iron rice bowl, lacked a national welfare system. The Maoist era iron rice bowl was actually firm-based welfare. Without the continued flow of funds from the upper levels, the poorly performing firms were no longer able to continue to provide benefits to their workers.[1] The resulting slow pace of restructuring amid the political constraints on the number of workers who could be laid off in the 1980s and early 1990s suggested that China might never be able fully to reform its publicly owned sector.

Yet, by mid-2006 a new day had dawned for China's SOEs. SOE restructuring, including privatization, began to accelerate rapidly in the late 1990s. Many of the earlier constraints on privatization, including the need to retain current workers, had disappeared. The number of state-owned firms dropped significantly as the majority of SOEs were corporatized or privatized. By the early to mid-2000s SOEs reported record profits as well as record tax payments to the state. During the three years "from 2004 to 2006, the revenue on

1 This is discussed in Jean C. Oi, "Patterns of Corporate Restructuring in China: Political Constraints on Privatization," *China Journal*, no. 53 (January 2005): 115–36.

core businesses of the central SOEs increased 78.8 percent . . . ; total profits increased 140 percent . . . ; taxes-paid increased 96.5 percent . . . ; the rate of preserving and increasing the value of state-owned assets reached 144.4 percent, and the returns on assets reached 10 percent, an increase of 5 percentage points. . . . The average annual increase of profits reached more than 100 billion RMB, and taxes-paid averaged an increase of 100 billion RMB annually. Thirteen central SOEs were ranked among in the world's Top 500 ... in 2006."[2] Although problems remain, there is a consensus that a remarkable turnaround has been achieved in China's state-owned sector.[3]

This chapter examines how these policy successes were achieved given the problems that plagued earlier SOE reforms. We will argue that China's restructuring process was slow in the initial stages to lay the necessary groundwork for future, more radical change. China's lack of supporting institutions prevented it from adopting the most economically efficient forms of restructuring when the reforms first began. As a result, China turned to shareholding rather than privatization and settled for partial reform. Politics prevented restructuring from being a one-step process, moving directly from public ownership to privatization. Instead, China took smaller, less invasive, and less ideologically alien steps in the direction of restructuring.[4] However, despite these constraints and the generally cautious approach, there was considerable room for more radical action in selected firms. Some SOEs were allowed to spin off parts of their state assets to form private companies and become listed firms. It is these SOEs that are now making record-breaking profits. China's had a two-track system for different classes of SOEs. Large, key SOEs received preferential access and were allowed to implement radical reforms while seemingly still adhering to the earlier socialist modes of industrial organization. Moreover, because the forms of restructuring adopted during the first phase of the reforms were second-best choices, as problems began to emerge and as conditions allowed the state to promote more radical policies, further restructuring was eagerly embraced. China's outwardly slow corporate restructuring process paved the political way and planted the seeds

---

2 News release from the press conference held by the Information Office of the State Council on General Information on Reform and Development of Central SOEs and Development of State-owned Assets Management System Reform, SASAC, December 19, 2006, at http://www.sasac.gov.cn/n2963340/n2964712/3059894.html, accessed September 4, 2010.

3 See, for example, Barry Naughton, "SOE Policy: Profiting the SASAC Way," and other articles in *China Economic Quarterly* 12, no. 2 (July 2008).

4 This is in accord with Yingyi Qian, "How Reform Worked in China," in Dani Rodrik, ed., *In Search of Prosperity: Analytic Narratives on Economic Growth* (Princeton, NJ: Princeton University Press, 2003), 297–333.

for the second stage of reform. In contrast to studies that focus on firm interests, we argue that the logic of China's corporate restructuring was based on the interests of the state and its agents at both the central and local levels.

The distinct phases and dramatic changes in China's pattern of corporate restructuring are evident in the results of two surveys carried out in 2000 and 2005,[5] on which this chapter is based. The surveys were conducted by the Institute of Economics of the Chinese Academy of Social Sciences. The 2000 survey involved five cities (Wuxi, Zhengzhou, Jiangmen, Hangzhou, and Yancheng) in four industrial sectors (textiles, machinery, electronics, and chemicals). The sample included 451 companies. The 2005 survey involved five cities (Wuxi, Zhengzhou, Jiangmen, Chengdu, and Shenyang) in five sectors (textiles, machinery, electronics, chemicals, and electricity). This sample included 1,022 enterprises.[6]

Not only do we have longitudinal data on the same sectors in the same three cities, but we also are able to track some of the same enterprises over time. A unique feature of our study is a longitudinal dataset of 145 enterprises that experienced property-rights restructuring during the 1994-2003 period. This dataset was created by returning in 2005 to three of the same cities (Wuxi, Zhengzhou, Jiangmen) and re-sampling the same firms as those surveyed in 2000 to see how they changed over time. We were only partially successful in our re-sampling because some of the original firms could no longer be located, either because they had been closed or because they had been merged under a different name. However, we did succeed in returning to a total of 208 firms in the three cities. After excluding those cases with missing values on corporate restructuring during the period of interest, we ended up with a panel dataset of 145 enterprises for a period of 11 years, 1994 to 2003 (our 2000 survey collected data dating from 1994). This dataset provides detailed information about corporate restructuring between 1994 and 2003, controlling for location, sector, and firm. With this dataset we are able to conclusively show the impact of restructuring on a number of variables, including the payment of taxes, thus directly testing assumptions of earlier studies.

Below we document the changes that occurred during China's corporate restructuring and then examine the logic of the policy shifts during the second phase of SOE restructuring.

5 The authors would like to thank Robby Shi for his assistance in processing the data from the 2005 survey.

6 The research was generously supported by funds from Stanford University and the Harvard Business School.

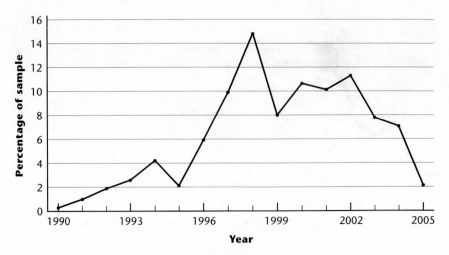

FIGURE 2.1 Most Important Firm Restructurings Since 1990
Source: Authors' Surveys.

Shifting Patterns of Corporate Restructuring

The late 1990s was the watershed period in China's corporate restructuring when the nationwide pattern and speed of reform changed markedly. Figure 2.1 shows a distinct upward tilt in restructuring beginning in 1995 and reaching a peak in 1998. The year 1997 was a crucial turning point when the Fifteenth Party Congress gave an official green light to privatization. The legitimacy of the private sector was reaffirmed and its importance for the development of the economy was expanded.[7]

But the difference was not only in the speed of the restructuring. In the sections that follow we will show that there were also significant shifts in the forms of restructuring, the number of workers laid off, the constraints on privatization, and the distribution of shares within the restructured firms.

Forms of Restructuring

In the 1990s only a limited number of firms were privatized or declared bankrupt; shareholding was much more common.[8] In this respect, there is consistency across the five cities we surveyed in 2000—privatization was the

7 See Heilmann's and Jung's chapters in this volume.

8 In spite of the policy to "grasp the large and let go of the small," the number "let go" was limited. Even when we disaggregate our data in the 2000 sample, we find that regardless of firm size, sales amounted to no more than 7 percent of the total. Further discussion of the 1990s can be found in Oi, "Patterns of Corporate Restructuring."

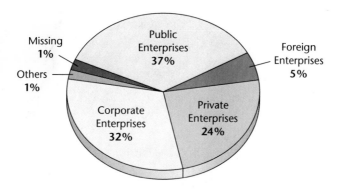

FIGURE 2.2 2004 Status of 521 Firms that Were Publicly Owned in 1990

Source: Authors' Surveys.

Note: Public Enterprises = state-owned enterprises + collective enterprises; Shareholding Enterprises = limited-liability companies + shareholding companies + other limited-liability companies; Private Enterprises = all types of private enterprises and stock cooperative enterprises; Foreign-invested Enterprises = Hong Kong-, Macao-, and Taiwan-invested enterprises and foreign-invested enterprises (exclusive of Hong Kong, Macao, and Taiwan); Other Enterprises = jointly operated enterprises + other domestic-invested enterprises.

last form of restructuring. There is also a relationship between ownership and type of restructuring: (1) collective firms were more likely to restructure. Less than one-fifth were not restructured. In contrast, more than one-third of the state-owned firms were not restructured. (2) Shareholding was the most popular form of restructuring for state-owned, urban collective, and rural collective firms; joint ventures with foreign firms were more likely to be adopted by pooled firms. (3) Collective firms were more likely than state-owned firms to be sold or leased.

By the mid-2000s significant change had taken place. Our 2005 survey shows a substantial increase in privatization of the formerly state-owned firms. As Figure 2.2 reveals, by 2004 a significant number of previously state-owned firms had privatized. Only 37 percent of the 521 firms that were publicly owned, i.e., state or collectively owned, in 1990 remained public in 2004.

Of course, there is regional variation with regard to privatization. In our 2005 survey Wuxi showed the greatest increase in private enterprises—the change was much greater than that for the sample as a whole.[9] In contrast, in Shenyang the restructuring of public firms was less than that for the sample as a whole, although there still was more than a 30 percent decrease in the number of state-owned firms. Although the precise triggers for

9 Wuxi, which is at the core of the Sunan model of collective development, similarly rapidly privatized its TVEs.

restructuring are closely linked to the political pressures that the locality imposes on local officials, as Zeng and Tsai argue in this volume, the relative delay in Shenyang, compared to the other cities in our sample, is not surprising given that Shenyang is at the heart of China's rust-belt and is home to many old state-owned enterprises. Even with the increased attention that Zeng and Tsai describe and in spite of the campaign-style implementation programs, this situation is not expected to change immediately.

Increased Managerial Control and Ownership

Along with the increased rate of restructuring and privatization, our 2005 survey data show an increase in the number of firms in which the managers are the controlling shareholders. In contrast to Russia where managers gained large blocks of shares from the beginning of the privatization process, China intentionally adopted a more egalitarian policy that prevented managers from immediately engaging in insider privatization. Walder argues that the Chinese case suggests that the speed it takes to achieve market transformation may affect the nature, degree, and consequences of insider privatization.[10] Our survey results bear this out (see Figure 2.3 below). The early forms of restructuring limited the number of shares that managers were allowed to buy. However, we also know from our 2000 survey that although the number of shares held by managers was limited, there were early efforts to increase managerial shareholding. After each restructuring, the share distribution between workers and managers tilted increasingly toward the managers. Even prior to 2001, after the different rounds of restructuring were implemented, the proportion of shares held by top managers had increased. The proportion increased from 21.5 percent at the time of the first restructuring to 24.8 percent after the subsequent restructuring.[11] The shares held by ordinary workers decreased from 16.3 percent to 14.7 percent.[12] Looking at the shareholding cooperatives, we find that 7 out of the 31 firms were restructured into shareholding cooperatives

10 For a comparative discussion of the different outcomes of privatization according to the speed and constraints, see Andrew G. Walder, "Elite Opportunity in Transitional Economies," *American Sociological Review* 68, no. 6 (December 2003): 899–916.

11   The t-test shows that the increase is statistically significant (t= −3.47, p= .0003). The increase in the top managers' share mainly occurred in limited-liability companies (an average increase of 3.45 percent), limited-liability shareholding companies (an average increase of 4.71 percent), and shareholding cooperative companies (an average increase of 4.88 percent). There was not much change in the other types of firms.

12   The t-test shows that the change is statistically significant (t= 2.06, p=.02).

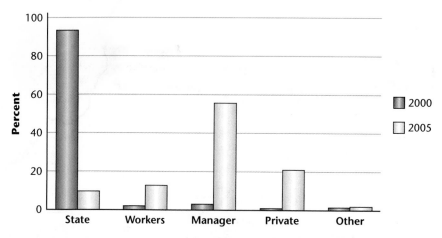

FIGURE 2.3 Change in Controlling Shareholder, 2000 and 2005
Source: Authors' Surveys.

Note: State includes state and public legal person shares; Workers include worker and manager shares, i.e., the entire enterprise.

with equal shareholding during the first round of reform; in the second step they were restructured into shareholding cooperatives where the manager held the controlling shares.

Putting the findings of our two surveys together, as the figure above shows, we see a significant increase in the percentage of managers as controlling shareholder between 2000 and 2004. Whereas in 2000 little over 4 percent of the managers were controlling shareholders, by 2004 after the later restructuring in these same factories, more than half of the managers had become controlling shareholders.[13] According to the 2005 survey, the most frequent type of restructuring involved managers holding a controlling share or purchasing the entire enterprise (26.4 percent). The second most frequent type of restructuring was workers holding a controlling share or purchasing the enterprise (20.2 percent).[14]

Interviews in 2005 suggest that in some parts of the country manager buyouts were initiated in the first round of restructuring, without going through the phase of equal shareholding. Local officials explained that this was necessary because effective corporate governance requires a major hands-on stakeholder.[15]

13 Survey I.
14 Survey II, Q2.
15 Jean C. Oi, China interviews, Shandong, June-July 2005.

Reduced Commitment to Retain Workers

Perhaps the most significant change was the commitment of would-be buyers to retain workers (see Figure 2.4). Because the CCP wanted to minimize the number of layoffs from the restructuring, as much as possible corporate restructuring was de-linked from layoffs.[16] In line with other studies,[17] our 2000 survey revealed that 75 percent of the firms in our sample were restructured but did not lay off any workers.[18] Moreover, when firms were restructured either to shareholding, sold, or formed joint ventures with foreign firms, the majority of the employees remained with the firms. Firms that were restructured and leased were more likely to retain only a portion of the employees, but the government took care of the remaining workers. To a lesser extent, this was also the case for joint ventures. If a firm went bankrupt, the government was more likely to step in and take care of all of the workers.[19] Similarly, an International Finance Corporation study found that there were fewer worker layoffs and unemployed workers in restructured firms than in non-restructured firms.[20] Thus, restructuring was distinct from layoffs and in some cases may have reduced the number of layoffs.

To help ensure that the number of layoffs was kept to a minimum, there were conditions attached to the sale of firms—what some have called "privatization with a tail."[21] The buyer had to make a commitment to retain all or a certain percentage of a firm's existing workers for a certain length of time. In our 2000 survey, 95.7 percent of the firms reported such a commitment. However, by 2005 only 11.28 percent of the firms had made this commitment.[22]

Although change has been dramatic, the political constraints on SOE restructuring that were so potent earlier did not entirely disappear. There is

16 See, for example, Oi, "Patterns of Corporate Restructuring."

17 Ross Garnaut et al., *China's Ownership Transformation: Process, Outcomes, Prospects* (Washington, DC: World Bank, 2005).

18 Lu Zheng provided assistance with the statistical analysis of the dataset. The research was generously supported by a grant from the Asian Development Bank Institute and a seed grant from the Stanford Institute of International Studies, Stanford University.

19 The patterns of corporate restructuring in the 1990s are discussed in Oi, "Patterns of Corporate Restructuring," upon which parts of this chapter are based.

20 Garnaut et al., *China's Ownership Transformation*, ch. 4. They also point out it is incorrect to simply look at the aggregate statistics on the changes in the number of workers in state-owned firms. Former state jobs may have been reclassified as private-sector jobs.

21 Stephen Green, "Privatization in the Former Soviet Bloc: Has China Learned the Lessons," in Stephen Green and Guy S. Liu, eds., *Exit the Dragon: Privatization and State Control in China* (London: Blackwell, 2005), 42–59.

22 The result of the binomial test shows this difference to be significant.

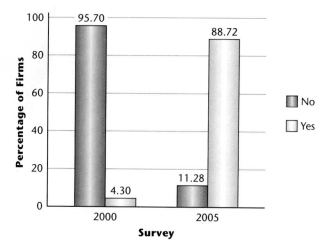

FIGURE 2.4 Firms that Were Required to Retain Existing Workers after Restructuring
Source: Authors' Surveys.

ample evidence to show that segments of the population, cadres and workers alike, remained opposed to more radical restructuring, including both manager buyouts (MBOs) and privatization more generally.[23] Recent press reports of Jilin steel workers who beat to death a private factory owner who was planning to buy a majority stake in a state-owned steel factory suggest that opposition to privatization still remains strong.[24] We should make clear that our findings do not reveal any information about worker opposition to these changes. However, we have found that the state no longer imposes constraints on potential buyers regarding worker retention.

Unpacking China's State-Led Restructuring

Unlike the situation described in much of the corporate restructuring literature, in China the state, not the individual firms, decides when and how the restructuring will take place. In the former Soviet bloc (FSB), the

23 Jean C. Oi, "Political Crosscurrents in China's Corporate Restructuring," in Jean C. Oi, Scott Rozelle, and Xueguang Zhou, eds., *Growing Pains: Tensions and Opportunity in China's Transformation* (Stanford: Walter H. Shorenstein Asia-Pacific Research Center, Stanford University, 2010), 5–25.

24 Tania Branigan, "Chinese State Steel Workers Beat Private Firm Boss to Death," at www.guardian.co.uk/world/2009/jul/26/china-steel-workers-riot, accessed July 26, 2009. Sales of other firms have been halted. See Keith Bradsher, "Bowing to Protests, China Halts Sale of Steel Mill," *New York Times*, August 16, 2009, at http://www.nytimes.com/2009/08/17/business/global/17yuan.html, accessed May 19, 2010.

generally weak states were unable or unwilling to manage the privatization process.[25] But under continued one-party rule, China sequenced the form and speed of restructuring to ensure that each step was aligned with the political and economic constraints. China's pattern of corporate restructuring was the result of a calculated state response to the changing political and economic contexts.

Our findings from the two surveys conducted during a five-year interval clearly show that the government is the main initiator of firm restructuring.[26] In both surveys, the government, i.e., the state bureaucratic authorities, initiated more than 60 percent of the restructurings.[27] Firm managers may initiate restructuring, but ultimately the decision must be approved by the level of government that "owns" the firm.[28] The frequency of external investors initiating restructuring rose significantly from 0.7 percent to 4.0 percent, but the low numbers still render these cases less important. Meanwhile, the frequency of public enterprise insiders who were the main initiators of restructuring dropped, from 32.9 percent to 25.2 percent, between our two surveys.

Local Resources and Variation in Restructuring

The central state gave a green light to restructuring, but implementation was left up to the localities. Local governments were the key decision makers regarding SOE reform within their respective localities. As McDermott shows in a comparative study of Poland and the Czech Republic, the role of local government may be a key variable in determining the longer-term success of privatization.[29] Granted, the local authorities in such post-Communist

25 For an insightful comparison of the differences in privatization between China and the FSB, see Green, "Privatization in the Former Soviet Bloc," 42-59. However, Gerald A. McDermott, "Institutional Change and Firm Creation in East-Central Europe: An Embedded Politics Approach," *Comparative Political Studies* 37, no. 2 (2004): 188 shows that there was in fact variation in the degree to which different governments were able to manage the process. This ability turns out to be key in determining the long-run success.

26 The findings from the 2000 survey can be found in Oi, "Patterns of Corporate Restructuring," 115–36.

27 We find an increase (from 60.7 to 62.6 percent) from 2000 to 2005, but the result of the binomial test shows that this is not statistically significant. The point is that the percentage did not decrease.

28 Firms in China are divided between those that are considered central-level enterprises (*zhongyang qiye*) and those owned by different levels of local government.

29 McDermott, "Institutional Change and Firm Creation in East-Central Europe," 188-217.

states were quite different from those in China. McDermott's point is to highlight the role that local authorities played in coordinating and providing institutional support for the privatization process. In China, local governments have played a much more direct and hands-on role in the process. Local officials crafted restructuring strategies that were suited to their localities' political and economic constraints. The need to heed these constraints, especially the political constraints, meant that the overall thrust of the reforms was necessarily slow and often appeared to be half-hearted during the early years. But such measures were due not to a lack of political will but rather to necessity. How quickly and enthusiastically the localities implemented restructuring was influenced by local incentives and resources.

Because no central funding was provided for restructuring, the central authorities were constrained in their ability to control how quickly and how many firms were restructured. The result was that some localities, regardless of how much they might have wanted to restructure, were too poor to reform because they lacked the resources to settle with those workers who would be displaced in the process. The forms and speed of the restructuring thus varied according to the political and economic constraints in each locality, as well as according to the incentives provided for restructuring opportunities. Our findings thus question earlier assumptions that governments could act on their interests.[30] Although all local governments may have had incentives to privatize, whether the local political actors could restructure, sell, or declare bankruptcy depended on the different constraints that they faced. If a locality was too poor to restructure, the incentives could not be acted upon. Restructuring in each locality was shaped by existing institutions and resource endowments. This means that different forms of restructuring could be selected to achieve economic or political goals at different stages of the process based on local conditions.

Generally, it was only when local authorities managed to resolve the political and economic limitations that the more radical reforms could be implemented. However, poor localities were not doomed to retain the old system even if they lacked resources. As Cai's chapter in this volume shows, the state could make strategic interventions. The upper levels could intervene to provide the needed funding to implement more radical, and likely more costly, forms of restructuring in important regions, for instance the Northeast rust-belt where there were many poorly performing firms, little new revenue,

30 See, for example, Yuanzheng Cao, Yingyi Qian, and Barry R. Weingast, "From Federalism, Chinese Style to Privatization, Chinese Style," *Economics of Transition* 7, no. 1 (1999): 103–31.

and much potential for unrest.[31] The restructuring was a process carefully calibrated and calculated at both the local and central levels.

The delay in China's SOE reforms is often compared to the rapid reforms in Russia and Eastern Europe. However, recent work, such as that by McDermott, shows that there was variation among the latter cases as well.[32] Poland, which at one time lagged behind the Czech Republic in terms of privatization, over the longer term has performed better. This suggests that China's slower approach may not be that unusual after all.

The Chinese state's ability to control the speed and the forms of restructuring allowed policies to be crafted and implemented in ways that intentionally thwarted potential critics of the reform and allowed the reform to move ahead, even if only slowly. The restructuring policies were not efficient but they were feasible and thus could be implemented. Although results were slow to occur, they came with a minimum of political instability and social dislocation. Restructuring in China was thus a multi-step process. Moreover, as we shall show below, there was still room for flexibility and more radical reform.

Variation and Hierarchy in Corporate Restructuring

Above we have argued that variation in restructuring resulted from differences in the constraints and resources across localities. Variation in restructuring also stemmed from the options available to firms of different size and importance. This differentiation reflected both the long- and short-term restructuring goals of the state. The state's multi-faceted agenda allowed restructuring to move forward more rapidly in key firms while moving more slowly in other enterprises.

As stressed above, prior to the late 1990s during the first phase of restructuring, the overall policy was to delay and minimize worker layoffs. Instead of rapid privatization, like that which occurred in Russia and Eastern Europe, most firms, regardless of size, that were restructured at that time became shareholding cooperatives, whereby the workers became shareholders. It was hoped that this form of restructuring would give the workers

31 A recently completed study by Jeremy Wallace goes further to show that the state is funneling increased fiscal transfers to cities that have a potential for instability and to rural areas near these localities. Jeremy Wallace, "Cities and Stability: Urbanization, Migration, and Authoritarian Resilience in China," Ph.D. diss., Department of Political Science, Stanford University, 2009.

32 McDermott, "Institutional Change and Firm Creation in East-Central Europe," 188-217.

more incentives to work hard, and it also provided a convenient and immediate source of credit for the firm, especially for poor-performing firms. The money paid by the workers for their shares went directly to the firm for needed capital.[33]

After 1997, restructuring more often took the form of privatization, but the policy was intended primarily for small and medium-sized firms. The policy was to "grasp the large and let go of the small" (*zhuada fangxiao*). Even in cases when firms were sold, as detailed above, it was not without conditions. Before a sale, the new owners had to agree either to provide an acceptable severance package or to retain all the workers for a certain amount of time. It was only later that these privatization "tails" were removed.

After 1997 more large SOEs were restructured, but they were not let go by the state. Rather, they were given special treatment so that they would be strengthened—here a more accurate definition of the term *zhua* is to "grasp," i.e., by the state. To illustrate how these larger firms were handled, let us elaborate on the distinction between privatization and corporatization. When large firms were restructured they were corporatized. Corporatization means that the state no longer was the sole owner but simply one of a number of owners.[34] In a corporatized firm, shares are sold, some to the workers and managers of the firm, but the state often holds a controlling number of the shares. In a privatized firm, the state does not own any shares.

The dramatic turnaround that is apparent today is due to what the state did with the corporatized SOEs. From the beginning, China has had a two-pronged or dual-track method for dealing with different types of firms.[35] Even during the earlier period when the government moved cautiously, China left room for a select group of strategically important enterprises—the largest and most important enterprises in key industries that are now considered strategic sectors, such as energy, communications, and heavy industry—to adopt much bolder reforms. In some of these firms, the best portions of their assets were spun off to form new, financially attractive entities. The new firms would then be listed on the stock market, while the parent firms remained state-owned entities. The latter is referred to as an enterprise group.[36]

China's strategy to spin off a new firm is not unique. In the United States, in an effort during the global financial crisis to restructure ailing firms like

---

33 For details, see Oi, "Patterns of Corporate Restructuring."
34 See Walter in this volume for more details on this distinction.
35 Oi describes some of these methods in her "Patterns of Corporate Restructuring."
36 For a more detailed discussion of enterprise groups, see Oi, "Patterns of Corporate Restructuring."

GM, a part of the old firm was spun off into a new entity. The latter was the healthiest part of the firm—the portion with the best chance for survival. Similarly, in China the best assets of a large state firm were spun off to form a new company, which then would attempt to be listed. But unlike at GM where the worse parts were sold off, in China it was the state that had to retain the worst parts of the firm. The original firm, what can be considered the parent company, remained a state-owned enterprise. China expects that the parent company will reform as well, but it is given a much longer time-line to become profitable. The parent company continues to carry the burden of the earlier debt—the least productive workers and many of the non-economic costs characteristic of China's *danwei* system. These burdens include the funding of schools, hospitals, and other public goods that in the United States are the responsibility of the local governments. In 2008 some SOEs were still responsible for schools and hospitals, costs that are considered public goods in other countries. This burden is compounded by holding the debt and having to support the less-skilled workers who remain with the parent firm and are left to work on more obsolete equipment.[37] This combination of strategies has resulted in a complex property-rights mix within a single enterprise group, thus masking the degree of change that might actually be taking place in China's SOEs.

This double-pronged strategy, although not the most economically effective way to reform, has allowed China to pursue the dual agenda of improving economic efficiency and advancing reform while still maintaining political stability in some of its most important SOEs. The restructuring process implemented in the large state-owned firms reflects both the need to create as little dislocation as possible and, at the same time, to allow for substantive reform. For example, only a portion of the large steel firms, like Wuhan Iron and Steel or Bao Steel with thousands of workers, underwent radical change—most of the firm moved at a much slower pace. In these instances, we find radical reforms and new ownership forms within an outwardly unreformed state-owned enterprise.

Incentives for Restructuring

Let us now address the question of why a one-party authoritarian state would want to restructure and give up ownership and control over firms,

37 This might seem like an untenable situation, but the parent-child relationship provides the old firm with some assistance. The strategy allows the parent company to benefit from the child both through shares in the newly spun-off firm as well as through less legal transactions. See Zheng and Kim in this volume for further details on how this works.

TABLE 2.1

Situation of Firms after Restructuring

Operative Situation	Frequency	Percent	Valid Percent
Improved	233	55.08	57.53
Worsened	16	3.78	3.95
No change	156	36.88	38.52
Total	405	95.74	100.00
Missing System	18	4.26	
Total	423	100.00	

Source: Authors' Survey.

either at the central or local level. The desire to reduce losses and subsidies is an obvious reason. The state wanted to stem the flow of red ink that was eating up local revenue.[38] The results from our 2005 survey of 1,000 firms suggest that China's corporate restructuring has had a direct positive impact toward achieving this goal (see Table 2.1). More than 50 percent of the firms felt that their performance had improved after restructuring. However, it should be remembered that these are self-reported assessments.

Although most studies measure the success of China's corporate restructuring by examining changes in profits,[39] focusing narrowly on profits may capture only some of the state's goals. Obviously, the state also wants the firms to be efficient and perform well. However, there is the possibility that the state pursues restructuring to serve its self-interests. We should remember that the state, at all levels, is a self-interested political actor. Keeping this caveat in mind, the overriding goal of the Chinese state in pursuing expanded restructuring may be to increase state revenues from the restructured firms.

From the comparative literature we know that FSB privatization was also undertaken to gain revenue from the sale of assets, although studies have shown that such revenue was often minimal. In some cases, more was spent than earned.[40] There is also the possibility that the Chinese state wanted to sell some of its assets to earn revenue. How much was made from such sales must be left to future research. We do know, as Walter shows in his chapter in this volume, that the state tried to use the sale of some of its shares in SOEs to fund the social security system.

Another plausible hypothesis for China's restructuring, including privatization, hinges not on revenue gained by the state from sales, but on gains

38 See Green, "Privatization in the Former Soviet Bloc."

39 See, for example, Liu Xiaoxuan, "The Effects of Privatization on China's Industrial Performance," in Green and Liu, eds., *Exit the Dragon*, 79-89.

40 See Green, "Privatization in the Former Soviet Bloc."

from the increased tax payments by restructured firms. We already know from earlier studies that localities, especially those at the county level, began to privatize their collectively owned township and village enterprises (TVEs) starting in the early to mid-1990s when it became clear that the TVEs were more of a liability than an asset.[41] Localities that privatized their TVEs earlier in the 1990s recognized that private firms were capable of providing as much, if not more, tax revenue than publicly owned firms.[42] Taxes from privately owned TVEs became a viable source of local county revenue. Our two surveys show that the same logic holds true for restructured SOE firms. As we have detailed elsewhere, our combined dataset shows that over time the same firms, once restructured regardless of the form of restructuring, paid more taxes than those that had not been restructured.[43]

Increased tax revenues thus should be a very strong incentive for local privatization. Of course, one can argue that the localities did not know that the restructuring would yield such high tax returns. Even though the TVE experience may have been a learning experience, the localities certainly knew that they had little to lose. Privately owned firms required no subsidies.

The Logic of China's Evolving Corporate Restructuring

The purpose of this chapter has been to identify the changes and the logic in the patterns of China's corporate restructuring. The chapters that follow will provide further pieces to the puzzle of China's SOE restructuring. Our piece of the puzzle has focused on key incentives and constraints on both the state and its agents at different levels. We have argued that such incentives and constraints shaped the process and outcome of corporate restructuring. This approach takes into account the changing political and economic contexts in which the corporate restructuring took place over time. We have stressed that corporate restructuring in China should not be understood as an all-or-nothing event. Restructuring has been a multi-step process. China ignored recommendations to adopt a big-bang approach, but reform occurred nonetheless. Despite the absence of the necessary institutions to

41 We should note that localities were less constrained in those instances because the workers were not contract workers and they held land rights because they held peasant household registrations. See Jean C. Oi, *Rural China Takes Off: Institutional Constraints of Economic Reform* (Berkeley: University of California Press, 1999).

42 See Oi, *Rural China Takes Off*.

43 These findings are presented in Han Chaohua and Dai Muzhen [Jean Oi], "Zhongguo Minyinghuade Caizheng Dongyin" [Fiscal Motivation for Property-Rights Restructurings of Public Enterprises in China], *Jingji Yanjiu* [Economic Research], no. 2 (February 2008): 56–68.

support effective corporate restructuring, China sought partial reforms and second-best solutions until more sustainable and efficient solutions could be adopted. Although China clearly lacked a social security system that is a prerequisite for rapid privatization, institutional deadlock or paralysis did not ensue. China successfully adopted a number of ad-hoc transitional measures that allowed it to move ahead with reform even in the absence of a unified social security system to provide a safety net for those losers from the reform. The state was able to time change in such a way so as to allow for the development of necessary institutions and to navigate the political crosscurrents that constrained China's corporate restructuring.

Second, our findings argue for a more complex understanding of the dynamics of corporate restructuring. They suggest that we need to take into account the complex agenda surrounding any reform measure. Shareholding was chosen over privatization because it was more compatible ideologically with China's adherence to socialism. It was a feasible policy option that served multiple objectives. Shareholding was a viable means to raise capital[44] and limit unemployment, while simultaneously beginning the process of ownership diversification. Once begun, shareholding turned into a useful political tool to move ahead with corporate restructuring. Diversification of ownership through shareholding altered the role of the state with regard to the SOEs—the state went from being the sole proprietor to being simply one of many investors. This led to an assessment of firm assets and the creation and distribution of shares to form shareholding companies, shareholding cooperatives, listed companies, and privately owned firms. This process of corporatization allowed for a clarification of state assets as well as property rights. Even though the state often still held a controlling share, a change in the state's ownership status meant that the state was no longer responsible for profits and losses and it no longer had to guarantee its earlier levels of funding. This hardened budget constraints and made the firm, not the state, responsible for taking care of its workers. It then opened the door for factories either to be shut down or sold and for workers to be fired or laidoff—a process that the state had long delayed.

Prolonging the restructuring process thus paved the way for future restructuring options. Through shareholding the state was able to end its implicit social contract with state workers. By allowing the workers to become investors through the shareholding system the state could claim that the workers had become, or had the right to become, owners of the public firms to which they had devoted their working lives.

44 In China, this was done primarily within factories—very few firms were actually listed.

We would argue that regardless of whether or not social security institutions were in place, the CCP needed to undergo what was a political as much as an economic process. As Oi has argued elsewhere, China had to limit the political costs of restructuring as it tried to move the process forward, treading hesitantly until the late 1990s when it took more decisive action at the Fifteenth Party Congress by giving a green light to privatization of large portions of state-owned enterprises. Workers became part-owners of the public assets to which they had devoted their working lives. Providing shares was a necessary and important political act by the state. Shares were distributed as political payoff to state workers for their previous service. Such distributions helped thwart charges of asset stripping and maintained political stability by appeasing the workers. Making the state workers shareholders changed their status—*shenfen*. They then had the right either to remain "owners" of the firm or to sell their shares for immediate cash and leave the firm—at which point their relationship with the firm (and the state) was terminated. The decision was up to the workers themselves. Although this was nothing more than a ritual, such acts were necessary to pave the way politically for the transformation from public to private ownership of the former state-owned assets.

Our finding that restructuring increased tax revenues for the state suggests that the state had greater flexibility to pay the costs of restructuring. Although we do not know how these increased revenues were used, the fact remains that restructured firms gave the state at all levels more resources and thus more flexibility to restructure the economy and maintain political stability through the strategies we have described above to end the social contract.

Finally, although our findings suggest that prolonging the restructuring process to pursue multiple agendas had its costs, such problems were an impetus for further reform. To China's credit, the costs of the earlier second-best solutions necessitated that the state move to the next stage in the corporate restructuring process. As firms have moved to the second or third phases of restructuring, the political concerns that originally steered the state to favor relatively equal worker-manager shareholding systems have become a problem obstructing further change. The shareholding system that began primarily as a scheme to raise money through the sale of shares to workers turned into a means by which the workers can now block further restructuring, including sales to both domestic and international companies.[45] The strength of this power remains to be investigated. The

45   A small percentage of our respondents replied that worker shares should be abolished.

local governments recognized that increases in the number shares held by managers and increases in the number of MBOs were necessary for effective corporate management.

Interviews in 2004 and 2005 suggest that enterprise managers were increasingly frustrated by the power of employee shareholder associations that were blocking opportunities for sales or joint ventures.[46] Some local authorities were so anxious to ensure that a firm could be sold that, based on years of service, they gave the workers money to buy extra shares, but then immediately turned around and offered to buy back all the worker shares—allowing the workers an opportunity to reap quick cash returns. One might ask why not just give the workers the extra money? When asked, the local authorities explained that a necessary step in the restructuring process was to give shares to long-time workers and then buy back the shares to mark the end of one stage in China's economic history and the beginning of another—from a socialist planned economy to a capitalist market economy.

46 For a different perspective on whether the employee shareholder associations have any influence, see Sally Sargeson and Jian Zhang, "Reassessing the Role of the Local State: A Case Study of Local Government Interventions in Property Rights Reform in a Hangzhou District," *China Journal*, no. 42 (July 1999): 77–99, especially 91–92.

3 The Local Politics of Restructuring State-owned Enterprises in China[1]

Jin Zeng and Kellee S. Tsai

Since China embarked on a series of market-oriented reforms in 1978, the tightly-knit institutions of its socialist-era economy have been unraveling. Reforms in the pricing system, the fiscal system, and the financial system have gradually altered the operating environment for state-owned enterprises (SOEs), which can no longer rely on the state for the allocation of raw materials, procurement of their products, fiscal subsidies, or unlimited access to bank loans. Amid fierce competition from the booming private sector, by the late 1990s the performance of a majority of the SOEs was deteriorating and the debt-laden SOEs had already ceased to be "cash cows" to local governments. However, the apparently straightforward solution of privatization did not follow reforms in associated dimensions of the economic system.

It was not until the late 1990s that the Chinese government began to depart from its piecemeal reforms and initiate ownership transformation of the SOEs. Like other transition economies, China embarked upon the process of reform in the absence of a range of complementary institutions. It did not establish a unified national SOE management system that could regulate and monitor privatization at the local levels until 2003. Independent asset valuation agencies were virtually nonexistent, leaving ample room for asset stripping and rent-seeking behavior. Most notably, the national

1 This chapter is based on fieldwork conducted by both authors—individually and jointly—from 2001 to 2006, and draws on material in Jin Zeng, "Performing Privatization—The Restructuring of Small and Medium Public Enterprises in China," Ph.D. diss., Johns Hopkins University, 2007. Zeng acknowledges financial support from the Social Science Research Council and the Institute of Humane Studies for her dissertation fieldwork.

social security system was inchoate in the late 1990s and therefore unavailable as an alternative source of pensions and unemployment insurance for laid-off workers after the old work-unit-based socialist welfare system was dismantled.

However, by the end of 2003 over 85 percent of small and medium industrial SOEs supervised by local governments had been restructured.[2] The apparent correlation between a rapidly growing private sector and the emergence of a large number of privatized firms in China since the mid-1990s has given rise to two popular arguments—first, private-sector development drives SOE restructuring, and, second, localities with a large private sector have been more proactive in restructuring their state sectors. These claims imply that privatization in China has been driven by economic incentives in a marketizing environment. Although the economic explanations have overall validity when it comes to explaining the motivations for the central leadership to promote SOE restructuring, they fail to describe the specific process of restructuring at the local levels, especially the timing mechanism for privatization. Similarly, by focusing on firm-level incentives for change, the varieties of capitalism literature provides little guidance to explain the timing of institutional change. In the case of China's privatization, it was the local state, rather than the SOEs, that was the most critical agent of change, and the timing of institutional change was closely related to the incentives of local officials for privatization. More specifically, our fieldwork in various Chinese cities reveals that local officials' motivations for restructuring were shaped by both economic and political logics, and that the booming private sector actually delayed the much-needed SOE restructuring in some localities. This observed divergence from conventional wisdom gives us an opportunity to reexamine the impact of private-sector development on SOE restructuring and the timing of major reforms. In so doing, this chapter addresses the following two questions: What explains regional variation in the timing of large-scale restructuring across Chinese cities? What factors motivated local officials to initiate large-scale restructuring?

Private-sector development and market competition changed the operating environment of state enterprises and squeezed the profit margins of SOEs. Saddled with a bloated workforce and outdated equipment, many SOEs were struggling to survive. However, the severity of the SOE problems was not uniform among the different localities. Even in cities with a large number of loss-making SOEs, local governments might not be expected to respond to the inefficient condition of the state sector with outright

---

2 Organisation for Economic Co-operation and Development, *OECD Economic Surveys: China* (Paris, 2005), 120.

privatization or job cuts, because carrying out costly reforms requires not only a sound economic rationale but also a strong political will. This chapter aims to explore *when* and *under what conditions* local officials acted on the dismal situation of a majority of the SOEs by initiating ownership transformation. We propose that the timing of large-scale SOE restructuring in a locality depends on the incentives of local officials for restructuring. These incentives, however, are mediated by the importance of private-sector development in the local economy and the political mandate to restructure SOEs from the upper echelons of the government. In localities where the private sector dominated the local economy during the early stages of SOE reform, local officials relied on the private sector to meet their key performance criteria, including local economic growth, job provision, and increases in local revenue. Therefore, in areas where the local economy had grown rapidly through private-sector development, local officials were not motivated to restructure the SOEs despite their sluggish performance. Although the existence of a vibrant private sector made *implementation* of local restructuring relatively easier by providing laid-off workers with alternative jobs, it negatively affected local officials' incentives for privatization by making *initiation* of restructuring a low priority.

However, when municipal governments set timetables for local SOE restructuring and included the speed of SOE restructuring as a measure for evaluating the performance of officials, local officials had strong political incentives to initiate local restructuring. In order to meet the deadlines imposed by the municipal governments while reducing insider opposition to privatization, local officials gave SOE insiders priority and discounts in the privatization process. As such, we argue that the relationship between the development of the private economy and restructuring is much more complex than earlier, economic-oriented arguments would suggest. This chapter underscores the importance of political motivations for restructuring, as our research indicates that the criteria used for evaluating local officials has had a more direct impact on the timing and strategies of large-scale restructuring in a locality than the level of local private-sector development.

China's privatization experience also illustrates how the Chinese government managed to move toward unprecedented state-sector reform when many of the complementary institutions thought to be necessary for a transition to a market economy were lacking. Instead of relying on market institutions to divest the SOEs, the Chinese Communist Party employed political and administrative means to orchestrate privatization at the local levels. As the above argument shows, the political mandate from the higher authorities to restructure state enterprises turned out to play a critical role in motivating local officials to initiate and implement large-scale ownership transformation. Although the mandate to privatize was given in the absence of supporting institutions for privatization, local officials made up for this deficiency by innovatively devising many ad-hoc practices or measures to cope with the restructuring of a large number of SOEs, including measures to maintain social stability by assisting laid-off workers. For these reasons, one of the analytic implications of our findings is that the firm-centric varieties of capitalism literature has limited explanatory relevance in specifying the actual politics and timing of China's privatization process. Instead, an examination of the local policy environment in which local officials are embedded proves to be more revealing given the reality of decentralized policy implementation in contemporary China.

To illustrate the logic of our arguments, this chapter examines three different developmental patterns—private sector–dominated, foreign sector–dominated, and state sector–dominated—as represented by the cities of Wenzhou, Xiamen, and Shenyang, respectively. The chapter consists of three major sections. The first section reviews the relevant literature on the relationship between private-sector development and privatization; the second section examines the privatization process in each of the three cities; and the third section analyzes the comparative implications of privatization in the three cases.

Definitional Issues

In 1997, the Fifteenth Party Congress endorsed the policy of "keeping the large and letting go of the small," which literally means retaining state ownership of large SOEs while allowing small and medium-sized firms to undergo ownership transformation. Although this policy signaled a relaxation of the party-state's official ideological stance, the word "privatization" remains politically sensitive in China. To avoid potential political problems, governments at all levels have thus adopted other terms to refer to the process of reforming SOEs, such as "restructuring" (*gaizhi*), "ownership transformation" (*suoyouzhi gaizao*), or "transformation of ownership to a joint-stock system" (*gufenzhi gaizao*).[3] The most frequently used term is "restructuring" (*gaizhi*), which refers to any structural change or ownership

---

3 As Steinfeld rightly points out, "One of the geniuses of Chinese economic reform has always been the tendency to blur semantic distinctions and sidestep inflammatory labels. . . . Ambiguous language has been extremely useful for establishing continuity with the past and shrouding revolutionary change in a veil of normality. Such language, however, causes considerable confusion in the area of enterprise reform, even with regard to the most basic questions of firm-level categorization." Edward S. Steinfeld, *Forging Reform in China: The Fate of State-Owned Industry* (New York: Cambridge University Press, 1998), 10.

transformation of a firm, including leasing, corporatization, sales, bankruptcy, mergers, and acquisitions.[4] In line with the central policy of "letting go of the small," this chapter focuses on the restructuring of small and medium-sized SOEs that have not been listed on domestic or international stock exchanges.[5]

This chapter uses the first major wave of restructuring in a locality to measure the timing of local SOE restructuring. We recognize that spontaneous or small-scale restructuring occurred in some areas in the early 1990s,[6] but our chapter focuses on large-scale restructuring at the local level after 1997. The timing of restructuring is important because the efficiency of local firms directly affects economic development and delays in restructuring are costly to the local economy. SOE losses have burdened the state-owned banks with non-performing loans and accumulated enormous contingent liabilities.[7] In particular, the problem of insider control and asset stripping in many SOEs has exacerbated operational inefficiencies and depleted state assets at an alarming rate, leaving local governments with fewer resources to compensate workers for severing ties with the SOEs.[8] The standards

4 Privatization is only one of several possible expressions of SOE restructuring. For more details, see Jean C. Oi, "Patterns of Corporate Restructuring in China: Political Constraints on Privatization," *China Journal*, no. 53 (January 2005): 115–36.

5 According to the State-owned Assets Supervision and Administration Commission (SASAC), by the end of 2003 there were about 150,000 SOEs, 98 percent of which were small and medium-sized. "Standards Released for SOE Buyouts," *China Daily*, April 15, 2005, at http://china.org.cn/english/government/125945.htm, accessed May 19, 2010.

6 There were only a few cases of small-scale privatization in the 1980s. In the early 1990s, several cities in China pioneered wholesale privatization. Local officials in Zhucheng, a city in Shandong, sold all municipally-owned state enterprises in 1992. Hence, the mayor of the city, Mr. Chen Guang, was nicknamed "Chen Sold Out" (*Chen Maiguang*). For an introduction to the privatization process in Zhucheng, see Zhang Wenkui and Yuan Dongming, *Zhongguo Jingji Gaige 30 Nian: Guoyou Qiye Juan* [Thirty Years of China's Economic Reform: Volume on State-Owned Enterprise] (Chongqing: Chongqing daxue chubanshe, 2008), 112–14.

7 Shahid Yusuf, Kaoru Nabeshima, and Dwight H. Perkins, *Under New Ownership: Privatizing China's State-Owned Enterprises* (Stanford: Stanford University Press, 2006), 216–17.

8 According to a rough government estimate, a daily average of over RMB100 million in state assets has been lost (*liushi*) since 1980, and the total loss of state assets has reached RMB1,000 billion. See Tian Guoqiang, "Guoyou Qiye Gufenzhi Gaige He Zhongguo Zhidu De Pingwen Zhuanxing" [Shareholding Reform of State-owned Enterprises and the Stable Institutional Transition in China], *Dangdai Zhongguo Yanjiu* [Modern China Studies], no. 2 (1998): 73–86. Some scholars have compared state assets to ice cream cones in the summer: "If you do not sell them now, then they will melt away quickly and nothing will be left."

for official compensation to SOE workers have increased every year, which raises the overhead costs of late restructuring to SOEs, and therefore to local governments. In addition, early SOE restructuring was desirable because in theory SOE restructuring improves resource allocation and economic efficiency, an issue that loomed as China prepared to accede to the WTO in the late 1990s.

The Local Politics of Re-structuring State-owned Enterprises

The worldwide spread of privatization in the 1980s and 1990s has given rise to many studies analyzing the reasons for ownership transformation. The following section outlines three types of theories that have been proposed to explain the cause(s) of privatization—namely, those highlighting private-sector development and market competition, political benefits, and the relaxation of political constraints by the central government, respectively.[9] Examining the relative strengths and weaknesses of these approaches enables us to provide an alternative explanation that challenges prevailing assumptions about the positive association between private-sector development and SOE restructuring. It is worth mentioning that none of the above-mentioned studies considers institutional complementarities as a precondition for privatization. While echoing this observation, we call attention to the issue of when local officials are likely to act upon political and economic incentives for restructuring despite the absence of supporting institutions for ownership transformation. Specifically, we propose that focusing on the political incentives faced by local officials provides more explanatory leverage when it comes to explaining the timing and pace of privatization in particular localities.

9 For example, Ross Garnaut et al., *China's Ownership Transformation: Process, Outcomes, Prospects* (Washington, DC: World Bank, 2005); Hongbin Li, "Government's Budget Constraint, Competition, and Privatization: Evidence from China's Rural Industry," *Journal of Comparative Economics* 31, no. 3 (2003): 486–502; Guoqiang Tian, "A Theory of Ownership Arrangements and Smooth Transition to a Free Market Economy," *Journal of Institutional and Theoretical Economics* 157, no. 3 (2001): 380–412; Henry Bienin and John Waterbury, "The Political Economy of Privatization in Developing Countries," *World Development* 17, no. 5 (1989): 617–32; Lin Bai, Gong Mu, and Zhang Gang, eds., *Wenzhou Moshi De Lilun Tansuo* [Theoretical Investigations of the Wenzhou Model] (Nanning: Guangxi renmin chubanshe, 1987); and Yongshun Cai, "Relaxing the Constraints from Above: Politics of Privatising Public Enterprises in China," *Asian Journal of Political Science* 10, no. 2 (December 2002): 94-121.

Market Competition as a Cause of Privatization

Most scholars view privatization as a market-driven process.[10] Guoqiang Tian's analysis of how the economic institutional environment affects the optimal choice of ownership arrangements typifies this market-competition-as-selection-mechanism thesis. Tian contends that when a market is well developed and when government intervention is minimal, private ownership arrangements are optimal, as firms do not need to rely on their external management ability to procure government-owned or -controlled resources.[11] Tian even predicts that the optimal timing of massive privatization is when the state-owned sector is only a small proportion of the economy (say, about 15 percent of the Gross National Product). His theoretical framework "regards an ownership arrangement not as given, or chosen directly by a social planner, but as an efficient response to the degree of economic liberalization and marketization."[12] His argument rests upon two key assumptions—that managers and workers of public firms have the autonomy to decide the ownership arrangements of the firms, and that they prioritize the firms' economic efficiency. However, these assumptions are not always empirically appropriate. In China, all SOEs are owned or supervised by different levels of government, which possess the ultimate authority to decide whether, when, and how to privatize a specific SOE. Although SOE managers and workers can propose to privatize their SOEs, such proposals are subject to the approval of local officials, as Oi and Han's study shows. Tian omits key actors, namely local officials, thus overlooking a basic causal dimension in the implementation of China's privatization process.

Relatedly, it may be unrealistic to assume that SOE managers and workers prioritize firm economic efficiency. In the course of our research, we found that they were more concerned about the individual distributional effects of privatization than collective efficiency gains from ownership transformation. Hence, we would expect workers to oppose privatization if they face the prospect of being laid off, and managers would probably sabotage privatization if they expect to be removed from their positions as a result of privatization via an outsider buyout.

10 Garnaut et al., *China's Ownership Transformation*; Li, "Government's Budget Constraint"; Tian, "A Theory of Ownership Arrangements"; Shaomin Li, Shuhe Li, and Weiying Zhang, "The Road to Capitalism: Competition and Institutional Change in China," *Journal of Comparative Economics* 28, no. 2 (2000): 269-92; and Yuanzheng Cao, Yingyi Qian, and Barry R. Weingast, "From Federalism, Chinese Style, to Privatization, Chinese Style," *Economics of Transition* 7, no. 1 (1999): 103-31.

11 Tian, "A Theory of Ownership Arrangements," 385.

12 Tian, "A Theory of Ownership Arrangements," 404.

Another influential contribution to the analysis of China's privatization process is a study commissioned by the International Finance Corporation.[13] The authors use firm-level data to analyze how the degree of private-sector development affects the extent of privatization,[14] and find that provinces with larger private sectors have privatized their state sectors more actively. Garnaut et al. reason that the public's acceptance of privatization is likely to be higher in cities with large private sectors because it is relatively easier for redundant workers to find new jobs. This reasoning appears plausible, but again, our fieldwork observations challenge its accuracy. The level of SOE workers' resistance to privatization in localities with large private sectors was not necessarily lower than that in localities with small private sectors. As Dorothy Solinger points out, the private sector generally has more job opportunities for rural migrants or the highly educated than for laid-off workers.[15] Moreover, irrespective of the level of private-sector development, SOE employees might strongly resist restructuring for various reasons, including, for instance, their preference for job security, the relatively higher benefits associated with some SOEs, the unattractive severance packages, and the dismal prospects of securing an alternative job.

Relaxation of Political Constraints as a Cause of Privatization

Instead of exclusively focusing on the economic rationale for privatization, Yongshun Cai argues that the relaxation of constraints by the central government provided political incentives for local officials to carry out widespread privatization in the late 1990s.[16] According to Cai, immediately after the central government relaxed the political constraints on privatization in 1997, "local governments seized this opportunity to privatize state and collective enterprises at an unprecedented pace."[17] Cai argues that local officials chose to adhere to government policy because it would not only benefit their localities economically, but also give them a chance to demonstrate their loyalty.[18]

Such a sweeping generalization assumes uniformity in the implementation of central policy and fails to capture regional variation in the timing of

---

13 Garnaut et al., *China's Ownership Transformation.*

14 They use the lagged employment share of the private sector in a province as the indicator of market liberalization.

15 Dorothy J. Solinger, "Labour Market Reform and the Plight of the Laid-off Proletariat," *China Quarterly*, no. 170 (June 2002): 405–32.

16 Cai, "Relaxing the Constraints from Above."

17 Cai, "Relaxing the Constraints from Above," 101.

18 Cai, "Relaxing the Constraints from Above," 102.

privatization. Although national policies provide a permissive political environment for privatization, our study shows how local state actors differed in their responses to the relaxation of political constraints on privatization, and how local officials' incentives for privatization were affected by a combination of the local economic structure and the criteria by which cadres are evaluated.

Political Benefits as a Cause of Privatization

The third perspective on privatization recognizes that it has political consequences. In examining the political economy of privatization in developing countries, Henry Bienen and John Waterbury contend that implementation of privatization will be tempered by political support for reform as well as by the leadership's desire to maintain control over economic resources and patronage: ". . . even in nonelectoral systems, leaders must find enough support or create new bases of support to sustain privatization policies."[19] Adopting this "political-benefit" perspective, Guy Liu, Pei Sun, and Wing Thye Woo develop a more sophisticated explanation of the motives of local Chinese officials for privatization.[20] We agree with the part of Liu et al.'s contention that "the combination of fiscal reform and intensified market competition itself is still not adequate to nurture the appropriate conducive institutional environment for privatization."[21] They suggest that the cadre management system during the reform era and the private benefits that local bureaucrats can capture from the state and privatized firms affect local officials' incentives for privatization. In particular, two elements of the cadre management system shape local officials' incentives for privatization: the fact that cadre performance is measured by the "hard target" (*ying zhibiao*) of local economic growth, whereas social stability represents a "priority target with veto power" (*yipiao fojue*).[22] This, according to Liu et al., means that China's cadre evaluation system "rewards the promotion of local growth *on the condition that* social stability is not in serious jeopardy."[23]

---

19 Henry Bienen and John Waterbury, "The Political Economy of Privatization in Developing Countries," *World Development* 17, no. 5 (May 1989): 629.

20 Guy S. Liu, Pei Sun, and Wing Thye Woo, "The Political Economy of Chinese-Style Privatization: Motives and Constraints," *World Development* 34, no. 12 (December 2006): 2016–33.

21 Liu, Sun, and Woo, "The Political Economy of Chinese-Style Privatization," 2020.

22 Liu, Sun, and Woo, "The Political Economy of Chinese-Style Privatization," 2022.

23 Liu, Sun, and Woo, "The Political Economy of Chinese-Style Privatization."

Due to "the political infeasibility of accessing the related data in China," however, Liu et al. acknowledge that their analysis lacks a convincing account of how private benefits affect local officials' incentives.[24] They claim that the outcome of local privatization is indirectly linked to local officials' political career advancement through the expected growth of local tax revenues from privatization and the preservation of social stability. Oi and Han provide evidence that tax revenues did increase with restructuring. But that is an expected reward in the future. Recent changes in the cadre evaluation criteria in some localities provide a much more immediate and direct incentive that has had a profound impact on the local restructuring process. Specifically, we found that *when the speed of local restructuring is adopted as a target for evaluating local officials' performance*, the incentive structure of local officials is substantially changed by directly connecting their political career advancement to the progress of restructuring.[25] The empirical cases in the next section illustrate this argument with the intention of casting new light on the impact of the cadre evaluation system and local private-sector development on the decentralized restructuring process. Contrary to the expectations of market-oriented analyses, we found that localities with the most developed non-state sectors, Wenzhou and Xiamen, experienced significant delays in privatization, in contrast to the locality in our study with the largest state sector, Shenyang. The reason for these counterintuitive findings may be traced to local political incentives—a variable that is absent from the literature on institutional complementarities that regards the firm as the major agent of change.[26]

SOE Restructuring in Wenzhou

Wenzhou is a mountainous locality with a population of 7 million people in the southeastern province of Zhejiang. Due to the Third Front (*sanxian*) development strategy and its propinquity to Taiwan, Wenzhou received

24 Liu, Sun, and Woo, "The Political Economy of Chinese-Style Privatization," 2025.

25 It is worth noting that our analysis takes the specific criteria for cadre evaluation as externally given. Explaining the change in cadre evaluation criteria at the municipal level would require additional data on the particular economic and political conditions for SOE restructuring and the orientation of municipal leaders toward SOE restructuring, such as how municipal leaders interpret central policies. Further research along these lines will enrich our understanding of the decision-making processes involved in restructuring China's SOEs at the intermediate level.

26 See Peter Hall and David Soskice, eds., *Varieties of Capitalism: The Institutional Foundations of Comparative Advantage* (Oxford: Oxford University Press, 2001).

little capital investment from the central government before the mid-1980s.[27] As a result, the state sector in Wenzhou was very small on the eve of the reform in the late 1970s. What set Wenzhou apart from other localities in the first decade of reform was the rapid growth of its private economy, coupled with a high degree of local initiative and even disregard for national regulations that stood in the way of its entrepreneurs.[28] In the late 1980s, Wenzhou was nationally known as a prosperous locality with a vibrant private sector based on household factories, specialized wholesale markets, informal financial intermediaries, and a steady supply of merchants who were willing to travel and live all over the country to market their products. In a series of reports and monographs, Chinese economists and policymakers began to refer to the rise of the "Wenzhou model."[29]

The vibrant growth of Wenzhou's private sector overshadowed its relatively insignificant and declining state sector. Table 3.1 shows that compared with the national average, the contribution of industrial SOEs to local gross industrial output was much smaller and it diminished more rapidly over the years from 1980 to 2004. Relatedly, the profits made by industrial SOEs as a

27 With the breakdown of the Sino-Soviet alliance in the early 1960s and concern about a possible war with Taiwan, in 1965 the Chinese State Planning Commission issued an economic program for military preparedness, in which the central government would devote its resources to building a strategic industrial base in China's hinterland, or what became known as the "third tier" or "third front." The so-called "first front," including the coastal areas, Xinjiang, and Inner Mongolia, was intentionally deprived of industrial investment. Barry Naughton, "The Third Front: Defence Industrialization in the Chinese Interior," *China Quarterly*, no. 115 (September 1988): 351–86; and Kellee S. Tsai, *Back-Alley Banking: Private Entrepreneurs in China* (Ithaca, NY: Cornell University Press, 2002), 49 n.48.

28 Kristen Parris, "Local Initiative and National Reform: The Wenzhou Model of Development," *China Quarterly*, no. 134 (June 1993): 242–53.

29 The phrase "Wenzhou model" first appeared in the Shanghai newspaper *Jiefang Ribao* [Liberation Daily] on May 12, 1985. Jian Xie, *Wenzhou Minying Jingji Yanjiu: Touguo Minying* [Research on Wenzhou's Private Economy: Penetrating the Private Sector] (Beijing: Zhonghua gongshang lianhe chubanshe, 2000), 37–38. Representative selections of other writings on the Wenzhou model include Lin, Gong, and Zhang, eds., *Wenzhou Moshi De Lilun Tansuo*; and Yuan Enzhen, ed., *Wenzhou Moshi Yu Fuyu Zhilu* [The Wenzhou Model and the Road Toward Affluence] (Shanghai: Shanghai shehui kexueyuan chubanshe, 1987). Articles written in 1986 by members of the Institute of Economics of the Chinese Academy of Social Sciences are translated into English and compiled in Peter Nolan and Fureng Dong, eds., *Market Forces in China: Competition and Small Business—The Wenzhou Debate* (London: Zed Books, 1989). For early journalistic discussions, see *Jingji Ribao* [Economic Daily], July 1986. In addition, newspaper articles from 1988 are collected in Yu Shizhang, ed., *Wenzhou Gaige Moshi Yanxin Yingxiang* [New Reflections on Wenzhou's Reform Model] (Wenzhou: Zhonggong Wenzhou shiwei xuanchuangu, 1989).

TABLE 3.1

Contribution of Industrial SOEs to Gross Industrial Output, 1980–2004
(unit: %)

	1980	1985	1990	1995	1997	1998	1999	2000	2004
Wenzhou	32.7	19.4	16.5	6.6	4.6	3.9	3.4	2.8	3.3
National level	76.0	64.9	54.6	34.0	31.6	28.2	28.2	47.3	35.2

Sources: 2005 Wenzhou Tongji Nianjian [2005 Wenzhou Statistical Yearbook] (Beijing: Zhongguo tongji chubanshe, 2005), 231; Zhongguo Tongji Nianjian [China Statistical Yearbook] (Beijing: Zhongguo tongji chubanshe), 1989 (pp. 224–25), 1992 (p. 365), 1995 (p. 375), 1999–2005.

percentage of profits made by all industrial enterprises in Wenzhou declined from 37.5 percent in 1980 to 8.4 percent in 1999.[30] Nevertheless, despite the small and declining contribution of the state sector, Wenzhou's GDP increased at an annual average of 18.6 percent during the period from 1980 to 2004, largely due to its rapidly growing private sector. Meanwhile, the share of employees in private enterprises and individual businesses (getihu) in Wenzhou jumped from a negligible 1.4 percent in 1978 to 41.9 percent in 2004.

Wenzhou achieved a high level of market development at a relatively early stage, as indicated by its various specialized wholesale markets. As early as 1994, there were already 513 commodity markets in Wenzhou, including 363 specialized markets, many of which had established international reputations.[31] The increasing number of private enterprises and growing competition from the private sector since the late 1980s dramatically changed the operational environment for the SOEs and greatly squeezed their profit margins. SOEs in Wenzhou experienced the "intrusion" of the private sector earlier than SOEs in other localities. They could barely survive in locally competitive sectors, such as garment making, lighter manufacturing, and shoe making. In 1990, over half of the 180 within-budgetary (yusuan nei) industrial SOEs were experiencing losses, and the aggregate level of their

30 The percentages are calculated by the authors with the data in Wenzhou Tongji Nianjian 2000 [Statistical Yearbook of Wenzhou 2000] (Wenzhou: Wenzhoushi tongjiju, 2000), 208.

31 Ma Jinlong, "Wenzhou Jingji Gaige De Lishi, Xianzhuang He Qianjing" [The History, Current Situation, and Prospects for Wenzhou's Economic Reforms], Jishu Jingji Yu Guanli Yanjiu [Technology, Economy, and Management Studies], no. 3 (1996): 15–18. For instance, in 1994 the button markets in Wenzhou's Qiaotou township constituted 70 percent of button output and 80 percent of button sales in China. In Wenzhou, there were over 3,000 manufacturers of lighter components in 1994, each specializing in one or two lighter components. The highly specialized markets and the large number of manufacturers for the same product indicate the high level of competition in Wenzhou's product markets.

losses reached RMB534 million, which exceeded the total profits of the 180 SOEs by RMB210 million.[32]

Given the predominance of the non-state sector in Wenzhou's economy since the early 1980s and the poor performance of its SOEs, some observers might have expected that local restructuring in Wenzhou would occur earlier and more rapidly. However, our research indicates that thriving private-sector development in Wenzhou was not accompanied by early SOE restructuring. Although there were sporadic cases of privatization throughout the 1990s, large-scale privatization did not occur until 2000. The Wenzhou Municipal Government proposed that the restructuring of the state sector be completed by the end of 2004,[33] and a city-wide survey conducted by the Wenzhou Statistical Bureau in 2004 reveals that there were 820 state-owned or -controlled enterprises in 2004, a net decrease of 510 SOEs compared with 2001.[34] Among the 209 SOEs and collective enterprises supervised by the Wenzhou economic and trade system (jingmao xitong), about 85.6 percent (179 SOEs and collectives) had been restructured by the end of 2004. The above data indicate that from 2000 to 2004 SOE restructuring in Wenzhou was an ongoing process.

Why did Wenzhou not restructure its SOEs earlier? One possibility is that it would have been politically risky to privatize SOEs without the central government's approval in the late 1980s and early 1990s when official ideological discrimination against private property was still palpable. But this does not explain why SOE restructuring was delayed until 2000 given that the Fifteenth Party Congress in 1997 formally endorsed the policy to restructure small and medium SOEs. We argue that there were three major reasons for the relative delay of SOE restructuring in Wenzhou. First, local officials lacked consensus on the desirability of SOE restructuring. Some local officials believed that the problems of SOEs arose from external environmental

32 Ma Jinlong, "Guanyu Wenzhoushi Guoying He Geti, Siying Qiye Waibu Huanjing De Bijiao Yanjiu" [Comparative Studies on the External Environment of State-owned Enterprises, Individual Businesses, and Private Enterprises in Wenzhou], *Jingji Gongzuozhe Xuexi Ziliao* [Study Materials for Economic Work] (1991).

33 "Wenzhou Zuida Guoqi Dongfang Jituan Fuzong Zisha Shijian" [The Suicide of the Vice President of the Largest State Enterprise in Wenzhou—Dongfang Group], July 15, 2003, at www.zj.xinhuanet.com/tail/2003-07/15/content_709874.htm, accessed May 19, 2010. This article quotes some data from a report on Wenzhou SOE restructuring and development. According to the report, by February 2001, among the 146 within-budgetary (yusuan nei) industrial SOEs, 70 had completed restructuring and 63 were at the implementation stage.

34 See Wenzhou Statistical Bureau, "Wenzhoushi Diyici Jingji Pucha Zhuyao Shuju Gongbao" [Bulletin of Major Data from Wenzhou's First Economic Survey], January 2, 2006, at http://www.wzstats.gov.cn/infoshow.asp?id=5545, accessed May 19, 2010.

conditions rather than from state ownership, and thus an effective way to invigorate SOEs would be to suppress the development of private enterprises so as to create a level competitive environment.[35] For instance, some officials argued that SOEs and private enterprises were not competing on an equal footing. SOEs normally had a heavier fiscal burden due to their welfare obligations; meanwhile, private enterprises usually evaded taxes.[36] In the absence of consensus on the desirability of SOE restructuring among local officials, a timetable for local restructuring was not set.

Second, SOE managers and workers in Wenzhou opposed local restructuring despite the existence of a strong local private economy. Since the late 1980s, a considerable number of SOE managers and skilled employees, attracted by the higher salaries or better opportunities for career development in the private sector, left the SOEs and joined the private enterprises. This self-selecting process of exit from the state sector actually increased the difficulties of restructuring SOEs, as the remaining employees chose to stay either because of their complacency with the status quo or their lack of competitiveness in the market economy.[37] As William Hurst points out, "Former SOE employees with, on average, a junior or senior high school education, and mostly aged between 35 and 50, were excluded from most types of both high-end and low-end employment in private or foreign-invested firms."[38] Given that private enterprises generally preferred to hire younger or more highly educated workers, laid-off workers had great difficulties in

35 For more details on the debate on the causes of the problems of the SOEs, see Ma Jinlong, "Guanyu Wenzhoushi."

36 Similarly, Justin Yifu Lin argues that privatization is not the solution for loss-making SOEs. He argues that the major causes of the SOEs' low efficiency are strategic, or the social burdens that most SOEs are shouldering, and SOE reforms, first and foremost, need to relieve the SOEs of these burdens. See Justin Yifu Lin, "Guoqi Zhengce Fudan Taizhong Siyouhua Bushi Gaige Fangxiang" [The Burdens SOEs Shoulder Are Too Heavy: Privatization is Not the Solution], January 12, 2005, at http://business.sohu.com/20050112/n223903598.shtml, accessed May 19, 2010.

37 Interview with a government official, Wenzhou, April 19, 2006. This official used the term "the old, the weak, the sick, and the handicapped" (lao, ruo, bing, can) to describe the majority of the remaining SOE employees.

38 William Hurst, The Chinese Worker After Socialism (New York: Cambridge University Press, 2009), 88. The following data on the makeup of the laid-off workers from the SOEs in 1999 indicate the average age and educational levels of SOEs workers in Wenzhou. In 1999, there were 10,943 laid-off workers from Wenzhou SOEs. Of the total number of those laid off in that year, 27.6 percent were under 35 years old; 51.7 percent were between 35 and 46 years old; and 20.7 percent were over 46 years old. In terms of their educational levels, only 1.7 percent had a college degree or above; 24.3 percent had a senior high-school diploma or the equivalent; and 74.1 percent had a junior high-school diploma or less. Wenzhou Tongji Nianjian 2000, 426.

securing alternative jobs in the private sector, and self-employment became an important avenue for their re-employment.[39] Hence, as long as the performance of SOEs allowed them to get by, managers and workers in SOEs resisted restructuring due to a fear of uncertainty.[40]

Meanwhile, government subsidies kept local loss-making SOEs afloat in the late 1980s and early 1990s, and few SOEs, even insolvent SOEs, were allowed to go bankrupt. Soft-budget constraints distorted the incentives for SOE managers, with some of them even preferring larger-scale losses to smaller losses. One SOE manager revealed the skewed reasoning, "If the SOE loses only one million RMB, then I have to beg the bank and the government for help, but if the SOE loses ten million RMB, then the bank needs to beg me to repay the outstanding loans and the government will have to come to our rescue (*kui 100 wan, wo qiu yinhang, zhengfu; kui 1000 wan, jiude yinhang qiuwo, zhengfu jiuwo*)."[41] Even when the government subsidies were reduced and the budget constraints hardened in the late 1990s, some loss-making SOEs subsisted on proceeds from leasing out their office space.

Third, local officials did not have much of an incentive to initiate SOE restructuring due to the relatively small contribution of the state sector to the local economy in terms of local SOE industrial output, employment, and fiscal revenue. This point is well-illustrated by the following case in the Yueqing district of Wenzhou. At the Tenth Plenary Session of the Third Conference of the Chinese People's Political Consultative Conference (CPPCC) in Yueqing in 2005, delegate Zhao Bailin put forward a proposal entitled, "SOE Reform Requires Attention" (*guoqi gaige, zaiyu zhongshi*).[42] Although the annual government reports always advocated SOE reform, Zhao observed that SOE restructuring in Yueqing lagged behind other districts in Wenzhou, and wrote, "I think government agencies [in Yueqing] did not pay attention to SOE restructuring due to the absence of a concrete timetable and pressure from higher levels of government." Zhao argued that without government-imposed deadlines and pressure, district officials would not take the initiative to restructure local SOEs for the following two reasons:

> First, the state sector is tiny in Yueqing, and local fiscal revenues do not rely on it at all. The existence or demise of the state sector does not matter that much to the local government. Second, SOE restructuring is inevitably associated

39 Hurst, *The Chinese Worker After Socialism*, 88–95.
40 Interview with a government official, Wenzhou, April 19, 2006.
41 Ma Jinlong, "Guanyu Wenzhoushi."
42 Zhao's proposal was available on the official Web site of the Yueqing government when we wrote this chapter. Unfortunately, the content was later removed.

with troubles and bad consequences, and government agencies do not want to deal with them. SOE restructuring requires the local government to allocate a certain amount of money, which is difficult to provide.

Zhao further argued that local SOE restructuring could not be implemented without the participation of the local government, as local officials play a decisive role in SOE restructuring.

Zhao's proposal effectively demonstrates the nature and necessary conditions for local SOE restructuring, which is far from being an automatic response to competition or market development. Furthermore, concerns about local revenues did not necessarily drive local officials to implement SOE restructuring. When the contribution of the local state sector to the local economy is negligible, and when local officials can rely on a prosperous private sector for revenue, they lack incentives to restructure the state sector, however trouble-ridden it may be, especially given the potential political costs that restructuring might bring.

As a result of the above three factors, most SOEs in Wenzhou were not restructured until they were barely functioning. But by then, privatization came too late to single-handedly revive loss-making SOEs burdened with outdated equipment and heavy debt. An official in Wenzhou labeled such restructuring, "crisis restructuring," and lamented, "Most SOEs missed their prime time to be restructured, and it is not surprising that the performance of most restructured SOEs was poor."[43] This official echoed the point made by Zhao Bailin. He remarked that SOE restructuring could not be accomplished in a spontaneous manner, and it was difficult to restructure SOEs without forceful top-down administrative pressure. Indeed, due to the combination of opposition from insiders and lack of consensus among local officials, private entrepreneurs were largely excluded from SOE privatizations.[44] As discussed above, there was no consensus among officials in Wenzhou on the desirability of SOE restructuring, and they did not have a strong incentive to initiate SOE restructuring due to the relative insignificance of the state sector in local economic development. One official frankly told us that few local SOEs improved performance after privatization. Hence, when

43 Interview with a government official, Wenzhou, April 19, 2006.

44 Our fieldwork in other Chinese cities indicates that given the lax regulatory environment for SOE restructuring, insider privatization was preferred by both managers and local officials because it provided local elites with opportunities for asset appropriation and self-enrichment. For a general theory on elite opportunities for asset appropriation in transitional economies, see Andrew G. Walder, "Elite Opportunity in Transitional Economies," *American Sociological Review* 68, no. 6 (2003): 899–916.

SOE managers and workers opposed restructuring, local officials, attaching a high priority to social stability, usually yielded to the pressure of insiders by postponing the restructuring.[45] To pacify insiders, local officials usually gave them priority to purchase the SOEs where they were employed, while outside investors were largely precluded from participating in the restructuring process.

SOE Restructuring in Xiamen

Xiamen is a coastal city in southeastern Fujian province, with a long history as one of China's leading trade ports and a population of 1.53 million in 2005.[46] Similar to the case of Wenzhou (though to a lesser extreme), Xiamen also received limited investment from the central government during the Mao era due to its proximity to Taiwan.[47] Once Xiamen was designated a special economic zone (SEZ) in 1980, however, its location and ties to overseas Chinese became valuable assets in the city's economic transformation as FDI poured in from Taiwan, Hong Kong, and other developed countries.[48] Foreign-invested enterprises (FIEs) became the engine of local economic growth.

Table 3.2 shows Xiamen's phenomenal annual growth in GDP and the FIE share of industrial output from 1983 to 2004. The contribution of FIEs jumped from nil in 1980 to 83.3 percent of Xiamen's total industrial output in 2004; and local GDP soared from RMB94.4 million in 1983 to RMB88.3 billion in 2004, an increase of nearly 93 times within two decades. Meanwhile, the steady decline of the once-important public sector contrasts

45 Interview with a government official, Wenzhou, April 19, 2006. His observation was echoed by our interviewees in other localities. Local officials tended to agree with managers and workers and rarely imposed a privatization strategy on the SOEs. When there was fierce insider resistance to privatization, local officials were likely to put off privatization to avoid an escalation of tensions with managers and workers.

46 For the history of economic development in Xiamen, see Jude Howell, *China Opens its Doors: The Politics of Economic Transition* (Boulder, CO: Lynne Rienner, 1993), 125–79; and David L. Wank, *Commodifying Communism: Business, Trust, and Politics in a Chinese City* (New York: Cambridge University Press, 1999), 17–22.

47 Compared to the northeastern and central industrial centers, Xiamen received minimal capital investment from the center during the Mao era, but in relative terms the amount of industrial output generated by the state sector on the eve of reform was higher in Xiamen than in Wenzhou (i.e., over 90 percent as compared to 32.7 percent).

48 The SEZ was originally confined to a small district and was not expanded to the entire island until 1984. The three other SEZs were in Guangdong province—Shenzhen, Shantou, and Zhuhai. Hainan became the fifth SEZ in 1988. For SEZ policy with reference to Xiamen, see Howell, *China Opens its Doors*, 125–79.

TABLE 3.2

Contribution of FIEs to Xiamen's Industrial Output,
1983–2004

Year	Annual GDP growth rate (%)	FIE industrial output value as % of total industrial output
1983	8.8	1.2
1985	49.4	18.5
1990	19.1	59.8
1995	34.0	70.9
1996	19.7	73.7
1999	9.3	84.0
2000	14.0	84.8
2001	11.3	83.8
2002	16.1	84.2
2003	17.2	84.6
2004	16.3	83.3

Sources: Jude Howell, "The Political Economy of Xiamen Special Economic Zone," in Y.M. Yeung and David K.Y. Chu, eds., *Fujian: A Coastal Province in Transition and Transformation* (Hong Kong: The Chinese University Press, 2000), 123; and *Xiamen Tongji Nianjian* [Xiamen Statistical Yearbook] (Beijing: Zhongguo tongji nianjian), various years.

with this otherwise impressive economic picture.[49] The industrial output of the public sector shrank from generating over 90 percent of total industrial output in 1983 to less than 16.7 percent in 2004.

The decline of Xiamen's public sector from 1978 to 2004 is also reflected in the decreasing percentage of employees in the state sector, which was accompanied by employment growth in the non-public sector, especially the foreign-invested sector (see Table 3.3). Before 1985, the non-public sector was almost negligible, but since the mid-1980s it has rapidly generated new jobs and by 2004 it accounted for about 75 percent of local employment. In contrast, the percentage of employees in the state sector dropped from 54.7 percent of total employees in 1978 to 26 percent in 2004.

Realizing the importance of the foreign-invested sector to the local economy and government revenue, local officials in Xiamen identified FDI as a developmental priority, and the amount of FDI introduced each year became one of the key indicators in evaluating cadre performance. Xiamen's heavy reliance on FDI has had mixed implications for the state sector. On the one hand, the booming foreign-invested sector, fueled by favorable municipal policies (such as land, credit, and tax policies), disadvantaged the state

49 The public sector includes both the state and collective sectors.

TABLE 3.3

Employment in Xiamen by Ownership Type (various years)

Year	Total Employees	% of state employees	% of collective employees	% of employees in the non-public sector	% of employees in the foreign-invested sector
1978	180,779	54.7	45.3	n.a.	n.a.
1980	206,345	59.9	40.1	n.a.	n.a.
1985	244,815	62	33.1	4.9	3.4
1990	299,680	58.2	26.9	14.9	13.4
1995	461,467	42.4	14	43.6	39
2000	501,398	33.1	8.9	58	48.9
2003	564,906	27.8	5	67.2	55
2004*	617,354	26	3.3	75	58

Source: *2005 Xiamen Jingji Tequ Nianjian* [2005 Xiamen Special Economic Zone Yearbook], at www.stats-xm
.gov.cn/tjxx/tqnj/2005/maino.htm, accessed September 4, 2010.

Note: *Due to data discrepancies in the employment figures in the 2005 *Xiamen Jingji Tequ Nianjian*, we found
that the percentages of employment in the three ownership categories of firms exceeded 100 percent in 2004.
The actual amounts of employment in the state sector, the public sector, and the non-public sector in 2004 were
160,747, 20,174, and 463,433, respectively.

sector, which was already troubled by over-employment and heavy social burdens. The rapid introduction of FIEs squeezed the profit margins of the SOEs. Most small and medium SOEs were struggling to survive amid fierce competition from giant multinationals, and some poor-performing SOEs became increasingly dependent on income generated by leasing office space.[50]

Again, contrary to the market liberalization argument that localities with a larger private sector have been more active privatizing,[51] the booming private sector has actually delayed the much-needed restructuring of the state sector. As in Wenzhou, Xiamen did not launch large-scale restructuring of its state sector until 2000, three years after the central government sanctioned the policy of "keeping the large and letting go of the small." Because the local economy had grown remarkably well, local officials in Xiamen, like those in Wenzhou, were not eager to restructure SOEs despite their poor performance. The steady growth in the fiscal power of local governments allowed local officials to act in an ad-hoc manner to bail out some insolvent SOEs. More importantly, the relatively small contribution of the

50 This observation does not preclude the possibility that some SOEs improved their efficiency under competitive pressure from FDI. However, such cases are rare among the small and medium-sized SOEs.

51 Tian Guoqiang, "A Theory of Ownership Arrangements and Smooth Transition to a Free Market Economy"; and Garnaut et al., *China's Ownership Transformation*, 38–45.

public sector to local taxes and industrial output did not give local officials a sense of urgency to restructure the public sector.

At a more fundamental level, however, disincentives for restructuring the public sector were inherent in Xiamen's cadre evaluation system prior to 2000. The major performance criteria (*kaohe zhibiao*) of local officials included annual GDP growth, annual industrial output, fiscal revenue, social stability, and the annual amount of contracted FDI, with the last two being the priority targets. These criteria to evaluate local officials determined their tenure in office and opportunities for career advancement.[52]

Given the importance of FIEs to the local economy, local officials were more eager to devote resources to attract FDI, which would have a more immediate and positive impact on local employment, annual industrial output, and local fiscal revenue. In contrast, restructuring the public sector seemed less important due to its small contribution to the local economy, as well as the political and economic constraints associated with the restructuring process.[53] SOE restructuring may not improve firm performance within a short period of time, but it is likely to create immediate problems of debt repayment, rising unemployment, and the need to compensate workers with adequate severance packages. Thousands of laid-off workers unleashed in the restructuring process could jeopardize social stability, which would "cancel out all other work performance [of local officials], however successful, in the comprehensive evaluation at the end of the year."[54] One official had his own interpretation of the "priority targets with veto power" for local officials: "If you work for the Communist Party, then it is your obligation to do one hundred things the right way, but if you do one thing the wrong way, then you are dismissed."[55] Therefore, local officials were cautious to avoid the risks associated with initiating large-scale restructuring.

The lack of relevant municipal policies guiding the restructuring process before 2000 also made it difficult for district officials to go forward with local privatization. As a local official voiced his concerns: "It was politically risky to restructure without the guidance of relevant policies. We could

52 For detailed case studies examining the link between the career advancement of township and village leaders and their performance in rural industry, see Susan H. Whiting, *Power and Wealth in Rural China: The Political Economy of Institutional Change* (New York: Cambridge University Press, 2001), 101–10; Maria Edin, "State Capacity and Local Agent Control in China: CCP Cadre Management from a Township Perspective," *China Quarterly*, no. 173 (March 2003): 35–52.

53 Oi, "Patterns of Corporate Restructuring in China," 135.

54 Edin, "State Capacity and Local Agent Control in China," 39.

55 Interview with a municipal official in Xiamen, December 2, 2006.

be accused of dissipating state assets, which is a serious crime."[56] In other words, despite the fact that the central government sanctioned restructuring small- and medium-sized enterprises, implementation of this central policy entailed an array of facilitating policies, although not necessarily complementary institutions, at the local level. The following section shows how the changed incentive structure for local officials in Xiamen triggered the initiation of large-scale local restructuring in 2000.

Insiders' Opposition to Restructuring in Xiamen

In the mid-1990s, the Xiamen Municipal Government supervised about 400 small and medium SOEs, with total assets of RMB9.8 billion. About half of them were insolvent or on the verge of bankruptcy.[57] Contrary to the argument that restructuring was a spontaneous process in China,[58] very few public enterprises initiated restructuring in Xiamen. Our interviews with local officials and former SOE managers reveal that most SOE managers and workers were unwilling to sever their ties with SOEs.

Four major factors underlie the opposition of former SOE workers and managers to restructuring. First, most SOE workers cherished the "iron rice bowl" and enjoyed the generous benefits provided by the SOEs.[59] Jobs in some SOEs, especially profitable ones, were considered less demanding but better paid than jobs in private enterprises.[60] Furthermore, as Smuthkalin's chapter in this volume details, the social security system in China remains underdeveloped, characterized by resource scarcity, low coverage, and administrative

---

56 Interview with a district official in Xiamen, December 13, 2005.

57 The poor performance of most small and medium-sized SOEs can be attributed to three major factors—the withdrawal of the government's financial commitment in the 1990s, difficulties in securing loans from state banks, and their declining capability to generate profits amid fierce competition from the private sector, Cao, Qian, and Weingast, "From Federalism, Chinese Style, to Privatization, Chinese Style."

58 Garnaut et al., *China's Ownership Transformation*, 38.

59 During our fieldwork in the three cities, we also learned of a few cases where workers supported privatization. Workers in insolvent SOEs or SOEs that had partially or completely halted production for many years might have favored privatization because these SOEs could hardly offer workers stable jobs, whereas privatization would provide them with a sum of money as severance compensation.

60 The following is an extreme example of the salary disparity between state and private enterprises. A security guard in a SOE in Xiamen was paid RMB3,000 per month, whereas a guard in a similar job in a private enterprise was paid RMB600 per month. When the municipal government imposed a deadline for this SOE to restructure, the former workers put up fierce resistance and lodged complaints with the municipal government. Interview with a municipal official, Xiamen, December 9, 2005.

incapacity. It can hardly serve as an alternative source of welfare for work-ers, who were accustomed to relying on individual work-units for pensions, health insurance, housing subsidies, and other welfare benefits.[61] The inade-quate social security system partially explains the workers' unwillingness to sever their ties with the SOEs and their strong resistance to the dismantling of the life-long employment system. Second, similar to the case of Wenzhou, although Xiamen had a thriving private sector, laid-off workers in their 40s and 50s faced difficulties in finding jobs in private enterprises or joint ven-tures that preferred low-wage migrant workers or high-skilled labor.[62] Third, even though former SOE workers would receive monetary compensation at the time of restructuring, in most cases the severance pay was only sufficient to cover their living expenses for two or three years. Fourth, having spent most of their adult lives in SOEs, these workers had developed a psychologi-cal attachment to their work-units and still clung to the cradle-to-grave wel-fare that the SOEs promised to provide. Some of them claimed, "I belong to the SOE. It needs to take care of me until I die."[63] Relatedly, years of public-sector employment made workers risk-averse. Some turned down the option of becoming shareholders in their former SOEs because they preferred not to risk their savings. For all of these reasons, although SOE restructuring in Xiamen started in the mid-1990s, the initial restructuring only involved several small SOEs and due to resistance from SOE managers and workers, the pace of restructuring was slow. About twenty municipally-owned SOEs were restructured from 1994 to 2000, representing a tiny fraction of the total number of SOEs supervised by the Xiamen Municipal Government.

61 For more information on China's inchoate social security system, see Solinger, "Labour Market Reform and the Plight of the Laid-off Proletariat."

62 The "40s-50s," commonly referring to the laid-off workers in their 40s and 50s, could not find suitable jobs due to their low skills and lack of competence. In comparison, there were 275,500 migrant workers employed by FIEs in 2005. FIEs preferred migrant workers because they asked for lower wages than native workers and also because they were young and willing to endure hardships. Data available on the official Web site of the Xiamen Statistical Bureau, at www.stats-xm.gov.cn/staanis/tjfx00149.htm, accessed May 19, 2010. For more information on the plight of laid-off workers, see Solinger, "Labour Market Reform and the Plight of the Laid-off Proletariat"; Dorothy J. Solinger, "State and Society in Urban China in the Wake of the 16th Party Congress," *China Quarterly*, no. 176 (December 2003): 943-59; Yongshun Cai, "The Resistance of Chinese Laid-off Work-ers in the Reform Period," *China Quarterly*, no. 170 (June 2002): 327-44; and Yongshun Cai, *State and Laid-off Workers in Reform China: The Silence and Collective Action of the Retrenched* (London: Routledge, 2006).

63 Interview with a district official in Xiamen, December 11, 2005.

The major wave of SOE restructuring at the municipal level in Xiamen was not launched until 2000 when the municipal government issued, "An Opinion on Deepening the Restructuring of Small and Medium SOEs in Xiamen." The Opinion set the goal that by the end of 2002 all state assets would have retreated from small- and medium-sized SOEs in all competitive sectors. To emphasize the importance of SOE restructuring, the Opinion further stipulated that each work-unit should include the speed of restructuring as one of the criteria for the annual cadre performance evaluation. It was this governmental stipulation, the prioritizing of the speed of SOE restructuring—not the rise of institutional complementarities for privatization—that directly changed the incentive structure for local officials.

SOE Restructuring in Shenyang

Shenyang has lagged behind Xiamen and Wenzhou in private-sector development. If the market-oriented argument that higher levels of private-sector development are associated with earlier SOE privatization is valid, then one would expect privatization to occur later in Shenyang than in Wenzhou or Xiamen. Yet our fieldwork revealed that SOE restructuring was launched earlier and more aggressively in Shenyang than in Wenzhou and Xiamen. How do we explain this puzzle?

Including the provinces of Heilongjiang, Jilin, and Liaoning, northeast China was a major industrial base for China prior to 1978.[64] The region was known for its large SOEs engaged in heavy industrial sectors, especially iron, steel, machinery, and petroleum. However, many of the traditional industrial enterprises established under the planned economic system in the 1950s lost their competitive edge during the reform era (see Cai's chapter in this volume). The total industrial output of the three northeast provinces declined from 16.5 percent of national industrial output in 1978 to 9.3 percent in 1998.[65] As a result, the region is popularly called the "industrial rust-belt of China."

The problems associated with a declining local state sector have been felt most seriously in Liaoning. With the highest concentration of SOEs

64 The northeast region contributed China's first batch of steel, machine tools, locomotives, and planes after the founding of New China in 1949.

65 See Zhang Nianqing, "Ziyuan Kujie Qiye Laohua, Dongbei Xianxiang Zhuanzhi Chengben Juda" [The Drain of Natural Resources and the Lagging SOEs: The Huge Cost of Restructuring the Dongbei Phenomenon], http://www.people.com.cn/GB/jingji/1045/2083471.html, accessed September 28, 2010.

in China during the 1950s and 1960s, Liaoning was slow in developing a market economy in the mid-1990s. By 1997, industrial SOEs in Liaoning province as a whole had been operating at a net loss for three consecutive years. Among the 926 large and medium SOEs in Liaoning in 1997, 491 SOEs (53 percent) were loss-making, and many SOEs had partially or completely halted production.[66] The developmental challenges faced by SOEs in Liaoning province are all present in Shenyang, the provincial capital with a population of 6.94 million in 2004. Most SOEs in Shenyang suffer from outdated technology and equipment, inferior product quality, inefficient organizational structure, and heavy social burdens.

Local Economic Structure and the Performance of Local SOEs

Before the 1990s, in sharp contrast to Wenzhou and Xiamen, Shenyang's economy was dominated by the state sector, whereas the private sector remained relatively small. In 2000, the non-public sector contributed only 48.4 percent of local GDP.[67] The predominance of the state sector in the local economy was reflected in its controlling share of employment, which was 63.7 percent in 1990 and remained over 50 percent as late as 2004.[68] Due to the poor performance of a large number of local SOEs, numerous incidents of workers' complaints in Shenyang erupted from wage arrears and workforce reductions, which posed a major headache for local officials. The SOEs, once the pride and backbone of the local economy, during the early to mid-1990s increasingly became a burden.

Figure 3.1 shows the dramatic decline of the once-important state sector in terms of industrial output from 1990 to 2004, especially during the period from 1993 to 1998. The share of SOE industrial output in Shenyang fell from 54.1 percent in 1990 to 12.8 percent in 1998 and to 4.4 percent in

66 On the official Web site of the Liaoning Provincial Party School, see "Sannian Tuokun Hou Liaoning Guoqi De Xianzhuang Ji Fazhan Silu" [The Current Situation and Thoughts on the Prospects for SOEs in Liaoning After the Three-Year Program to Relieve SOE Difficulties], June 13, 2002, at http://www.lndx.gov.cn/text%5C2004-7/2002613132002.htm, accessed May 19, 2010.

67 "Baoliu Yancong Yu Dongbei Laogongye Jidi Zhuanxing" [Keep the Chimney and the Restructuring of the Northeast Traditional Industrial Base], 21 Shiji Jingji Daobao [Twenty-first Century Economic Herald], August 13, 2003, at http://news.sina.com .cn/c/2003-08-13/16081536442.shtml, accessed May 19, 2010.

68 "Shenyang Bianjian" Bianweihui, comp., Shenyang Tongji Nianjian 2004 [Shenyang Statistical Yearbook 2004] (Shenyang: Shenyangshi tongjiju, 2004). Note that the data on the number of SOE employees may include laid-off workers who had not cut ties with their original firms and were not counted as unemployed.

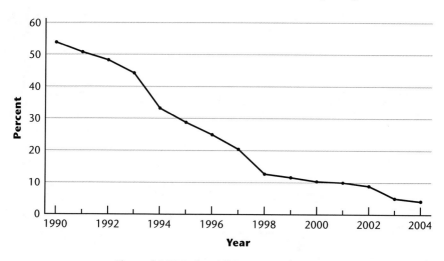

FIGURE 3.1 Share of SOE Industrial Output in Shenyang (1990-2004)

Source: Shenyang Tongji Nianjian 2004 [Shenyang Statistical Yearbook 2004]
(Beijing: Zhongguo tongji chubanshe, 2004).

2004. Yet in 2000, state assets still constituted 75.5 percent of all industrial assets; the large gap between total industrial assets and the share of industrial output is indicative of the extreme inefficiency of the state sector. Juxtaposing the small contribution of SOEs to local industrial output in 1998 with the large number of SOE employees in the same year (about 64 percent of local employment) reveals the severity of the inefficiencies associated with excessive employment in the state sector. As one former SOE manager put it, "In our enterprise, only one-third of the employees actually did their jobs, one-third were retired, and the other third were administrative staff. Therefore, in essence one-third of the employees were feeding the other two thirds."

Relatedly, industrial SOEs in Shenyang had suffered a net loss for three consecutive years—RMB900 million in 1995, RMB839 million in 1996, and RMB523 million in 1997.[69] Given the negligible industrial contribution of the state sector and its dismal performance as a whole, it became increasingly difficult to justify its occupation of an overwhelming amount of the city's industrial assets and over-employment of the local workforce. Furthermore, the predominance of the state sector in Shenyang's local economy severely constrained market development, as the SOEs were tying up a

69 *1998 Shenyang Tongji Shouce* [1998 Shenyang Statistical Manual] (Shenyang: Shenyang Statistical Bureau, 1999), 78.

large amount of valuable resources, including land, office space, bank credit, production materials, and human resources.

Local Cadre Evaluation System

In July 1997, then premier Zhu Rongji visited the traditional industrial base of Liaoning province. On behalf of the central government, he put forth the goal of "getting most SOEs out of difficulties within three years" (*yong sannian shijian, shi daduoshu guoyou qiye zouchu kunjing*). The goal of "three years to relieve difficulties" (*sannian tuokun*) was further elaborated by then president Jiang Zemin at the Fifteenth Party Congress in September 1997. With the highest concentration of SOEs among all provinces in China, Liaoning became a pilot province for SOE restructuring, and, according to local officials, Liaoning's success or failure in achieving the goal of *sannian tuokun* would have a decisive impact on the overall process of SOE restructuring nationwide. Rather than market competition or local private-sector development, as suggested by earlier theories about the reasons for privatization, the Shenyang case suggests that it was Premier Zhu's 1997 visit, together with Liaoning's newly-acquired status as a pilot province for restructuring, that created strong political incentives for Liaoning officials to launch and accelerate local restructuring.

In December 1997, the Liaoning Party Committee and the Liaoning Provincial Government issued a joint circular on concrete strategies for alleviating the difficulties of large and medium SOEs within three years. The policies at both the central and provincial levels set the stage for large-scale SOE restructuring in Shenyang. To achieve the ambitious three-year goal of alleviating SOE difficulties, in 1997 the municipal government in Shenyang clearly mandated that district governments impose rapid restructuring on small and medium SOEs, thus ushering in the first major wave of privatization in Shenyang.[70] District governments were required to sign responsibility contracts with the municipal government and to commit to restructuring 90 percent of the local SOEs by the end of 1998. The actually completed quota became a criterion for evaluating the performance of local officials. Although this performance criterion was not directly linked to their remuneration or promotion, district officials were extremely sensitive to the new performance indicator because it would affect their tenure in office

---

70 There were two major waves of SOE restructuring in Shenyang. The second wave took place from 2001 to 2003, when the focus was on SOEs that had been administratively transferred to district governments from the Shenyang Municipal Government. This chapter mainly discusses the first wave of SOE restructuring. See Zeng, "Performing Privatization," for more details on the dynamic process of local SOE restructuring.

and opportunities for promotion. One district official quoted a threat from his superior, "Can you promise to finish restructuring by the end of this year? If not, then we will replace you with someone else" (*Neng bu? Buxing, huanren*).[71] When asked if there was a clear reward and penalty system attached to meeting the restructuring quota, this official replied,

> SOE restructuring is a soft target that government officials in the higher echelons of the hierarchical regime may use to make promotion decisions. If a district leader fails to finish the task, then it indicates his incompetence (*meiyou nengli*), and his superiors may remove him from the position. But if he can get this job done nicely, then he may have a greater chance of being promoted. . . . Therefore, we need to ensure the security of our own jobs first before thinking about building grand careers (*xianbao zhiye, zaigan shiye*).

Another district official sharply pointed out that local officials were motivated by accumulating "political credits" (*zhengji*): "The campaign-style restructuring was implemented in a top-down manner, and local officials were trying to present a nice performance report (*shuzhi baogao*) by finishing the task imposed by their superiors."[72] According to him, hard-budget constraints did not necessarily drive local officials to promote SOE restructuring, as restructuring insolvent SOEs entailed capital infusions from the local government to repay debts and compensate workers, which in the short term worsened the local fiscal situation rather than improving it.

Although local economic growth remained an important cadre evaluation criterion, SOE restructuring became a priority target for local officials in Shenyang in 1997, creating strong incentives for district officials to promote local restructuring. By linking the job performance of local officials to the progress of SOE restructuring, the Shenyang Municipal Government was trying to achieve the ambitious goal of alleviating SOE difficulties within three years, as put forth by Premier Zhu. A former manager of a collective enterprise indicated that during the first wave of restructuring, the head of the district faced "restructuring criteria" (*gaizhi zhibiao*), which replaced the former "profit criteria" (*lirun zhibiao*).[73] The changed ranking of performance criteria reflected the priorities of municipal leaders and was one means of conveying these priorities to local officials at different levels and eventually to former SOE managers and workers. This former manager remarked, "The district officials talked me into buying the firm. If I had refused to buy it, then

71 Interview with the head of a district industrial bureau, Shenyang, August 3, 2005.
72 Interview with a district official of an economic and development bureau, Shenyang, August 5, 2005.
73 Interview with a former manager of a collective enterprise, Shenyang, August 12, 2005.

I would have been removed from the position of manager. I tried to help out the government by making acceptable arrangements for the workers."[74]

Implementing SOE Restructuring

Similar to the case of Xiamen, local SOEs in Shenyang were under supervision of different government agencies and there was no one overarching supervisory institution overseeing local state assets. To guide SOE restructuring at the district level, major leaders from the district party committee, district government, local national people's congress, and the district-level Chinese People's Political Consultative Conference participated in the process. The district government also formed a "property-rights leading group" (*chanquan lingdao xiaozu*), comprised of leaders from several district-level agencies, including the economic bureau, land bureau, audit bureau, inspection bureau, and workers' union. The "property-rights leading group" helped to coordinate policy-making and implementation among the different government agencies.

In one of Shenyang's districts, 280 public enterprises, representing about 90 percent of the total enterprises supervised by the district government, were restructured during the first wave of SOE restructuring (1997-1998).[75] In another district in Shenyang, 234 public enterprises, or about 98 percent of the total number supervised by the district government, were restructured from 1997 to 1998. The large number of SOEs restructured within one year illustrates the aggressive and rapid character of local restructuring in Shenyang. A district official described the swift change in the status of former SOE managers from government officials to new owners of privatized firms in the following way: "Overnight hundreds of red capitalists were born."[76] The sudden implementation of large-scale SOE restructuring in Shenyang challenges economic theories of restructuring that focus on the causal impact of either intensified competition or the level of market development. This phenomenon also challenges the characterization of local officials as being revenue-driven and/or efficiency-oriented.[77] The findings from our fieldwork support the argument that local officials were motivated

74 Interview with a former manager of a collective enterprise, Shenyang, August 12, 2005.

75 In this section "public enterprises" include both SOEs and collective enterprises in urban areas.

76 Interview, Shenyang, August 10, 2005.

77 Li, Li, and Zhang, "The Road to Capitalism"; Cao, Qian, and Weingast, "From Federalism, Chinese Style, to Privatization Chinese Style"; and Liu, Sun, and Woo, "The Political Economy of Chinese-Style Privatization."

to promote local restructuring because their personal career advancement was connected with the speed of local restructuring.

Explaining Regional Variation in the Timing of SOE Restructuring

The three empirical cases yield new insights into the impact of private-sector development on local SOE restructuring. In direct contrast to the expectations of market-oriented analyses, we found that the locality with the largest state sector, Shenyang, implemented restructuring with greater vigor and speed than the localities with the most developed non-state sectors, Wenzhou and Xiamen. These findings support our argument that the timing of large-scale SOE restructuring in a locality depends on the incentives of local officials for restructuring, which, we argue, are intimately tied to the political pressures to privatize, especially the specific cadre evaluation criteria at the local level. The impact of private-sector development on SOE restructuring depended on the importance of the state sector in local economic development. Although the existence of a developed local private economy made it relatively easy to take care of laid-off workers, by finding them jobs and paying severance, it also worked in the opposite manner by making restructuring a lower priority for local officials. This situation changed when there was a specific local policy providing strong incentives for local officials to initiate privatization by linking their job performance with restructuring progress. Thus, our three case studies show that the relationship between the development of the private economy and restructuring is much more complex than earlier, simple economic arguments suggest.

Table 3.4 summarizes the impact of the specific cadre evaluation criteria and local private-sector development on the timing of large-scale restructuring in a locality. The success of private-sector development and the minimal

TABLE 3.4

Explaining Regional Variations in the Timing of Local Restructuring

City	Level of local private-sector development	Specific cadre evaluation criteria	Timing of large-scale local SOE restructuring
Wenzhou	High	No strict timetable	2000–2004
Xiamen	High	2000: the speed of local restructuring became a criteria for cadre evaluation	2000
Shenyang	Low	1997: the speed of local restructuring became a criteria for cadre evaluation	1997

Source: Authors' Fieldwork.

contribution of the state sector to the local economy failed to provide local officials in Wenzhou and Xiamen with strong incentives to restructure the declining state sector. In the absence of strict timetables for local restructuring in Wenzhou, large-scale local restructuring did not take place until 2000, when the Wenzhou Municipal Government began a three-year effort (2000–2002) to restructure local SOEs.

Local officials in Xiamen were not motivated to restructure local SOEs until 2000, when the municipal government attached priority to the speed of local restructuring and explicitly specified that the speed of local restructuring would be included as a criterion for cadre evaluation. This change in performance criteria directly connected local officials' career advancement with the progress of local restructuring, and created strong incentives for local officials to initiate the restructuring of local SOEs. Therefore, we observe a strong correlation between the timing of large-scale local SOE restructuring and the timing of municipal policies that imposed timetables for restructuring.

In contrast, the rapidly deteriorating performance of a large number of SOEs in Shenyang posed a formidable obstacle to local economic development and the dire situation of the state sector propelled local officials to restructure local SOEs at an early stage. To achieve the goal of "relieving difficulties in three years" (*sannian tuokun*), the Shenyang Municipal Government imposed timetables for local restructuring and evaluated local officials' performance against the "restructuring criterion." In response to the municipal government's mandate, district officials launched large-scale local restructuring in Shenyang in 1997, making the restructuring process more rapid and aggressive in Shenyang than it was in the other two cities.[78]

There were two unintended consequences of setting timetables for local restructuring. First, privatization, instead of the pursuit of economic efficiency, became a goal in itself, and second, local officials pursued the speed of local restructuring without due consideration for workers' welfare and the sustainability of privatized firms. Local officials' drive for the speed of restructuring had a great impact on the choice of privatization strategies. One interesting finding from our fieldwork is that regardless of the level of local private-sector development, insider privatization was a prevalent strategy across the three cities. In order to meet the deadlines for local restructuring while preserving social stability, local officials gave insiders priority and discounts to purchase their SOEs.

78 This statement does not mean that compared to other cities in China the restructuring process in Shenyang was completed earlier. See Oi and Han's chapter in this volume.

A related implication of our research is that the varieties of capitalism literature is orthogonal to the fundamentally political nature of the economic reform processes in contemporary China. Focusing on the firm is analytically limited because China's SOEs lack the autonomy to initiate major reforms. By the same token, examining institutional complementarities cannot explain the timing of institutional change. Ultimately, the absence of certain institutions may be either enabling or constraining. On the one hand, decentralization and the absence of a national system for management of state assets before 2003 allowed local officials ample autonomy to decide when, to whom, how, and at what price a local SOE should be sold. At the same time, the lax regulatory environment and the lack of independent asset valuation agencies at the initial stage of privatization gave rise to rampant rent-seeking behavior and a prevalence of insider privatization. On the other hand, the lack of a national social security system constrained local officials' options for proceeding with privatization in a radical and massive manner. Without adequate pensions and unemployment insurance to fall back on, massive layoffs could trigger social unrest. Local officials thus tried to cushion SOE workers' resistance to restructuring by setting up reemployment centers, targeting insiders as buyers of their SOEs, and offering monetary compensation to workers for severing ties with their SOEs. In other words, the concept of institutional complementarities is indeterminate when it comes to detailing the local causal mechanisms and timing of privatization. Instead, in our study the local policy environment emerges as the critical variable defining how motivated local officials were to implement SOE restructuring.

In sum, we wish to highlight the critical importance of local officials in China's process of SOE restructuring by specifying *when* they are likely to initiate and implement large-scale restructuring at the local level. Although local private-sector development helped absorb some laid-off workers, thus facilitating local restructuring, it may have negatively affected the incentives of local officials for restructuring. Our study demonstrates that the specific cadre evaluation criteria had a more direct impact on the timing and strategies for large-scale restructuring at the local level than the extent of local private-sector development. This finding embodies an important policy implication—although economic or institutional changes may necessitate certain reforms, it is important to provide incentives to key actors (i.e., local officials) for initiating and implementing socially costly reforms. Given that our research is based on an examination of only three cities, larger-scale studies may subject our argument to more systematic empirical testing as local-level data become more widely available.

4 Distinguishing Between Losers

INSTITUTIONALIZING INEQUALITY IN CHINA'S
CORPORATE RESTRUCTURING

Yongshun Cai

Economic restructuring inevitably invites resistance when it sacrifices the interests of those subject to reform. Since the mid-1990s, China has taken unprecedented measures to reform inefficient public firms. From 1997 to 2002, the number of public enterprises declined by 85 percent, and the number of employees in the public sector (i.e., mainly public firms) decreased by 55.9 million. or 41 percent.[1] Given the inadequate welfare system before the early 2000s, these reform measures affected a vast number of employees in public firms. Workers' grievances translated into numerous incidents of resistance, becoming the major sources of social unrest in China at that time.[2] But, although workers' resistance posed a serious concern for the Chinese government, economic restructuring continued. After 2001, the Chinese government began to stop the transitional measures designed to help laid-off workers, signaling the end of the most difficult period of industrial restructuring faced by the government.[3]

---

1 National Bureau of Statistics, *Xin Zhongguo Wushiwu Nian Tongji Ziliao Huibian* [Fifty-five Years of Statistics in New China] (Beijing: Zhongguo tongji chubanshe, 2005), 48.

2 Yongshun Cai, *State and Laid-Off Workers in Reform China: The Silence and Collective Action of the Retrenched* (London: Routledge, 2006); William Hurst, "Understanding Contentious Collective Action by Chinese Laid-Off Workers: The Importance of Regional Political Economy," *Studies in Comparative International Development* 39, no. 2 (2004): 94–120; Ching Kwan Lee, "From the Specter of Mao to the Spirit of the Law: Labor Insurgency in China," *Theory and Society* 31, no. 2 (April 2002): 189–228; William Hurst and Kevin J. O'Brien, "China's Contentious Pensioners," *China Quarterly*, no. 170 (June 2002): 345–60; Feng Chen, "Subsistence Crises, Managerial Corruption and Labour Protests in China," *China Journal*, no. 44 (July 2000): 41–63.

3 *Zhongguo Qingnian Bao* [China Youth Newspaper], October 29, 2003.

Much has been written about the serious pressures arising from the industrial restructuring that China's government faced due to workers' widespread grievances and resistance.[4] This chapter examines how the Chinese government managed to successfully address the threat of massive layoffs and eventually complete the task of restructuring in spite of limited institutional capacity. A key part of the answer is that the impact of restructuring varied across regions and among different types of workers. I focus on one of the most seriously affected areas—China's rust-belt, the three northeastern provinces of Liaoning, Jilin, and Heilongjiang—to illustrate the disparities and the solutions. The government adopted a variety of policies to mediate the political and fiscal pressures on government in this blighted area.[5] However, I will show that even within a hard-hit locality, the state did not treat all of the affected workers equally.

Public enterprises in China consist of state-owned enterprises (SOEs) and collective enterprises. When economic restructuring began, the central government made commitments only to state-owned enterprises, especially large ones. By discriminating among different types of workers, the government reduced its political and financial pressures. Although laid-off workers from urban collective enterprises accounted for a significant portion of the total number of laid-off workers, they were almost entirely ignored by the central and local governments during the initial years of the reform. The governments were able to ignore the workers in collective enterprises because they were politically weak.

The unequal treatment of workers in the state and collective sectors is a practice that extends back to the pre-reform period. This chapter examines the consequence of this historical legacy both in terms of the ability of different groups of workers to generate pressure on the government and how the government then treated these workers. It suggests that China's hierarchical welfare policies helped mediate the political impact of the restructuring by placating the laid-off workers who were the most politically threatening. Even without necessary supporting institutional complementarities,[6] and without a developed social security system, the state was able to continue and eventually succeed in its restructuring. The Chinese reform experience suggests that, as elsewhere, a government's reform policy is shaped both by state

4 Dorothy Solinger, "Labour Market Reform and the Plight of the Laid-off Proletariat," *China Quarterly*, no. 170 (2002): 304–26.

5 Jean C. Oi, "Patterns of Corporate Restructuring in China: Political Constraints on Privatization," *China Journal*, no. 53 (2005): 115–36.

6 Peter Hall and David Soskice, eds., *Varieties of Capitalism: The Institutional Foundations of Comparative Advantage* (Oxford: Oxford University Press, 2001).

power and by the power of the victims or losers of the reform. It also reveals that in a non-democratic system it is possible to implement reform by sacrificing the interests of the politically weak groups regardless of their number.

Economic Restructuring and its Uneven Impact: Resource-Dependent Cities

The inefficiency of public enterprises in China became an increasingly serious problem in the 1990s.[7] As Oi and Han document, the Chinese government launched unprecedented efforts to address this problem through a series of reform measures, including reorganizing, streamlining, and eventually privatizing, declaring bankruptcy, or closing the affected firms. In the mid-1990s massive layoffs began to take place. Among these layoffs, the collective sector was harder hit than the state sector. As Figure 4.1 shows, the number of employees in the state and urban collective sectors has continued to decline since 1993. From 1995 to 2000, the number of employees in the state sector declined by 28 percent, whereas the decline in the urban collective sector was 63 percent.[8] The drop is most obvious between 1997 and 2000 when the annual number of laid-off workers (i.e., including unemployed laid-off workers and newly laid-off workers) was between 10 million and 13 million.

When the economic restructuring was carried out, China did not have an adequate welfare system (i.e., a pension system or an unemployment insurance system), and workers' welfare depended on the individual firms. Many workers, including retired workers, failed to receive living allowances or pensions because their firms were unable to pay them.[9] In 1997 half of the 12.7 million laid-off workers failed to find jobs, and half of the unemployed did not receive living allowances.[10] Meanwhile, the simultaneous layoffs of such a large number of workers also created a difficult re-employment environment. The re-employment rate of laid-off workers declined from 50 percent in 1997 to 40 percent in 1998 and 27 percent in the first half of 1999.[11] Consequently, an increasingly large number of employees and their families faced economic difficulties.[12]

7 National Bureau of Statistics, *Da Toushi* [A Comprehensive Perspective] (Beijing: Zhongguo fazhan chubanshe, 1998), 216.

8 National Bureau of Statistics, *Xin Zhongguo*, 48.

9 Also see Smuthkalin's chapter in this volume.

10 State Statistical Bureau, comp., *Zhongguo Laodong Tongji Nianjian 1998* [China Labor Statistical Yearbook 1998] (Beijing: Zhongguo tongji chubanshe, 1998), 431–32.

11 *China Daily*, August 30, 1999.

12 Solinger, "Labour Market Reform and the Plight of the Laid-off Proletariat"; Cai, *State and Laid-Off Workers in Reform China*, ch. 2.

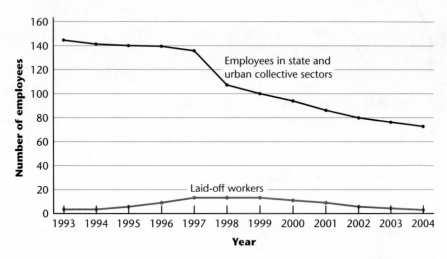

FIGURE 4.1 Number of Employees and Laid-Off Workers in China (million)

Source: Compiled from State Statistical Bureau, comp., *Zhongguo Laodong Tongji Nianjian* [China Labor Statistical Yearbook], various years (Beijing: Zhongguo tongji chubanshe, 1997–2005).

The impact of industrial reform was most serious in China's three northeastern provinces (Jilin, Liaoning, and Heilongjiang), which formerly had been China's industrial base and had contributed significantly to the country's economic and industrial development. In the First Five-Year Plan of socialist China that started in 1953, the central government chose 156 heavy industry projects as priorities for industrial development, 58 of which were located in the Northeast which was rich in natural resources, especially coal, oil, gas, and wood.[13] By 1995, the number of large- and medium-sized SOEs in the Northeast accounted for 13 percent of the national total.[14] However, when the central government discouraged problem-ridden banks from continuing to put money into inefficient SOEs, many of the enterprises had to cease production, close their factories, or declare bankruptcy, in addition to undergoing privatization. Between 1998 and 2002, the number of laid-off workers from state-owned enterprises in the three northeastern provinces accounted for more than 25 percent of all laid-off workers in China, whereas the populations of the three provinces accounted for only about 8.4 percent

13 Chen Yongjie, "Dongbei Jiben Qingkuang Diaocha Baogao" [An Investigation into the Basic Situation in the Northeast], at http://unpan1.un.org/intradoc/groups/public/documents/APCITY/UNPAN015994.pdf, accessed September 28, 2010.

14 *Zhongguo Tongji Nianjian 1996* [Chinese Statistical Yearbook 1996] (Beijing: Zhongguo tongji chubanshe, 1996), 408.

of the national total.[15] This concentrated impact is also reflected in the difference in poverty rates. Whereas the poverty rate in the country as a whole was 4 percent, it was 8 percent in the three northeastern provinces in the early 2000s.[16]

Layoffs

The situation was especially serious in the northeastern cities where industry depended on natural resources (*ziyuanxing chengshi*), such as coal. There are five such cities and four county-level cities in Liaoning, five in Jilin, and seven in Heilongjiang. The total urban population of these resource-dependent cities accounted for about 32 percent of the total urban population in the three provinces by 2000.[17] A common problem facing these cities was the declining deposits of natural resources and the increased costs of exploiting these resources. As a result, these were destined to be sunset sectors providing few options for generating new employment.

In Liaoning, for example, four of the five resource-dependent cities faced this problem.[18] The results are evident in the higher number of layoffs in these areas. While the urban population of the four cities (Fushun, Benxi, Anshan, and Fuxin), accounted for 22 percent of the urban population in the province, their laid-off workers made up 38 percent of the laid-off workers in the province in 2001.[19] In Fushun city, the urban unemployment rate was 31 percent in 2000, the highest in the country. By 2001, laid-off workers in the city accounted for 16 percent of the total urban population.[20] Of the 400,000 workers in the coal bureau in Fuxin, half were laid off, accounting for 45

15 State Statistical Bureau, comp., *Zhongguo Laodong Tongji Nianjian 2004*, 134; *Zhongguo Tongji Nianjian 2003*, 100.

16 Chen Yongjie, "Dongbei Jiben Qingkuang Diaocha Baogao."

17 *Liaoning Tongji Nianjian 2000* [Liaoning Statistical Yearbook 2000] (Beijing: Zhongguo tongji chubanhe, 2000), 56; *Heilongjiang Tongji Nianjian 2000* [Heilongjiang Statistical Yearbook 2000] (Beijing: Zhongguo tongji chubanshe, 2000), 43; *Jilin Tongji Nianjian 2000* [Jilin Statistical Yearbook 2000] (Beijing: Zhongguo tongji chubanshe, 2000), 47.

18 The fifth city is Panjin. A relatively new city established in 1984, Panjin does not face the problem of a serious decline in natural resources (i.e., oil and gas). *Zhongguo Huanjing Bao* [China Environment News], April 9, 2004.

19 *Liaoning Tongji Nianjian 2000*, 52, 68.

20 Wu Yaowu, Zhao Quan, Zhang Dandan, and Wang Zhiyong, "Ziyuan Kujie Haishi Tizhixing Zhang'ai?" [The Depletion of Resources or Institutional Obstacles?], in Research Center, *Guoqing Diaoyan* [Investigation of the National State of Affairs] (Ji'nan: Shandong renmin chubanshe, 2005), 257–324.

percent of the urban labor force.[21] According to a survey of about 1,000 laid-off workers in Benxi, Fushun, Fuxin, and Liaoyang in 2002, approximately 80 percent reported that their living standards were at the bottom of society. The survey also showed that more than 80 percent believed that society was unfair. When asked whether they would participate in collective petitions if they were asked to do so, about 28 percent answered positively.[22]

Worker Resistance

Workers' layoffs did lead to social unrest. Various studies have documented worker resistance, including by unpaid retirees, from the mid-1990s to the early 2000s throughout the country.[23] In 1996, about half of the instances of social unrest occurred because workers or retired workers had failed to receive salaries, pensions, allowances, or medical care.[24] In my earlier study, I found that the number of collective petitions (per 10,000 citizens)[25] in 1998 was positively and strongly correlated with the proportion of the urban population in 40 cities.[26] Collective petitioning is the most basic mode of collective action in China. The trend has continued in the 2000s. In 2001, instances of social unrest arising from conflicts related to

21   *Nanfang zhoumo* [Southern Weekend], February 21, 2003.

22   Si Ren, "Liaoning Si Chengshi Xiagang Zhigong Qingkuang Diaocha" [Survey of Laid-off Workers in Four Cities of Liaoning], in Lu Xin, Lu Xueyi, and Li Peili, eds., *2003 Nian: Zhongguo Shehui Xingshi Fenxi Yu Yuce* [2003: An Analysis and Prediction of China's Social Situation] (Beijing: Shehui kexue wenxian chubanshe, 2003), 162-68.

23   Cai, *State and Laid-Off Workers in Reform China*; Hurst, "Understanding Contentious Collective Action by Chinese Laid-Off Workers," 94-120; Lee, "From the Specter of Mao to the Spirit of the Law," 189-228; Hurst and O'Brien, "China's Contentious Pensioners," 345-60; Chen, "Subsistence Crises, Managerial Corruption and Labour Protests in China," 41-63. But also see Marc Blecher, "Hegemony and Workers' Politics in China," *China Quarterly*, no. 170 (2002), 283-303.

24   Yang Yiyong et al., *Gongping Yu Xiaolü* [Equality and Efficiency] (Beijing: Jinri Zhongguo chubanshe, 1997), 78.

25   Chen Jinsheng, *Quntixing Shijian Yanjiu Baogao* [Research Report on Instances of Collective Action] (Beijing: Qunzhong chubanshe, 2004), 59-60.

26   The 1999 yearbook for each city. The 40 cities are: Fushun (21.04 collective petitions per 10,000 citizens), Benxi (11.21), Harbin (9.99), Fuxin (9.43), Siping (5.67), Anshan (4.82), Jinzhou (4.56), Daqing (4.12), Taiyuan (3.79), Jiyuan (3.79), Ji'nan (2.82), Zhaozhuang (2.77), Zhenjiang (2.57), Rizhao (2.47), Changchun (2.4), Anyang (2.27), Yangzhou (2.24), Guiyang (2.22), Qingdao (2.04), Guining (1.85), Qinhuangdao (1.79), Zhengzhou (1.65), Jingzhou (1.61), Xiangfan (1.57), Yichang (1.51), Xuzhou (1.46), Luoyang (1.45), Wuxi (1.37), Weihai (1.32), Suzhou (1.25), Zhuzhou (1.23), Xiangtan (1.23), Nantong (1.22), Weifang (1.17), Weinan (1.12), Changzhi (1.09), Changsha (0.93), Yueyang (0.9), Xinyang (0.6), and Yibin (0.52).

workers' welfare or the reform of public enterprises accounted for 37.6 percent of the total instances of collective action in China.[27] This connection is found in both the industrial and the agricultural provinces. For example, in Jiangxi, an agricultural province, 985 instances of social unrest occurred between 1998 and 1999. Those involving workers or retired workers accounted for 52 percent and those involving peasants accounted for 22 percent.[28]

Not surprisingly, with high rates of layoffs, the northeastern provinces saw widespread resistance. Although not all collective petitions were presented by workers, failure to receive salaries, subsistence allowances, pensions, or reimbursement for medical expenditures were the most common reasons for the large number of petitions.[29] According to statistics that I collected on nine provinces, the average number of collective petitions directed at county-level authorities and above was 1.8 per 10,000 citizens in 1998, as opposed to 4.7 per 10,000 citizens in Jilin.[30] The other two provinces, Liaoning and Heilongjiang, do not report on the number of collective petitions in their yearbooks. But the 2000 yearbook for Heilongjiang province shows that the number of petitions (i.e., letters and petitions) in 1999 was even higher than that in Jilin, reaching 264 for every 10,000 citizens, as opposed to 154 for

27 He Zuowen, "Zhengque Renshi He Chuli Woguo Xianjieduan De Liyi Guanxi Maodun" [Properly Understand and Handle the Conflicts in our Country at the Current Stage], *Kexue Shehuizhuyi* [Scientific Socialism], no. 2 (2005): 8-11.

28 Conflicts arising from housing demolition accounted for 14 percent. Chen Jinsheng, *Quntixing Shijian Yanjiu Baogao*, 60.

29 Jilinsheng difangzhi bianzuan weiyuanhui, *Jilin Nianjian 1999* [Yearbook of Jilin Province 1999] (Changchun: Jilin nianjianshe, 2000), 116; Jilinsheng difangzhi bianzuan weiyuanhui, *Jilin Nianjian 2002* [Jilin Yearbook 2002] (Changchun: Jilin nianjianshe, 2003), 53.

30 See Jilinsheng difangzhi bianzuan weiyuanhui, *Jilin Nianjian 1999*; Nei Menggu zhizhiqu difangzhi bangongshi, *Nei Menggu Nianjian 1999* [Yearbook for Inner Mongolia 1999] (Beijing: Fangzhi chubanshe, 2000); Zhongguo gongchandang Zhejiangsheng weiyuanhui zhengce yanjiushi, Zhejiangsheng renmin zhengfu jingji jishu shehui fazhan yanjiu zhongxin, *Zhejiang Nianjian 1999* [Yearbook of Zhejiang 1999] (Hangzhou: Zhejiang renmin chubanshe, 2000); Henansheng difangzhi bianzuan weiyuanhui, "Henan nianjian" bianjibu, eds., *Henan Nianjian 1999* [Yearbook of Henan 1999] (Zhengzhou: Henan nianjianshe, 2000); Jiangsu nianjian bianzuan weiyuanhui, *Jiangsu Nianjian 1999* [Yearbook of Jiangsu 1999] (Nanjing: Nanjing daxue chubanshe, 2000); Hebei nianjian bianzuan weiyuanhui, ed., *Hebei Nianjian 1999* [Yearbook of Hebei 1999] (Beijing: Hebei nianjianshe, 2000); Shanxisheng difangzhi bianzuan weiyuanhui, *Shanxi Nianjian 1999* [Yearbook of Shanxi 1999] (Taiyuan: Shanxi renmin chubanshe, 2000); Anhui nianjian bianweihui, *Anhui Nianjian 1999* [Yearbook of Anhui 1999] (Hefei: Anhui renmin chubanshe, 2000); Sichuan nianjian bianji weiyuanhui, *Sichuan Nianjian 1999* [Yearbook of Sichuan 1999] (Chengdu: Sichuan nianjianshe, 2000).

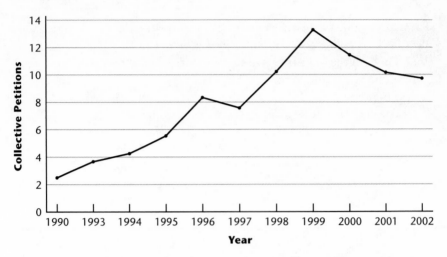

FIGURE 4.2 Collective Petitions in Five Northeastern Cities (per 10,000 citizens)
Source: Calculated from the Anshan, Benxi, Fushun, Fuxin, and Jinzhou yearbooks (1991–2003).

every 10,000 citizens in Jilin.[31] From the evidence we have been able to gather, we know that collective action by workers in Jilin and Liaoning accounted for 40 percent of the total nationwide instances of collective action, mainly by workers in the oil, coal, mine, forestry, and textile industries.[32] In 2002, Liaoning reported the most people in the country approaching the central authorities with petitions.[33]

The increase in collective petitions is particularly obvious in some northeastern cities. As Figure 4.2 shows, the number of collective petitions in the five northeastern cities increased from 1997 and reached a peak in 1999, with 13.3 per 10,000 citizens. The 40 cities mentioned earlier included nine in the Northeast. The average number of collective petitions per 10,000 citizens in the 40 cities was 3.2 in 1998, as opposed to 8.1 in the nine northeastern cities. The top eight cities were all in the Northeast, with the average number of collective petitions per 10,000 citizens at 8.9. The city that witnessed the highest number of petitions (i.e., 21) was Fushun, one of the resource-dependent cities.[34]

31 Heilongjiang nianjian bianzuan weiyuanhui, *Heilongjiang Nianjian 2000* [Yearbook of Heilongjiang 2000] (Ha'erbin: Heilongjiang renmin chubanshe, 2001), 93; Jilinsheng difangzhi bianzuan weiyuanhui, *Jilin Nianjian 2000* [Yearbook of Jilin 2000] (Changchun: Jilin nianjian chubanshe, 2001), 47.

32 Qiu Zeqi, "Baofadian Zai Naili" [Where are the Trigger Spots?], *Yunnan Daxue Xuebao* [Journal of Yunnan University], no. 5 (2003): 21-26.

33 *Heilongjiang Gongren Bao* [Heilongjiang Workers Paper], December 17, 2003.

34 Anshanshi shizhi bangongshi, *Anshan Nianjian 2001* [Yearbook of Anshan 2001] (Shenyang: Liaoning minzu chubanshe, 2002), 48.

Political Pressures and Government Responses

The many problems faced by laid-off and retired workers as well as their resistance attracted serious concern from the central government. Central leaders at the time, including Jiang Zemin and Zhu Rongji, paid close attention to the workers' problems. In 1999, Jiang inspected a number of provinces and chaired five meetings attended by the provincial party secretaries on the reform of state-owned enterprises. At the fifth meeting, in Liaoning in August 1999, which was attended by eight provincial party secretaries, including the three from the Northeast, Jiang said that the working class was the main force determining social stability in China. He declared that the government must correctly handle the relationship between reform, development, and stability, and prevent the reform and the speed of development from exceeding the tolerance of society. The party committee and government at each level were given the task of taking care of the laid-off workers' lives and employment. Jiang made clear that this was a serious political task to be carried out by all possible means.[35]

Zhu Rongji was similarly visible. From 1997 to 2002, Zhu inspected the Northeast almost every year. As Zeng and Tsai detail (see Chapter 3 in this volume), Zhu was instrumental in promoting restructuring in Shenyang. And as Jung argues (see Chapter 6 in this volume), Zhu was eager to speed up the corporate restructuring process. However, once restructuring was accelerated and layoffs increased beginning in 1997, Zhu was careful to show concern for those displaced. In Jilin province in March 1998, on behalf of Jiang and the central authorities, Zhu chaired a meeting on re-employment attended by the major local leaders of the three northeastern provinces and Inner Mongolia. He pointed out that the livelihood and re-employment of laid-off workers "affected not only the success of the reform of state enterprises but also social stability and consolidation of the socialist regime."[36] In April 2000, Zhu conducted a nine-day visit to Liaoning where he acknowledged that "Some laid-off workers have not received the regulated amount of subsistence allowance, and others have failed to receive a subsistence allowance. Collective petitions and instances of social unrest have occurred repeatedly." He ordered that the party committee and government at each level accept their "unshakable duty to establish an adequate welfare system and a stable social environment."[37]

35 *Renmin Ribao* [People's Daily], August 13, 1999.
36 *Renmin Ribao*, March 28, 1998.
37 *Renmin Ribao*, May 28, 2000.

Unfunded Mandate to Restructure

Central leaders ordered governments at each level to take care of the dislocated, but it was local governments that were under constant pressure as the laid-off and retired workers approached them with their complaints. It was common in the Northeast for workers and retired workers to take their collective petitions all the way to the provincial authorities. Between January and August 2002, such petitions constituted more than 50 percent of the total petitions received by the provinces. Disaggregating these figures we see that salary or pension payments, labor relations of laid-off workers, and ownership reform constituted 60 percent of the petitions in Jilin province and a slightly lower 54 percent in Liaoning province.

Pressures on local governments in the resource-dependent cities were particularly great. According to local officials in Fushun and Fuxin that relied heavily on the coal industry, the office compounds of the city authorities were surrounded by workers at least 15 to 20 days each month after the restructuring reforms began.[38] For example, in 1999 Fushun city authorities held frequent meetings to discuss citizens' petitions and social stability. The city leaders had to deal with the people (i.e., mainly workers) who were blocking traffic or bridges. This occurred 34 times in 1999 when the city party committee and the government received about 1,900 collective petitions. In 340 of the collective petitions, the number of participants exceeded 50; in 195 of the collective petitions, the number of participants exceeded 100. Petitioners blocked the office compounds of the city authorities, surrounded and attacked the leaders, cursed cadres in the complaints bureau, blocked traffic, and stopped trains and trucks.[39] The city mayor admitted that he had become the head of a "fire brigade"—the "fire" being the worker resistance. This happened so often, he said, that he "did not have any time free of pressure."[40]

The former governor of Liaoning province, Bo Xilai, admitted that in Fuxin, a city with fewer than one million people but where miners and their family members accounted for almost half of the population, "resentment among laid-off workers is high, and the police must be on high guard to detect potential organizers of protests."[41] In other resource-dependent cities

38 Wu Yaowu et al., "Ziyuan Kujie Haishi Tizhixing Zhang'ai?" 297.

39 Fushunshi shehui kexueyuan, Fushunshi renmin zhengfu difangzhi bangongshi, *Fushun Nianjian 2001* [Yearbook of Fushun 2001] (Shenyang: Liaoning minzu chubanshe, 2002), 119–20.

40 *Jingji Ribao* [Economic Daily], August 22, 2004.

41 "Guojia Touzhi Dongbei Fangfa Bu Mingzhi" [It is Not a Wise Choice for the Government to Invest in the Northeast], at http://business.sohu.com/2004/01/13/80/article 218478035.shtml, accessed October 6, 2010.

such as Benxi in 1997 and 1998, annually there were more than 40 blockades of highways or roads and more than 50 invasions into the compounds of the city and provincial governments by petitioners.[42] In Anshan, petitioners demanded to see the major local leaders. They surrounded, attacked, or cursed lower-level cadres who tried to talk with them. In 130 cases, after collective petitions were lodged, participants blocked the compounds of the city party committee and the government and the railways and highways.[43]

Central Bailouts

The serious pressures due to the grievances of laid-off workers and their resistance forced central and local governments to respond. The center left it up to the localities to restructure and take care of worker discontent, but it became increasingly clear that meeting the workers' demands was often beyond the financial ability of the local governments. When radical forms of restructuring were pursued, such as bankruptcy, in which many workers were displaced at once and the potential for disruption was great, the central government intervened. For example, in Jilin in 2001, four mines with 13,000 employees were declared bankrupt. The local government needed 553 million yuan to pay the bank loans, overdue salaries, and severance allowances to the workers. On average, each worker was owed 7,070 yuan in back salary, and the average severance pay for each worker was about 5,750 yuan.[44] The central government stepped in to allocate funds to allow the bankruptcy to go forward.[45] Similarly, in 2004 the central government intervened by allocating 16.3 billion yuan to the three northeastern provinces so as to close or declare bankrupt more than 60 enterprises. These central-level funds accounted for 23.3 percent of the total funds allocated nationwide for bankruptcy.[46]

42 Benxishi dangshi difangzhi bangongshi, *Benxi Nianjian 1998* [Yearbook of Benxi 1998] (Dalian: Dalian chubanshe, 1999), 119; Benxishi dangshi difangzhi bangongshi, *Benxi Nianjian 1999* [Yearbook of Benxi 1999] (Dalian: Dalian chubanshe, 2000), 142.

43 Anshanshi shizhi bangongshi, *Anshan Nianjian 1999* [Yearbook of Anshan 1999] (Shenyang: Liaoning minzu chubanshe, 2000), 42.

44 Jilinsheng difangzhi bianzuan weiyuanhui, *Jilin Nianjian 2002* (Yearbook of Jilin 2002) (Changchun: Jilin nianjianshe, 2003), 80.

45 In 2002, the central government allocated 1.23 billion yuan to Heilongjiang for the bankruptcy of two mines involving 34,000 workers, and 5.5 billion yuan to Jilin for the closure and bankruptcy of fourteen programs or firms. Heilongjiang nianjian bianzuan weiyuanhui, *Heilongjiang Nianjian 2003* [Yearbook of Heilongjiang 2003] (Ha'erbin: Heilongjiang renmin chubanshe, 2004), 160-61; Jilinsheng difangzhi bianzuan weiyuanhui, *Jilin Nianjian 2003* [Yearbook of Jilin 2003] (Changchun: Jilin nianjianshe, 2004), 105.

46 *Renmin Ribao*, January 16, 2005.

Bankruptcy was but one source that consumed the limited financial resources of the central and local governments. When the central government proposed the establishment of re-employment service centers in 1998 to help laid-off workers (see below), the local governments, insurance organizations, and SOEs were each expected to contribute one-third of the funds needed for the operations of the centers. In Liaoning, because most SOEs could not provide such funds, the governments paid 70 percent (the central government paid 40 percent and the local governments paid 30 percent). There was also a huge amount of overdue insurance premiums. The governments paid these premiums for the SOEs (i.e., the central government paid 75 percent and the local governments paid 25 percent). The central government continued to provide financial aid to cover the shortfall when there was a gap between the amount collected and the amount paid.[47] There was also the problem of severance pay. By 2001, half a million laid-off workers from SOEs in Liaoning had had their labor relations terminated. The central government provided 36.4 percent of the severance pay required at that point. Several years later, the number of workers from SOEs who had their labor relations terminated had grown to 1.76 million, and in the early 2000s the severance pay per capita was 8,700 yuan. The central and provincial governments shouldered much of the financial responsibility for this reform measure.[48]

Because both central and local governments were stretched in their ability to fund restructuring, the local governments had an interest in maximizing their use of limited funds, whether provided by the center or the locality. Given their limited capacity to accommodate all the grievances, government policy and practice distinguished among the laid-off workers, providing different treatment for the workers in state and collectively owned enterprises. This distinction followed the precedent set during the pre-reform period when workers in SOEs received better economic treatment than workers in collective enterprises. Continuing this distinction shaped the local government response to workers during corporate restructuring.

Government Response: One Class, Two Groups

Beginning in 1997 the central government issued a number of policies to deal with the issue of laid-off workers and unpaid retired workers.[49] In

47 Zhao Xiaojian and Hu Yifan, "Shiye Zhiyou" [Worry over Unemployment], *Caijing* [Finance] (September 24, 2002): 27-53.

48 *Ershiyi Shiji Jingji Baodao* [Twenty-first Century Business Herald], May 12, 2004.

49 For the various policies, see Ministry of Labor and Social Security and Document

June 1998, the State Council issued the most important document to date to address the welfare of the laid-off workers. The directive stated, "In recent years, the issue of laid-off workers has become increasingly salient and has attracted the attention of society." The key point of this directive was the establishment of re-employment service centers in SOEs.

These re-employment service centers served as a transitional arrangement to provide living allowances to laid-off workers and to pay their pensions, unemployment, and medical insurance premiums to make up for China's inadequate welfare system. They were also meant to help train workers and assist them in securing new jobs. A laid-off worker was allowed to stay at a center for a maximum of three years. If he/she was unable to find a job after three years, his/her labor relations with the firm were terminated. Thereafter, the worker would be considered unemployed, i.e., the relationship with the firm was severed and there were no more unemployment benefits. Funding for the re-employment centers was provided by the local governments, social insurance organizations (and donations), and firms. In addition, the central government took steps to help laid-off workers seeking employment. For example, those firms that hired a certain number of laid-off workers enjoyed certain tax breaks. As discussed below, although government measures failed to solve the economic plight of laid-off workers entirely, the re-employment centers proved to be helpful in addressing the problem of layoffs and allowing industrial reform to continue by reducing worker resistance.[50]

In 2000, the State Council issued other directives to ensure that laid-off and retired workers from the SOEs would be paid. In a February directive, in addition to urging local governments and SOEs to pay the laid-off workers, the central government also tackled the issue of retired workers. The central government decided to pay a large portion of the overdue premiums of many of the SOEs that had failed to pay their employees. In addition, the central government set the goal that by year-end 2000, 80 percent of the retired workers should receive their pensions from insurance organizations rather than from individual firms. In other words, pensions would be guaranteed.

Research Office of the Central Communist Party Committee, eds., *Xinshiqi Laodong He Shehui Baozhang Zhongyao Wenxian Xuanbian* [Selected Important Documents Regarding Labor and Social Security] (Beijing: Zhongguo laodong shehui baozhang chubanshe, 2002). Also see Lei Guang, "Broadening the Debate on *Xiagang*: Policy Origins and Parallels in History," in Thomas B. Gold et al., eds., *Laid-Off Workers in a Workers' State* (New York: Palgrave MacMillan, 2009), 15-37.

50 Gold et al., eds., *Laid-Off Workers in a Workers' State*, ch. 3.

Institutionalized Inequality

To be sure, there were problems with implementation of these policies intended to protect all laid-off state workers and pensioners.[51] We have long known that Chinese SOEs differed in their access to financial resources, aid from the government, as well as their profitability. Not surprisingly, the fate of their laid-off workers was no different. Workers in large SOEs who were recipients of aid from the government fared better than workers in small SOEs.[52] For example, the generally large SOEs owned by the central government had more resources to pay their laid-off workers. As Table 4.1 shows, in 1997 more than 56 percent of the laid-off workers in small industrial SOEs who were not re-employed had not been paid, whereas only 21 percent of the laid-off workers in SOEs under the central government had not been paid. That laid-off workers in small and medium SOEs were less likely to be paid continued after 1997.[53] However, as Table 4.1 also shows, the situation for all workers laid-off from SOEs improved somewhat in subsequent years after the intervention of the central government.

Disparities between the State and Collective Sectors

Although there were disparities within the SOE sector, the difference between SOE- and collective-sector workers was even greater. In comparison with laid-off workers in SOEs, those in urban collective enterprises fared much worse in terms of welfare provision, with the differences continuing over time. As presented in Table 4.1, in 1998 41 percent of the laid-off workers in collective enterprises who failed to be re-employed had not been paid subsidies, as opposed to 8 percent of the laid-off workers in SOEs. In 1999, 20.6 percent of the laid-off workers in collective enterprises were either underpaid or not paid at all.[54]

Table 4.2 compares the monthly allowances provided to laid-off employees in the state and collective sectors, indicating a striking gap. In the Northeast, because the limited resources were mostly allocated to laid-off workers from the SOEs, the disparity in the treatment of workers is obvious. As Table 4.2 shows, the gap was larger in the Northeast than the national average. In Liaoning, there was a 10-fold gap in 2003 and 12.5-fold in 2004. Between 1998 and 2002, the average monthly allowance received by

51 Solinger, "Labour Market Reform and the Plight of the Laid-off Proletariat."
52 National Bureau of Statistics, *Da Toushi*, 214–15.
53 Cai, *State and Laid-Off Workers in Reform China*, 116.
54 State Statistical Bureau, comp., *Zhongguo Laodong Tongji Nianjian 2001*, 402.

TABLE 4.1

Comparison of Subsistence for Unemployed Laid-Off Workers

	1997 Unpaid	1998 Unpaid	1999 Partly Paid	1999 Unpaid
SOEs (%)	48.8	8.0	11.1	6.3
Under the central government	20.7	4.1	8.9	1.7
Large and medium industrial SOEs	37.2	4.7	—	—
Small industrial SOEs	56.2	—	—	—
Urban collective enterprises (%)	—	40.8	20.6	25.7

Source: Calculated from State Statistical Bureau, comp., *Zhongguo Laodong Tongji Nianjian* [China Labor Statistical Yearbook], various years (Beijing: Zhongguo tongji chubanshe, 1998–2000).

TABLE 4.2

Monthly Allowances to Laid-Off Employees in the State and Collective Sectors (yuan)

	National		Northeast		Liaoning	
	State	Collective	State	Collective	State	Collective
1998	121	57	71	18	84	29
1999	150	61	99	18	111	28
2000	178	68	24	22	139	31
2001	208	67	39	23	148	34
2002	258	69	78	24	198	29
2003	299	73	09	23	264	27
2004	350	74	45	22	338	27

Source: State Statistical Bureau, comp., *Zhongguo Laodong Tongji Nianjian* [China Labor Statistical Yearbook], various years (Beijing: Zhongguo tongji chubanshe, 1997–2005); *Liaoning Nianjian* [Liaoning Yearbook] (1997–2005).

a worker laid-off from a collective firm in Fushun never exceeded 16 yuan per month. A report on the workers' situation in the city states: "Between 1995 and 2000, the salaries of those working in the collective sector decreased, and even workers' salaries or laid-off workers' subsistence allowances were not guaranteed, not to mention other welfare benefits. They were living in an entirely different world, compared with employees in state-owned enterprises."[55] Given the limited compensation received by workers, especially those in collective enterprises, the number of people requiring a minimum subsistence allowance in Fushun increased from 52,000 in 2000 to 156,000 in 2002.[56]

55 Fushunshi shehui kexueyuan, Fushunshi renmin zhengfu difangzhi bangongshi, *Fushun Tongji Nianjian 2001*, 63.

56 Liaoning nianjian bianwei huibian, *Liaoning Nianjian 2003* [Yearbook of Liaoning 2003] (Beijing: Zhongguo tongji chubanshe, 2004), 254, 262.

Government Policies and the Plight of Workers
in Collective Enterprises

The plight of laid-off workers in collective firms was partly due to the fact that they were largely ignored by both the central and local governments. They were either excluded from the central government's policies or were urged to solve their problems through their individual enterprises. The central government refused to make any commitment to the urban collective enterprises in the important 1998 directive cited above. The last paragraph of the directive contains one sentence about laid-off workers from urban collective enterprises: "As to the basic living allowance and re-employment of laid-off workers from urban collective enterprises, the provincial-level party committees and the provincial governments can make policies based on their own local situations." This implied that the local governments were also free to make no policy. Hence, although the establishment of re-employment service centers was compulsory for SOEs, whether collective enterprises established service centers was left entirely up to the firms. Workers in collective firms continued to receive their benefits from the outdated firm-based welfare system.

The welfare of laid-off workers from collective enterprises was never a priority of central government policy. In the directive promulgated in February 2000, the central government urged local governments and SOEs to guarantee payments for laid-off and retired workers from SOEs, but the directive failed to even mention the unpaid retired workers in urban collective units. Not until May 2000 was there any mention of the unpaid retired and laid-off workers from urban collective enterprises. The directive stated that, "if retired workers and laid-off workers from urban collective enterprises have not participated in insurance programs, they will be covered by the minimum subsistence program." This program was established in the 1990s to help the urban poverty-stricken population as a whole. In theory, these collective workers should have received help, but in practice the program in a number of cities was plagued by a lack of funding.[57] For example, over the years Benxi Steel Company had many collective enterprises that provided jobs for more than 60,000 people. By 2002, the company still had 168 collective enterprises that owed their employees 200 million yuan in insurance premiums and 307 million yuan in salaries. Although 460 workers were entitled to the minimum subsistence, only 6.5 percent received it.[58] Hence, the government commitment to collective workers was largely symbolic or absent in cities with insufficient funding.

57 Solinger, "Labour Market Reform and the Plight of the Laid-off Proletariat."
58 Chen Yongjie, "Dongbei Jiben Qingkuang Diaocha Baogao."

In the early 2000s, the central government decided to end the establishment of the re-employment service centers. Newly laid-off workers and those who had stayed at the re-employment service centers for three years were treated as unemployed. Their labor relations with their firms were terminated. But these workers were paid a severance pay, often based on the number of years they had worked. This compensation was clearly stated in a directive issued by the Ministry of Labor and Social Security in September 2003. The practice of terminating labor relations with severance pay had been carried out much earlier in certain places. In Liaoning province, it began in 2001 with the support of the central government. But again, there were no regulations stating whether or not the laid-off workers from the collective enterprises were entitled to severance pay. Not surprisingly, few laid-off workers from collective enterprises were offered this type of severance pay.[59]

By 2004, most collective enterprises and small SOEs in China had been privatized, closed, or declared bankrupt; this was also true for many medium-sized SOEs. From 1995 to 2004, the number of employees in the urban collective sector declined 72.3 percent, from 30.8 million to 8.5 million, whereas in the state-owned sector, the number declined 41 percent, from 109.6 million to 64.4 million.[60] Although governments at all levels managed to buy out workers from the SOEs, they offered very limited if any help to those from the collective enterprises. Many of these workers thus became part of the urban poverty-stricken population.[61] It was not until more recently that governments at both the central and local levels began to tackle the problems faced by these workers. In the cities, poverty-stricken workers are now included in the urban subsistence allowance scheme. Under this system, urban citizens whose incomes fall below a certain level can receive aid from the government.

Workers' Power and Welfare

Workers in collective enterprises were largely ignored by government policies but not because their numbers were too small. For example, in Liaoning province between 1998 and 2003 laid-off workers from collective enterprises accounted for from 38 percent to about 47 percent of the total number of laid-off employees.[62] Between 1998 and 2002 the proportion in

---

59 The policy did not change until 2005. *Zhongguo Shuiwu Bao* [China Taxation News], February 14, 2006.

60 National Bureau of Statistics, *Xin Zhongguo*, 8.

61 Cai, *State and Laid-off Workers in Reform China*, ch. 2.

62 *Liaoning tongji nianjian* (1999–2005).

Fushun city ranged from 46.4 percent to 54.5 percent.[63] The lack of attention to workers from collective enterprises was due to both the government's traditional commitments as well as the workers' lack of power to resist.

Limited Government Obligation

The employment system in Communist regimes had always been regarded as a moral arrangement in which the government ensured the livelihood of workers in exchange for their compliance and contribution.[64] However, there was always a distinction between state and collective-sector workers. The Chinese government made only limited commitments to urban collective enterprises and their workers. The social contract between the government and collective enterprises was less binding. The reason for this can be traced back to the origins of the collective firms. Urban collective enterprises in China were established for two major reasons. One was to collectivize (individual) family businesses in the cities in the 1950s, and the other was to create jobs.

In the late 1970s and early 1980s, the government needed to provide jobs for 17 million young people, some of whom had returned from work in the countryside. Establishing urban collective enterprises became an important way to create employment. From 1978 to 1984, the number of employees in the urban collective sector increased by 11.2 million.[65] In the Northeast, many SOEs established collective enterprises to create employment for local people. By 2002, the number of urban collective enterprises established in the Northeast by large- and medium-sized SOEs totaled 1,433, and these enterprises employed 506,000 workers and 120,000 retired workers, respectively.[66]

Because collective enterprises were mainly established to create jobs, they were not included in the state budget. As Walder suggests, under the planned economy the funds for welfare and insurance benefits were generated by the profits of the collective factories and were not a fixed portion of the state wage bill. Few collective enterprises were able to provide the services and distributions provided in the state sector—enterprise housing, daycare centers, hospitals and clinics, kindergartens, and a wide range of supplements and extra rations for consumer items and foodstuffs.[67]

63   *Fushun tongji nianjian* (1999–2003).

64   Linda J. Cook, *The Soviet Social Contract and Why it Failed: Welfare Policy and Workers' Politics from Brezhnev to Yeltsin* (Cambridge, MA: Harvard University Press, 1993); Andrew Walder, *Communist Neo-Traditionalism* (Berkeley: University of California Press, 1986).

65   National Bureau of Statistics, *Xin Zhongguo*, 8.

66   Chen Yongjie, "Dongbei Jiben Qingkuang Diaocha Baogao."

67   Walder, *Communist Neo-Traditionalism*, 43-48.

Yet, under the planned economy, although collective enterprises were not included in the state budget, their survival was not a problem because their production was often included in the plan. But with market-oriented reform as well as declining profitability, public firms began to face pressures to survive, especially after the government imposed serious restrictions on state banks regarding lending. Like many small SOEs, collective enterprises had to become self-supporting. Budget constraints forced many collective enterprises to stop production and thus to stop paying their employees. Collective enterprises were also less able to receive aid from banks or the government. This explains why compared with workers from SOEs, those from collective enterprises were more likely to be laid off. [68] In the 1,433 collective enterprises in Liaoning province, two-thirds had difficulties surviving and 527 had stopped production either entirely or partly by 2002. More than 700 enterprises owed their employees one year of back salaries. Not surprisingly, 56 percent of the workers were not covered by any pension scheme, 70 percent were not covered by the unemployment insurance system, and most had no medical insurance coverage. Among the half million employees in the collective sector, about 70 percent were laid off.[69]

The governments' selective commitment was also reflected in the ways they dealt with the disgruntled workers. For example, a factory in a northeastern city had about 10,000 workers, including several thousand workers in its collective enterprises. Because of its poor performance, by 1998 the factory had failed to pay its workers for more than a year. In September 1998, workers blocked the streets on three consecutive days. The city government and the factory eventually agreed to pay each worker 176 yuan per month. But workers in the collective units were not entitled to this pay. According to city government policy, when the re-employment service center was established to help the laid-off workers in this company, the laid-off workers from the state-owned units would receive 220 yuan per month in the first year, 196 yuan in the second year, and 188 yuan in the third year. After three years, they would receive a severance pay of 596 yuan for each year served. But workers in collective units were excluded. By 2002, more than 2,000 workers in the collective units in this factory were told to take unpaid leave without receiving any subsidies.[70]

---

68 Simon Appleton et al., "Labor Retrenchment in China: Determinants and Consequences," in Li Shi and Hiroshi Sato, eds., *Unemployment, Inequality and Poverty in Urban China* (London: Routledge, 2006), 19-42.

69 See Chen Yongjie, "Dongbei Jiben Qingkuang Diaocha Baogao."

70 Wu Qingjun, "Zou Xiang Jiti Pinkun" [Falling into Collective Poverty], ms., Beijing, 2006.

Unequal Threats of Resistance

The government's obligation is relative to the power of the workers. Compared with the laid-off workers from the SOEs, those from the collective enterprises were weak. Most collective enterprises were small and their workers were less able to stage large-scale resistance. Take industrial enterprises as an example. Nationwide, by 1995 industrial SOEs accounted for 73 percent of the large industrial enterprises in the country, whereas collective enterprises accounted for only 8.3 percent. By comparison, collective enterprises accounted for 74 percent of the total number of small-sized enterprises. Among the medium-sized enterprises, SOEs accounted for 65 percent and collective enterprises accounted for 21 percent.[71] Hence, as Table 4.3 shows, in 1995 the average number of employees (i.e., 41) in the collective enterprises was much smaller than that in the SOEs (i.e., 504). This difference was particularly great in those enterprises owned by governments at the city level and above. In the Northeast, in 1997 the average number of employees was 704 in the state-owned enterprises, whereas it was only 80 in the collective enterprises.[72]

Existing research shows that the pace of reform, such as privatization, tended to be slower in those provinces where more workers from the large and medium-sized SOEs were laid off and not paid.[73] This is because workers from larger firms were better able to stage large-scale and forceful resistance. In China, the impact of a social group's resistance is determined by the frequency of resistance and the number of large-scale incidents. In individual incidents of resistance, the size of the protesting group is often the most important determinant of the power of resistance.[74] In worker resistance, cross-firm collective action is still uncommon, and most instances of large-scale action have been taken by workers from individual large firms.[75] As a result, compared with laid-off workers from collective enterprises, those from SOEs generally were more able to stage large-scale resistance.

Collective petitions are a good example. My 1999 survey of more than 740 laid-off workers in five provinces shows that laid-off workers from both SOEs and collective enterprises presented collective petitions.[76] But

71 National Bureau of Statistics, *Da Toushi*, 34–35.

72 *Zhongguo Gongye Jingji Tongji Nianjian* 1998 [Statistical Yearbook of the Chinese Industrial Economy 1998] (Beijing: Zhongguo tongji chubanshe, 1998), 106, 109.

73 Yongshun Cai, "Relaxing the Constraints from Above: Politics of Privatising Public Enterprises in China," *Asian Journal of Political Science* 10, no. 2 (2002): 94–121.

74 Yongshun Cai, "Power Structure and Regime Resilience: Contentious Politics in China," *British Journal of Political Science* 38, no. 3 (July 2008): 411–32.

75 Cai, *State and Laid-Off Workers in Reform China*, ch. 7.

76 The survey was conducted in 16 cities and 11 counties of 5 provinces.

TABLE 4.3

Details on Industrial Enterprises in China (1995)

	SOEs	Collective Enterprises[1]
Number of firms (10,000)	11.8	147.5
Total number of employees (million)	59.5	60.5
Average number of employees (million)	504	41
• In central-level firms	1,490	—
• In provincial-level firms	83	150
• In city-level firms	76	180
• In county-level firms	66	106

Source: Compiled from National Bureau of Statistics, *Da Toushi* [A Comprehensive Perspective] (Beijing: Zhongguo fazhan chubanshe, 1998), 30, 33.

Note: [1] These include enterprises established by governments below the county level.

proportionally more workers in the SOEs had resisted and, equally important, their resistance was more likely to succeed. Workers in the SOEs were better able to stage large-scale actions (i.e., with more than 100 participants). Whereas such large-scale actions accounted for 17 percent of the total number of petitions submitted by laid-off workers from the SOEs, they accounted for only 5 percent of the total number of petitions submitted by workers in the collective enterprises. None of the collective petitions by workers in collective enterprises claimed more than 500 participants. Before 2004, the media both inside and outside China reported on at least twelve large-scale worker protests (i.e., with at least 5,000 participants),[77] and all of these were staged by workers from SOEs. Six of the protests took place in the Northeast, with 10,000 participants or more in each protest. Large-scale protests often occurred because a large number of workers were affected simultaneously due to certain reform measures, such as bankruptcy. This was more likely to be the case in large SOEs.[78]

77 The twelve large protests (1997–2004) were in: Nanchong in Sichuan (20,000 participants), Zhangjiakou in Hebei (5,000), a factory in Liaoning (10,000), Huludao in Liaoning (20,000), Sulan mine in Jilin (15,000), Liaoyang in Liaoning (10,000), Daqing in Heilongjiang (30,000), Fushun in Liaoning (10,000), Xiangfan in Hubei (10,000), Xiangyang in Shaanxi (6,000), and Bengbu in Anhui (5,000).

78 For example, in Yangjiazhangzhi town of Liaoning province in February 2000, over 20,000 miners, joined by thousands of family members, smashed windows, blocked traffic, burned cars, and confronted armed police for days. Order was restored after the government sent in the army and police. The cause of this unrest was workers' resentment over the small amount of compensation (i.e., 560 yuan for every year served) after their mine was declared bankrupt. James Kynge, "Chinese Miners Riot over Severance Pay," *Financial Times*, April 3, 2000.

TABLE 4.4

Workers' Collective Petitions by Ownership Type of their Enterprises

	Collective Enterprises	SOEs
Number of workers	130	594
Participation in collective petitions (%)	15	26
Petitions with more than 100 participants (%)	5	17
Petitions with more than 500 participants (%)	0	6
Usefulness (%)	16	35

Source: Author's Survey, 1999.

Based on the incomplete information that we have, we know that the average size of worker collective action is limited. According to one account of seven provinces, the average number of participants in 3,600 collective actions was only 81 in 1999. In Liaoning province, more than 863,000 people took part in more than 9,000 protests in 1999, with the average number of participants over 90.[79] If most of the workers in each firm were mobilized, this average number apparently would be within the reach of workers in many collective enterprises (e.g., at the county level and above). But workers in collective enterprises were less capable of staging large-scale resistance (e.g., with more than 500 participants) that was more effective in receiving a government response (see Table 4.4).

It was this stronger power of workers in the SOEs that put their counterparts in the collective enterprises at a constant disadvantage in competition for the limited financial resources. This explains why the gap between the living allowances received by laid-off workers from the state sector and by those from the collective sector remained strikingly large over the years. In those places where the number of laid-off workers was large, the gap in welfare provisions between the two groups of workers was even greater. This is because those from the collective enterprises could be entirely ignored by the government.

Conclusion

The massive retrenchment due to the economic restructuring was a serious challenge to the Chinese government, but it was not insurmountable. After 2002, the issue of laid-off workers was not as serious as it had been earlier. The Chinese government was able to successfully address this issue because of its power and because of the composition of public enterprises in China. When the reforms began, Chinese workers did resist, but their

79 Murray Scot Tanner, "China Rethinks Unrest," *The Washington Quarterly* 27, no. 3 (2004): 137–56.

resistance differed in its effectiveness. This difference allowed the government to distinguish between two kinds of losers and to ignore the weakest (i.e., those from collective enterprises and some small SOEs). This approach to reform was particularly obvious (and important to the government) in the restructuring in the Northeast rust-belt. Although this targeted approach saved huge costs for the central and local governments in the initial years of the reform, it also drove many laid-off workers into poverty. Compared with workers from SOEs, laid-off workers from urban collective enterprises were disadvantaged under both the old welfare regime and the new policies. Theirs had become an institutionalized inequality.

The Chinese reform experience reveals that the government's reform policy is affected by both the legacies of past polices and the power of the losers. More specifically, workers faced different welfare institutions, which both shaped their access to welfare benefits and reflected their political power. There was a social contract between the state and SOE workers. Because of this relationship, when the reforms began, SOE workers expected that the government would take responsibility to address their problems. It was their due. In comparison, the government had only a limited commitment to workers in urban collective enterprises. Thus, the government felt less moral pressure when dealing with collective-sector workers. Moreover, as a result and, perhaps, more importantly, because of their weak political power the government tended to ignore workers from collective enterprises. Although the number of laid-off workers from urban collective enterprises was not small, their power of resistance was limited. Collective-sector workers also might have had lower expectations of the government, knowing that they were less able than workers from state-owned enterprises to stage powerful resistance. Consequently, despite the lack of adequate welfare institutions, the powerlessness of a large segment of the laid-off workers made it possible for the government to use a "divide-and-rule" strategy to move forward with corporate restructuring.

Nevertheless, the reform of public firms in China points to the problems in government policy-making. Although the government succeeded in removing the financial burdens arising from subsidizing public firms, the costs paid by laid-off employees were simply too high. It is very clear that the reform of public firms in China was far from well planned by policymakers. As a result, politically weak groups, such as laid-off workers from collective firms, suffered tremendously. But sacrificing the interests of the weak groups in a society characterized by rising inequality certainly damages the legitimacy of the reform. Such pent-up grievances may motivate people to challenge the regime whenever such opportunities arise. Therefore, policymakers need to balance their policy goals with the interests of even the weak groups in society in order to achieve long-term political stability.

5 Experience First, Laws Later

EXPERIMENTATION AND BREAKTHROUGHS IN THE
RESTRUCTURING OF CHINA'S STATE SECTOR[1]

Sebastian Heilmann

The reorganization of large state-controlled enterprises arguably has been the toughest job for Chinese policymakers over the last three decades. State-sector reorganization has been subject to very strong political inertia and opposition that are inherent in a socialist and post-socialist political economy. Traditional socialist ideology stresses the dominant role of public ownership, the central position of the industrial working class in the political economy, and the redistributive goals of economic planning and policy-making. All three ideological elements have continued to be highly contested issues in the politics of corporate restructuring in China. Each of them became a line of defense for powerful interest groups. The managers of state-owned enterprises (SOEs) lobbied their political-bureaucratic superiors to keep budget constraints soft and access to preferential loans open. Public-sector workers and pensioners protested against the risks, burdens, and manipulations they faced with the reorganization or close-down of their long-time workplaces. Containing the social repercussions of SOE restructuring and dampening ideological controversies about the appropriate extent of state control in the economy therefore have been pushed to the top of policymakers' agenda since the 1980s.

In addition, contrary to what one might expect, decision-making at the apex of China's political system is hampered by informal consensus rules.

1 The research for this article was supported by the German National Research Foundation (DFG). The author is especially indebted to Jean Oi for encouraging this study of the state sector and to Nancy Hearst, the librarian of Harvard University's Fairbank Collection in the Fung Library, who provided precious sources and proofread an initial version of the manuscript.

Controversial policy proposals are rarely pushed through by a lone decision by the Communist Party's general secretary or by a majority vote in the Politburo. Rather, they are postponed until a consensus among major policy-makers can be reached. Such decision-making rules are not conducive to producing determined and consistent national policies in a highly controversial and ideologically charged policy domain such as state-sector restructuring. Moreover, institutional rivalries among entrenched national bureaucracies (more or less reformed socialist-era commissions and ministries) and the emergence of increasingly assertive new players in national policy-making (in particular the Standing Committee of the National People's Congress as a legislative body; the Supreme People's Court as a quasi-policymaker through judicial interpretations for insolvency proceedings; and since 2003 the State-Owned Assets Supervision and Administration Commission [SASAC] as a new regulatory body) complicated the formulation and revision of restructuring policies.

Against this background of reform inertia, one central puzzle in China's restructuring efforts is how policymakers managed to overcome the constraints and promote the new policies and institutions that changed the rules of the game. Differences in initial conditions and economic structure may explain why China had the potential to introduce market competition with less disruption than the former socialist economies of Eastern Europe.[2] But initial conditions do not determine how effectively policymakers make use of them. In order to explain China's remarkable "adaptive efficiency"[3] in promoting growth, investment, and trade, changing the behavior of state and market actors, and establishing new economic institutions we must take a careful look at the policy processes that have propelled restructuring in spite of the severe reform inertia.

In SOE reform, as in most domains of China's economic reform since 1979, policy changes were produced according to a process whereby central policymakers encouraged local experimentation to generate novel policy options that could then be fed back into national policy-making. Experimentation served as a crucial means for avoiding policy deadlock and reducing the frictions and delays characteristic of top-level consensus-building and inter-agency accommodation. It helped to reduce the risks in policy-making, stimulate policy entrepreneurship, and contribute to the

2 For an influential analysis along these lines, see Jeffrey Sachs et al., "Structural Factors in the Economic Reforms of China, Eastern Europe and the Former Soviet Union," *Economic Policy* 9, no. 18 (April 1994): 102–45.

3 See Douglass C. North, *Institutions, Institutional Change and Economic Performance* (New York: Cambridge University Press, 1990), 80–81; *Understanding the Process of Economic Change* (Princeton, NJ: Princeton University Press, 2005), 154.

fine-tuning of policy content and implementation. In policy domains in which new actors, interests, and ideologies entered national policy-making, such as foreign trade and investment or private business during the 1990s, experimentation went beyond incremental adaptations and resulted in trans-formative departures marked by the emergence of novel policy regimes with new constellations of actors, interests, institutions, and ideologies.[4]

Proceeding from "experimental points" (*shidian*) to broader policy in-novation was possibly the only way to introduce a vital pioneering element into the rigidly organized polity. The "experimental point" method was ca-pable of contributing to substantial policy innovation over time precisely because it fit so well into the logic of the Chinese political economy with its mixture of rigid formal-hierarchical and more flexible informal-institutional elements. Experimentation served as a method for political management of rapid change that utilized, rather than destroyed, existing formal and infor-mal rules of the policy-making game to introduce a strong innovative ele-ment into the bureaucratic polity.

China's ability to experiment with policy prior to the actual formulation and passage of policies or laws allowed a highly unusual degree of policy flexibility. It is well known that in China's state sector powerful vested in-terests and socialist ideological concerns stood in the way of transformative change. From 1978 to the mid-1990s, recurrent rounds of experimentation resulted in protracted policy tinkering with bureaucratic and financial incen-tives or formal corporate reorganization, yet without touching the politi-cally protected and financially privileged status of the SOEs in the economy. Incrementalist reforms minimized political conflict and social disruption but perpetuated the misallocation of resources, subsidies, and loans and therefore were wasteful in narrow economic efficiency terms. Seen from the perspective of the evolution of the political economy and policy learn-ing, however, the contribution of experimental tinkering to transform the policy-making context of local and central decision-makers was essential. It provided test-runs for novel administrative and business practices, initi-ated learning processes and behavioral changes, and thereby undermined entrenched ideologies, attitudes, and interests. In short, policy experimenta-tion helped to "smuggle changes into the system."[5] Experimental tinkering in combination with transnational push factors such as the Asian financial

4 For a study of the varying functions, patterns, and effects of experimentation in ma-jor economic policy domains, see Sebastian Heilmann, "Policy Experimentation in China's Rise," *Studies in Comparative International Development* 43, no.1 (March 2008): 1–26.

5 This is how Charles E. Lindblom characterizes the tactics of introducing indirect change over time in American politics; see his article "Still Muddling, Not Yet Through," *Public Administration Review* 39, no. 6 (November-December 1979): 517–526, at 521.

crisis and WTO accession negotiations provided the policy planks for broad reform departures in 1997 and 2001.

In the sections below, I will first briefly contrast the distinctive policy cycle that we find in China with the conventional process of policy-making. To examine the implications of the experimentation-based approach for state-sector restructuring, I identify the general constraints inherent in this policy domain. To illustrate what this meant for policy change, I will turn to a case study of bankruptcy regulation, which has been a particularly contested issue for more than two decades. I look at how the changes proceeded but also consider the political and economic drawbacks of state-sector experimentation. In the concluding sections, I expound on how experimentation laid the groundwork for the post-1997 policy breakthroughs and why experiment-based institutional innovation is superior to the synoptic policy-making approaches that are implied in the institutional complementarities framework.

China's Experimentation-Based Policy Process

The Chinese experience in developing and implementing economic reforms differs in fundamental respects from standard assumptions about policy-making. The conventional model of the policy process holds that policy analysis, policy formulation, and embodiment in legislation *precede* implementation. One core principle of policy-making in rule-of-law systems is that administrative implementation must come after parliamentary legislation or executive regulation and must be based on formalized, publicized, and therefore verifiable and actionable general rules. The priority of the law and the principle of law-bound administration basically rule out discretionary and experimental administrative measures in advance of the enactment of laws and regulations. One striking feature of this legislation-centered policy process is that the potential impact of the policies under deliberation has to be assessed *ex ante*, without being able to test the new policies (or at least some key elements) in practice beforehand and thereby obtain realistic information about the potential effects.

In China's reform experience, many successful innovations have been the result of administrative "groping along," that is *experimentation during implementation*.[6] Frequently there was little, if any, policy impact assessment, administrative coordination, and consensus-building in advance

6 For general features of this mode of administrative experimentation, see Robert D. Behn, "Management by Groping Along," *Journal of Policy Analysis and Management* 7, no. 4 (Summer 1988): 643–63.

of the testing of new policies. Policy analysis and codification came only after experience, and after it could be determined what would work in the administrative reality. This mode of policy-crafting is the main source of the unorthodox regulatory practices and unclarified property-rights regime that have accompanied the strong economic growth in China.[7] Thus, discretionary administrative experimentation *in advance* of legislation plays a crucial role in China's policy process. In general, universal rules are made only after real-life test-runs and after obtaining experience about which ways to handle problems will work in practice. In short: experience first, laws later.

The mode of central-local interaction that we find in China's policy cycle does not easily fit into conventional social-science models of policy implementation and central-local relations. In research on China's reform, administrative decentralization is often cited as the key change that triggered local state activity. However, Chinese reform of governance goes beyond sweeping administrative decentralization and spontaneous diffusion of successful experiments. It requires the authority of the central government. The Chinese pattern of *experimentation under hierarchy* focuses on finding innovative policy *instruments*, rather than defining policy *objectives*, which remains the prerogative of the top political leadership. With regard to the means of reform, the experimental process is decidedly open and regularly leads to decentralized initiatives that are not anticipated by the center. Political actors at various levels thereby become initiators and active participants in the reform drives.[8] But ultimate control over confirming, revising, terminating, and spreading local policy experiments rests with higher-level decision-makers.

In the making of China's economic reform policies, experimentation has been much more prevalent and institutionalized than the available literature suggests. It has provided policymakers with a veritable laboratory for policy innovation. In this laboratory, the constant search for new policy solutions is not driven by the *ex ante* policy debate and impact assessments that are

---

7 Sharun W. Mukand and Dani Rodrik, "In Search of the Holy Grail: Policy Convergence, Experimentation, and Economic Performance," *American Economic Review* 95, no.1 (March 2005): 374–83, make a similar basic point, albeit without scrutinizing the particular policy process behind experimentation. For the unorthodox development of China's property-rights regime, see Andrew G. Walder and Jean C. Oi, "Property Rights in the Chinese Economy: Contours of the Process of Change," in Jean C. Oi and Andrew G. Walder, eds., *Property Rights and Economic Reform in China* (Stanford: Stanford University Press, 1999), 1–24.

8 Thomas G. Rawski, "Implications of China's Reform Experience," *China Quarterly*, no. 144 (December 1995): 1155, states that "the mix of top-down initiative and bottom-up reaction is itself a variable element within the reform mechanism."

typical of democratic law-making. Instead, policy adaptation is built into administrative practice and made a permanent enterprise. It is based on the administrative discretion and entrepreneurship exercised by local officials. This clearly contradicts law-based administration. But in developing new and practical policy options, this approach to reform has provided policy-makers with a much broader and more flexible range of instruments than the legislation-centered policy processes in democratic polities such as Japan or South Korea since the 1990s.

Experimentation, Inertia, and Complementarities

Almost all crucial economic reform initiatives in post-Mao China were prepared and tried out by means of "experimental points" (pilot projects) before they were universalized in national regulations. This applies to SOE restructuring in particular (see Table 5.1). I need not go into the policy history of restructuring since the crucial steps and advances in restructuring are elaborated in Oi and Han's contribution to this volume.[9] What I want to stress here is the importance of local "experimental point work" and central adoption of "model experiments" for national economic regulation. China's experience with policy-based bankruptcy regulation from 1984 to 2007 is one major example of this type of policy process.

Designed as a response to chronic SOE deficits, the experimental programs of the 1980s were mainly oriented to providing additional incentives and decision-making powers to SOE managers, albeit without transforming the bureaucratic institutional set-up outside of the companies. Reformist experimentation met with strong reservations from parts of the policy-making community, industrial bureaucracies, and the national legislature. In effect, SOE restructuring that aimed at full-scale corporate reorganization turned out to be unachievable during the 1980s and the early 1990s.[10]

In the mid-1990s, an ambitious new attempt to transform SOE operations was undertaken with the "modern company system" (MCS) experimental program. In the face of increasing debts in the state sector, a consensus for thoroughgoing SOE restructuring was taking shape among

9 For brief policy histories of SOE restructuring written by Chinese scholars, see Ding Xiaozhi and Ji Liuxiang, "1978 Nian Yilai Guoyou Qiye Chanquan Gaige Jincheng Ji Xiaolü Pingxi" [Evaluation of the Process and Effectiveness of Property-Rights Reform of State-Owned Enterprises], *Zhongguo Jingjishi Yanjiu* [Research on Chinese Economic History], no.1 (2005): 69-77; Wang Haibo, "Zhongguo Guoyou Qiye Gaige de Shijian Jincheng (1979–2003 nian)" [The Experience of the Process of State-Owned Enterprise Reform (1979–2003)], *Zhongguo Jingjishi Yanjiu*, no. 3 (2005): 103-12.

10 Cf. Murray Scot Tanner, *The Politics of Lawmaking in Post-Mao China* (Oxford: Clarendon, 1999), 167-205.

TABLE 5.1

Application of the "Experimental Point" Method in SOE Restructuring since 1978

Delegation of greater autonomy to enterprises	1978–1980
Delivery of contract profits to the state	1981–1982
Substitution of profits with taxes	1983–1986
Transformation of SOEs into shareholding companies	1984–1997
Bankruptcy regulation	1984–2007
Preparation of a national SOE law	1984–1988
SOE responsibility contracts	1987–1993
Establishment of enterprise groups	1991–
"Grasp the large and let go of the small [SOEs]" (Chongqing experiments)	1994–1995
"Modern company system" (corporatization of large SOEs)	1994–1997
Deepening corporate governance reform in large SOEs	2003–
Complete transfer of the social functions of large enterprises to local governments	2004–2005

Source: *Zhongguo Jingji Tizhi Gaige Nianjian, 1988–2006* [Yearbook of Economic Structural Reform in China, 1988–2006] (Beijing: Gaige chubanshe, 1989–2007).

top policymakers. As a result, the new Company Law that was passed in 1993 envisaged the transformation of SOEs into modern business entities with transparent structures of corporate governance, but still shunning the privatization of state assets. Policy implementation became based on "post-law experimentation": MCS experiments were designed to smooth the implementation of a reformist national law. However, experimental points established between 1994 and 1997 revealed how tacit resistance from SOE managers and their supervisory agencies produced a heavily bureaucratized design for experimentation and consequently meager results. An evaluation of MCS implementation in the 100 centrally supervised experimental companies at year-end 1996 concluded that "almost no experimental enterprise had achieved the minimum standards of a modern corporation."[11]

Overall, experimental programs undertaken in the state sector appeared inhibited and clumsy in comparison to the pioneering experimentation that was possible in policy domains driven by rapidly ascending new economic actors such as foreign investors or private business. China's state sector represented a policy domain that remained under the control of vested interests. Established actors of the state sector sought to lock in partial reforms and allow only incremental change. By the mid-1990s, as a result of more than a decade of incremental change, SOE management had moved away

11 Jinglian Wu, *Understanding and Interpreting Chinese Economic Reform* (Mason, OH: Thomson, 2005), 155; *Zhongguo Jingji Tizhi Gaige Nianjian 1995* [Yearbook of Economic Structural Reform in China 1995] (Beijing: Gaige chubanshe, 1995), 138–41; 1996, 222–26.

from the coordinated plan of earlier times, but it was still dominated by the socialist legacy of soft-budget constraints.

A special challenge in the reform of SOEs was the necessity for "comprehensive coordinated reform" (*zonghe peitao gaige*) due to the fact that socialist SOEs were not only firms but, with regard to their extensive social functions (including kindergardens, schools, hospitals, pension funding, administration, and so forth), were comparable to self-contained municipalities. As Oi highlights in Chapter 1 of this volume, this characteristic rendered system restructuring necessary to achieve effective corporate restructuring. Therefore, corporate reorganization and bankruptcy posed many more difficulties than they did in Western political economies because they had to go far beyond the transfer of ownership rights, debt restructuring, or liquidation.[12] There was institutional complementarity but it was to the planned political economy from which China sought to transition. One of the most pressing challenges was the close interrelation between SOE debt and China's state-controlled banking system, which was manifest in the huge amount of non-performing loans. Thus, radical SOE restructuring would possibly lead to massive social unrest and the bankruptcy of state banks. Many crucial institutions in China's political economy had to be reformed in a coordinated fashion so as to contain the social and financial repercussions of SOE reform.

As early as the mid-1980s, selected municipalities were designated as experimental sites for coordinated reform. But local experimenters were not in a position to deal effectively with the overarching institutional deficiencies regarding state functions in the economy or the social insurance system whose transformation was indispensable for meaningful SOE reform.[13] Up to 1997, reforms of the state economic bureaucracy were implemented as a formalistic exercise based on re-naming and re-arranging old structures and redistributing their staff but without transforming government operations.[14] In the mid-1990s, state-sector restructuring appeared to be stuck.

The sluggish policy regime in China's state sector was eventually broken up due to the confluence of a number of developments. As Jung will further discuss in this volume, reformers took advantage of the Asian financial crisis

12 See Charles D. Booth, "Drafting Bankruptcy Laws in Socialist Market Economies: Recent Developments in China and Vietnam," *Columbia Journal of Asian Law* 18, no.1 (Fall 2004): 94–147.

13 Zhang Zhuoyuan, ed., *20 Nian Jingji Gaige: Huigu Yu Zhanwang* [Twenty Years of Economic Reform: Reflections and Prospects] (Beijing: Zhongguo jihua chubanshe, 1998), 65–66.

14 Pan Xining, "Gaige Shidian Chengbai Bian" [Debating the Success and Failure of Experimental Points for Reform], *Fazhan* [Development], no. 2 (1995): 28.

to solve the mounting debt problems. The improved fiscal capacity of the central state also made it possible to compensate the losers from restructuring. Finally, a forceful policy entrepreneur, Premier Zhu Rongji, used this policy window to achieve a reform breakthrough. In 1997 China's central policymakers mustered the determination and means to move beyond incremental reform and to deal with the intertwined policy reforms simultaneously. They adopted a plethora of transformative policies to turn around the SOEs—including large-scale mergers, management and employee buyouts, takeovers of small SOEs by private investors, complete closures, mass layoffs, entry of foreign strategic partners, and exposure to international competition through WTO accession. The impacts of these developments are explored in various chapters in this volume.

The policy breakthroughs of the late 1990s, which displayed the potency of a broad approach to tackle corporate, administrative, and social reforms simultaneously, might be taken as support for the institutional complementarities argument that posits that it is not feasible to achieve systemic restructuring by introducing successive piecemeal reforms. The end result (broad complementary reforms), however, must be seen as very different from the extended piecemeal process (non-complementary) that produced the results. The breakthroughs in SOE restructuring had been prepared by a series of limited reorganization experiments that helped policy-makers and administrators understand the cost and risk structure of SOE reform and craft low-risk policy approaches that would have the potential to work in the Chinese context. The preparatory steps in SOE restructuring thus were segmented and non-complementary. From 1978 to the mid-1990s, SOE restructuring was not implemented as a holistic, universal, or law-based policy package. Rather, it was achieved through a policy-based ad-hoc approach to solve the problems of individual enterprises at an opportune point in time. The policies that were part of the post-1997 breakthrough in restructuring (including the approach of "grasping the large and letting go of the small," which had been tested beforehand in the large diverse state sector of Chongqing municipality in 1994–95) had already been tried out in experimental sites in the preceding years and therefore constituted policy approaches with risks that were regarded as calculable. A series of experimental point programs had already tested the waters and prepared the ground for "proceeding from point to surface" as soon as a policy window opened. Post-1997 restructuring, though still costly, discretionary, and controversial, was thus based on the local knowledge, administrative experience, and policy learning that had been obtained from the earlier decentralized experimentation. China's experience with the regulation of corporate insolvencies is a striking example of this approach.

Defying Bankruptcy Orthodoxy: Insolvency by Policy, 1984–2007

Insolvency regulation can be seen as a major test case for how serious and effective state-sector restructuring was pursued and how it came about at the end of the 1990s. Insolvency provisions are characterized by international organizations and their economic advisors as a central pillar of a modern corporate structure to safeguard the interests of creditors and investors, and as an indispensable instrument for restructuring either through corporate rehabilitation or liquidation, especially in the case of insolvent SOEs in the post-socialist economies.[15] After the Asian financial crisis (1997–99), insolvency and related laws were presented as "vital to economic development and stability" by the international bodies that had to deal with the fallout from the crisis. Under the buoyant economic conditions that had prevailed prior to the crisis, governments had neglected to regulate and administer insolvency effectively.[16] According to a strongly worded G-22 working group report, the Asian financial crisis highlighted

> the critical importance of strong insolvency and debtor-creditor regimes to crisis prevention, crisis mitigation and crisis resolution. Effective national insolvency regimes contribute to crisis prevention by providing the predictable legal framework needed to address the financial difficulties of troubled firms before the accumulated financial difficulties of the corporate sector spill over into an economy-wide payments crisis.[17]

According to this approach, indispensable institutional features of an effective insolvency regime include consistent national legislation that protects the interests of creditors and investors, independent courts that handle insolvency proceedings in a competent and reliable way, and a government that takes a neutral position on bankruptcy filings and proceedings.

China defied this kind of "bankruptcy orthodoxy" in managing state-sector restructuring and instead applied a seemingly inconsistent and ineffective "insolvency by policy" approach during a very long period. From 1984, when the first local experiments with bankruptcy began, until June 2007, when the national law on corporate bankruptcy finally came into effect, bankruptcy proceedings were ruled by experimental and makeshift central and local policies and ad-hoc bailouts (see Table 5.2).

---

15 Booth, "Drafting Bankruptcy Laws in Socialist Market Economies," 94.

16 Asian Development Bank, "Insolvency Law Reforms in the Asian and Pacific Region," *Law and Policy Reform at the Asian Development Bank* 1 (April 2000): 11-12.

17 "Report of the [G-22] Working Group on International Financial Crises," Basel, October 1998, 9.

TABLE 5.2

China's Approach to Bankruptcy: Local Experiments and Central Regulation

	Local Experimentation	Central Regulation and Law-Making
1984–1986	Four municipalities experiment with bankruptcies based on local initiative and with informal backing by individual central policymakers.	
1986	Formal central approval of local experiments.	National bankruptcy law passed "for experimental implementation."
1986–1993	Law never applied nationally. Instead, selective local experiments are sponsored.	
1991		Supreme People's Court provides extensive judicial interpretation of 1986 law.
1993	Shenzhen adopts local bankruptcy provisions that go beyond the 1986 law.	
1994	State Council circular on trial implementation of new insolvency procedures in 18 cities (experimental points).	Drafting of revised national bankruptcy law is initiated. 1994–2008: "insolvency by policy" approach, based on centralized coordination and government-supported mergers and insolvencies.
1996	SETC/PBOC circular on trial implementation of new merger and insolvency procedures in 56 cities (experimental points).	
1997	State Council supplementary circular on trial implementation of merger, bankruptcy, and re-employment procedures in 117 cities (experimental points).	Newly formed inter-agency "National Leading Small Group" put in charge of coordinating policy-based insolvencies.
1998–	Nationwide application of the 1994, 1996, and 1997 circulars on debt restructuring.	
1994–2002	Local governments issue implementation measures for SOE bankruptcies based on post-1994 central policies.	
2002		Supreme People's Court provides extensive judicial interpretation of bankruptcy regulation (106 articles).
Feb. 2005		National Plan for Enterprise Closures and Insolvencies, 2005–2008.
Aug. 2006		New Bankruptcy Law adopted, entering into effect in June 2007.
2008	Deadline to terminate policy-based bankruptcies and to make the transition to law-based bankruptcy regulation.	

Sources: Compiled by the author based on coverage in Chinese media and on Xianchu Zhang and Charles D. Booth, "Chinese Bankruptcy Law in an Emerging Market Economy: The Shenzhen Experience," *Columbia Journal of Asian Law* 15, no.1 (Fall 2001): 1–32; and Charles D. Booth, "Drafting Bankruptcy Laws in Socialist Market Economies: Recent Developments in China and Vietnam," *Columbia Journal of Asian Law* 18, no.1 (Fall 2004): 94–147.

The regulation of bankruptcies has belonged to the most controversial issues of economic policy-making in China, starting in 1983 when the issue was first brought onto the policymakers' agenda. Controversies revolve around safeguarding state assets in liquidations and reorganizations and, even more pressing from a political perspective, containing the social and financial repercussions of SOE insolvencies. Dealing with massive unemployment and re-arranging the social functions of SOEs (the provision of pensions, health care, housing, schools, kindergartens, and so forth) proved to be an extremely difficult task that required huge budgetary outlays and a bundle of reforms beyond simply firm insolvency.

The political controversies and drafting processes surrounding the 1986 "Experimental Bankruptcy Law"[18] and the finalized 2006 "Bankruptcy Law" are rather well documented in Chinese and Western research.[19] However, one of the most striking and under-explored aspects of Chinese bankruptcy regulation is the extensive use of centrally sponsored, locally implemented experimentation to find ways to deal with the social and fiscal repercussions of thousands of SOE insolvencies. Local experience was used by central policymakers in their arguments about the necessity and content of bankruptcy regulation. Local governments were clearly interested in being relieved of the task of paying endless subsidies to unprofitable and wasteful SOEs. At the same time, they had to worry about the consequences of bankruptcy on their political-administrative power base and potential mass unrest among workers.

The first attempt at national bankruptcy regulation began with ideologically charged political controversies (1983–1986), became stuck in the middle of law-making due to political opposition in the Standing Committee of the National People's Congress (in 1986), and resulted in a compromise "Experimental Bankruptcy Law" (1986) that was applied only in selected localities and enterprises and never nationwide. Bankruptcy regulation therefore was in a state of limbo until a centrally sponsored policy push introduced a new phase in 1994.

From 1989 until 1993, China's courts accepted only about 1,150 bankruptcy cases whose outcomes are not documented in detail. However, in the early 1990s, rapidly mounting state enterprise debts and debt chains among enterprises and state banks emerged as a top-priority problem among policymakers who shared the view that a turn-around and reorganization of the SOEs was needed. Led by the major economic policymaker of the 1993–2002 period, Zhu Rongji (vice premier 1993–98, premier 1998–2003), it was

18 Official title: "Enterprise Bankruptcy Law (for Experimental Implementation)."
19 Tanner, *The Politics of Lawmaking in Post-Mao China*, 135-66; Booth, "Drafting Bankruptcy Laws in Socialist Market Economies."

decided to begin drafting a new national bankruptcy law that would support the new strategic goal of establishing a "socialist market economy," as
laid down by the Communist Party's Central Committee in fall 1993. Zhu
started a virtual crusade against debt chains among SOEs and state-owned
banks and managed to raise the issue to the top of the national economic
agenda. In this undertaking, he apparently enjoyed strong backing from a
broad spectrum of top-level policymakers, all of whom agreed that something had to be done about the debt chains. At the same time, however, there
was no consensus about how the drastic restructuring should proceed. In
this political context, the "experimental point" method proved to be an approach that could break the national policy-making deadlock.

Starting in fall 1994, a series of central government circulars initiated a
new wave of local bankruptcy experiments, based on what Charles Booth
aptly terms an "insolvency by policy" approach:[20]

- In August 1994, the State Council decided to initiate a "Capital
  Structure Optimization" program in order to achieve "key breakthroughs" in SOE reform. The measures encouraged raising new
  capital, company reorganization, staff diversion, and bankruptcy.
  The State Economy and Trade Commission (SETC) was charged
  with formulating specific measures in coordination with eight other
  departments.[21]

- In October 1994, the State Council issued a circular on trial implementation of SOE bankruptcy in eighteen pilot cities (including
  Shanghai) to test new methods to deal with the resettlement of
  employees in insolvent industrial enterprises. Land-use rights were
  to be sold by auction or tender and the proceeds were to be used for
  resettling laid-off workers.

- In July 1996, the SETC and the People's Bank of China issued a
  joint circular on trial implementation of mergers and insolvencies
  of SOEs in fifty-six experimental units. State-owned banks were
  ordered to play an active role in arranging debt restructuring.

20 This section is mainly based on the highly instructive study by Booth, "Drafting
Bankruptcy Laws in Socialist Market Economies,"100-2. See also Xianchu Zhang and
Charles D. Booth, "Chinese Bankruptcy Law in an Emerging Market Economy: The Shen-
zhen Experience," *Columbia Journal of Asian Law* 15, no.1 (Fall 2001): 1-32, esp. 13.

21 See *Renmin Ribao* [People's Daily], August 27, 1994, 2. A sober critique of this
program from the perspective of a state bank is found in Hu Liang, "Youhua Ziben
Jiegou Shidian Zhong Mianlin De Wenti Ji Jianyi" [Problems We Are Facing in the Experimental Points for Optimizing the Capital Structure and Related Proposals], *Jinrong
Yu Jingji* [Finance and Economics], no.9 (1997): 8-9.

- In March 1997, the State Council issued a supplementary circular on trial implementation of merger, bankruptcy, and re-employment measures in SOEs, establishing a National Leading Small Group for restructuring work and officially designating 111 additional experimental units. Coordinated by the SETC, a list of enterprises in the trial cities was drawn up for merger, bankruptcy, and rescue.[22]

Based on these policy documents, the national government issued general guidelines on basic priorities and approaches to handle enterprise insolvencies. Local governments were encouraged to come up with innovative solutions to debt restructuring, mergers, closures, and employee resettlement. In the process, the central government selectively extended substantial financial support to local restructuring. Examples in cases of bankruptcy are provided in Cai's contribution to this volume. Because national social insurance programs were still at an experimental stage when these policies were being initiated, bailouts had to be paid to laid-off workers from local and central coffers or new bank loans. This is an example of how the state intervened to provide an intermediate solution to a longer-term institutional problem that had not yet been resolved, in this case the building of a social security system. As Oi and Han point out succinctly, local officials, caught between financial and political pressures, had to work out "ad-hoc strategies either to cut job losses or to provide for displaced workers." This approach produced "significant local variation in the timing, speed, and content of reform in different cities" and restructuring remained a "patchwork of solutions that pushed the limits of reform but then had to be reined back to accommodate the political as well as the economic realities that existed in different localities."[23]

Based on the stipulations of the above-mentioned policy documents, 2,982 SOE restructuring projects, involving mergers, insolvencies, and re-employment, were commenced between 1994 and 1997. By year-end 1997, 2,393 of these projects were already completed, among which there were 585 enterprise bankruptcies and 1,022 mergers.[24] In 1998 the experience obtained from the experimental implementation of these policy documents was promoted as the basis for nationwide debt restructuring in SOEs. In their

22 See *Renmin Ribao*, April 21, 1997, 1.

23 Jean C. Oi and Han Chaohua, "Political and Institutional Complementarities: The Evolution of Corporate Restructuring in China," unpublished paper, 4.

24 *Zhongguo Qiye Guanli Nianjian 1998* [Yearbook of Chinese Enterprise Management 1998] (Beijing: Qiye guanli chubanshe, 1998), 217, quoted in Ding Xiaozhi and Ji Liuxiang, "1978 Nian Yilai Guoyou Qiye Chanquan Gaige Jincheng Ji Xiaolü Pingxi," 71.

chapter in this volume Oi and Han stress the sequencing of the forms of re-structuring. Part of what determined movement to the next phase was gaining sufficient knowledge about what could work, or not, and in what kind of context. Local solutions that appeared socially and economically tenable to the top leadership were promoted as models from which other jurisdictions should learn. Restructuring then gained momentum on a nationwide scale. To accelerate the restructuring process, the Fourth Plenum of the Fifteenth CCP Central Committee (fall 1999) adopted a decision with far-reaching impact that ordered banks to increase their bad-debt write-offs so as to support the merger and bankruptcy of large and medium-sized SOEs and to convert SOE debts into equity (debt-equity swaps). Four national asset management companies were created at that time to re-package and sell the non-performing loans taken over from the state-owned commercial banks.

The policies crafted between 1994 and 1998 and the experience obtained through local implementation experimentation were used as the main national guidelines for dealing with insolvency throughout the country until 2006. The number of insolvencies (including proceedings formally completed by Chinese courts) increased from 1,232 in 1995 to 3,296 in 2000.[25] Overall, the central government pursued a policy of administratively guided and planned bankruptcy that was shaped and refined based on test-runs in a large number of centrally designated experimental units. In the course of this experimentation process, China's insolvency system came to constitute a patchwork of overlapping legal and policy documents: the vague, brief, and outdated 1986 "Experimental Bankruptcy Law"; extensive judicial interpretations by the Supreme Court in 1991 and 2002 to clarify bankruptcy proceedings in China's courts; the series of path-breaking policy decrees, issued by the central government since 1994, to deal with specific methods of debt restructuring, enterprise reorganization, and employee resettlement, mainly based on administrative guidance; and local regulations for corporate insolvency and reorganization, with a pioneering role played by the Shenzhen Special Economic Zone (SEZ) in testing an approach that was more court-based and market-oriented than the widespread administrative-guidance approach.[26] This patchwork of regulations and regulatory practices left many legal gaps but at the same time provided leeway for innovative policy solutions and, most importantly, allowed the process of corporate restructuring to move forward.

---

25 Supreme People's Court data, quoted in Booth, "Drafting Bankruptcy Laws in Socialist Market Economies," 95 and 101.

26 Booth, "Drafting Bankruptcy Laws in Socialist Market Economies," 97–102.

The evolution of these insolvency policies shows how changing economic and political conditions affect policy-making. Beginning in 1984,
probably the most consistently contested legal issue in Chinese bankruptcy
regulation revolved around the priorities of debt settlement. In the liquidation of assets, should priority protection be given to creditors or to employees? Chinese policy-making underwent several shifts to deal with this
issue, which is particularly delicate in a "socialist market economy" that
was expected to respect workers' interests but lacked an effective social
security system. Although the 1986 "Experimental Bankruptcy Law" was
more creditor-friendly, in reality the administrative practice of dealing with
insolvent enterprises favored employees. This was formalized by the 1994
State Council circular that "provided workers' resettlement rights with a
first claim on the land-use rights of SOEs in priority to the preexisting rights
of secured creditors."[27] This priority scheme was practiced in thousands of
cases thereafter. Local experience clearly demonstrated that, due to rising
labor protests and public discontent, it was politically inadvisable and practically impossible to reduce employment in state firms without granting locally negotiated more or less generous compensation packages to employees.

Further shifts in the priority scheme occurred in the process of drafting
the new bankruptcy law. A 2002 draft placed the burden of providing compensation to employees of insolvent enterprises explicitly on local governments. In a very employee-friendly October 2004 draft that was circulated
during heated debates about social inequities in China, workers were given
first priority over the rights of secured creditors, thereby going beyond the
preferential treatment that workers received under the 1994-99 policy decrees.[28] However, this policy shift in favor of protecting workers was not
retained in the final version of the new Bankruptcy Law, adopted in August
2006, that was presented as in keeping with international standards of priority protection for creditors and investors (whereas employee compensation
was implicitly arranged through government bail-outs).

This sequence of rather drastic policy shifts makes it clear that
experimentation-based discretionary bankruptcy regulation helped to con-
ceal and manage fundamental political-ideological controversies that were
at the heart of the delayed law-making. Policy experimentation during the
course of twenty-three years allowed recurrent adaptations in the application of the basic priority scheme and thereby helped to avoid open policy
conflicts and allowed localities to proceed with restructuring.

27 Booth, "Drafting Bankruptcy Laws in Socialist Market Economies," 139.
28 Booth, "Drafting Bankruptcy Laws in Socialist Market Economies," 140–41.

The unorthodox approach to bankruptcy regulation taken by Chinese policymakers reveals the key guiding role that government organs and administrative actions play in the management of the state sector: "SOE restructuring in China is not a firm-level decision."[29] Formal bankruptcy court proceedings played a minor role during the crucial period of SOE restructuring from 1994 to 2007. Instead, Chinese policymakers used alternative ways to reorganize and turn around the SOEs. Corporate rescue measures were not undertaken primarily through bankruptcy proceedings but through a variety of flexible, inconsistent, but, from a policy-making perspective, much less painful policies. Central and local policymakers shared the view that bankruptcy was neither the most politically palatable, nor the most effective means for dealing with state-sector restructuring. Bankruptcy was merely used as one of several instruments to manage state-sector debts, "along with asset management companies, debt-equity swaps, mergers and acquisitions and other devices, in order to see which works best."[30]

A political imperative to avoid sweeping liquidation of state assets through bankruptcy prevented a comprehensive regulation and propelled a lengthy search for alternative policy solutions to allow state assets and state control in the economy to survive in a new form. The process was not about finalizing policy at certain points in time but about re-shaping available imperfect solutions over and over again until politically acceptable and economically bearable solutions were found and until a conducive economic and fiscal environment made it possible to buffer the social repercussions of more comprehensive restructuring. This lies at the heart of the sequencing process that Oi and Han describe as the pattern of China's corporate restructuring.

Whereas policy experimentation was part of a highly politicized and conflict-ridden process at the central level of policy-making, it was predominantly driven by economic and fiscal exigencies at the local administrative levels. Local policy experimentation contributed to a series of makeshift, half-way restructuring measures since the mid-1980s. Between 1994 and 1997, the number of experimental sites for the management of bankruptcies was constantly expanded. Thereafter, restructuring measures in large SOEs were implemented as part of national plans that stipulated which

29 Oi and Han, "Political and Institutional Complementarities: The Evolution of Corporate Restructuring in China," 3.

30 This is how one experienced lawyer specializing in bankruptcies and mergers, Ta-kuang Chang, characterizes the policy choices made in China. See his "Ten Lessons of the GITIC Bankruptcy," *Asian Wall Street Journal*, January 12, 2001.

enterprises in which industries should be strengthened, merged, or closed down within a certain period. These plans were then carried out by state investment and administrative allocation.[31] After 1998, decentralized experiments in handling insolvencies no longer re-defined national policy goals but contributed to fine-tuning the implementation of employee resettlement and financial arrangements.

For the 2005–8 period, a national plan on closures and bankruptcies was drafted and implemented under the auspices of an inter-agency Leading Small Group for Enterprise Mergers, Bankruptcies, and Staff Re-Employment that had been formed in 1997 to coordinate the restructuring process (see Table 5.2). The 2005–8 plan on bankruptcies was presented as the concluding step in state-guided insolvency management to deal with the "historical burdens" of the SOEs. By this point, experimentation no longer had a role to play. In 2008, policy-based insolvencies were terminated to allow for law- and court-based procedures.

The history of bankruptcy management in China from 1984 to 2007 reveals that two central institutional elements that are taken for granted in "bankruptcy orthodoxy" simply could not be applied to China's political economy: a government that takes a neutral, passive role in insolvency proceedings, and an independent, effective court system.[32] China's insolvency by policy approach generated particular costs and distortions due to government domination in handling the proceedings and fear of the fall-out from corporate bankruptcies.[33] But for central and local policymakers, economic inefficiencies associated with insolvency by policy were part of the "necessary transaction costs to maintain political stability and social cohesion."[34] For them, China's experimentation-based approach to insolvency was an indispensable instrument to promote and manage systemic change. And for political scientists, this approach constitutes an original policy methodology in the restructuring of a socialist economy.

31 For a critical view of this state involvement and an assessment of the transition to a more market-based system, see Wu, *Understanding and Interpreting Chinese Economic Reform*, 191-92.

32 Shahid Yusuf, Kaoru Nabeshima, and Dwight H. Perkins, *Under New Ownership: Privatizing China's State-Owned Enterprises* (Washington, DC: World Bank, 2005), 104.

33 Chen Zhisen et al., "Zhengcexing Guanbi Pochan Hequ Hecong?" [What Course Should be Followed for Policy-Based Closures and Insolvencies], *Dangdai Jingji* [Contemporary Economics], no.11 (2004): 9.

34 Oi and Han, "Political and Institutional Complementarities: The Evolution of Corporate Restructuring in China," 21.

Experimentation and Reform Breakthroughs

In democratic polities, which are characterized by extensive institutional checks, regular electoral and leadership changes, contentious public-policy debate, and a constantly shifting mix of policy priorities, experimentation is subject to narrow limitations:

> By the time a policy has reached the statute books, its content (and often its methods of delivery too) have run the gauntlet of parliamentary debate, media examination, pressure from lobbies and scrutiny by committees. Emerging from this process, the final version of a policy may well incorporate numerous carefully worked compromises, which are by then far too complex to be re-opened.[35]

Under these conditions, pilots that are designed to contribute to developing major policies (*before* binding policy compromises have been made) are rare. Pilots mainly contribute to optimizing methods of implementation for policies whose content has been hammered out beforehand. This is fundamentally different in China, where policy is developed through experimentation and policy departures are prepared and justified on the basis of prior experimentation.

Ambitious structural reformers utilized experimental programs, such as the insolvency, merger, bankruptcy, and re-employment procedures implemented locally from 1994 to 1997, as an effective method to introduce ultimately radical policy goals in the guise of incremental trial measures, thereby reducing risks while increasing the "controllability" (*kekongxing*) of the reforms.[36] Through decentralized experimentation, policy deadlock was frequently overcome and the achievements of the reform were expanded "far beyond what could have been accomplished by top-down initiatives dependent on political consensus among national leaders."[37]

An underrated effect of policy experimentation is in the consequences that come to light only over time and go way beyond the initial intentions of the policymakers who initiated the experimentation. The economic opening of the SEZs and fourteen coastal cities, for instance, was originally justified by Deng Xiaoping as a limited experiment. At that time, foreign trade and foreign direct investment were not intended to increase the competitive

---

35 Roger Jowell, *Trying It Out: The Role of "Pilots" in Policy-Making* (London: Government Chief Social Researcher's Office, 2003), 9-10.

36 Liu Zhao, Wang Songqian, and Huang Zhanfeng, "Lun Gonggong Guanli Shidian Zhong De 'Shidian Fangfa'" [On the "Pilot Method" in Public Management Practice], *Dongbei Daxue* [Journal of Northeastern University], no. 4 (2006): 281.

37 Rawski, "Implications of China's Reform Experience," 1162.

pressures on China's state enterprises. But over the course of the reforms they exerted increasing influence on the policies crafted for SOE restructuring through selective mergers and acquisitions involving foreign investors. Similarly, China's initial experiments with the transformation of SOEs into shareholding companies were primarily used as an avenue for raising capital. But during the 1990s, policymakers began to use the shareholding system for other purposes: first to change the status of state responsibility in the former SOEs and to find ways to end the state's "implicit social contract with state workers";[38] and second, and belatedly, to improve overall corporate governance with the help of more hands-on shareholders at home and abroad.[39] In these cases, policy approaches that initially appeared rather conservative paved the way for more radical approaches through experimentation and the learning processes they stimulated. Therefore, experimentation often resulted in changes that went beyond the original policy intentions.

Some of the distinctive traits of China's policy-making approach to state-sector restructuring have been pointed out in this chapter. The main components are summarized in Table 5.3. Beyond the growth imperative, no preconceived reform strategy (such as "privatization") was laid down. The means to achieve economic growth and efficiency gains was largely left open. A fundamental difference compared to Japanese and South Korean policymakers since the 1980s is the *time horizon* and the secure political position of Chinese policymakers that facilitated "institutional displacement" and "institutional layering."[40] Newly emerging elements in the political economy "outgrew" the older elements over an extended period. The main precondition for such a policy-making approach, as opposed to policy-making in democratic rule-of-law systems where there are recurrent electoral campaigns, is the long time horizon of the Chinese policymakers who, in the context of the authoritarian polity, do not have to face organized opposition and electoral competition and therefore can afford to wait for conditions to "mature" and for local experience to accumulate. Moreover, the protracted process of policy learning was made possible by the massive growth of nonstate economic activity that reduced the pressures for immediate structural

38 This intriguing point is made by Oi and Han in "Political and Institutional Complementarities: The Evolution of Corporate Restructuring in China," 14–15.

39 See Yusuf, Nabeshima, and Perkins, *Under New Ownership*, 72–73.

40 For a systematic study of incremental but transformative institutional change, see Wolfgang Streeck and Kathleen Thelen, "Introduction," in Streek and Thelen, eds., *Beyond Continuity: Institutional Change in Advanced Political Economies* (Oxford: Oxford University Press, 2005).

TABLE 5.3

Foundations of Policy-making for System Restructuring in China since 1978

Strategy: Beyond the growth imperative, no preconceived reform strategy (such as "privatization") was predetermined. The means to achieve economic growth was largely left open.

Time horizon: The policymakers' secure political position facilitated institutional displacement and institutional layering ("dual track": the new system outgrows the old system) over an extended period.

Experimentation: Decentralized policy experimentation and jurisdictional competition (including technically illegal local policy initiatives) were stimulated and tolerated by the top policy-makers.

Experience first, law-making later: Information about local policy experiments regarded by decision-makers as economically successful and politically acceptable was selectively disseminated and the experiments were expanded "from point to surface" in official pilot programs. Economic legislation usually came as a result of this experimentation process.

Reserve capacities: In periods of "extraordinary politics" (1992–93, 1997–98, 2001–2) when big reform pushes were undertaken by the central policy-makers, Communist Party institutions fulfilled a key role by imposing top-level policy initiatives and institutional reorganization.

Two-level games: Policy-makers played a two-level game during the WTO negotiations so as to intensify transnational adaptive pressures and accelerate state-sector restructuring.

Source: Author.

reform in the public sector[41] and thereby provided Chinese policymakers with an unusually opportune environment for learning and adaptation over an extended period of time.

Opportunistic timing of major policies has been a constant feature of China's state-sector reform. As Jung also stresses, the breakthrough for SOE corporatization came in 1997–98 when top decision-makers were willing to entertain radical restructuring measures due to the shock of the Asian financial crisis. At the same time, economic growth and improved tax collection provided the central government and some local governments with the fiscal means to pave the way for the SOEs to be relieved of their costly "social functions" and to lay off millions of workers at the expense of government coffers. The years of large-scale SOE restructuring after 1998 benefited from a highly opportune economic and fiscal environment that buffered the painful process through government bailouts.[42] The Chinese government was in a position to make determined use of this opportunity not only due to decisive leadership, but also because a plethora of restructuring policies had

41 Specific cases of the variations in leeway that the various localities had in deciding whether to restructure SOEs are detailed in the contribution by Zeng and Tsai in this volume.

42 Cf. Oi and Han, "Political and Institutional Complementarities: The Evolution of Corporate Restructuring in China," 20–21.

been tried out in diverse SOEs and localities beforehand, namely, in the massive, largely ineffective, yet highly instructive 1994–97 experiments introducing a modern company system.

Learning *ex negativo*, that is, by failed experiments, played a crucial role in overcoming the piecemeal approach to restructuring pursued prior to 1997. Negative lessons from failed local experiments, for example those provided by the 1994–97 "modern company system" experimental program, constituted a much less risky mode of policy learning than the enactment of national laws that were not tried out in key elements beforehand and therefore might have produced unintended adverse results. From the perspective of national policy-making, the limited costs attached to the failure of local experiments appear to be much less significant than the experience and knowledge that the failed experiments provide and that may help to avoid national policy disasters. Thus, on the basis of the sobering lessons from earlier restructuring measures, reformers found themselves in the position in 1997-98 to win support for a much more drastic approach to restructuring as soon as the Asian financial crisis opened a window of opportunity for comprehensive SOE reform.

Institutional Complementarities and the Limits of Synoptic Policy-making

Political economy models that stress institutional complementarities call for optimizing the coherence of policy and institutional changes in system restructuring. From this perspective, smartly coordinated restructuring programs are the only way to keep reforms in different policy domains compatible with one another.[43] Yet, as Braybrooke and Lindblom point out in their pioneering and still valid analysis, such synoptic, rationalistic-deductive conceptions of policy-making are generally untenable since they assume, first, that the entire spectrum of alternative policies is somehow known to the analyst and, second, that the ultimate objectives of policy-making are well defined and stable.[44]

Both assumptions are implausible and detached from the reality of policy-making. A central proposition of policy studies that has been bolstered by

43 For such an approach, see Fan Gang and Wing Thye Woo, "The Parallel Partial Progression (PPP) Approach to Institutional Transformation in Transition Economies: Optimize Economic Coherence, Not Policy Sequence," *Modern China* 35, no. 4 (July 2009): 352-69.

44 Cf. David Braybrooke and Charles E. Lindblom, *A Strategy of Decision: Policy Evaluation as a Social Process* (New York: The Free Press, 1963), ch. 3.

broad empirical evidence from all types of polities over recent decades states that policy is "made and re-made endlessly. Policy-making is a process of successive approximation to some desired objectives in which what is desired itself continues to change under reconsideration."[45] Interlinked institutional and policy reforms therefore represent "wicked problems"[46] that are characterized by extensive uncertainty about the feasibility and consequences of interventions, pervasive ambiguity, controversy, and indecision on the part of policymakers, unique and rapidly shifting conditions for intervention and interaction, multiple unforeseeable feedbacks, as well as unexpected endogenous and exogenous developments or shocks that can transform the entire playing field within a short period of time.

China's experience with systemic restructuring is characterized overall by an unsynchronized, piecemeal process of reform-making whose *strength is not its coherence but its openness to unexpected and tentative policy solutions that are seized upon when they come up.* Broad-based tinkering effectively enriched and transformed the economic policy know-how of local and central decision-makers and administrators. Protracted policy learning was helped immensely by the massive growth in private and transnational economic activity that lessened pressures for immediate structural reform in the public sector and thereby provided policymakers with an opportune environment for adaptation over an extended period. Reform breakthroughs that contained interlinked restructuring policies came in 1992-93 (the program for market-oriented restructuring), 1997-98 (SOE and financial industry reform), and 2001-2 (foreign trade and investment liberalization) when external push factors (the Soviet collapse, the Asian financial crisis, and WTO negotiations, respectively) propelled top-level policy decisiveness that could build on the diverse experiences obtained through the years of piecemeal tinkering.

From the mid-1980s China's policymakers stated again and again that they saw "comprehensive coordinated reform" as the optimal way to deal with the administrative and welfare impacts of SOE reform. But they could not, and still cannot, build a policy consensus, vision, or agenda about what the state sector should look like at the end of its transformation since sweeping privatization seemed neither desirable nor acceptable to most policymakers. Beyond ultimate policy goals, they also were not sure about the

45 Charles Lindblom, "The Science of 'Muddling Through'," *Public Administration Review* 19, no. 2 (1959): 86, 88.

46 Cf. Horst Rittel and Melvin Webber, "Dilemmas in a General Theory of Planning," *Policy Sciences* 4, no. 2 (June 1973):155-69.

policy instruments. They did not know what types of policies would solve the most pressing deficiencies of the state sector without losing control.

Instead of settling for a deadlock in economic reform as occurred in Brezhnev's Soviet Union, Chinese policymakers tinkered with incoherent, yet still instructive, piecemeal restructuring. In the end, they seized the opportunity for decisive reform only when they were driven forward by exogenous events, felt sufficiently confident to know what might work and what should be avoided due to previous experimentation, and could afford to pursue a proactive fiscal policy that allowed them to placate the losers of state-sector reform through ad-hoc compensation. *The essential fluidity and unpredictability of the policy environment must be taken seriously as a universal constraint for any attempt to design comprehensive reform packages in dealing with institutional complementarities.*

Context-driven expectations are crucial to understanding the distinctive behavior of policymakers and experimenters in China's polity. Whereas policymakers, administrators, and citizens in advanced political economies, such as Japan, tend to view experimental policy departures as risky, destabilizing, and threatening to their stakes in the status quo, political actors in less advanced, yet rapidly growing economies with successful reform records, such as China, tend to display more confidence in the benefits that policy change may bring. Therefore, they may perceive policy experimentation more as a chance than as a risk. Seen from this perspective, in addition to the distinctive policy process, expectations among experimenters and policymakers about the potential gains are a crucial factor that explains the unusual productivity of policy experimentation in China.

6 Reinvented Intervention

THE CHINESE CENTRAL STATE AND STATE-OWNED
ENTERPRISE REFORM IN THE WTO ERA[1]

Joo-Youn Jung

Since China began economic reform and opening in the late 1970s, the underperformance of its state-owned enterprises (SOEs) has put a drag on the prospects for the entire Chinese economy. The problem is that restructuring China's gigantic public corporate sector, once the backbone of its socialist planned economy, is a very sensitive political move that could directly contradict the socialist ideals and thus undermine the legitimacy not only of the market-oriented economic reforms but also of the Chinese Communist Party (CCP). Yet, in the mid-1990s, Chinese SOEs finally began to go through the long-delayed restructuring. A critical turning point came in 2001 with China's accession to the World Trade Organization (WTO). The WTO accession was a loud and clear signal that the Chinese economy will be even more closely tied to the global economy. It further implied that China could no longer muddle through with lukewarm and partial economic reform. One can interpret the acceleration of SOE restructuring during the last decade[2] as the loosening of the state's tight grip over the economy, allowing more comprehensive marketization and institutional reform to take place in an era of neoliberal economic globalization and rapid domestic economic transition. Dominant state ownership and control of the corporate sector, in the end, might not be compatible with efficient capitalist economic development

The comprehensive restructuring of the Chinese central economic bureaucracy, carried out in 2003 after WTO accession, seems to effectively corroborate

---

1 A large portion of this chapter relies on Joo-Youn Jung, "Retreat of the State? Restructuring the Chinese Bureaucracies in the Era of Economic Globalization," *China Review* 8, no. 1 (Spring 2008): 105–25.

2 See Chapter 1 in this volume by Jean C. Oi.

this interpretation. During this round of bureaucratic restructuring, there was a significant institutional change: the State Economic and Trade Commission (SETC), a supra agency responsible for the SOEs, was dismantled. In charge not only of the SOEs but also of industrial policy-making, sectoral planning, and macroeconomic coordination within the Chinese central bureaucracy, the SETC had been a top central economic agency during the 1990s. When it was dismantled, its central function, i.e., SOE management, was transferred to a new, much smaller, agency, the State-owned Assets Supervision and Administration Commission (SASAC), designated as the representative of government interests as "investor" in the SOEs. The transformation of the powerful SETC into the investor SASAC appeared to symbolize momentous changes in the Chinese central state, at least in relation to the SOE sector. The state seemed to be downsizing, retreating from the SOE sector, and redefining its role as the regulator of the SOEs.

This chapter provides a very different perspective from such a dominant view. Instead of focusing simply on the ostensible outcome of SETC restructuring in 2003, it pays attention to the institutional history of the SETC and investigates the political logic of the SETC's rise and fall since the early 1990s. Illuminating the political logic of the SETC's institutional reform will shed light on how the economic role of the Chinese central state has been changed and what the continuity or discontinuity in the state role implies for SOE reform in the context of China's transitional economy.

The following section utilizes the concept of institutional complementarities to discuss why the reform of China's central economic bureaucracy was a critical part of the broader system restructuring that was required for effective SOE reform. The next two sections analyze the role of the domestic political leader as well as WTO entry in the institutional changes of the SETC since the early 1990s. WTO accession was key, not by forcing the state to retreat from the SOEs but by enabling Premier Zhu Rongji to pursue a politically sensitive agenda, such as SOE reform, with the support of the reinforced SETC. The fifth section confirms this by showing that the new economic agencies created in the place of the SETC hardly portend a retreat of the Chinese interventionist state bureaucracy from the SOEs. They simply represent a different type of state intervention, which seems to be more efficient and focused than that in the past.

SETC dismemberment indicates neither the transformation of the Chinese central state into a regulatory state nor its retreat from the corporate sector. The active manipulation of the SOE reform rhetoric by the top political leaders in the SETC restructuring process and the persistence of bureaucratic control over the SOEs after the SETC dismemberment suggest that, despite China's economic globalization and rapid domestic economic transition, the

Chinese SOE sector is not likely to experience a dramatic state retreat and off-equilibrium market-driven reform, at least in the near future.

The Central Economic Bureaucracy in the Chinese Transitional Economy

A national economic system is a tightly woven web of interdependent institutions. A useful concept to portray such an institutional interconnectedness is "institutional complementarities." Institutions are interconnected or tightly coupled as part of a national economic system, creating "ensembles" that link institutions in one issue area within a system to those in other issue areas.[3] A high level of institutional interdependence means that breaking the solid institutional status quo in one subsystem is limited without changes in other related subsystems. In addition, the complementary subsystems are subordinated to the institutional logic of the national economic system.[4] Combined, these two characteristics show that strong institutional path dependency is created within a national economic system. For the ensembles of the complementary institutions to loosen up and for off-equilibrium development of a subsystem such as the SOE sector to take place, either comprehensive and simultaneous reform of all the major subsystems or significant changes in the core institution that coordinates and defines the nature of the interactions among the major sectors within the national economic system are necessary.[5]

As is well known, China has avoided the dramatic "big-bang" approach and instead has pursued incremental institutional reform. For significant restructuring of the SOE sector without a big bang, changes in the core coordinating institution are critical. The key institution that has characterized the China's socialist economic system is the state, which has been the planner, executor, monitor, and coordinator of the national economy. With the

---

3 Colin Crouch, "Complementarity and Fit in the Study of Comparative Capitalisms," in Glen Morgan, Richard Whitley, and Eli Moen, eds., *Changing Capitalisms? Internationalization, Institutional Change, and Systems of Economic Organization* (New York: Oxford University Press, 2005), 167–89.

4 Richard Deeg, "Path Dependency, Institutional Complementarity, and Change in National Business Systems," in Morgan, Whitley, and Moen, eds., *Changing Capitalisms? Internationalization, Institutional Change, and Systems of Economic Organization*, 21–52.

5 For more detailed discussion on institutional complementarities and application of the concept to the Korean case, see Joo-Youn Jung, "State Coordination in Transition and Corporate Restructuring in South Korea," in Byung-Kook Kim, Eun-Mee Kim, and Jean C. Oi, eds., *Adapt, Fragment, Transform: Corporate Restructuring and System Reform in South Korea* (forthcoming 2011).

rapid transition of the Chinese economy, a redefinition of the role of the state is a central issue that can either facilitate or hamper reforms in any particular sector and in the end can transform the nature of the entire economic system. The state's withdrawal from the economy and the reduction in state ownership are often considered essential prerequisites or inevitable consequences of China's successful transition to a market economy. An underlying preconception of this logic is that active state intervention is incompatible with the market. Effective SOE restructuring is possible only when accompanied by a dramatic reduction in the state's direct management of the SOEs or ultimately a major privatization of the SOEs.

It is in this context that the dismemberment of the SETC becomes important. The restructuring, and more importantly downfall, of the top central agency in charge of SOEs has significant implications for understanding the changing role of the Chinese state in a transitional economy. Beginning in the 1990s, the official goal of bureaucratic restructuring was explicitly to transform state functions to meet the needs of the now officially accepted "market economy." Under this goal, structural changes of the central economic bureaucracy in direct control of the socialist planned economy were undertaken. Since the 1990s, the crucial changes in the central economic bureaucracy evolved around the SETC.

The SETC was not a completely new agency. It was an incarnation of the State Economic Commission (SEC), which had been abolished in 1988 but then revived in 1991. The SEC was formally transformed into the SETC in 1993. After its establishment, the SETC rapidly expanded its portfolio. In 1998, the SETC incorporated six line ministries in charge of domestic industries and became a supra agency in charge of industrial policy-making and coordination within the central bureaucracy. Whereas the State Development and Planning Commission (SDPC), the successor to the State Planning Commission (SPC) and a symbol of China's socialist planned economy, was experiencing a significantly reduced portfolio and reduced organizational power, the SETC's portfolio expanded considerably. In charge not only of the SOEs but also of industrial policy-making, sectoral planning, and macroeconomic coordination within the Chinese government, the SETC became a powerful agency that rose to the position of a "little State Council" during the 1990s.[6]

However, as noted earlier, the SETC was suddenly dismantled in 2003. The SETC's SOE management functions were transferred to a new agency, the

6 Yongnian Zheng, *Globalization and State Transformation in China* (New York: Cambridge University Press, 2004), 83; Alice L. Miller, "The 10th National People's Congress and China's Leadership Transition," *China Leadership Monitor*, no. 7 (Summer 2003): 6.

State-owned Assets Supervision and Administration Commission (SASAC), a much smaller and weaker version of its predecessor. The role of the SASAC was to be representative of government interests as "investor." The demise of the powerful SETC and its replacement by the SASAC appeared to be a clear signal that the Chinese central state was finally being transformed into a regulator of the economy and in this process reform of the SOEs would be compatible with China's rapidly rising market economy and would enable survival in the global competition of the WTO era.

Existing studies support this view. The 2003 government restructuring has been described as an "apparent effort to manage the impact on China's domestic economy of China's entry into the WTO, especially for the state-owned enterprise sector,"[7] that aimed at creating "a regulatory state administration that fundamentally transforms and limits the roles and reach of government and that uses only indirect levers to guide a largely autonomous market economy."[8] The goal was "to make the Chinese government significantly stronger as a regulatory body and reduce direct government management of businesses."[9]

However, this interpretation leaves a number of puzzles unresolved. If the reform goal was to reduce the state's hands-on management of the SOEs, why was the SETC highly empowered during the 1990s and then abolished in 2003, seemingly at the peak of its institutional power? In addition, an often ignored fact is that the SDPC was re-strengthened as a result of the 2003 bureaucratic restructuring and reborn as the powerful State Development and Reform Commission (SDRC). If the SETC was dismembered to reduce state economic intervention due to the WTO challenges, then why was the SDPC, a rival agency of the SETC and an agency symbolic of China's planned economy, given greater power and an extended portfolio in place of the SETC? To answer these questions, one needs to look behind the façade of the reform rhetoric into the processes of the rise and fall of the SETC.

Zhu Rongji and the SETC

A closer look at the institutional development of the SETC reveals an important factor relevant to the SETC's institutional fate: Zhu Rongji's political power. Table 6.1 summarizes the rise and fall of the SETC's institutional

---

7 Alice L. Miller, "The Hu-Wen Leadership at Six Months," *China Leadership Monitor*, no. 8 (2003).

8 Miller, "The 10th National People's Congress and China's Leadership Transition."

9 Barry Naughton, "Government Reorganization: Liu Mingkang and Financial Restructuring," *China Leadership Monitor*, no. 7 (2003).

TABLE 6.1

The Rise and Fall of the SETC and Zhu Rongji

Year	SETC	Zhu Rongji
1979	SEC re-established	Worked at the SEC (1979-87)
		Vice Minister (1983-87)
1988	SEC abolished	Shanghai Mayor (1987-91)
1991	SEC revived as Production Office	Vice Premier
1992	Economic and Trade Office established	Promoted to the No. 5 position at the 14th CCP National Congress
1993	SETC established	First Vice Premier
1998	SETC strengthened by incorporating industrial ministries	Premier
2003	SETC abolished	Out of Power

Source: Compiled by the author.

power within the context of the rise and fall of Zhu Rongji. The two clearly coincide, revealing how tightly the fate of the SETC was tied to that of its political patron, Zhu Rongji.

As noted earlier, the SETC was an incarnation of the SEC that had been abolished in 1988. The SEC had been in charge of production coordination, annual production planning, resource distribution and transportation planning, and macro-management of the economy. Zhu Rongji originally built his career in the SEC beginning in 1979, and served as a vice minister of the SEC between 1983 and 1987 until he left the commission in 1987 to become mayor of Shanghai.

In July 1991, only four months after his return to the State Council, Zhu Rongji established the Production Office (PO) in the State Council as a partial revival of the former SEC. In May 1992, the PO was upgraded to the State Council Economic and Trade Office (ETO), with Zhu Rongji as its leader. The ETO revived most of the former functions of the SEC. It participated in the SPC's long-term, mid-term, and annual planning and industrial policy-making, and coordinated implementation of annual planning. Within the boundaries of the annual planning, the ETO managed and coordinated the production, transportation, and resource distribution related to industry, transportation, commerce, and international trade. It also was in charge of technological advancement policies for enterprises.

Zhu formally established his leadership in the economic field at the Fourteenth CCP National Congress in October 1992. At this National Congress, Zhu was promoted to Politburo Standing Committee member, becoming the number-five figure in the CCP, after Jiang Zemin, Li Peng,

Qiao Shi, and Li Ruihuan. Thereafter, at the Eighth National People's Congress (NPC) in March 1993, Zhu became the first vice premier directly under Li Peng, securing a position to take drastic measures in terms of economic policy.[10] It was also in March 1993 at the Eighth NPC that the ETO was upgraded to the SETC, a state commission and a supra-ministerial agency. The SETC was placed under the direction of Zhu's associate Wang Zhongyu, who later became State Council secretary general when Zhu assumed premiership. The main functions of the SETC were to deepen the economic reforms (especially reform of the SOEs) and strengthen macroeconomic coordination.[11]

In March 1998, Zhu Rongji became premier. With the rise of its patron's political power, the institutional power of the SETC was greatly enhanced. The most striking change in the bureaucratic restructuring of 1998 was the demise of most industrial line ministries, which had been the bulwark of the centrally planned economic system and a mechanism designed to manage the economy in minute detail.[12] The SETC incorporated six line ministries in charge of domestic industries,[13] along with two industrial associations

10 Yasuo Onishi, "The 16th Congress of the Communist Party of China and Prospects of Market Economy with Chinese Characteristics," in IDE-JETRO (Institute of Developing Economies-Japan External Trade Organization), ed., *Spot Survey No. 26: China's New Leadership*, 2003, at http://www.ide.go.jp/English/Publish/Download/Spot/26.html, accessed September 28, 2010; Yongnian Zheng, *Zhu Rongji Xinzheng: Zhongguo Gaige De Xin Moshi* [The New Politics of Zhu Rongji: A New Model for Chinese Reform] (River Edge, NJ: Bafang wenhua qiye gongsi, 1999), 46.

11 For more detailed discussion on the functions of the SETC and its institutional evolution since the 1990s, see Joo-Youn Jung, "When Nonliberal Economies Meet Globalization: The Transformation of Interventionist States in East Asia," Ph.D. diss., Department of Political Science, Stanford University, 2006.

12 John Abbott Worthley and King K. Tsao, "Reinventing Government in China: A Comparative Analysis," *Administration & Society* 31, no. 5 (1999): 571–87.

13 These are the Ministries of Electric Power Industry, Coal Industry, Machinery Industry, Chemical Industry, Metallurgical Industry, and Internal Trade. An exception is the Ministry of Information Industry. The Ministry of Information Industry was separately created based on a merger between the Ministry of Posts and Telecommunications and the Ministry of Electronics Industry. The Ministry of Radio, Film, and Television, the General Company of Aviation Industry, and the information and network management function of the General Company of Aviation Industry were also incorporated into the new ministry. Guowuyuan Bangongting Mishuju, Zhongyang Jigou Bianzhi Weiyuanhui Bangongshi Zonghesi [State Council Secretariat Office and Central Bianzhi Committee Office], *Zhongyang Zhengfu Zuzhi Jigou 1994* [Central Government Organizational Structure 1994] (Beijing: Zhongguo fazhan chubanshe, 1994), 12; and Dali L. Yang, *Remaking the Chinese Leviathan: Market Transition and the Politics of Governance in China* (Stanford: Stanford University Press, 2004).

and two SOEs.[14] With the line ministries downgraded to the bureau (*ju*) level under the SETC,[15] the voices of each industry that had been directly represented in the State Council by the line ministries were now coordinated and represented by the SETC. This meant that the SETC became a supraministerial agency in charge of industrial production and domestic trade in both name and reality.

The rise of the SETC changed the balance of power within the central economic bureaucracy. In addition to incorporating the industrial ministries, the SETC absorbed key functions of the SDPC, a long-time rival agency of the SETC. Such functions included industrial policy-making, adjusting the industrial structure, and guiding financial investment.[16] The SETC was now called the "little State Council," where Zhu formed and implemented the major economic reform policies.[17] In contrast, the power of the SDPC, formerly in charge of the Chinese planned economy as the top economic agency, decreased considerably. Functions related to industrial policy-making and implementation were transferred to the SETC, and the SDPC's role was defined not as a powerful planning agency governing the entire Chinese economy but as a macroeconomic coordination agency in charge of analyzing and recommending economic and social development strategies, making long-term plans, maintaining general economic equilibrium, and conducting structural adjustments of the economy.[18] Some

14 The two associations are the National Councils of Light Industry and Textile Industry and the two SOEs are the General Company of Petroleum and Gas and the General Company of Petroleum and Chemical Industry. See Yang, *Remaking the Chinese Leviathan* and Zheng, *Globalization and State Transformation in China*.

15 Zheng, *Globalization and State Transformation in China*, 105, 25.

16 Guowuyuan Bangongting Mishuju, Zhongyang Jigou Bianzhi Weiyuanhui Bangongshi Zonghesi [State Council Secretariat Office and Central Bianzhi Committee Office], *Zhongyang Zhengfu Zuzhi Jigou 1998* [Central Government Organizational Structure 1998] (Beijing: Gaige chubanshe, 1998).

17 Zheng, *Globalization and State Transformation in China*, 83; Miller, "The 10th National People's Congress and China's Leadership Transition," 6; Kjeld Erik Brødsgaard, "Institutional Reform and the Bianzhi System in China," *China Quarterly*, no. 170 (2002): 361–86.

18 Stoyan Tenev, Chunlin Zhang, with Loup Brefort, *Corporate Governance and Enterprise Reform in China: Building the Institutions of Modern Markets* (Washington, DC: International Finance Corporation, 2002), 58; Yang, *Remaking the Chinese Leviathan*; Worthley and Tsao, "Reinventing Government in China"; Joseph Fewsmith, *China Since Tiananmen: The Politics of Transition* (New York: Cambridge University Press, 2001), 574; Guowuyuan Bangongting Mishuju and Zhongyang Jigou Bianzhi Weiyuanhui Bangongshi Zonghesi, *Zhongyang Zhengfu Zuzhi Jigou*.

observers saw the 1998 reform as a signal of the SDPC's demise and transformation into a research and advisory body.[19]

By February 2001, measures to strengthen the SETC were pushed even further. Eight of the SETC's industrial bureaus were abolished and transformed into sectoral industrial associations (*hangye xiehui*) that were no longer part of the State Council.[20] This meant the end of an era when the fragmented central line ministries directly controlled (and protected) their own constituent industries. At the same time, the macroeconomic coordination function of the SETC, encompassing production and trade in focused industrial sectors, was further enhanced.

However, this power concentration in the SETC ended in two years when Zhu Rongji was out of power. In March 2003, a new generation of leaders emerged. Wen Jiabao, succeeding Zhu Rongji as premier, initiated another round of central government reform and the central economic bureaucracy went through another restructuring. The most striking change was the dismemberment of the SETC, the top economic coordination agency under Premier Zhu. The restructuring divided the SETC's extensive portfolio into two already existing economic agencies—the SDPC and the Ministry of Foreign Trade and Economic Cooperation (MOFTEC)—leaving SOE management to the SETC's successor, the SASAC. The SDPC was expanded into the SDRC, as noted earlier, and the MOFTEC became the Ministry of Commerce (MOC) in charge of international and domestic trade. This ended ten years of SETC supremacy.

The Political Logic of SETC Dismemberment

The previous section shows that the institutional fate of the SETC fluctuated with the rise and fall of Zhu Rongji's political power. Zhu Rongji was widely known as the patron of the SETC. For him, the SETC was a

19 Zheng Yongnian, *Zhu Rongji Xinzheng*, 175.

20 According to the author's interviews, this does not mean that the personnel who were previously at the industrial ministries were off of the central government payroll. The personnel were "pushed out" of the State Council to show off the dramatic reduction in the number of employees, bureaus, and ministries, but they mostly remained inside the boundary of the state, often in various *shiye danwei* (non-profit government-funded organizations), which include industry associations, research institutes, educational institutions, hospitals, and so forth. This shows the difficulties of laying off government employees in China and the limited reforms aiming at "smaller government" (author's interview). For a good discussion of the recent *shiye danwei* reform, see Yang, *Remaking the Chinese Leviathan*, 49–53.

vanguard agency that not only made and implemented his preferred economic policies but also provided an organizational power base within the government to support his economic reform agenda.[21] With Zhu's support and protection, the SETC quickly expanded its organizational power and arguably became the most prominent agency in the State Council within a few years after its establishment. But with the decline of its patron's political power, the power of the SETC also waned.

However, the significance of Zhu Rongji to the SETC's institutional fate does not imply that the personal preference of an individual leader alone can explain away the institutional transformation of the state bureaucracy and thus the future of SOE reform. Nor does it imply that WTO entry did not play an important role in the bureaucratic institutional reform process. Despite the authoritarian nature of the regime and the centralization of decision-making power in a few political figures, decision-making power in China was not monopolized by one or two paramount leaders but rather shared among several top leaders.[22] The emphasis on consensus-making among the top leaders meant that even as vice premier and then premier in charge of economic issues, Zhu Rongji's power was confined by China's divided decision-making structure. Thus, Zhu's preferences alone do not explain why the SETC could expand its organizational portfolio in such an impressive way. This is where WTO entry played a key role.

WTO entry opened a window of opportunity for Zhu Rongji, who faced a deadlock in his domestic reform agenda both inside and outside the government. He actively utilized the WTO negotiations to justify not simply his support for the SETC but also his domestic reform agenda that was endorsed by the SETC. It is known that when Zhu first became premier, he was not enthusiastic about joining the WTO. In charge of the SOE reforms, Zhu maintained that it was too early to open up domestic industries to international competition. However, stiff domestic resistance against the restructuring of domestic industries and the limits of the moderate SOE reform led Zhu to regard the pressures from the WTO as a useful impetus

21 This point was repeatedly confirmed at various interviews with Chinese economic bureaucrats, not only former SETC officials but also current and former bureaucrats in other economic agencies who unanimously concurred that there was such a close relationship between the SETC and Zhu Rongji. Zheng makes the same argument in *Globalization and State Transformation in China*.

22 For more detailed discussion, see Joo-Youn Jung, "China's National Security Policymaking: Waning Military Representation and Shifting Policy Priorities," *Korean Journal of Defense Analysis* 19, no. 3 (Fall 2007): 77–98.

to weaken domestic resistance to SOE reform.[23] Although SOE reform was a key precondition for enhancing the efficiency of the economy, it was also an extremely delicate political issue. Restructuring the problematic SOEs eventually would lead to the dissolution of the remnants of the *danwei*, or collective production system, removing social security and preferential protection for urban workers and creating many urban layoffs, as demonstrated in other chapters of this volume. Such a measure that would generate many losers in the name of economic efficiency could effectively shake the ideological legitimacy of the CCP and threaten regime stability by creating large dissident groups in the urban areas.

The WTO enabled Zhu to blame foreign forces as the source of the problems and to guard himself from political attacks from both within the leadership group and society. It was not Zhu but the exogenous pressures that made the painful SOE reform unavoidable. Furthermore, as Gallagher effectively shows, WTO entry created a powerful rationale for a reform based on nationalism—building a strong, healthy corporate sector that could withstand foreign enterprises became a matter of national survival, even if it meant the sacrifice of less competent enterprises.[24] WTO entry also provided Zhu with an effective rationale for SETC expansion. The SETC with its reinforced organizational power greatly enhanced Zhu's authority within the government and reduced the ability of other ministries to obstruct the progress of the WTO negotiations.[25]

Therefore, it is inaccurate to argue that the purpose of SETC dismemberment was to withdraw the central bureaucracy from SOE management and eventually to allow market-oriented SOE reforms to take place in the face of the inevitable challenges of economic globalization, such as WTO entry and the needs for a successful domestic economic transition. Rather,

23 Joseph Fewsmith, "The Politics of China's Accession to the WTO," *Current History* 99, no. 638 (September 2000): 268–73; David Zweig, "China's Stalled 'Fifth Wave': Zhu Rongji's Reform Package of 1998–2000," *Asian Survey* 41, no. 2 (March-April 2001): 234; Margaret M. Pearson, "The Case of China's Accession to GATT/WTO," in David M. Lampton, ed., *The Making of Chinese Foreign and Security Policy in the Era of Reform, 1978–2000* (Stanford: Stanford University Press, 2001), 364; Seung-Wook Baek, "Junggukui WTO Gaipgua Segyegyongjeroui Pyonip" [China's Accession to the WTO and Its Incorporation into the World Economy], in Il-Yeung Lee, ed., *WTOro Ganeun Jungguk* [China Entering the WTO] (Seoul: Park yeong ryul chunlpansa, 2002); Nam-Joo Lee, "Jungguk WTO Gaibui Jongchi Nonli" [The Political Logic of China's WTO Entry], in Lee, ed., *WTOro Ganeun Jungguk.*

24 Mary Gallagher, *Contagious Capitalism: Globalization and the Politics of Labor in China* (Princeton, NJ: Princeton University Press, 2005).

25 Fewsmith, *China Since Tiananmen*, 575.

reform-oriented Zhu Rongji utilized these challenges to push through the difficult state-led reform of the SOEs with fewer political risks and resistance.
The retreat of the state from the SOEs or their privatization was not Zhu's
primary intention. Rather, the strengthened and enlarged SETC centralized
and rationalized the bureaucratic management of the SOEs that had formerly been compartmentalized by the line ministries.[26]

The New Economic Agencies

Even more convincing evidence that betrays the state retreat hypothesis
can be found in the establishment of the new economic agencies that replaced the SETC, especially the SDRC and the SASAC.

As noted earlier, the expansion of the SDPC, the symbol of powerful
state economic control and planning, into the SDRC cannot be explained
if the intention behind the SETC dismemberment was to reduce the role of
government in SOE management and to enhance the role of markets in SOE
restructuring.[27] The SDPC, the successor to the SPC that had been the top
planning agency of the Chinese planned economy since 1952, was the greatest beneficiary of the 2003 restructuring. With the dismemberment of the
SETC, the SDPC recovered its old territory. Furthermore, its organizational
power increased considerably, taking expanded planning and regulatory
roles and incorporating the SETC's important industrial policy and regulatory functions. Such functions included industrial planning and policy-
making, economic operations and controls, supervision of investment in
technological innovation, macroeconomic policy guidance for enterprises of
all ownership types, promotion of small and medium-sized enterprises, and
planning for the import and export of raw materials.[28]

The rise of the SDRC suggests that the Chinese central bureaucracy re-
claimed some of its control over the economy. In fact, the SDRC's intervention in the economy has sharply increased in recent years.[29] The most
important tool for SDRC economic intervention is its power to approve

26 For more detailed discussion on Zhu Rongji and WTO entry, see Jung, "Retreat
of the State?"

27 This chapter focuses on explaining the downfall of the SETC and only briefly
touches on the new agencies. For a detailed discussion on the new agencies and the political dynamics behind their creation, see Jung, "When Nonliberal Economies Meet
Globalization."

28 Shanghai Shehui Kexueyuan Minzhu Zhengzhi Yanjiu Zhongxin [Shanghai
Academy of Social Sciences, Democracy Research Center], *Zhongguo Zhengzhi Fazhan
Jincheng 2004* [The Process of Chinese Political Development 2004] (Beijing: Shishi chu-
banshe, 2004); and Yang, *Remaking the Chinese Leviathan*, 62.

29 Jung, "Retreat of the State?"

investment projects as part of its macroeconomic coordination. Project approval rights (*shenpi quan*) are one of the most effective tools of the Chinese government over the SOEs. With regional development programs, such as the southern area development, drawing more and more resources, the SDRC gained clout in those regions through its decisions on infrastructural investment projects.[30] The attempt to correct the overheating of the macroeconomy since 2004 also increased the SDRC's power. The SDRC fanned out across the country, telling local governments and businesses which investment projects could be continued.[31]

The establishment of the SASAC, the successor to the SETC, is often considered a measure to reduce the state's direct control over the SOEs. However, the SASAC, although attempting to play a redefined role for the state in SOE management, did not aim to reduce the role of the state.

The SASAC redefined the central government's role from being the public manager of society to being the representative of government interests as an "investor" and an owner of state assets.[32] According to its official mission statement, the SASAC "performs the responsibilities of an investor, guides and pushes forward the reform and restructuring of SOEs, supervises the preservation of an increase in the value of state-owned assets, advances the establishment of a modern enterprise system in SOEs, perfects corporate governance, and propels the strategic adjustment of the structure and layout of the state economy." It also "dispatches supervisory panels to some large enterprises on behalf of the state" and "takes charge of daily management work of the supervisory panels."[33]

These new functions for the SASAC were supported by several other institutional changes. First, the SASAC was directly subordinate to the State Council and not part of the line-up of ministries and commissions. This gave the SASAC a status different from that of a typical bureaucracy, enabling it to act more like an "investor." Second, the part of the Ministry of Finance that had acted as a de facto equity owner of the SOEs was merged into the SASAC, giving it the power to register and approve equity transactions such as mergers. This meant that the SASAC combined both ownership and

---

30 Alice L. Miller, "Commemorating Deng to Press Party Reform," *China Leadership Monitor*, no. 12 (Fall 2004).

31 Barry Naughton, "Changing the Rules of the Game: Macroeconomic Recontrol and the Struggle for Wealth and Power," *China Leadership Monitor*, no. 12 (Fall 2004); Barry Naughton, "Hunkering Down: The Wen Jiabao Administration and Macroeconomic Recontrol," *China Leadership Monitor*, no. 11 (Summer 2004).

32 Barry Naughton, *The Chinese Economy: Transitions and Growth* (Cambridge, MA: MIT Press, 2007).

33 See http://sasac.gov.cn.

regulatory functions.[34] Third, the SASAC was given personnel power over some of the SOEs. Although the CCP continued to exercise dominant control over the career paths of SOE managers at the core SOEs,[35] the SASAC could appoint or remove key figures below the vice ministerial level at the SOEs and could evaluate their performance through statutory procedures.[36]

These changes suggest efforts to establish a more effective mechanism for SOE management and monitoring by adjusting the division of labor within the economic bureaucracy and focusing SOE management tools in one agency. The SASAC was established to strengthen the control of the economic bureaucracy over the SOEs by combining central government ownership with central government control over personnel assignments. In addition, the SASAC followed the strategy of "selection and concentration."[37] It focused on restructuring SOEs under its control by discarding non-core businesses and building strong, competitive firms around a few national champions.[38] At the time of its establishment, the central SASAC was in charge of 196 SOEs. A series of mergers and consolidations reduced the total to 136 as of August 2009. These included the largest companies in China, especially

34 Barry Naughton, "SASAC Rising," *China Leadership Monitor*, no. 14 (2005).

35 The CCP retained direct appointment power over the top jobs at 53 of the 196 enterprises managed by the central government's SASAC and delegated appointment power for the other top jobs to the Communist Party Committee within the SASAC. Naughton, *The Chinese Economy*.

36 Before the establishment of the SASAC, personnel power over the SOEs was vested in the CCP, whereas oversight of state property was left to the line ministries or weak government auditors. Authority over different decision areas has continued to be diffuse and imprecise. See Barry Naughton, "The Emergence of Wen Jiabao," *China Leadership Monitor*, no. 6 (Spring 2003). The SASAC draws manpower and responsibilities from the Central Enterprise Work Committee (CEWC, *Zhongyang Qiye Gongwei*), which, as of March 2003, oversaw 195 large SOEs with 12,000 subsidiary corporations. The CEWC appointed top managers and dispatched supervisory boards to the major SOEs. Under the direct control of the Politburo Standing Committee, the CCP used the CEWC to retain power to appoint the leaders of the key SOEs that were subject to government regulation. Now that personnel power has been at least partially moved to the SASAC under the State Council, the party and the State Council have reached a new balance with respect to SOE control. See Barry Naughton, "The State Asset Commission: A Powerful New Government Body, " *China Leadership Monitor*, no. 8 (Fall 2003); and Yang, *Remaking the Chinese Leviathan*.

37 See Jean C. Oi, "Patterns of Corporate Restructuring in China: Political Constraints on Privatization," *China Journal*, no. 53 (January 2005): 115–36.

38 Barry Naughton, "The New Common Economic Program: China's 11th Five Year Plan and What It Means, " *China Leadership Monitor*, no. 16 (Fall 2005); Naughton, *The Chinese Economy*.

those in strategically important areas such as natural resources, transportation, and the machinery and chemical industries.[39]

Therefore, the demise of the SETC and the creation of the SASAC do not necessarily mean that the central government's control over the SOEs was diminished. Although the scope of the central state's direct control might have been narrowed, the efficiency and intensity of state control and monitoring over targeted SOEs have increased. "A stronger SASAC foreshadows a stronger role for the bureaucracy" in the Chinese economic transition.[40]

Conclusion

China's thus far successful economic transition is facing the ultimate task of institutional transformation that is more compatible with capitalism. The pressures from economic globalization, represented by China's WTO entry in 2001, provided an important impetus and rationale for accelerating such a transformation. Will the deepening marketization of the Chinese economy make dramatic privatization and fundamental restructuring of the SOE sector possible, breaking the equilibrium in the Chinese economic system? Even though a big bang might not take place, is the retreat of the state from the SOEs not inevitable, if China wants to make a successful transition toward a capitalist economy? On the surface, a series of restructurings of the Chinese central economic bureaucracy since the 1990s, and particularly the dismemberment of the SETC in 2003, appears to prove that the Chinese interventionist state is finally attempting to retreat from the SOE sector, slowly handing the SOEs over to market logic.

However, as this chapter demonstrates, such an interpretation is impetuous and incorrect. The façade of the political rhetoric coincides with neither the intention behind nor the real consequences of the rise and fall of the SETC. Critical to the rise of the SETC was the role of the top political leader, Zhu Rongji, who actively reinterpreted the nature of the new economic challenges and buttressed the SETC as a vanguard agency that supported his vision of SOE reform and served as his power base in the bureaucracy. Similarly, the decision to dismantle this once powerful state economic apparatus was not intended for the state to withdraw from the SOEs nor did it portend deregulation in the SOE sector.

The renewed power of the SDRC after the downfall of the SETC shows that SETC dismemberment was pursued to redistribute power and functions

39 For a complete list, see www.sasac.gov.cn/n1180/n1226/n2425/index.html, accessed May 19, 2010.

40 Naughton, "SASAC Rising."

within the economic bureaucracy following the political downfall of Zhu Rongji and the rise of new leaders. The SASAC's enhanced monitoring power over SOEs demonstrates that the Chinese central state is now pursuing a more focused and efficient mode of intervention, especially for SOEs in key issue areas. The discrepancy between the façade of state withdrawal and the actual reinvention of central state intervention suggests that despite the accelerated economic opening and marketization, the Chinese central state has retained close control and monitoring of the state sector. As long as the state successfully maintains its control over the SOEs through reinvented intervention, off-equilibrium development in the SOE sector that loosens the tight ensemble of complementary institutions in the Chinese economic system is unlikely to occur.

7 FDI and Corporate Restructuring in China

IS THE MEDICINE WORSE THAN THE DISEASE?

Mary E. Gallagher and Yue Ma

Attracting foreign direct investment (FDI) has been an integral part of the Chinese reform program since its earliest inception in the late 1970s. China's success in the global economy is directly related to the large FDI inflows since the 1990s that have built export powerhouses in the development zones along China's coast from Dalian in northeastern Liaoning province to Zhuhai in southern China's Guangdong province. One of the most successful policies of the reform era, opening to foreign trade and investment was not uncontested and even today continues to create divisions within the leadership and intellectual policy circles.[1] Although some of the fruits of foreign investment seem clear—increased employment opportunities, absorption of technological and managerial know-how, integration into global production networks, and vastly increased trading power—the Chinese government continues to worry about the effects of FDI-spawned competition on the creation of "national champions" and its ability to constrain foreign influence in strategic sectors, from finance to the media.[2] These concerns about the health of the state sector are also related to the government's drive for systemic restructuring, in particular the restructuring of state-owned enterprises (SOEs) and the creation of globally competitive Chinese companies.

---

1 Joseph Fewsmith, *China Since Tiananmen: The Politics of Transition* (New York: Cambridge University Press, 2001).

2 Peter Nolan, *China and the Global Economy: National Champions, Industrial Policy and the Big Business Revolution* (New York: Palgrave, 2001) and Eric Thun, *Changing Lanes in China: Foreign Direct Investment, Local Governments, and Auto Sector Development* (New York: Cambridge University Press, 2006).

In this chapter we explore the effects of FDI on SOE restructuring. We find that FDI inflows contributed greatly in both direct and indirect ways to fundamental reform and ownership change in large swathes of the SOE sector. The economic literature shows that restructuring, as measured by labor productivity, changes in assets, firm size, and qualitative shifts in employee management, has been significant. There is also evidence that the presence of FDI has a disciplining effect on SOEs. In some research, this effect is captured as the "crowding out" of SOEs in competitive sectors. The number of SOEs has been reduced, either due to closure or absorption into the private sector. In other cases, the remaining SOEs are strengthened and rationalized by the competition emanating from the foreign presence. Our exploration of FDI effects supports the general finding in the literature that the presence of FDI disciplines SOEs and provides competitive pressures on SOEs in the same sector. We also show through case studies and system-wide policy changes that FDI has had important qualitative effects on corporate governance, labor relations, and notions of property rights. In the later period focused on here, from 1999 to 2005, we do not find significant evidence that FDI is crowding out SOEs but rather that the presence of competition from foreign enterprises improves the performance of those SOEs that have survived the winnowing reforms of the late 1990s.

The causal mechanisms of FDI influence on SOE restructuring are three-fold: through cooperation, through copying, and through competition. Although they are not mutually exclusive and may occur simultaneously, we argue that competition has become more important over time. Changes in the importance of each mechanism are linked to the different manifestations of FDI during the reform period. There were three major "waves" of FDI activity in China.[3] The earliest period of cooperation was defined by the joint-venture (JV) system in which foreign investors were legally restricted to JVs. A middle period of increased foreign autonomy and control came in the form of rapid expansion of wholly foreign-owned enterprises (WFOEs). During this period, SOEs were able to view up close how a fully capitalist firm behaves in the Chinese market, accelerating mimicry and demonstration effects as well as important legal and policy changes. Finally, most recently, an acquisition stage in which foreign firms acquire or merge with existing Chinese firms has picked up speed. The dramatic increase in merger and acquisition (M&A) activity has accompanied the more general trend of SOE corporatization, as foreign equity has played an important role in the restructuring of the corporatized SOEs. This dynamic process of shifting

3 Kim Woodard and Anita Qingli Wang, "Acquisitions in China: A View of the Field," *China Business Review* 31, no. 6 (November/December 2004): 34.

manifestations of FDI has had important consequences for SOE restructuring, with the later periods greatly increasing the FDI competitive pressures on SOE performance. With the change to M&As as the main vehicle for investment, competition can also lead to the absorption of Chinese firms into the foreign sector. Thus, FDI has been a remedy to discipline and improve the health of the state sector, but large inflows of FDI, in the later period in particular, have also led to the transformation of many state firms into FIEs (foreign-invested enterprises) and rising social and political concerns about dependency on foreign capital, especially in certain sectors.

This chapter details these three mechanisms in separate sections, providing evidence through case studies, instances of important policy and legal changes, and finally through a quantitative analysis of FDI's competitive and disciplining effects on SOEs in the most recent years of reform. We begin with a short but necessary description of the evolution of FDI inflows in the Chinese economy. Our overview focuses on the dynamic changes in FDI over time, including liberalization across spatial regions (from tightly controlled "special economic zones" to nationwide FDI) and ownership regimes (from constrained JVs to foreign acquisitions of Chinese firms).

Foreign Direct Investment in China

Figures for FDI inflows into the Chinese economy are impressive. Although inflows increased slowly from 1978 to the early 1990s, they expanded greatly after Deng Xiaoping's Southern Tour in 1992 signaled the government's renewed commitment to economic reform in the aftermath of the 1989 Tiananmen crackdown. By the late 1990s China was attracting more FDI than all other developing countries and in some years it surpassed the United States as the most-favored destination for FDI bar none. Utilized FDI increased from $38 billion in 1995 to over $92 billion in 2008. (See Figure 7.1.) Some of the top investors in China come from Hong Kong, the British Virgin Islands, South Korea, Japan, Singapore, and the United States. Taiwan is not far behind the United States and several other tax havens are also heavily invested in the Chinese economy. It is widely assumed that at least some of the capital coming from Hong Kong and these havens is the result of "round-tripping" in which domestic Chinese capital is routed through a foreign destination and returns as foreign capital.[4] This allows domestic investors to take advantage of the preferential policies offered to foreign investors, a topic that is discussed further below.

4 Yingqi Wei, "Foreign Direct Investment in China," Lancaster University Management School Working Paper, no. 53 (2003).

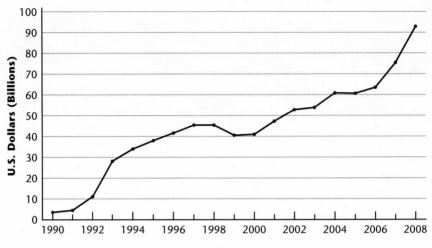

FIGURE 7.1 Utilized Foreign Direct Investment, 1990–2008
Source: Authors.

Global flows of FDI fell by 20 percent in 2008 due to the sharp con-
traction in economies around the world. Despite the crisis, FDI in China
increased 23 percent over 2007. Although FDI in China continued to be
heavily concentrated in the coastal provinces and in manufacturing, in 2008
we began to see more investment in services and in inland areas that were
less dependent on labor-intensive export manufacturing, which was the sector hardest hit by the economic crisis. China's liberalization of its economy
following its accession to the World Trade Organization in 2001 also led to
increased foreign investment in the services and financial sectors.

Two important trends in FDI inflows are the growing autonomy of foreign investors and foreign-invested enterprises and the increased ability of
foreign investors to participate fully in the privatization and restructuring of
Chinese state-owned enterprises. FDI has played a central role in the reform
process since 1978, but its role and its linkages to the domestic economy
have changed dramatically over time. Although the beleaguered Beijing Jeep[5]
story of the 1980s typifies the challenges and constraints on foreign investors in the early years, the expansion and penetration of FDI in more recent
years have led to growing concern among Chinese policymakers that foreign
investors are too dominant and have too much control over individual firms,
and, in some cases, over entire sectors.

5 Jim Mann, Beijing Jeep: A Case Study of Western Business in China (Boulder, CO:
Westview, updated ed., 1997).

TABLE 7.1

Evolution of Foreign Direct Investment Liberalization, 1979–present

Period	1979–1986	1986–1992	1992–1997	2001–
Spatial Limitations	Special Economic Zones	Coastal Development Strategy	Coastal Cities, Border Cities, Yangtze River Delta	WTO Accession, National Openness
Ownership Limitations	Joint Venture Model	JVs, WFOEs	JVs, WFOEs, Limited Stock Investment	JVs, WFOEs, Expanded Stock Investment, M&As

Source: Compiled by authors.

The increased importance of FDI to the Chinese reform program generally and to SOE restructuring specifically can be attributed to two distinct types of liberalization: "competitive liberalization"[6] across China's regions and liberalization of ownership, which includes both the introduction of new types of industrial firms and "ownership recombination"[7] (see Table 7.1). These liberalizing trends across regions and ownership regimes led not only to regional competition for investment inflows but also to competition between individual firms for foreign investment and competition between foreign-invested firms and state firms for skilled labor.[8] These different modes of competition increased the importance of FDI in China's domestic economy by encouraging regions and firms to liberalize competitively so as to become more attractive to potential investors. Competition between foreign and domestic firms also created internal support within the SOE sector for a "level

6 See Dali Yang, *Beyond Beijing: Liberalization and the Regions in China* (New York: Routledge, 1997). We use Yang's "competitive liberalization" here but the concept is similar to Zweig's "segmented deregulation." It can be argued that Zweig's definition is more comprehensive because the notion of deregulation focuses attention on the power and rents that accrue to the "gatekeepers" of the deregulation process. Despite these different emphases, we use these terms more or less interchangeably to convey the notion of uneven liberalization across regions. See David Zweig, *Internationalizing China: Domestic Interests and Global Linkages* (Ithaca, NY: Cornell University Press, 2002).

7 David Stark and László Bruszt, *Postsocialist Pathways: Transforming Politics and Property in East Central Europe* (New York: Cambridge University Press, 1998), 143. Recombinant property is defined as "novel forms of interorganizational ownership that blurred the boundaries of public and private, as well as the boundaries of the enterprises themselves."

8 Shaomin Li, Shuhe Li, and Weiying Zhang, "The Road to Capitalism: Competition and Institutional Change in China," *Journal of Comparative Economics* 28, no. 2 (June 2000): 269–92; Wei, "Foreign Direct Investment; and Mary Elizabeth Gallagher, *Contagious Capitalism: Globalization and the Politics of Labor in China* (Princeton, NJ: Princeton University Press, 2005).

playing-field." This level playing-field involved the extension of preferential policies and laws applicable to foreign-invested enterprises to the state sector. Preferential laws included the more lax employment regulations that guided labor relations in the FIEs, allowing FIEs to offer short-term contracts to workers, whereas SOEs were still subject to "iron rice bowl" employment relations that made it difficult to fire workers. More recently, SOEs have lobbied for changes to the tax code and the elimination of tax breaks to foreign companies that made their effective tax rates about one-third lower than that of the SOEs. After several years of debate among relevant ministries, the National People's Congress approved a unified tax code in 2007.

Regional Competition

The decentralization of the economy and the devolution of authority and decision-making power to local governments are key characteristics of the Chinese reforms, as other chapters in this volume detail. Decentralization, at times described as an informal version of federalism, was key in granting local governments the ability and necessity to contribute to the growth of the economy, as the central government cut spending and support and hardened the budget constraints of local governments.[9] Liberalization of the foreign investment and trade regime in China was not a uniform policy of national liberalization and integration with the outside world. Initially, it consisted of a policy of insulated laboratories that allowed limited contact with the external capitalist economy in rural or suburban areas isolated and separate from the urban core of public ownership.[10] Benefits that came from the extension of these policies led other regions that had been excluded to push for further liberalization.[11] Liberalization of the foreign investment and trade regimes sparked regional competition for inflows of both foreign and domestic capital, further enhancing the bargaining power of capital.

Ownership Liberalization

"Segmented deregulation" of foreign investment and the spread of these policies through a dynamic of competitive liberalization are one crucial part

9 Gabriella Montinola, Yingyi Qian, and Barry Weingast, "Federalism, Chinese Style: The Political Basis for Economic Success in China," *World Politics* 48, no. 1 (October 1995): 50–81.

10 Jung-Dong Park, *The Special Economic Zones of China and their Impact on its Economic Development* (Westport, CT: Praeger, 1997).

11 Yang, *Beyond Beijing.*

of the story of FDI policy liberalization.[12] A second equally important dimension includes the changes that took place in ownership, including both the expansion of new types of enterprise ownership and the "recombination" of public and private (often foreign) ownership in the form of hybrid firms.[13] China's avoidance of shock therapy–style privatization masks the very radical changes that occurred in lieu of privatization and that were realized by tapping the huge labor supply in the rural areas.

Evolution of foreign ownership in China took place on two fronts: first, there was increased choice in the type of foreign investment vehicle and the range of domestic partners. Second, through this expansion of choice, there was a steady increase in the degree of managerial autonomy and the degree to which foreign investors could control enterprise decision-making. As with the liberalization of policies across regions, policies that dictated the permissible types of foreign investment vehicles and the allowable domestic Chinese partners were gradually yet radically liberalized over time. The 1978 containment of foreign capital to the joint venture framework by 1997 had become permission to sell off SOEs to foreign and private investors.[14] These rules were formalized in 2003 and again in 2006, with specific regulations on mergers and acquisitions (M&As) involving foreign investors.[15] As investor autonomy and control increased, changes in firm management and restructuring that had earlier been in effect only at the margins (through the formation of JVs) were now taking place in the core public sectors. In some

12 Zweig, *Internationalizing China*; Yang, *Beyond Beijing*.

13 Some of the initial consequences emanating from ownership changes are noted by Naughton. See Barry Naughton, "Implications of the State Monopoly over Industry and Its Relaxation," *Modern China* 18, no. 1 (January 1992): 14–41. In an important early article on ownership liberalization, Naughton focuses on the fiscal consequences of the growing non-state sector.

14 Robert P. Weller and Jiansheng Li, "From State-Owned Enterprise to Joint Venture: A Case Study of the Crisis in Urban Social Services," *China Journal*, no. 43 (January 2000): 83–99; Feng Chen, "Industrial Restructuring and Workers' Resistance in China," *Modern China* 29, no. 2 (April 2003): 237–62; and X.L. Ding, "The Illicit Asset Stripping of Chinese Firms," *China Journal*, no. 43 (2000):1–28.

15 In August 2006 the Ministry of Commerce replaced the 2003 *Interim Provisions on Mergers and Acquisitions of Domestic Enterprises by Foreign Investors* with the *Regulations on the Acquisition of Domestic Enterprises by Foreign Investors*. The 2006 regulations are more restrictive than the 2003 interim provisions, requiring an additional layer of government approval to protect China's "national economic security." This more restrictive trend reflects the higher degree of suspicion toward foreign investment in recent years.

TABLE 7.2

Foreign Direct Investment by Vehicle Type, 1996–2008

	EJVs	CJVs	WFOEs	SHEs w/FDI	WFOEs Share of Total FDI
1996	12,628	2,849	9,062	NA	36.9%
1997	9,046	2,371	9,694	6	45.6%
1998	8,146	2,010	9,674	9	48.7%
1999	7,050	1,656	8,201	3	48.4%
2000	8,560	1,755	12,199	9	54.1%
2001	8,895	1,589	15,640	11	59.8%
2002	10,380	1,595	22,173	19	64.8%
2003	12,521	1,547	26,943	37	65.5%
2004	11,570	1,343	30,708	43	70.3%
2005	10,480	1,166	32,308	47	73.4%
2006	10,223	1,036	30,164	50	72.7%
2007	7,649	641	29,543	38	78%
2008	4,612	468	22,396	38	81.3%

Source: Table compiled by the authors using data from the U.S.-China Business Council, http://www.uschina
.org/info/index.php#foreigninvestment, accessed November 9, 2010.

Notes:
EJVs = equity joint ventures
CJVs = contractual joint ventures
WFOEs = wholly foreign-owned enterprises
SHEs = shareholding enterprises

regions where the reforms surfaced as spontaneous innovations by local elites, this transformation occurred much earlier in the early 1990s.[16]

These changes in ownership can be partially demonstrated by tracing the decline in the joint venture model over time. By 2000, wholly foreign-owned enterprises had become the main vehicle for FDI in China (see Table 7.2).

The first two waves of FDI in China, the JV wave and then the WFOE wave, were followed by a much deeper and more significant impact on the domestic economy in general and on SOE restructuring in particular. In the previous waves, by design the entities set up were isolated and hived off from the domestic economy and the Chinese partners (if a JV). A joint venture was a new entity, often located in a greenfield industrial site; it was both

16 Edward X. Gu, "Foreign Direct Investment and the Restructuring of Chinese State-Owned Enterprises (1992–1995): A New Institutionalist Perspective," *China Information* 12, no. 3 (Winter 1997–98): 46–71; Shu-Yun Ma, "Foreign Participation in China's Privatisation," *Communist Economies and Economic Transformation* 8, no. 4 (December 1996); and Yasheng Huang, "Ownership Biases and FDI in China: Evidence from Two Provinces," paper presented at the conference on China's rise, Tuck School of Business, Dartmouth College, Hanover, NH, May 13–14, 2006.

legally and spatially separate from the Chinese partner's main enterprise. A WFOE was a wholly owned subsidiary of a foreign corporation. WFOEs in China were required to be heavily invested in the export sector, using China as a base for cheap manufacturing for other global markets. In the third wave of FDI, however, foreign investors bought equity in existing Chinese firms and took part directly in the corporatization and restructuring of SOEs. Foreign M&A activity was part of a more general increase in restructuring and consolidation of the Chinese economy. Changes in the regulatory environment made it easier for foreign companies to participate in this process. In recent years, M&As as a proportion of total FDI have sharply increased, though they are still much lower than the proportion of M&As in foreign direct investment between the developed countries. The Economist Intelligence Unit estimates that inward M&A deals in China reached $13 billion in 2005, about 22 percent of the total FDI that year. By 2006, the American Chamber of Commerce in China estimated that one-third of total FDI inflows during that year were in the form of M&A transactions. In 2001, M&A deals accounted for only 5 percent of total FDI.[17]

Cooperation, Copying, and Competition: Mechanisms of "Contagious Capitalism"

Liberalization across regions and ownership structures increased the importance of FDI in China's domestic economy as actors competed for access to foreign funding and technology. The uneven playing-field between FIEs and SOEs also led to increased lobbying efforts by state managers to extend preferential policies, for instance, relaxed labor regulations and lower tax rates, to the public sector. In the section below, we specify how FDI affected the course of SOE restructuring through cooperation (using the JV structure), through copying (as wholly foreign-owned companies began to operate fully in the domestic economy), and through competition (as foreign investors were allowed to acquire and merge with existing Chinese enterprises). These mechanisms are not mutually exclusive; rather they occurred simultaneously and in a cumulative fashion have had important effects on SOE restructuring. We argue, however, that the competitive mechanism has become central to SOE restructuring as the barriers to foreign participation in the corporatization of SOEs have been reduced.

17 Economist Intelligence Unit, "The Great Buy-Out: M&A in China," 2006, at http://www.eiu.com/site_info.asp?info_name=eiu_The_great_buy_out_MnA_in_China&rf=0, accessed September 4, 2010; "Mergers and Acquisitions," *China Insight* (Shanghai: American Chamber of Commerce, 2007).

Mechanisms of Cooperation

Cooperation through Joint Ventures—Shanghai Auto Case

At the beginning of the economic reforms, foreign capital was permitted to enter China only through the formation of JVs or licensing. This forced foreign investors to cooperate with local enterprises, almost exclusively SOEs, either through co-investments or business contracts. At the same time, foreign investors took advantage of their cooperation with local enterprises to gain local expertise and, more importantly, political connections that were key to their operations under the still largely unreformed economic system. For these reasons, having a local partner was attractive for some foreign investors, even after the 1990s when the Chinese government removed the JV requirement for most foreign capital ventures.

The main initial intention of the Chinese government of forcing foreign investors to cooperate with local enterprises was to encourage technology transfers that would benefit China's domestic industries. After the end of the Cultural Revolution in the late 1970s, China's leaders were painfully aware of China's backwardness in comparison to the West and even to its neighbors. The backwardness was partially blamed on the country's lack of advanced technology and management skills. The leadership set out to acquire these skills through cooperation with foreign capital. At the time, thorough restructuring of the corporate governance system and changes in the ownership of state enterprises overwhelmingly were considered contradictory to the socialist ideology. Therefore, involvement of foreign capital in the corporate restructuring of Chinese SOEs was not the leadership's initial intention.

Because of the ideological restrictions, early cooperation between foreign investors and local SOEs was designed to achieve the original goal of technology transfer. This cooperation was marked by certain related characteristics:

1. It occurred mostly in sectors that were relatively technology-intensive, where the country intended to catch up with the Western economies, such as the automobile and consumer electronics industries.

2. State enterprises that formed joint ventures with foreign enterprises usually did so by establishing new subsidiaries with their foreign partners, instead of allowing the injection of foreign capital into the SOE. This type of cooperation excluded the ability of foreign companies to directly own shares and to exert an influence on the management systems of the existing SOEs.

Due to this second characteristic, any intended effect of cooperation with foreign enterprises on the corporate restructuring of Chinese SOEs was limited during the early years of the reform. However, the unintended effects of the cooperation were huge as the SOEs involved in cooperation with foreign enterprises were impressed by the advanced business strategies and efficient corporate structures of their foreign partners and started to absorb features of their foreign partners and to replicate them in their own business models.[18] The Shanghai Auto case described in the next section is a typical example of such changes. At the bottom level, state enterprises started to adopt the efficiency-enhancing labor-reward systems already in place in their JV subsidiaries. At the top, these enterprises replicated the cost-saving mechanisms of their foreign partners. In this way, the copying mechanism described below actually began early in the reform era as the SOEs adopted practices of the JVs. In addition, competition to cooperate with foreign enterprises stimulated the SOEs to adopt more Western-like management models. These changes in the SOE internal management structure marked a step forward in the gradual restructuring of SOEs.

Even in the 1980s when neither government officials nor SOE managers were contemplating systemic restructuring of the state sector, foreign capital was already playing an important role in the early changes in the corporate structure of the SOEs, as the case of Shanghai Auto presented below reveals. This early influence served as a prelude to the restructuring in the later periods.

A good example of SOE cooperation with foreign capital in the 1980s is the case of Shanghai Volkswagen, a JV co-established by Shanghai Automotive Industry Company (SAIC) and Volkswagen.

SAIC is one of the oldest automotive companies in China. It started in 1958 under the name Shanghai Automotive Machinery Manufacturing Company (Shanghai Dongli Jixie Zhizao Gongsi). For several decades, it operated under the command economic system as one of the largest production bases for automotive vehicles in China.

In 1983, SAIC was contracted by Volkswagen to produce the first Santana vehicles in Shanghai and in 1985 it entered into a joint venture with Volkswagen to establish Shanghai Volkswagen. Volkswagen invested in 50 percent of the shares and SAIC 25 percent. The remainder was owned by the Bank of China (15 percent) and the China National Automotive Industry Corporation (10 percent).[19] This ownership structure, bringing in the participation of a major state bank as well as the national shareholding company in the industry, was not unusual at the time.

18 Doug Guthrie, *Dragon in a Three-Piece Suit: The Emergence of Capitalism in China* (Princeton, NJ: Princeton University Press, 1999).

19 "After Attaining its Monthly Production Target of 700 Vehicles for the First Time in May, Shanghai Volkswagen is Hoping to be Able to Record a Profit for this Year," *Asian Wall Street Journal*, June 18, 1986.

Despite the significant achievements of the new joint venture in the first year of operations, some major difficulties arose due to the mismatch between Volkswagen's Western management style and SAIC's Chinese SOE structure. The German management team found it extremely difficult to train and work with the local workers, most of whom were veteran SAIC workers who were used to the "iron rice bowl" of state ownership. Mr. Martin Portch, deputy managing director of Volkswagen, said that, "if he was back in Germany, he would have laid off 80 percent of the workers."[20]

Volkswagen gradually managed to modify the governance system in the Shanghai JV, starting with implementation of a more efficient reward system that changed the incentive structure for workers. Over the years, more elements of Western corporate governance strategies were injected into the joint venture, greatly improving enterprise efficiency. Shanghai Volkswagen is now one of the most successful joint ventures in China, producing and selling over 300,000 cars per year.

Satisfied with the results of cooperating with Shanghai Auto, in 1991 Volkswagen went on to enter into another joint venture with the First Automotive Works (FAW, another old SOE in the auto sector) to form FAW-VW, mainly for the production of high-standard cars under VW's Audi brand. Volkswagen now controls 17 percent of the Chinese auto market and is the second largest foreign automaker in China. The Chinese market is also Volkswagen's second largest market, behind only that of Germany.

At the same time, SAIC benefited enormously from its experience of cooperating with a top international auto producer. Early exposure to foreign investment gave the state enterprise an advantage in the later stage of the reforms. When the wave of corporate restructuring hit the state sector in the second half of the 1990s, it was less of a surprise for Shanghai Auto, which for years had observed a Western-style corporate governance system in its joint venture subsidiary. This made restructuring smoother and less costly for the Shanghai automaker. In 1997, Shanghai Auto established another joint venture with the American automaker General Motors, creating Shanghai General Motors Company.[21] The company funded the new JV by issuing its first IPO, from which it raised RMB2.1 billion.[22] By 2007, the company was

20 James Rusk, "VW-Chinese Venture Counts on Profit," *Globe and Mail*, July 5, 1986.

21 "China: Shanghai Auto's Stature, Prospects Grow With GM Deal," Dow Jones International News, June 13, 1997.

22 Foo Choy Peng, "Shanghai Auto's IPO Gets into Gear," *South China Morning Post*, November 6, 1997, 5.

the third largest auto company in China and thirtieth largest in the world,[23] generating about $4 billion per year in total sales revenue.[24]

Cooperation through Acquisition—The Case of the Guangdong Development Bank

In the late 1990s, Chinese SOEs suffered their most serious financial losses and operational failures in history. According to data published by the State Statistical Bureau's Research Team for State-Owned Large and Medium Enterprises, of the 14,923 state-owned large- and medium-sized industrial enterprises existing in 1997, 6,042 (40.5 percent of the total) were operating at a loss. Losses in these enterprises totaled RMB58.91 billion.[25] Policymakers and corporate leaders gradually realized that technology alone would not turn around the state enterprises and that a complete restructuring of their governance structure and even of their ownership was necessary. It was at this point that Chinese policymakers recognized the important role that foreign capital could play in the rescue and restructuring of state-owned enterprises. Compared to the relatively weak domestic private sector, foreign enterprises were much better capitalized and equipped with mature and well-implemented corporate governance systems. On the one hand, they had sufficient capital resources to acquire and provide cash for the immediate needs of the newly acquired state enterprises, most of which faced serious liquidity problems due to years of capital losses under state ownership. On the other hand, their management and marketing systems had been developed and tested for decades in their home countries and could be implemented to replace the old style corporate governance system that the SOEs had inherited from the planned economy.

Taking this into account, the Chinese government began to encourage foreign capital to gain ownership control over state enterprises through partial or entire acquisitions. This policy was enforced gradually, with approvals granted on a sector-by-sector basis.[26] Those sectors considered less important for national security were the first to be approved to utilize

23 Deloitte & Touche, LLP, *Annual Report of Shanghai Automotive Industry Corporation*, 2007.

24 Deloitte & Touche, LLP, *Annual Report of Shanghai Automotive Industry Corporation*, 2006.

25 Yunhua Liu, "A Comparison of China's State-owned Enterprises and their Counterparts in the United States: Performance and Regulatory Policy," *Public Administration Review* 69 (December 2009): 46–52.

26 Winston Yau, "Regulator Issues Fresh Acquisition Rules," *South China Morning Post*, October 9, 2002, 4.

foreign investment in existing SOEs. Since then, cooperation with foreign capital has directly impacted the corporate restructuring of Chinese SOEs.

The cooperation mechanism after the late 1990s significantly promoted corporate restructuring. The partial or entire acquisition of existing state enterprises by foreign investors allowed foreign enterprises to intervene directly and to reshape governance and operations of the SOEs. Following acquisition, the foreign enterprises usually sent a board of directors and executives to help with the restructuring of the existing business model and with the implementation of a Western-style management system. This process is clearly reflected in the acquisition of Guangdong Development Bank (GDB) by Citibank as described below, where the participation of a large multinational corporation improved the management system of the state-owned bank enormously, turning a bank at the edge of insolvency into a profit-making financial institution. In order to prepare themselves to be more attractive to foreign bidders, SOEs voluntarily adopted a higher degree of transparency, disciplined financial spending, clarified their ownership structures, improved their management systems, and carried out a series of restructuring procedures.[27]

The case of the GDB is a typical example of cooperation between FDI and a Chinese state-owned enterprise through a partial acquisition. The acquisition of 85 percent of GDB shares by a Citibank-led consortium in 2006 played an important role in the restructuring of the state-owned bank.

Guangdong Development Bank was a shareholding commercial bank operating mainly in Guangdong province. It was established in 1988 by 55 state-owned entities, including the provincial financial bureau, state-owned companies, and government banks. Before restructuring, the provincial financial bureau and its related parties were the bank's largest shareholders, directly controlling 24 percent of the shares.[28] Guangdong-based entities (including the provincial financial bureau) owned 70 percent of all the shares, and the Bank of China owned 11 percent.[29] Since its inception, GDB had always been under de-facto control of the provincial government.

The banking sector was one of the last sectors to allow the restructuring of SOEs and the introduction of FDI. This was due to the importance of the banking system to the entire state-owned economy. When the government

27 The "preparations" usually came with the support of the government, as illustrated in the GDB case.

28 Kate Lin, Charlene Chu, and Lynda Lin, "Fitch Report: Guangdong Development Bank 2006" (Fitch Ratings, 2006), http://www.fitchratings.com.

29 Arthur Lau, Delis Mok, and David Marshall, "Fitch Report: Guangdong Development Bank 2001" (Fitch Ratings, 2001), http://www.fitchratings.com.

stopped subsidizing SOEs in the early 1990s, it relied on state-owned banks to continuously pump cash into the SOEs to ensure state-sector survival. As Steinfeld points out, by the mid- to late 1990s, SOEs accounted for less than half of net asset industrial growth, yet they consistently consumed 70–80 percent of the credits extended by the financial system.[30] For a long period, due to both government intervention and poor credit management, state-owned banks extended "policy loans" to the largely inefficient SOEs. This seriously hurt the quality of the bank assets. According to the China Banking Regulatory Commission (CBRC), 16.61 percent of the loans in the Chinese banking system were classified as non-performing.[31] Other sources have quoted even higher figures, ranging from 25 percent to 40 percent.[32]

Although established in the 1980s and technically a shareholding bank, Guangdong Development Bank had all the shortcomings of most state-owned banks. A market-oriented governance system and an efficient risk management system were lacking. Since its inception, the GDB's official task was to "support the economic development of Guangdong province."[33] Consequently, the bank's lending policy was biased toward government-sponsored projects and state-owned enterprises in the province. Prior to 1998, 90 percent of the bank's credit portfolio was used to fund development projects within Guangdong province.[34] Moreover, the GDB's ability to determine interest pricing was limited given the government's control over interest rates. Hence the bank did not receive appropriate rewards for concentrating its portfolio in the province's highly inefficient public sector. Assuming the high risks of a concentrated portfolio, in 1999 the bank's returns on assets (ROA) were only 0.24 percent.[35]

Like most other Chinese banks prior to 1995, the GDB was a victim of the decentralized branch system. Headquarter control of the branches

30 Edward S, Steinfeld, "Moving Beyond Transition in China: Financial Reform and the Political Economy of Declining Growth," *Comparative Politics* 34, no. 4 (July 2002): 379–98.

31 "NPLs of Major Commercial Banks as of March 31, 2004," China Banking Regulatory Commission Statistics, at http://www.cbrc.gov.cn/english/home/jsp/docView .jsp?docID=724, accessed November 12, 2010.

32 Fitch Analysts, "The Chinese Banking Industry: Recent Developments" (1998), http://www.fitchratings.com.

33 Lu Yanzheng and Xueqing Long, "Guangdong Fazhan Yinhang Zhongzu Yibo San Zhe" [The Twists and Turns in the Restructuring of the Guangdong Development Bank], *Caijing*, August 22, 2005, at *Renmin wang*, August 25, 2005, http://finance.people .com.cn/GB/1040/3643302.html, accessed August 16, 2010.

34 Lu Yanzheng and Xueqing Long, "Guangdong Fazhan Yinhang Zhongzu Yibo San Zhe."

35 KPMG, "Financial Statement of Guangdong Development Bank" (1999), http:// www.fitchratings.com

throughout the province was very limited. Branches at the municipal level were under the direct command of the city governments and were usually forced to play important roles in the local financing of development projects and enterprises owned by the local governments.[36] The branches turned into "piggy banks" for the local governments and further increased the GDB's exposure to risky and low-quality policy loans.

Furthermore, the GDB was used by the government as a vehicle to absorb failed state-owned financial institutions. In 1996, as mandated by the People's Bank of China, the GDB acquired the bankrupt China Finance Trust and Investment Corporation. The acquisition cost GDB over RMB5 billion,[37] significantly increasing the bank's leverage. Thereafter, the bank was entrusted by the Guangdong government to manage twenty failed local commercial banks and credit cooperatives.[38] As Walter argues more generally about problems in the banking system, these government-directed acquisitions and administrative agreements further eroded the GDB's financial strength and hurt the bank's normal operations.

In the late 1990s, Guangdong province was seriously affected by the Asian financial crisis. Many enterprises, including state-owned enterprises, became insolvent. As a result, the low-quality loan portfolio that GDB had built up during the previous years was affected. Impaired loans soared.

According to the GDB's financial statements, in 2000 23 percent of the bank's loan portfolio, amounting to RMB17.6 billion, was considered impaired. Meanwhile, lacking an effective loss assessment mechanism, GDB reserves to cover the losses were very low. The bank had only set aside an amount equivalent to 1.08 percent of its portfolio as loss reserves, covering 4.68 percent of its impaired loans. The total amount of impaired loans net of loss reserves was equivalent to 411 percent of the bank's equity.[39] In other words, the bank was technically insolvent.

This situation persisted for several years as the bank continued to operate with its inefficient system. Loan impairment was 16 percent, 28 percent, and 18 percent of total loans in 2001, 2002, and 2003 respectively. Net impaired loans were equivalent to 294 percent, 633 percent, and 557 percent

36 "Guangdong Yin Bianlian: Wei Shenme Zhongzu Guang Fayin" [The Changing Face of the Guangdong Bank: Why Reorganize the Guangdong Development Bank], *Nanfang Zhuomo* [Southern Weekend], February 22, 2002, at http://business.sohu.com/20060222/n241966483.shtml, accessed August 16, 2010.

37 Zhang Lisheng. "Guangdong Bank Goes All Out," *China Daily*, March 27, 2000.

38 Lau, Mok, and Marshall, "Fitch Report: Guangdong Development Bank 2001."

39 KPMG, "Financial Statement of Guangdong Development Bank" (2000), http://www.fitchratings.com

of the bank's equity at the respective year-ends, leaving the bank's equity persistently under water. [40]

It is worth noting that the bank's loan portfolio grew at an average speed of 37 percent per annum during these three years.[41] Evidently, the bank continued to expand its portfolio even though it was suffering enormous asset impairment. This reflected the state-owned bank's credit inefficiencies and slack budget constraints. According to Mr. Zhang Guanghua, then president of the GDB, since 1999 the bank had moved away from its original strategy of supporting big SOEs and had focused on SMEs.[42] However, from the perspective of asset quality, the move did not improve the credit efficiency of the bank.

Years later, loan impairment gradually turned into net losses for the bank. In 2005 and 2006, the GDB recorded net losses of RMB692 million and RMB450 million respectively.[43] After years of financial losses and loan impairment, the GDB's capital level was devastated. In 2005, the regulatory capital ratio of the GDB was 3.9 percent,[44] far below the 8 percent required by the country's banking regulatory authorities.

The inefficiencies and problems faced by the GDB were characteristic of those faced by most state-owned banks prior to restructuring. With the WTO's 2005 deadline for China to open up its banking market to foreign banks rapidly approaching, the need to restructure the inefficient state-owned banks became urgent.[45] Starting in the early 2000s, the People's Bank of China, the CBRC, and the government of Guangdong province considered several ways to restructure the GDB, including government capital injections, public listings, or selling shares to a domestic private company.[46] In 2005, however, encouraged by Newbridge Capital's acquisition

40 KPMG, "Financial Statement of Guangdong Development Bank" (2001–2003), http://www.fitchratings.com

41 KPMG, "Financial Statement of Guangdong Development Bank" (2001–2003).

42 Shaq Wang, "China's Guangdong Dev Bank Posts 120 Billion Yuan Outstanding Loans by November End," Xinhua Financial Network News, December 13, 2002.

43 KPMG, "Financial Statement of Guangdong Development Bank" (2005–2006), http://www.fitchratings.com

44 KPMG, "Financial Statement of Guangdong Development Bank" (2005), http://www.fitchratings.com

45 Mark T. Fung, "Review: Banking Reforms and Monetary Policy in the People's Republic of China: Is the Chinese Central Banking System Ready for Joining the WTO?" *Journal of Asian Studies* 62, no. 4 (November 2003): 1218–19.

46 Yue Gang, "Huaqi Shougou Qianzhuan: Guang Fa Yin Zhongzu Dangnian Shi" [The Story Before Citigroup's Acquisition: Guangdong Development Bank Restructuring in 2004], *Jingji Guancha Bao* [Economic Observer], December 2, 2006.

of Shenzhen Development Bank and HSBC's recent capital injection into China Communication Bank, the authorities decided to restructure the GDB by introducing a foreign strategic partner.[47]

In preparation for the restructuring, the government transferred a massive amount of non-performing loans (NPL) from the GDB to state-owned asset management companies. As a result, the GDB's NPLs were reduced from 18.32 percent of the total loans in 2003 to only 4.47 percent in 2005.[48] The government cleaned up the bank's balance sheet, making it more appealing to investors and then held open bidding for 85 percent of the GDB's shares. After a lengthy process of due diligence, bidding, and approval seeking, a consortium led by Citibank, with the participation of three state-owned enterprises and IBM, emerged as the winner. The acquisition was completed in December 2006. The Citibank-led consortium acquired 85 percent of GDB's shares for a total cost of about $3.1 billion.[49]

According to CBRC policy, foreign investors could hold no more than 25 percent of a Chinese bank, and no single foreign investor could hold more than 20 percent. Hence, Citibank had to limit its holdings to 20 percent. The remaining 65 percent of the bank was shared by the other participants in the consortium: State Grid Corporation held 20 percent, Citic Trust and Investment held 20 percent, China Life Insurance Company held 20 percent, and IBM Credit held 5 percent. Although it owned only 20 percent of the bank, Citibank obtained effective management control. All other major shareholders delegated their authority to Citibank, which appointed six out of the nineteen members on the board of directors as well as all the key managers.[50] It also appointed Michael Zink, then senior executive vice president of Citibank South Korea, as new president of the GDB.

Even though 60 percent of the shares were still owned by three state-owned companies, management was largely in the hands of Citibank. Government intervention in bank operations was minimized, allowing Citibank to completely reshape the management and operating systems of the bank. As the FDI shareholder of the GDB, Citibank assisted GDB in risk management, internal auditing, corporate governance, treasury management, asset-liability management, human resources, IT, and financial

47 Yue Gang, "Huaqi Shougou Qianzhuan."

48 KPMG. "Financial Statement of Guangdong Development Bank" (2003–2005), http://www.fitchratings.com

49 "Citigroup Leads China Bank Purchase," *Calgary Business*, December 19, 2006.

50 "Citigroup Completes Guangdong Development Bank Transaction," *The Asian Banker Interactive*, December 31, 2006.

innovation.[51] It also shared its credit management system and procedures with the GDB, effectively controlling the bank's lending quality and avoiding an increase in impaired loans. It introduced a risk-reward concept to determine products and strategies that would bring in profits. These moves ended the highly inefficient and government-directed operating procedures under which the bank had operated during the past eighteen years. Furthermore, Citibank shared its technological systems, employee training programs, as well as innovative financial products.[52] The restructured state-owned bank benefited greatly from Citibank's market experience and technical expertise as a leading global financial institution.

The benefits of Citibank's participation were rapidly reflected in the balance sheet and income statement of the restructured GDB. In 2007, the first year after Citibank's takeover, the bank generated a net income of RMB2.5 billion, reversing the losses of the previous two years. In 2008, net income increased to almost RMB4 billion. Meanwhile, NPLs were reduced from 5.84 percent of gross loans in 2006, to 4 percent of gross loans in 2007. In 2008, NPLs were further reduced to 2.85 percent of the gross loan portfolio.[53] The bank managed to maintain a conservative cushion to protect its equity against actual or potential loan impairments. In 2008, the loan loss reserves that the bank had set aside covered 150 percent of the total NPLs. Due to the reduced loan impairments and enhanced profitability, the bank's regulatory capital ratio reached 11.6 percent, well above regulatory requirements.[54] In April 2008, Fitch upgraded the GDB from E to D/E, citing "positive internal reform and noteworthy improvements in asset quality and capitalization."[55]

Citibank's acquisition and restructuring of the GDB was one of the most influential FDI acquisitions in the Chinese financial industry. For the Chinese authorities, it was a trial cooperation with FDI to restructure SOEs in the banking sector. It was also a big step forward for the gradual opening

51 Mai Dongyan, "Huaqi Yinhang Ru Tou Guangdong Fazhan Yinhang Anlie Yanjiu" [A Case Study of Citigroup's Stake in the Guangdong Development Bank], *Xiaofei Daokan* [Consumer Guide], no. 18 (2008).

52 Mai Dongyan, "Huaqi Yinhang Ru Tou Guangdong Fazhan Yinhang Anlie Yanjiu."

53 KPMG, "Financial Statement of Guangdong Development Bank" (2008), http://www.fitchratings.com

54 KPMG, "Financial Statement of Guangdong Development Bank" (2008).

55 Charlene Chu, Chunling Wen, and Peter Marshall, "Fitch Upgrades Guangdong Development Bank's Individual Rating to D/E" (April 9, 2008), http://www.fitchratings.com

of the Chinese banking sector to FDI participation. As indicated by the financial and operational results noted above, the reorganization of the GDB through cooperation with a foreign strategic partner was very successful.

Based on this case, we can summarize the following advantages of restructuring a state-owned bank through a foreign acquisition:

1. Compared to domestic enterprises, foreign investors are more likely to run the restructured bank independent of undesired government intervention. Given the large influence of the Chinese government in the domestic corporate sector (both public and private), it would have been difficult for a domestic owner to completely change the GDB's lending practices.

2. The transfer of Citibank's superior business model, credit culture, and management expertise was very important to improve the state-owned bank's efficiency during the post-acquisition period. Domestic investors, either public or private, would not possess those intangible resources that Citibank had as a leading international financial institution.

It is also worth noting that the government played an important and generally supportive role in the process of restructuring the GDB and introducing a FDI partner.

First, foreseeing the potential benefits, the CBRC, the People's Bank of China, and the government of Guangdong province made a key decision to introduce a FDI partner into the restructuring of the GDB. Although the decision process was mostly carried out behind closed doors, from what little information can be obtained, it is evident that these government institutions actively supported the proposal amid skeptical voices from the general public about putting a state-owned bank in the hands of a foreign company.[56]

Second, in order to make the state-owned bank appealing to foreign investors, the government spent RMB30 billion to recapitalize the bank and to separate its large impaired assets.[57] This move removed the legacy of the state-owned bank that would have worried any potential foreign investor.

56 Skeptical voices regarding Citibank's acquisition of the GDB were strong both within the bank and on the Chinese Internet. See, for example, Ding Yanao, "Guangfa Yin Gao Guanli Zhiyi Huaqi Zhongzu Cheng Gongsi Zheng Biancheng Huaqi Fenhang" [Citigroup Executives Questioned; Guangdong Development Bank Says the Bank was Reorganized into a Branch of Citibank], *Shanghai Zhengquan Bao* [Shanghai Securities News], September 19, 2007.

57 Bei Hu, "Province Picks up Lender's Problem Loans; Guangdong Development Bank Sells 35b Yuan of Assets to Municipal Firm after Failure to Reach Deal with Asset Managers," *South China Morning Post*, January 2, 2006.

Third, after the acquisition, even though 60 percent of GDB's shares were still owned by SOEs, the three participating SOEs basically delegated their shareholding authority to Citibank. They had little impact on the appointment of key managers and even less on the day-to-day operations of the bank. This allowed the GDB to operate under the almost exclusive guidance of Citibank and its appointed management board. None of this would have been possible without endorsement by the Chinese government.

However, government support of FDI participation in the state-owned bank was not without reservations. The 25 percent cap on foreign ownership of Chinese banks demonstrated the Chinese government's unwillingness to allow a rapid increase in FDI participation within certain sectors.

Copying Mechanism

Cooperation between foreign investors and Chinese companies through joint venture structures evolved in the late 1980s and early 1990s as foreign investors struggled for greater autonomy and control.[58] As noted above, the proportion of JVs to WFOEs changed with greater liberalization, as foreign investors either chose to establish WFOEs outright or bought out equity from their Chinese partners to achieve a controlling interest in an already established JV. These changes meant a greater foreign presence in the Chinese economy because 100 percent foreign-owned subsidiaries were allowed to function in the domestic economy. WFOE rights expanded over time as restrictions on marketing and distribution were phased out and WFOEs became more integrated into the domestic economy, although they continued to make large contributions to the export sector.

We argue that this middle stage of FDI utilization stimulated "copying" of foreign practices and management systems. Copying occurred at two distinct levels: at the firm level SOE managers adopted "scientific management" methods, some corporate governance practices, and innovations in marketing and sales borrowed from the foreign enterprises and investors operating in the Chinese economy. At the macro level of policy-making and legal development, laws and regulations originally adopted to regulate the foreign sector were extended to the entire economy. The copying mechanism often occurred in concert with the other mechanisms for cooperation and competition. For example, as in the GDB example above, one reason for rescuing the GDB through an infusion of foreign capital was to encourage the adoption of Citibank's corporate governance and internal management structures.

58 Gallagher, *Contagious Capitalism.*

In 1999 Guthrie argued that "[a]s they struggle to survive in the increasingly uncertain and turbulent markets of China's transition economy, Chinese firms mimic the examples of market actors that they view as being the most market-savvy, namely, foreign investors."[59] SOEs in the 1990s were squeezed at both the bottom and the top. Township-village enterprises (TVEs) took market share and profits through their ability to meet consumer demand because they did not bear the legacy of the SOE burdens, whereas FIEs increased their dominance in the high-tech and export sectors. But TVEs were no model for the leadership's oft-touted "scientific management" and "modern enterprise system." For these, the SOEs had to look abroad and to the FIEs already operating on Chinese soil.

SOE adoption of foreign management practices and strategies was often sparked by the presence of a JV. Guthrie's research finds that SOEs with a JV relationship were significantly more likely to put in place formal institutions for decision-making, dispute resolution, and employee participation.[60] Based on research at a large SOE conglomerate in Hebei province, we found that the presence of a JV could often spark changes in the larger enterprise system because particularly difficult and sensitive reforms were promoted first in the foreign part of the firm.[61] In this case, labor discipline regulations that significantly changed the work environment were first justified on the basis that the Hong Kong boss demanded them. Female workers from the original SOE were forced to adapt to new Tayloristic methods of worker control, such as limiting their movement at the machines to enhance speed, tightly controlling bathroom and rest breaks, and punitive regulations to reduce tardiness and absenteeism. The previous lax SOE work environment gave way to a workplace with greater productivity and intensity. The SOE gradually began to utilize such labor practices in its other subsidiaries.

The SOE's attention to foreign practices and management styles was also stimulated when the sector absorbed an increasing amount of foreign capital and technology. In the Hebei SOE that produced high-quality cement for the domestic construction sector, attention to foreign management was heightened when a large Sino-Japanese cement plant was established in Qinhuangdao, a nearby city. The competitive threat from this FIE was due not only to its higher technological capacity, but also to its ability to manage its workforce more effectively and to reach out to export markets.

59 Guthrie, *Dragon in a Three-Piece Suit*, 3.
60 Guthrie, *Dragon in a Three-Piece Suit*.
61 Gallagher, *Contagious Capitalism*.

Therefore, there is an obvious connection between firm-level differences among SOEs and FIEs and the larger macro regulatory and legal environments. The legal environment for foreign investors was initially hived off from the domestic Chinese economy. Foreign investors were subject to different legal requirements and were administrated by laws specifically created for the foreign sector, such as the 1979 Sino-Foreign Equity Joint Venture Law, the 1986 Law on Wholly Foreign-Owned Enterprises, and other regulations that stipulated how FIEs could operate in China. However, as Clarke, Murrell, and Whiting argue, over time convergence between the foreign sector and the domestic economy generally went in one direction, with the foreign sector setting an early example for later convergence:

> As reforms in China's domestic economy progressed, however, it became increasingly apparent that the segregated legal system did not make sense over the long term. The effect of unifying the separate legal regimes has generally been to make the regime for Chinese parties look more like the one for foreigners, not the other way around.[62]

In addition to certain labor practices such as short-term labor contracts, which were first extended to JVs in the early 1980s, other notions such as compensation for expropriation,[63] limited liability, and legal personhood were first instituted in the foreign legal framework and only later extended to domestic Chinese firms. The foreign sector's role as a laboratory for sensitive and difficult reforms is evident here, as changes both to social protection and to notions of property and ownership were first felt in the foreign sector and later extended to the larger domestic economy.

Competition Mechanism

Empirical research on the competitive effects of FDI on domestic firms yields interesting and complex results. Most studies examine two main theoretical propositions on the effect of FDI on domestic firms. The first is the "spillover effect," which is the ability of FDI to transmit positive effects to home-country firms, such as technology transfer, increased efficiency, and manufacturing, marketing, and distribution linkages. The second effect, "crowding out," captures the negative ramifications of foreign investment, in particular the crowding out of domestic firms in the bid for capital

---

62 Donald Clarke, Peter Murrell, and Susan H. Whiting, "The Role of Law in China's Economic Development," in Loren Brandt and Thomas Rawski, eds., *China's Great Economic Transformation* (New York: Cambridge University Press, 2008), 380.

63 Clarke, Murrell, and Whiting, "The Role of Law in China's Economic Development."

investment, market share, or skilled labor. The literature on China's experience with FDI finds evidence of both effects. Some studies have found that SOEs are indirectly or directly influenced to pursue higher productivity and efficiency. Particularly after the acceleration of SOE restructuring in 1997,[64] there is evidence that both collective and state enterprises were positively affected by inward FDI, achieving higher sales per employee when FDI was present. However, earlier research using 1995 data finds some evidence of a "crowding out" effect on SOEs by overseas Chinese investment, that is, the presence of investment by overseas Chinese was negatively correlated with SOE productivity in the same sector. However, these differences over time may show that FDI-spawned competition led to the rationalization of certain industries and the closure of poorly performing SOEs.[65] Using data up to 1996 it has been found that the profitability of state firms is positively correlated with the entry of new firms into the sector. This includes effects from both foreign-invested firms and private domestic companies. A later study by Hu and Jefferson, however, finds evidence of both positive effects and "crowding out." Firms that are directly affected by FDI through the absorption of FDI show higher labor productivity, whereas domestic firms without FDI are negatively affected by the presence of FDI. These findings with both positive and negative implications for SOE performance are not contradictory when we consider their effect on restructuring. In fact, they may demonstrate how FDI has shaped the restructuring process over time. An earlier "crowding out" effect may have led to the closure of poorly performing firms. In the later period, the surviving domestic companies were strengthened and improved by the competition. As Hu and Jefferson comment, "this finding indicates that in some industries, some domestic Chinese firms—those that are able to survive in the face of competition from FDI firms—seem able to capture some of the technology and know-how that are introduced to the industry from abroad."[66]

If we are looking for the effects of FDI on corporate restructuring (and not on growth or productivity), these results confirm the argument put forth

64 Peter J. Buckley, Jeremy Clegg, and Chengqi Wang, "The Relationship Between Inward Foreign Direct Investment and the Performance of Domestically-owned Chinese Manufacturing Industry," *Multinational Business Review* 12, no. 3 (Winter 2004): 23–40.

65 Gary H. Jefferson et al., "Ownership, Productivity Change, and Financial Performance in Chinese Industry," *Journal of Comparative Economics* 28, no. 4 (December 2000): 786–813.

66 Albert G.Z. Hu and Gary H. Jefferson, "FDI Impact and Spillover: Evidence from China's Electronic and Textile Industries," *The World Economy* 25 (2002): 1075.

here that FDI has had a large effect on SOE restructuring, but this effect has changed over time. The negative findings on productivity and growth (evidence of "crowding out") can be taken as evidence that FDI competition culls poorly performing domestic firms, but it may also lead to the strengthening of the remaining firms in the sector that survive this process.

In the analysis below, we examine how FDI has affected Chinese SOEs in terms of efficiency, overall number, total assets, and average size. By identifying the pattern of the FDI impact, we are able to assess the level of the positive impact (spillover) and/or negative impact (crowding out) of FDI inflows on the performance and restructuring of Chinese SOEs. After a summary of the main findings, we discuss how these results help us interpret the spillover and crowding out effects and how they inform our main topic of corporate restructuring.

Methodology and Data.   We assume that Efficiency, Total Number, Total Assets, and Average Size of Chinese SOEs are functions of FDI inflows into the country. We therefore try to find the correlation between FDI inflows and each of these indicators through linear regressions, using empirical data across the 39 main industrial sectors in China. FDI inflow is measured by the share of foreign assets in the total assets of the sector. SOE efficiency is defined as the average labor productivity of the SOEs in the sector. The number and total assets of SOEs are self-explanatory variables. The average size of SOEs in a given sector is obtained by dividing the total assets of the SOEs in the sector over the number of SOEs in the sector.

Because we are considering data from a wide array of industrial sectors, which differ significantly from one another, sector biases may produce misleading results. In order to minimize the possibility of mixing sectoral biases into our findings, all our regressions are based on proportional changes in the values (from 1999 to 2004) rather than the actual values of the indicators.

Table 7.1A in the Appendix documents the changes in FDI share and SOE efficiency from 1999 to 2003 in the 39 main Chinese industrial sectors. Table 7.2A in the Appendix records the changes in FDI share, SOE assets, and SOE average size in the 39 main Chinese industrial sectors from 1999 to 2004.

The data used in this research were collected by China's National Bureau of Statistics (NBS), based on the "Year Reports of Industrial Statistics," which are provided by the statistical bureaus of all provinces, autonomous regions, and municipalities. These data are published by the National Bureau of Statistics in the annual *China Statistical Yearbook*.

Empirical Findings

TABLE 7.3
Regression 1—Effect of FDI Inflows on the Efficiency of SOEs

Variables Entered/Removed[b]			
Model	Variables Entered	Variables Removed	Method
1	Change FDIshare[a]		Enter

[a]All requested variables entered
[b]Dependent Variable: ChangeProductivity

Model Summary				
Model	R	R Square	Adjusted R Square	Std. Error of the Estimate
1	.269[a]	.073	.046	********

[a]Predictors (Constant), ChangeFDIshare

ANOVA[b]						
Model		Sum of Squares	df	Mean Square	F	Sig.
1	Regression	.632	1	.632	2.737	.107[a]
	Residual	8.086	35	.231		
	Total	8.719	36			

[a]Predictors: (Constant), ChangeFDIshare
[b]Dependent Variable: ChangeProductivity

Coefficients[a]						
		Unstandardized Coefficients		Standardized Coefficients		
Model		B	Std. Error	Beta	t	Sig.
1	(Constant)	1.028	.088		11.716	.000
	ChangeFDIshare	.250	.151	.269	1.654	.107

[a]Dependent Variable: ChangeProductivity

Regression 1 (Table 7.3) shows a statistically significant positive coefficient of 0.25, indicating that sectors with faster increases of FDI experienced relatively higher growth in efficiency from 1999 to 2003. This implies that FDI indeed contributed to improvements in the efficiency of domestic SOEs. This finding confirms the argument that FIEs are able to yield positive spillover effects on local enterprises.

TABLE 7.4

Regression 2—Effect of FDI Inflows on the Number of SOEs

Variables Entered/Removed[b]			
Model	Variables Entered	Variables Removed	Method
1	Change FDIshare[a]		Enter

[a]All requested variables entered
[b]Dependent Variable: ChangeSOE#

Model Summary				
Model	R	R Square	Adjusted R Square	Std. Error of the Estimate
1	.486[a]	.236	.213	********

[a]Predictors (Constant), ChangeFDIshare

ANOVA[b]						
Model		Sum of Squares	df	Mean Square	F	Sig.
1	Regression	.333	1	.333	10.495	.003[a]
	Residual	1.079	34	.032		
	Total	1.412	35			

[a]Predictors: (Constant), ChangeFDIshare
[b]Dependent Variable: ChangeSOE#

Coefficients[a]						
		Unstandardized Coefficients		Standardized Coefficients		
Model		B	Std. Error	Beta	t	Sig.
1	(Constant)	−.505	.035		−14.524	.000
	ChangeFDIshare	.193	.059	.486	3.420	.003

[a]Dependent Variable: ChangeSOE#

Regression 2 (Table 7.4) produces a statistically significant positive coefficient of 0.193. This indicates that sectors with larger increases in the share of FDI experienced a relatively moderate drop, if not an increase, in the number of SOEs compared to other sectors. Unlike some of the earlier studies, we did not find that FDI crowds out domestic SOEs, at least in the later period under scrutiny here. Rather, there is a weak positive relationship between FDI inflows and the number of SOEs. Although there was a sharp drop in the number of SOEs in most sectors as well as in the national total (see Table 7.2A in the Appendix), this drop is unrelated to the presence of FDI.

TABLE 7.5

Regression 3—Effect of FDI Inflows on the Total Assets of SOEs

Variables Entered/Removed[b]			
Model	Variables Entered	Variables Removed	Method
1	Change FDIshare[a]		Enter

[a]All requested variables entered
[b]Dependent Variable: ChangeSOEasset

Model Summary				
Model	R	R Square	Adjusted R Square	Std. Error of the Estimate
1	.180[a]	.032	.004	********

[a]Predictors (Constant), ChangeFDIshare

ANOVA[b]						
Model		Sum of Squares	df	Mean Square	F	Sig.
1	Regression	.129	1	.129	1.132	.295[a]
	Residual	3.863	34	.114		
	Total	3.991	35			

[a]Predictors: (Constant), ChangeFDIshare
[b]Dependent Variable: ChangeSOEasset

Coefficients[a]						
		Unstandardized Coefficients		Standardized Coefficients		
Model		B	Std. Error	Beta	t	Sig.
1	(Constant)	.056	.066		.858	.397
	ChangeFDIshare	.120	.113	.180	1.064	.295

[a]Dependent Variable: ChangeSOEasset

Regression 3 (Table 7.5) shows a positive coefficient of 0.12, but it is not statistically significant. Although we cannot confirm that sectors where the share of FDI increased more rapidly showed higher growth in the total assets of SOEs than other sectors, we also do not find evidence of "crowding out." This further confirms the argument that we drew from Regression 2 (Table 7.4), rejecting the predictions of the "crowding out" argument. It is enough to demonstrate that FDI did not play a negative role in affecting the total assets of SOEs.

TABLE 7.6

Regression 4—Effect of FDI Inflows on the Average Size of SOEs

Variables Entered/Removed[b]			
Model	Variables Entered	Variables Removed	Method
1	change FDIshare[a]		Enter

[a] All requested variables entered
[b] Dependent Variable: changeAssetperente

Model Summary				
Model	R	R Square	Adjusted R Square	Std. Error of the Estimate
1	.368[a]	.135	.110	********

[a] Predictors (Constant), changeFDIshare

ANOVA[b]						
Model		Sum of Squares	df	Mean Square	F	Sig.
1	Regression	.957	1	.957	5.325	.027[a]
	Residual	6.110	34	.180		
	Total	7.067	35			

[a] Predictors: (Constant), changeFDIshare
[b] Dependent Variable: changeAssetperente

Coefficients[a]						
		Unstandardized Coefficients		Standardized Coefficients		
Model		B	Std. Error	Beta	t	Sig.
1	(Constant)	1.131	.083		13.659	.000
	ChangeFDIshare	−.327	.142	−.368	−2.308	.027

[a] Dependent Variable: changeAssetperente

Regression 4 (Table 7.6) produces a statistically significant negative coefficient of −0.327, indicating that sectors with faster growth in FDI recorded a slower increase in the average size of SOEs. This implies that the presence of FDI is associated with limitations on increases in the size of domestic SOEs. It is interesting to note that the average size of SOEs increased in most sectors as well as in the national average (see Table 7.2A in the Appendix). However, as indicated by the regression, this increase has nothing to do with the effect of FDI, which is negatively related to the growth in the size of SOEs.

Discussion

Testing the spillover effect. From the results of Regression 1 (Table 7.3), we can conclude that FDI inflows are associated with improved performance of Chinese SOEs. This may be evidence of spillovers in sectors with large amounts of FDI. The finding accords with some of the earlier research. Based on their superior performance, foreign firms have created a better economic environment in the sectors in which they are heavily invested. SOEs have benefited from this investment. At the same time, by cooperating with foreign companies, many Chinese SOEs have absorbed new technology and management know-how from their foreign partners, thus improving their efficiency. In addition, the competition presented by the FIEs has forced many SOEs to adopt more efficient production, marketing, and financial strategies.

As mentioned in the literature review, some previous studies find that FDI inflows have had a negative impact on the productivity of Chinese SOEs. These studies, however, are based on empirical data from the early to mid-1990s. Our argument does not necessarily contradict these findings, given that the effect of FDI may have changed over time as weak firms left the scene due to their being unable to survive the competition in the early years of the reform and the surviving state firms responded more positively to competitive pressures. Since the data used here date from 1999 to 2005, the enterprises that we observe are possibly those that had already survived the crowding-out phase, becoming stronger and more sensitive to the positive spillover effect of FDI.

Testing the "crowding out" effect. Spillover and crowding-out effects of FDI on domestic firms are not mutually exclusive. They can, or indeed tend to, occur concurrently in developing economies. After showing the possibility of a spillover effect on Chinese SOEs from the presence of FDI in the first part of our quantitative analysis, regressions 2 and 3 (Table 7.4 and Table 7.5) allow us to test whether the crowding-out effect is also present.

According to the results obtained from regressions 2 and 3, the crowding-out effect, which is noted in some of the earlier studies using data from the mid-1990s, is not confirmed. Instead, contrary to our expectations, FDI is associated with an increase in SOEs, at least in number if not total assets.

This unexpected result perhaps reflects the particular competitive environment in China that is shaped by government policy in a transitional economy. In other developing countries, FDI crowds out domestic enterprises through competition for financing, raw materials, skilled labor, and market dominance. However, foreign firms in China face a competitive environment that differs from that faced by foreign firms in other developing countries. As Yasheng Huang points out, FIEs may only be able to compete with SOEs for market share (not bank loans or other resources), whereas SOEs are able to take advantage of their privileged position in the "political pecking order" of firms.[67]

In other economies, by taking some of the bank credit and capital-market funds in the country, foreign firms make borrowing more difficult and costly for domestic enterprises. In China, equal competition for bank credit and capital-market funding between FIEs and SOEs is nonexistent. Due to government policies and regulations, SOEs have much better access to domestic financing and capital markets. Government control of the banking system and of the capital markets yields lending and funding requirements that are biased in favor of the SOEs, making it impossible for foreign firms to drive the SOEs out of the market by monopolizing funds.

Although to a lesser extent than the financial market, the demand market for raw materials in China also is far from competitive. Preferential government policies and direct ties with suppliers (which usually are other SOEs) provide most SOEs with sources of raw materials that are segmented from the raw materials market where the FIEs get their supplies. Therefore, the ability of foreign firms to crowd out state enterprises through competition for the supply of raw materials is minimal.

The only ground where FIEs in China can compete on a relatively equal basis with the SOEs is in the battle for control of the sales market and in attracting skilled labor. This competition has been effective in forcing SOEs to speed up their restructuring process. However, it has not been able to drive a significant number of local SOEs out of the market. Hence, the crowding-out effect of foreign firms that is usually found in other developing markets did not occur in China, at least during the later years of reform.

It is worth noting that, in contrast to the SOEs, private enterprises in China do compete with foreign firms on an equal, or even disadvantaged, footing. As previous studies have demonstrated, foreign firms may crowd out domestic private enterprises in China.[68] But we do not explore this relationship in this chapter.

At the same time, we do not rule out the possibility that some SOEs were crowded out of the market by the presence of foreign capital in the early years of the reform. As we noted in our discussion about productivity and the spillover effect, the early competitive effects of FDI inflows might have been

67 Yasheng Huang, *Selling China: Foreign Direct Investment During the Reform Era* (New York: Cambridge University Press, 2003).

68 Huang, *Selling China*; Huang, "Ownership Biases and FDI in China: Evidence from Two Provinces."

different from those during the period under study here; as weak SOEs exited the scene, the SOEs that responded most positively to the spillovers remained.

If this assumption is true, it further explains why in the later (post-1999) stage of the reforms, the SOEs have been waning away more slowly in sectors with greater growth in foreign capital. This may be related to the earlier crowding-out effect of FIEs on SOEs in these sectors, with the trend attracting the attention of state corporate leaders and policymakers. Their worries about state enterprises being completely driven out of certain sectors may have contributed to the decision to proceed with corporate restructuring more quickly as a way to rescue the firms. This would explain why stronger and more competitive SOEs were less likely to be crowded out by FDI during the 1999 to 2005 period examined in this study.

It is also important to point out, as we note from the reduction in the absolute number of SOEs between 1999 and 2005, a significant number of SOEs were indeed crowded out of the market. Nevertheless, this crowding out was unrelated to the presence of foreign capital. A more plausible explanation is that instead of being driven out of the market by the inflow of FDI, those SOEs were crowded out by local non-state enterprises, such as township and village enterprises and private enterprises, which over the years gained an increasingly stronger position in the Chinese economy. The government's decision in the late 1990s to allow small and medium state-owned enterprises either to compete or to fail also explains their sharp decline during the period of intense SOE restructuring.

The positive correlation between the number of SOEs and the presence of FDI might even suggest that in some sectors larger competitive pressures from FIEs helped SOEs reshape their corporate structures and achieve more efficient operations before the emergence of the domestic private sector. This might have saved some of these SOEs from being crowded out by the non-state sectors after the private sector began to emerge more aggressively.

Overall, our findings show that current arguments and worries about the crowding-out effect that FDI has on Chinese SOEs have overwhelmingly overstated the magnitude and implications of such an effect. We argue that at least since the later years of the reforms, the crowding-out effect of FDI on state enterprises has been well under control and has not superseded the spillover effect.

Testing the Effects on Restructuring

If the empirical findings in the text above only show the influence of FDI on the general performance of SOEs, the following analysis links the presence of FIEs to the "restructuring" of SOEs and examines their impact.

Through regression 4 (Table 7.6), we observe that although the average size of SOEs increased significantly in most sectors during the period from 1999 to 2004, the presence of FDI is associated with limitations on the average size of SOEs in the same sector. This finding has relevant implications for the restructuring of SOEs.

Over-expansion is a manifestation of the inability of Chinese SOEs to adapt to the rules of the new economic environment.[69] During the early years of the reform, as a legacy of the planned economy the performance of state enterprises was measured largely by their size and output level, rather than by their profitability. Due to systemic mechanisms, funds from the government and state-owned banks were more likely to flow to SOEs with larger outputs and assets.[70] Under this size-focused system, SOE managers were induced to build up output through massive acquisitions and irrational investments, paying little attention to cost-savings. Meanwhile, the soft-budget constraints under traditional state ownership provided the means for inefficient over-expansion.[71] This over-expansion became one of the major problems for Chinese state enterprises and was also one of the main reasons for their failure in the late 1990s. The case of China Worldbest Group Corporation (CWGC, otherwise known as Hua Yuan) is a clear example of failure due to over-expansion. The firm started in Shanghai in 1992 as a state enterprise directly controlled by the central government. Within less than thirteen years, it had expanded from a mid-size company, with barely $17.5 million in assets, into one of the largest enterprises in the country, with total assets of over $6.8 billion.[72] During the process, the firm carried out over 70 direct acquisitions, gaining predominance in three industrial areas: textiles, pharmaceuticals, and agro-machinery.[73] However, the enterprise ended up becoming a victim of its over-expansion. The newly acquired assets were largely unprofitable. After being unable to fulfill its huge debt responsibilities that had accumulated from the expansion, China Worldbest was forced to

69 Yue Ma, "Ineffective Restructuring of SOEs through Acquisition and Outsider Control," undergraduate honors thesis, 2006, Department of Political Science, University of Michigan, Ann Arbor.

70 Edward S. Steinfeld, *Forging Reform in China: The Fate of State-Owned Industry* (New York: Cambridge University Press, 1998).

71 Ma, "Ineffective Restructuring."

72 Jiang Bo, *Zai Kaifang De Guotu Shang: Hua Yuan Moshi Toushi* [On the Open Territory: Perspective on the Hua Yuan Model] (Shanghai: Shanghai kexue puji chubanshe, 2000).

73 Based on an interview with Minming Fan, co-chair of the board of directors, CWGC, July 30, 2005.

accept acquisition and restructuring by another enterprise.[74] The failure of this enterprise is a typical case of the over-expansion chaos in Chinese SOEs.

As Yue Ma points out in an earlier paper, adequate corporate restructuring is the only way of stopping the rapid, yet inefficient expansion of SOEs. Once an efficient corporate governance system is in place, enterprise operations as well as managerial behavior will be monitored internally (by the board of directors representing the shareholders) and externally (by creditors and the media). This monitoring will impose a higher level of financial discipline, tighten budget constraints, and make firms more cost-conscious. Hence, restructured enterprises will typically abandon the expansionary business model that pursues high output and high investment and will shift to a more stable and cost-efficient model of development.[75] The increase in the average size of SOEs observed during the 1999–2005 period in our data shows that despite the restructuring efforts that took place since the late 1990s, over-expansion still remained a problem. However, the negative relationship between the presence of FDI and the average size of SOEs that we observe in regression 4 implies that a relatively larger FDI presence can moderate the over-expansion of SOEs in certain sectors.

The underlying logic of this finding is that in order to compete more effectively with the technologically advanced and cost-efficient FIEs, SOEs critically need a more stable, profit-oriented (rather than size-oriented) business model. As noted above, under the old corporate structure SOE managers were encouraged to promote rather than to control over-expansion. In other words, inefficient over-expansion can only be controlled by an effective restructuring that completely reshapes the governance system of state enterprises. Competitive pressures from FIEs force SOEs to proceed with such a restructuring more rapidly in order to avoid being driven out of the market. Thus, FDI contributes to the acceleration of SOE restructuring.

Although the evidence provided here is still preliminary, this positive effect on SOE restructuring and corporate governance is intriguing and deserves further study. In the current Chinese political environment, where officials, intellectuals, and the media view foreign capital with suspicion, this kind of subtle, but positive, effect of FDI is often ignored.[76]

---

74 He Wannan, "Binggou Zhiguo: Hua Yuan Weiji" [Result of Acquisition: Hua Yuan Crisis], *Zhengquan Shichang Zhoukan* [Securities Market Weekly], November 26, 2005.

75 Ma, "Ineffective Restructuring."

76 For discussion of the debate on foreign capital, see Peter A. Neumann and Tony Zhang, "China's New Foreign-funded M&A Provisions: Greater Legal Protection or Legalized Protectionism," *China Law and Practice* 20, no. 8 (2007): 21–30; "Mergers and Acquisitions," *China Insight*.

Conclusion

FDI inflows have contributed greatly in both direct and indirect ways to fundamental reform and restructuring of the state sector in China. In particular, we find evidence that in recent years, the presence of FDI has had a disciplining effect on SOEs through competitive pressures emanating from increased foreign participation in China's domestic economy. Although the competitive effect of FDI seems to be the most important mechanism affecting future corporate and system restructuring in China, we also emphasize that foreign capital has played an important cooperative role in the reshaping of the Chinese economy by transferring new practices and strategies to domestic industries. The presence of foreign capital also stimulated legal and policy changes that were initially created to regulate the foreign economic sector but ultimately were extended to domestic economic actors as well.

With the move to M&As as a main vehicle for investment, the competitive pressures from foreign capital will be felt more acutely and may lead to a backlash against foreign capital specifically and globalization more generally. Even though FDI has been a remedy to discipline and improve the health of the state sector, large inflows of FDI is also leading to the transformation of many state firms into FIEs. The FDI medicine works for some patients, but also leads to their absorption into the private and foreign sectors through privatization and M&A activity. For a leadership and society that is still invested in the creation of global *Chinese* companies, these issues will continue to raise concerns.

The overarching theme of this volume focuses on the link between firm-level restructuring and complementary institutions in other realms, but the utilization of foreign capital as an engine of domestic reform shows the advantages of allowing institutional frictions and competition among different economic systems. Chinese socialist firms and their entire institutional environment were reformed through cooperation, copying, and competition with capitalist FIEs. This gradual reform process began at the firm level but led to important changes in the larger institutions managing the market, including the legal system and corporate governance. Change was the result of institutional frictions rather than the sudden importation of a new set of institutions, shock-therapy style.

It is difficult to measure whether foreign involvement in China's SOE restructuring is excessive or undesirable. It is the subjective judgment of the political leaders as there is no predetermined level of optimal foreign ownership. Even though foreign acquisitions of Chinese domestic firms accounted for over one-third of the total FDI in 2006, this is still well below the average in the OECD states where over 50 percent of FDI arrives as M&As. We also find little evidence that FDI is currently crowding out SOEs, though it may help to discipline their behavior and expansion activity. However, foreign participation in restructuring may impede the development of a Chinese domestic private sector if the domestic private sector is discriminated against due to the "political pecking order" of firms.[77]

The logical next question is whether such FDI is in the interest of the Chinese Communist Party (CCP). If FDI serves as a substitute for a powerful private sector, perhaps this indicates that the regime is willing to sacrifice some healthy Chinese firms in exchange for weaker Chinese firms that remain state-owned. If biases still persist against domestic private firms, as Huang and others argue, then the Chinese government has chosen the retention of state ownership with a large foreign role over the retention of Chinese ownership with a more minimal foreign role. This is strikingly different from the developmental trajectories of China's Northeast Asian neighbors where FDI was carefully restricted so as to allow for the development of domestic firms that could compete in global markets. Given the changes in the global economy, however, this level of protectionism is no longer a realistic option. SOE restructuring and economic liberalization have proceeded apace, with the Chinese government using FDI to discipline SOEs in the hopes that what does not kill them will make them stronger.

77 Huang, *Selling China*.

TABLE 7.1 APPENDIX

Changes in FDI Share and SOE Efficiency

	Change in FDI Share 1999–2003	Change in SOE Efficiency 1999–2003
National Total	0.181806417	1.436866564
Grouped by Sector		
Mining and Coal Washing	−0.169708074	1.328558219
Extraction of Petroleum and Natural Gas	1	1.393224118
Mining and Processing of Ferrous Metal Ores	2.607519374	1.058602832
Mining and Processing of Non-ferrous Metal Ores	0.263196165	0.777661223
Mining and Processing of Non-metal Ores	−0.098266569	0.805945922
Mining of Other Ores		0.619061453
Processing of Food from Agricultural Products	0.235247806	0.956689087
Manufacture of Foods	−0.036537396	0.973103309
Manufacture of Beverages	0.017609091	0.749384814
Manufacture of Tobacco	−0.312771458	1.362872222
Manufacture of Textiles	0.206070132	0.531626002
Manufacture of Textile Apparel, Footwear, and Caps	−0.013673738	0.474800784
Manufacture of Leather, Fur, Feathers, and Related Products	0.022655756	0.662498301
Processing of Timber, Manufacture of Wood, Bamboo, Rattan, Palm, and Straw Products	−0.109821595	0.766906496
Manufacture of Furniture	0.158567923	0.271884228
Manufacture of Paper and Paper Products	0.180776388	1.778309746
Printing, and Reproduction of Recording Media	0.218466076	1.116434682
Manufacture of Articles for Culture, Education, and Sports Activities	0.067600466	0.658328989
Processing of Petroleum, Coking, and Nuclear Fuel	1.64383652	2.041532499
Manufacture of Raw Chemical Materials and Chemical Products	0.259787534	1.608341546
Manufacture of Medicines	−0.110364184	0.833434062
Manufacture of Chemical Fibers	−0.191819696	0.170110044
Manufacture of Rubber	0.215055705	1.621965297
Manufacture of Plastics	0.088465947	1.266024208
Manufacture of Non-metallic Mineral Products	−0.016586991	0.991429705
Smelting and Pressing of Ferrous Metals	0.640906131	1.948921049
Smelting and Pressing of Non-ferrous Metals	−0.011273942	1.389107595
Manufacture of Metal Products	−0.00139891	1.362844116
Manufacture of General-Purpose Machinery	0.235174553	1.696501753
Manufacture of Special-Purpose Machinery	0.435908694	1.073497755
Manufacture of Transport Equipment	0.233776841	2.06889979
Manufacture of Electrical Machinery and Equipment	0.1235178	1.020722244
Manufacture of Communication Equipment, Computers, and Other Electronic Equipment	0.136010694	1.168135934
Manufacture of Measuring Instruments and Machinery for Cultural Activities and Office Work	0.310092451	1.005194136
Manufacture of Artwork and Other Manufacturing		n.d.
Recycling and Disposal of Waste		n.d.
Production and Distribution of Electric Power and Heat Power	−0.084345817	0.556541013
Production and Distribution of Gas	0.504496263	1.235870923
Production and Distribution of Water	0.520381859	0.207342105

Source: "Year Reports of Industrial Statistics," National Bureau of Statistics.

TABLE 7.2 APPENDIX

Changes in FDI Share, SOE Average Size, and SOE Total Assets

	Change in FDI Share 1999–2004	Change in the Average Size of SOEs 1999–2004	Change in Total Assets of SOEs 1999–2004	Change in # of SOEs 1999–2004
National Total	0.247863918	1.437517015	0.262478022	-0.482063914
Grouped by Sector				
Mining and Washing of Coal	0.426859457	1.428629987	0.66142679	-0.315899582
Extraction of Petroleum and Natural Gas	1	0.062760821	0.304297371	0.227272727
Mining and Processing of Ferrous Metal Ores	2.198118683	0.69620391	0.13992198	-0.327956989
Mining and Processing of Non-ferrous Metal Ores	0.401489004	1.060133936	0.072606607	-0.479351032
Mining and Processing of Non-metal Ores	-0.086964836	1.375702558	0.181215238	-0.502793296
Mining of Other Ores	n.d.	n.d.		
Processing of Food from Agricultural Products	0.239180621	0.832695028	-0.398927913	-0.672028309
Manufacture of Foods	-0.070721262	1.98767183	-0.001356985	-0.665644172
Manufacture of Beverages	0.023274859	1.539267407	-0.064612948	-0.631631135
Manufacture of Tobacco	-0.360436775	1.82571946	0.640740331	-0.419354839
Manufacture of Textiles	0.28447117	0.442310381	-0.389736491	-0.57684756
Manufacture of Textile Apparel, Footwear, and Caps	0.00366951	0.852491557	-0.223450509	-0.580808081
Manufacture of Leather, Fur, Feather, and Related Products	-0.036899279	0.385765341	-0.616149506	-0.723004695
Processing of Timber, Manufacture of Wood, Bamboo, Rattan, Palm, and Straw Products	-0.131103009	1.384051174	-0.068194378	-0.609150327
Manufacture of Furniture	0.186445082	1.051023024	-0.14096763	-0.581168831
Manufacture of Paper and Paper Products	0.262624038	1.723820154	0.11070582	-0.592224979
Printing, and Reproduction of Recording Media	0.247969338	0.928436361	0.050583735	-0.455214724

Manufacture of Articles for Culture, Education, and Sports Activities	0.068690747	0.861046575	-0.375648891	-0.66516129
Processing of Petroleum, Coking, and Nuclear Fuel	1.70295629	0.38223525	0.107589158	-0.198697068
Manufacture of Raw Chemical Materials and Chemical Products	0.335604637	1.164848936	0.0573108	-0.511600656
Manufacture of Medicines	-0.139616007	1.251408096	0.263641484	-0.438732815
Manufacture of Chemical Fibers	-0.097949522	0.373391047	-0.440079034	-0.592307692
Manufacture of Rubber	0.335231673	0.546922227	-0.238543826	-0.507760532
Manufacture of Plastics	0.064328798	1.432115852	0.061438877	-0.563573883
Manufacture of Non-metallic Mineral Products	-0.002455283	0.846905898	-0.12169364	-0.524444444
Smelting and Pressing of Ferrous Metals	0.877923136	1.352902239	0.347058785	-0.427490542
Smelting and Pressing of Non-ferrous Metals	0.059866343	0.98271783	0.426218807	-0.280674847
Manufacture of Metal Products	0.013201865	1.211806209	-0.122546363	-0.603286385
Manufacture of General-Purpose Machinery	0.276275217	1.203351957	0.2289777	-0.44222361
Manufacture of Special-Purpose Machinery	0.616832086	1.557638912	0.285635283	-0.49733511
Manufacture of Transport Equipment	0.357259808	1.526553376	0.547627435	-0.3745508
Manufacture of Electrical Machinery and Equipment	0.120297955	0.795702155	-0.073572554	-0.484086242
Manufacture of Communication Equipment, Computers, and Other Electronic Equipment	0.2079045	1.028209453	0.219954905	0.398506449
Manufacture of Measuring Instruments and Machinery for Cultural Activities and Office Work	0.420862836	0.666874241	0.030393654	-0.381840796
Manufacture of Artwork and Other Manufacturing	n.d.	n.d.	n.d.	n.d.
Recycling and Disposal of Waste	n.d.	n.d.	n.d.	n.d.
Production and Distribution of Electric Power and Heat Power	-0.08313192	0.93874023	0.693016178	-0.126744186
Production and Distribution of Gas	0.875096654	0.614408576	0.475126267	0.0862745 1
Production and Distribution of Water	0.405767107	0.812369061	0.716727412	0.052771619

Source: "Year Reports of Industrial Statistics," National Bureau of Statistics.

8 The Politics of Social Security Reform in Corporate Restructuring in China

Worawut Smuthkalin

China's transition from a command economy to a socialist market economy has created major problems in the country's corporate sector. To improve the productivity and maximize the efficiency of Chinese business enterprises, experts and scholars of corporate governance in less-developed markets, including transitional economies, have called for a complete overhaul of the system restructuring. Specifically, they have called for reforms in the related institutions of the financial sector, investment and banking policies, ownership and property rights issues, as well as government and business relations. Needless to say, the future of the social security system is a key determinant of the success of corporate restructuring in China. More importantly, it is also one of the most critical institutions maintaining the legitimacy of the Chinese Communist regime. The Chinese Communist Party (CCP) came to power claiming to protect the proletariat class against capitalist forces. In doing so, the Maoist system of labor protection tied urban workers to their state-owned enterprises with promises of job security and other welfare-related provisions. The dependence of workers on their host firms adds to the already cumbersome challenge of corporate restructuring in China not only because of the heavy financial burden for labor welfare services that enterprises must bear but also because labor immobility undermines the effective and appropriate allocation of workers' skills, which in general can raise the efficiency of the corporate sector.

This chapter attempts to explain the recent outcomes of the reform and, more importantly, the conflicts of interest that arose among the related actors that have limited the progress of the reform. Social security reform in China is a state-led process, meaning it is planned and regulated by the central government, and it complies and is implemented by the local authorities. It is beyond the scope of this chapter to provide a complete evaluation of the variety of policies implemented at the local levels. Instead, this chapter focuses on the overall reform plan projected in the regulations issued by the central authorities. These directives, I argue, represent the interests and reflect the incentives of the central government in Beijing as well as the central government's compromises with other sectors of the state and society more broadly. In the end, despite central directives to create a more effective labor protection institution to facilitate the corporate restructuring of the state-owned enterprise sector, non-economic factors—political, fiscal, and administrative—have also played an integral role in shaping and constraining the direction, sequencing, and extent that China's social security reform has taken. Consequently, these constraints limit the optimal utilization of the social security reform to accommodate corporate restructuring in China.

To elaborate on the points noted above, this chapter is organized as follows. Section 2 provides a brief background of China's social security system before the economic reform and examines its distinctive characteristics. The section also explains the degree to which the Maoist social security institution is embedded in the corporate sector of the country and how this existing arrangement undermines the progress of corporate restructuring efforts. Two broad strategies to approach the problem of China's corporate-based social security provisions are debated in Section 3. The reform plan can take either a "privatization" or a "socialization" route, both of which aim to transfer welfare-related burdens away from the enterprises. This section also discusses the attempts by the Chinese government, roughly divided into two main episodes, to reform its social security system. The first period, from the 1980s until the early 1990s, had a distinct privatization direction to social security reform, whereas the second period, starting around the mid-1990s, was characterized by a socialization approach. Focusing primarily on the outcome of the reform during the second episode, Section 4 addresses the difficulties of the reform plan to formulate an integrated Chinese social security institution due to the conflicts and cleavages among the different sectors in the state and society over the outcome of the reform. Using health insurance and pension reform as examples, I argue that the economic reform and social security reform policies during the 1980s widened the gap in socio-economic conditions in Chinese society and loosened the central government's control over financial resources, making the plan to pool resources and risks from diverse sectors and localities more difficult. As elaborated on in Section 5, the central government has recognized the limits of the reform initiatives and has increasingly come to rely on transitional strategies

requiring large central government subsidies to support the poorly performing localities and sectors. The final section concludes by summarizing the arguments in this chapter and exploring the context of the reform in broader
comparisons with such reforms in Japan and Korea.

China's Social Security System before the Economic Reform

In order to examine the process and outcome of social security reform in
China, we first need to understand what kind of social security institution
was in place prior to Deng Xiaoping's economic reforms.[1] By and large, the
Maoist social security system was heavily geared toward urban workers in
public (state- and collectively-owned) enterprises who were considered to be
the privileged group in the Chinese Communist regime. In comparison, welfare services that the state provided to the rural population were marginal.[2]
In order to place this discussion in the context of corporate restructuring,
this chapter focuses primarily on the urban-based social security institution
rather than the rural-based social welfare system. Also referred to as the
"iron rice bowl" system, the provision of welfare benefits in urban China
was guaranteed to public enterprise workers from "cradle to grave." We can
broadly divide the welfare provisions into four main programs,[3] 1) housing,
2) medical care, 3) elder care, especially old-age pensions, and 4) job security.[4] Disaggregating the Chinese social security system into specific programs
instead of considering it as a whole is crucial to understand the process of

---

1 For a detailed description of China's social welfare system prior to the era of economic reforms, see, for example, John Dixon, "China," in John Dixon and Hyung-Shik
Kim, eds., *Social Welfare in Asia* (London: Croom, Helm, 1985).

2 Gordon White, "Social Security Reforms in China: Towards an East Asian Model?"
in Roger Goodman, Gordon White, and Huck-ju Kwon, eds., *The East Asian Welfare
Model: Welfare Orientalism and the State* (New York: Routledge, 1998), 176. Also see,
for example, Xinping Guan, "China's Social Policy: Reform and Development in the
Context of Marketization and Globalization," in Huck-ju Kwon, ed., *Transforming the
Developmental Welfare State in East Asia* (New York: Palgrave, 2005), 231–56, and Table
10.1 in the Kwon volume for a concise comparison of the welfare policies provided for
urban and rural residents in China.

3 Edward Gu identifies housing, medical care, and pensions as the three elements in
the urban social security system during the Mao era; see Edward X. Gu, "Dismantling
the Chinese Mini-Welfare State? Marketization and the Politics of Institutional Transformation, 1979–1999," *Communist and Post Communist Studies* 34, no. 1 (2001): 93.
I argue that the guarantee of life-long employment to enterprise workers is a fourth element: labor security against the risk of unemployment.

4 Instead of an unemployment insurance program, the Communist Party guaranteed life-time employment to employees in the formal sectors of the economy.

the reform. During the reform period, each program did not proceed in the same direction or at the same pace and did not achieve the same progress.

In addition to welfare provisions, the distinctive institutional character-istics of the Maoist social security system are also relevant, especially the mechanisms that financed and distributed these welfare benefits to the work-ers. The arrangement of the Maoist social security system was somewhat unusual. One can say that it was a hybrid between a centralized and a firm-based arrangement and its welfare distribution was a mix of egalitarianism and stratification. At the core of China's socialist system was a centrally-planned economy characterized by two fundamental institutional structures. First, the system called for social ownership of the means of production (from which emerged the publicly-owned enterprises) and resource alloca-tion decisions that were made in response to the will of the planners rather than in response to market signals, i.e., prices. Second, many resources were concentrated in the hands of planners and utilization and redistribution of resources were controlled from the top through a highly centralized hier-archical political structure.[5] Because welfare-related expenses for urban workers were disbursed by the planners in Beijing, the Maoist social secu-rity system was highly centralized. Yet, it was the work-unit, or the *danwei*, that administered and handled the actual distribution of welfare-related re-sources.[6] Decision-making power was at the firm level, even though all re-lated budgets required approval and supervision by the upper levels. In other words, within the approved budget, work-unit heads had the autonomy to allocate resources for welfare-related purposes. The work-units are consid-ered by some China scholars to be micro or mini welfare states within the welfare state.[7]

To remain egalitarian, a core principle of the socialist ideology,[8] the state guaranteed workers in the urban areas comprehensive welfare benefits. Countrywide, work-units provided a similar set of welfare benefits and ser-vices based on state guidelines. However, it is inaccurate to argue that all workers in China enjoyed the same quantity and quality of welfare services. Chinese workers did not escape a stratified system of welfare provision, even

5 Barry Naughton, *Growing Out of the Plan: Chinese Economic Reform 1978–1993* (New York: Cambridge University Press, 1995), 26–27.

6 White, "Social Security Reforms in China," 177.

7 Gu, "Dismantling the Chinese Mini-Welfare State?" 91–111.

8 As a socialist country, China strived to achieve a modern developed socialist soci-ety as a first step toward a future egalitarian society. For detailed discussion, see John E. Dixon, *The Chinese Welfare System: 1949–1979* (New York: Praeger, 1981), 3–24.

though stratification was based on status in the social structure of the CCP.[9] In China, social stratification was largely shaped by the structural conditions of the work-units rather than the economic profiles of individual workers, i.e., skill level, job status, or position, as in the capitalist economies.[10] These *danwei*-related conditions depended on the type of enterprises, the size of the firms, and at which administrative level they operated. There were two main types of urban industrial enterprises in China: state-owned and collectively owned. State firms were normally larger, capital-intensive modern enterprises. They also provided better and more generous welfare benefits than collective firms, which were mainly composed of smaller, labor-intensive, and technologically basic factories.[11] The size of the enterprise also mattered. The larger the firm, the better and more numerous the fringe benefits, especially in firms that fostered business relations with ministerial, provincial, or municipal plants. Also, it was more likely that state enterprises owned by higher administrative echelons, i.e., by national ministries, provinces, or large cities, offered more complete benefits than those administered by small cities or counties.[12]

In a broad sense, the Maoist social security system resembled a "pay-as-you-go" system in a capitalist welfare state regime. In contrast to a "partially-funded" or a "fully-funded" system, a "pay-as-you-go" system has no reserve funds for financing welfare benefits.[13] In this system the current year liabilities were financed by the current year receipts.[14] Although the management of welfare funds in Maoist China took place at the workplace level, no substantial funds were collected and remained therein as the central planning system required that all resources be remitted to the center and reallocated back to the lower echelons after a unified decision at the central government level.

9 For a brief discussion of social stratification and welfare states, see Gøsta Esping-Andersen, *The Three Worlds of Welfare Capitalism* (Princeton, NJ: Princeton University Press, 1990), 23–26.

10 China shared with the capitalist economies the determination of job status based on the degree of welfare benefits. By job status, I do not mean the title or the position of the job, but whether workers were permanently or temporarily employed. The former group enjoyed a higher level of welfare provision than the latter. For further reading, see Andrew G. Walder, *Communist Neo-Traditionalism: Work and Authority in Chinese Industry* (Berkeley: University of California Press, 1986), 40–43 and 48–54.

11 For a comparison of welfare benefits between the state and collective sectors, see Table 3 in Walder, *Communist Neo-Traditionalism*, 44–45.

12 Walder, *Communist Neo-Traditionalism*, 67.

13 For definitions of these terms and other welfare-related terms, see Isabel Ortiz, ed., *Protection in Asia and the Pacific* (Manila: Asian Development Bank, 2001), Appendix 2.

14 "Pay-as-you-go" is the term used most widely for a pension insurance system. In terms of the pension, the current workers pay for the pension benefits of the current retirees.

The Reform of the Maoist Social Security System in the Context of Corporate Restructuring

Corporate restructuring aims to promote governance that enhances productivity, increases economic efficiency, and reduces unnecessary costs for firms. The concept, originating in the West, singles out two main actors in the corporate world: firm managers and investors.[15] The term captures a process in which the ability of investors to control firm management is increased in order that they receive a maximum return on their capital. Despite this narrow interpretation, corporate governance generally implies the pursuit of profit-maximization.

Following this broad conceptual analysis of corporate governance, we can argue that the Maoist social security system impeded the performance of the Chinese corporate sector in three fundamental ways. First, Chinese public enterprises, acting on behalf of the state, guaranteed welfare provisions for their employees. Their welfare-provision function exhausted the firms' resources and overshadowed their economic functions. In fact, during the Maoist era, making profits or increasing productivity may not have been the most important goals of the enterprises. A state-owned firm in the planned economy was not only an economic enterprise but, more importantly, a social and political institution.[16] For an authoritarian regime commanding a territory as large as China, social control is crucial to effectively govern the country. The *danwei* system divided society into manageable cellular units where the unified collective actions of the citizens against the state could be controlled and even prevented. At the same time, work-unit heads, as representatives of the state, provided their workers with fringe benefits in exchange for compliance. China's specific demographic pressures, particularly urban overpopulation, further enhanced the "organized dependency" system that tied workers and their life chances strictly to their workplaces. It not only prevented the illegal migration of workers from rural to urban areas, but also provided the surplus laborers in the cities with basic living arrangements.[17]

As social security benefits for urban workers were tied to individual firms, the corporate-based labor protection system limited the flexibility of the Chinese labor market and reduced the efficiency of labor inputs. With the understanding that quitting or changing jobs meant losing the welfare benefits that each firm exclusively provided, workers were unwilling to search

---

15 For a review of the general theory of corporate governance and corporate restructuring, see, for example, Andrei Shleifer and Robert W. Vishny, "A Survey of Corporate Governance," *Journal of Finance* 52, no. 2 (June 1997): 737–83.

16 Walder, *Communist Neo-Traditionalism*, 28–29.

17 Walder, *Communist Neo-Traditionalism*, 35–38.

for employment for which they might have been better suited. In addition, as employment and other welfare benefits were state-guaranteed, firm managers were reluctant to fire their employees, making it difficult to improve firm performance. To make things worse, the central planning system, in which the planners controlled the budgets and everything was subject to negotiation, underwrote all of the expenditures of local governments and work-units, creating the problem of "soft-budget constraints."[18] Discrepancies in the management of funding and distribution in the Maoist social security system resulted in waste and inefficient spending. Because firms did not benefit from their output and they were not responsible for their expenditures, they lacked material incentives to pursue economic efficiency.

The *danwei*-based social security system has to be followed by a system that separates the welfare-providing responsibility of firms from their profit-maximizing or productivity-enhancing function. To select a suitable social security institution, we should first acknowledge the various forms of social security institutions. Social security systems are arranged in various ways. To simplify, I map them in a two-dimensional space as shown in Figure 8.1. Fundamentally, there are two key aspects in the formation of a social security system. The horizontal axis represents the demand side of the system. It is labeled "the degree of risk redistribution." An essential element of the social security system is risk-pooling. To be included in the risk pool means to be eligible for compensation benefits during or after a particular risk. To be cost-effective in insuring against social risks, the size of the risk pool, which determines who is included, is important. The size can range from a party of one (self-insured) to an entire nation. A larger risk pool does not necessarily mean better or cheaper social insurance benefits for each insured person. There is always a tradeoff when including one additional person to the pool. One must weigh that one person's ability to contribute to the pooled fund and the probability of that person's incidence of risk. If the latter offsets the former, including that person in the pool may not be worthwhile. Along this axis, four levels of risk redistribution are ordered roughly by the size of each pooled fund. Three out of the four levels—individual, firm-based, and national—are self-explanatory. The other level—sectoral or local—requires some elaboration. At this level, a pooled fund can range from an industrial sector, such as mining, to a local administrative unit, such as a city or a province.

Labeled "the level of fund control," the vertical axis captures the supply side of the social security system. Regardless of institutional form, all social security systems require funding, which can come from direct payments

18 Popularized in Janos Kornai, *Economics of Shortage* (New York: North-Holland, 1980).

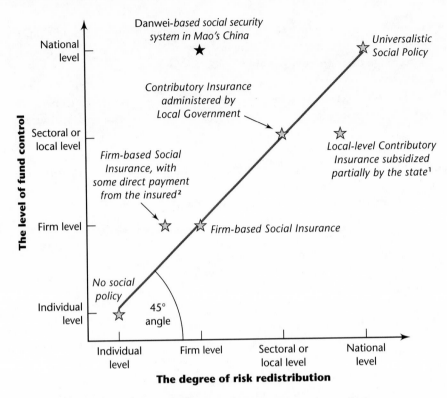

FIGURE 8.1 Social Policy Space According to the Level of
Fund Control and the Degree of Risk Redistribution[19]

Notes: 1. In this type of social security system, the insurance fund is administered at the local level. But, with some subsidies from the state, it helps share the risk of the insured at the sectoral/local level, making the system move slightly to the right of the sectoral or local level in the direction of the national level along the horizontal axis.

2. In this system, the insurance fund is controlled at the firm level. But with the individual insured paying the extra contribution for himself/herself, he/she becomes more responsible for his/her own risk, making the system move slightly toward the left of the system of firm-based social insurance in the direction of the individual level along the horizontal axis.

Source: Author's mapping.

by the insured person, contributions from employers and/or employees, or from general taxation. Those who administer the funds have a clear advantage. We can think of them as extra financial resources and they can be used not only to compensate for social risks but also for other purposes, such as investment. Four values are specified on the axis, indicating the level at which the social security fund is administered and controlled. At an individual level, each insured person manages his or her own resources. Firm-level

19 The theory of the structural formation of a social security system is adopted from Isabela Mares, *The Politics of Social Risk: Business and Welfare State Development* (New York: Cambridge University Press, 2003), 15, fig. 2.1.

social security funds are generally controlled by the employers or the trade unions in that particular firm, or both. Local authorities manage social security funds at the local level, whereas the central government oversees national social security funds.

It is only rational for those who contribute to the fund to demand that they are involved in managing and utilizing the resources. As a consequence, these two elements coexist in the most general forms of social security institutions. As shown in the diagram in Figure 8.1, these social security systems are positioned along a 45 degree angle. However, it does not mean that systems positioned away from the line do not exist. The *danwei*-based system in China prior to the reforms is but one example.

Broadly speaking, two major approaches can be adopted for social security reform in China. One option is privatization, in which the responsibility for welfare services is passed down from the firm to the individual. The approach conforms to a neo-liberal model. An extreme version of this approach eliminates a state-guaranteed or state-provided social policy; each worker is individually responsible for insuring against his or her own social risks. The alternative approach for *danwei*-based social security reform takes an opposite position regarding public integration of the social security system. The result is a national pool where all social risks are redistributed among the largest-sized population of the insured.

As illustrated in Figure 8.2, China has experimented with both reform alternatives. Despite the risk of oversimplification, the reform of the Chinese social security system can be roughly divided into two phases, each with its own predominant orientation. The first phase relies more on the privatization approach, whereas the second predominantly applies a socialization approach. Not all programs were subject to reform during each period. For example, only the housing program and a part of the health insurance program made some progress based on the privatization approach promoted during the first phase. Other programs, including unemployment insurance, health insurance, and old-age pensions, were postponed until the second phase, during which time social security reform proceeded in the direction of socialization.[20]

It is fascinating to observe the trends and sequencing of China's social security reform, as shown in Figure 8.2. Based on this observation, there are a number of puzzles regarding the overall reform, none of which can be answered satisfactorily solely in the context of its relationship with corporate restructuring. First, since there are two routes to reform the *danwei*-based social security system, how can we predict which direction will be chosen?

20 See, for example, Xinping Guan, "China's Social Policy."

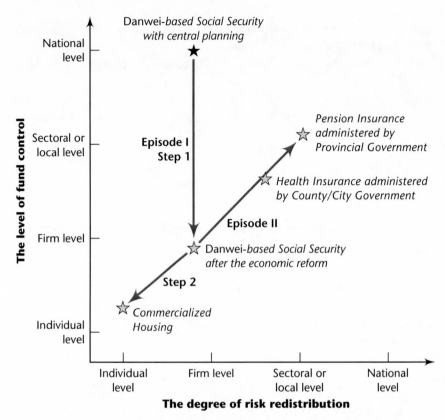

FIGURE 8.2 Directions and Outcomes of Social Security Reform in China
Source: Author's mapping.

In fact, China has tried both. The next question concerns the sequencing of the reform: why did the Chinese government decide to adopt the privatization approach and then change to the socialization approach? Third, why did some programs follow the privatization route whereas others seemed to proceed in the opposite direction? The last puzzle focuses on the socialization approach of the reform. In general, it would be the most economically efficient for the Chinese corporate sector to have a national social security system. Not only would the costs of financing the system be spread evenly across the country, but the degree of labor mobility would be maximized. But why does a national pension program seem impractical in China at this time? Furthermore, why do we observe risk-pooling of the pension program at the provincial levels whereas risk-pooling of the health insurance program takes place at the city/county level?

To answer these questions, we need more than an economic explanation. Additional factors are required to understand how China's social security reform has thus far complemented the overall reform of the corporate sector. Answering all of these questions is beyond the scope of this chapter. I will instead focus on the last puzzle. In Section 4 where I address in detail the outcomes of the pension and health insurance systems in the late 1990s, I emphasize three important factors: 1) the state's concern about political stability, 2) the state's concern about the financial situation, and 3) the state's administrative capacity to execute its plan.

The Role of Political, Fiscal, and Administrative Factors in the Reform of China's Social Security System

The discussion in this section revolves around the unified regulations issued by the Chinese central government during the second half of the 1990s regarding two major programs for social welfare provision: old-age pensions and health insurance. Beijing formulated a series of guidelines for local authorities to reform the social security system within their jurisdictions. According to the guidelines, the institutional features of China's new social insurance system showed signs of moving in the direction of socialization. Table 8.1 summarizes the main features of the pension and health insurance reforms in the urban sector during the 1990s.

Three specific elements in the institutional design of these two programs should be stressed. First, neither program reached an ideal socialization

TABLE 8.1

Unified Regulations for Pension and Health Insurance Reforms in the 1990s

Pension	Health Insurance
Compulsory old-age insurance for most urban employees at the provincial level.	Compulsory social health insurance for most urban employees at the municipal/city level.
Employers pay 20% of their total wage bill into a local pooled fund and the individual savings accounts of their employees. Employees pay 8% of their wages into their individual accounts.	Employers pay 6–8% of their total wage bill into a local insurance fund and the individual insurance accounts of their employees. Employees pay 2% of their wages into their individual accounts.
From the local pooled fund, retirees receive 20% of the average provincial wage for 15 years of contributions; retirees receive nothing for less than 15 years of contributions.	Patients use their individual accounts for outpatient care and the local insurance fund for inpatient care.
From the individual accounts, retirees receive 1/120 of the total sum for 15 years of contributions, or a lump-sum payment equal to the account balance for less than 15 years of contributions.	Co-payments are required for each patient, but the co-payment declines as the cost of treatment increases. The local insurance fund is limited to four times the average annual wage.

Source: Author.

model. In other words, they did not provide risk-pooling at the national level. Second, the development of the pension system surpassed that of health insurance as the pension fund was pooled at the provincial level whereas the health insurance fund was pooled at the city or county level. Third, both programs combined a socialized social insurance system and an individual savings account.

The Politics of Pension Reform in China

Pension reform in China during the late 1990s was driven by rising fiscal and political pressures. The inherent financial problem of the existing pension institution became apparent as soon as CCP leaders began pursuing the economic reform policies in the late 1970s. During the economic reform period of Deng Xiaoping, the fiscal decentralization of the pension scheme effectively undercut cross-subsidization among work-units; and in areas with diverse risk incidence and resources it eliminated the state's guaranteed underwriting under the central planning system. One might argue that the Chinese leaders expected the market economy to have a self-correcting mechanism and a trickle-down effect to correct social inequalities. However, China in the 1990s proved otherwise. By the end of the 1990s, state enterprises were deteriorating rather than improving. Report after report was filed about loss-making SOEs and the impact they had on the distribution of pension payments to retired workers.[21]

Although capitalism was increasingly dominant in China during the last two decades of the twentieth century, the CCP did not completely marketize industrial labor relations. In fact, the CCP, i.e., the central government, maintained the existing "social contract" that it implicitly had signed with the formal workers of the urban sectors and continued to provide them with fringe benefits out of fears of regime instability. The "social contract" refers to the promise made by the CCP to provide the most basic set of material rewards in exchange for loyalty and service to the regime.[22] Urban workers did not expect all of the fringe benefits and material

21 Loraine A. West, "Pension Reform in China: Preparing for the Future," in Sarah Cook and Margaret Maurer-Fazio, eds., *The Workers' State Meets the Market: Labour in China's Transition* (London: Frank Cass, 1999).

22 The concept of a "social contract" was introduced in the context of Soviet-style management of labor relations. For discussion of this concept, see, for example, Jan Adam, ed., *Economic Reforms and Welfare Systems in the USSR, Poland, and Hungary: Social Contract in Transformation* (London: Macmillan, 1991) and Linda J. Cook, *The Soviet Social Contract and Why It Failed: Welfare Policy and Workers' Politics from Brezhnev to Yeltsin* (Cambridge, MA: Harvard University Press, 1993).

rewards. However, they did believe that they would continue to be provided with at least the most basic benefits. Such subsistence claims included wages for those who were still employed, new jobs or alternative means of survival for those who were laid off or unemployed, and pension benefits for current retirees.[23] On the surface, the SOEs' inability to meet welfare needs did not seem to affect the state, especially the central government, as it already had transferred its responsibilities as welfare provider to authorities at the sub-central levels. Upon closer inspection, however, the central government was deeply impacted both politically and financially by the reform. The majority of failing enterprises facing complaints from workers were state-owned. Despite the fiscal decentralization policy, the state had not been able to escape bailing out troubled enterprises. As Edward Gu points out in cases of enterprises running at a loss, welfare expenditures were subsidized by the state, with the amount determined through bargaining between the enterprises and the government.[24]

The widespread violation of the rights of retired workers by state-owned enterprises led to an increasing number of protests against their former enterprises and even against their local government authorities throughout the 1990s. The number of protests officially acknowledged by the CCP nearly quadrupled, from 8,700 to 32,000.[25] These retirees saw their demonstrations as acts of "rightful resistance." After all, their pension benefits had been promised and endorsed by the CCP central government.[26] As Elisabeth Croll argues, Chinese citizens, especially those who experienced state socialism firsthand during the Maoist period, continued to have a sense of entitlement to social security and other social services that the state was obligated to provide.[27] The incidents of workers' protests were serious enough to cause concern amongst the central leadership to the point where they "now rate labor strife a major threat to social stability."[28]

23 According to a survey of Chinese and foreign newspapers from 1996 to 2001, cited in William Hurst and Kevin J. O'Brien, "China's Contentious Pensioners," *China Quarterly*, no. 170 (June 2002): 346, of the sixty-two documented protests in China, virtually all of them focused on benefits for laid-off workers (29 percent), wages (34 percent), or pensions (42 percent).

24 Edward X. Gu, "Market Transition and the Transformation of the Health Care System in Urban China," *Policy Studies* 22, nos. 3–4 (September 2001): 197–215.

25 Indira A.R Lakshmanan, "Coping With Broken Promises as Many Suffer in China's Transition, Party to Get New Chief," *Boston Globe*, November 2, 2002, A1.

26 Kevin J. O'Brien, "Rightful Resistance," *World Politics* 49, no. 1 (1996): 31-55.

27 Elisabeth Croll, "Social Welfare Reform: Trends and Tensions," *China Quarterly*, no. 159 (1999): 684-99.

28 Hurst and O'Brien, "China's Contentious Pensioners," 345.

TABLE 8.2

Average Wage Levels and Number and Ratio of Pensioners in Different Types of Firms, 1978–1998

Year	Wage (yuan)				Number of Pensioners (10,000 persons)				Ratio of employees to pensioners			
	Total	State-owned units	Collectively owned units	Other types of units	Total	State-owned units	Collectively owned units	Other types of ownership	Total	State-owned units	Collectively owned units	Other types of ownership
1978	615	644	506	–	314	284	30	–	30.3	26.2	68.3	–
1980	762	803	623	–	816	638	178	–	12.8	12.6	13.6	–
1985	1148	1213	967	1436	1,637	1,165	467	5	7.5	7.7	7.1	8.8
1986	1329	1414	1092	1629	1,805	1,303	496	6	7.1	7.2	6.9	9.2
1987	1459	1546	1207	1879	1,968	1,424	538	6	6.7	6.8	6.5	12.0
1988	1747	1853	1429	2382	2,120	1,544	568	8	6.4	6.5	6.2	12.1
1989	1935	2055	1557	2707	2,201	1,629	562	10	6.2	6.2	6.2	13.2
1990	2140	2284	1681	2987	2,301	1,742	566	11	6.1	6.0	6.3	14.9
1991	2340	2477	1866	3468	2,433	1,833	588	12	6.0	5.8	6.2	17.3
1992	2711	2878	2109	3966	2,598	1,972	609	17	5.7	5.5	5.9	16.6
1993	3371	3532	2592	4966	2,780	2,143	596	41	5.4	5.1	5.7	13.1
1994	4538	4797	3245	6303	2,929	2,249	619	60	5.1	4.8	5.2	12.5
1995	5500	5625	3931	7463	3,094	2,401	621	72	4.8	4.6	5.0	12.2
1996	6210	6280	4302	8261								
1997	6470	6747	4512	8789								
1998	7479	7668	5331	8972								

Source: *Zhongguo Tongji Nianjian 1996* [China Statistical Yearbook 1996] (Beijing: Zhongguo tongji chubanshe, 1996), 737.

We first need to acknowledge that not all Chinese retirees failed to receive their pension payments. This problem arose only in relatively poor-performing enterprises and in poor regions. Better-performing enterprises or better-off regions could still afford to pay their retired workers. With the increasing divide between the haves and have-nots, it was a logical choice for the state to create a system that could pool the risks and resources of both the under-performing and better-performing enterprises and also the poor and more prosperous areas. In search of viable options to both finance and sustain pension benefits, the first strategy adopted by the Chinese state was to consolidate the existing pension schemes. The central government strategically expanded the pension scheme to include those whose participation would raise the fund reserves. Including workers in private-owned and foreign-owned firms was the most important strategic choice made by the central government to minimize the costs of the program and to lessen the state's burden. As shown in Table 8.2, the average incomes of workers in the non-state-owned enterprises were much higher than those of workers in the state-owned and collective-owned enterprises. Also, the ratio of current pensioners to current employees was much lower in the private sector, making employees of private firms a perfect set of benefactors to be included in the social insurance scheme.[29]

The two-tiered pension scheme, which reflected the incorporation of the social pooling fund (*shehui tongchou zijin*) with the individual savings fund (*geren zhanghu*), requires some explanation. This combination does not entirely fit with the socialization approach. The social pooling fund reflects the mechanism of risk redistribution whereas the individual savings account does not. Because by law the savings account belongs to the individual program participant, it is the narrowest form of social security and does not serve any redistributive purposes. The second deviation concerned the level of the scheme integration. Ideally, pension fund pooling would be centralized at the national level to maximize its redistributive effect. But the government regulations apply only to provincial-level scheme consolidation. Although this is a great improvement from the previous enterprise-based pension schemes, it does not seem to adequately meet the demands of state leaders regarding minimizing financial involvement in the program. To understand why the Chinese state decided to opt for these specific choices, we

29 In fact, the Chinese government also sought to restructure the funding mechanism of the system from the implicit state-funded method (in the disguised form of the state's guarantee of pension payments to workers by their SOEs) to a contribution-based method that included the insurers as contributors. In doing so, the central government limited its financial responsibility and its responsibility for pension-fund subsidies.

need to look at the reactions of the relevant groups of societal actors and state agents, particularly the local authorities, to explain these deviant outcomes in the pension reform plan.

In the late 1990s, the State Council suggested that individual savings might not be necessary to increase national savings. The saving rates in China are relatively high compared to those of other major countries. In comparison to the United States where the savings ratio is only about 15 percent of the gross domestic product, China has a 40 percent national savings rate. According to my interviews, individual savings accounts have to remain because they attract workers' participation in the program. Workers are given a sense of control at least over their own contributions, which motivates them to remain in the state-offered pension scheme.[30] Although the state has not achieved the best-case scenario for having only a social pooled fund, this is better than completely losing the potential benefactors of the program. Without the individual savings accounts that have no resource- or risk-sharing mechanisms, the state would find it difficult to gain the participation of the segment of society it sought to subsidize the pension program.

The existence of a societal divide along the private and public urban sectors with regard to pension reform in China implies that there is a cross-class alliance between workers and their employers within the same sector. Throughout the 1980s and the 1990s, there have been reports of cross-class conflicts between workers and their enterprises regarding delays or avoidance of pension payments and other welfare benefits, in both the private and public sectors. Protests by retirees throughout the country serve as key evidence of how business owners have mistreated their employees. However, on the particular issue of extending coverage and integrating pension funds, employers and employees seemed to have formed alliances along sectoral lines. It is widely thought that workers in the private sector did not inform the authorities when employers missed pension payments to the designated agencies in their areas. The unwillingness of the workers to file complaints may have stemmed from a fear of repercussions from their employers. They may also have believed that there was nothing to be gained from joining the old-age insurance scheme. The individual savings accounts were created in order to break, or at least to weaken, the coalition between workers and employers in the private sector. As workers have exclusive ownership of their individual accounts, they are quick to insist that pension-related deposits be put in their accounts by their employers.

Beijing's "ideal plan" met with more resistance from the local authorities than from societal groups, with provincial government leaders at the

---

30 Author's interview, December 16, 2004.

forefront. Social policy experts and government technocrats alike agreed that in terms of redistribution the pooling of pension funds would be best at the national level.[31] But there have also been debates highlighting the downsides of this national integration option as well as the timeframe for implementation. Although some observers point to the massive population of the country as one of the reasons why the central government cannot implement a nationally integrated pension scheme, one of my informants at the Ministry of Labor and Social Security (MoLSS) reported that this was not the main reason. He believed that China possesses the capabilities and skills to successfully implement a nationally integrated pension scheme. But in his opinion what prevented the country from integrating the scheme was the huge gap between the provinces and regions in terms of socio-economic structure and performance.[32]

I argue that the decision to deviate from the "ideal plan" of national integration of the pension scheme occurred primarily as a result of conflicts among provincial authorities regarding their social policy preferences. In Table 8.3, I use per capita annual income data and the age dependency ratio of each province to show the provincial diversities in terms of level of income and probable social policy expenses. I further group these provincial-level statistics into three regions: eastern, central, and western. In 1994, the average per capita annual income in the eastern region was more than two times higher than that in the central or western regions. With regard to level of income, the eastern provinces would not be willing to participate in fund pooling with the central and western regions. Based on information from one of my interviewees in the MoLSS, the eastern provinces were most strongly opposed to national unified pension fund pooling.[33] However, data on the age dependency ratio, which illustrate the likelihood of the level of social policy expenses for each province and region, weaken this argument. The level of social policy expenses were positively correlated with the level of income in all three regions. The eastern region had the highest income per capita but also ranked number one in terms of the dependency ratio. In contrast, the western region had the lowest income per capita but also had the lowest dependency ratio. The high social policy expenses in the eastern provinces seem to suggest that those in the eastern region were willing to share the risks and resources, even in moderation, with other sectors that exhibited lower cost-related trends. Perhaps the eastern provinces were

31 Author's interviews, November 12, 2004 and December 20, 2004; World Bank, *China: Reforming Social Security in a Socialist Economy* (Washington, DC, 1990).

32 Author's interview, November 12, 2004.

33 Author's interview, December 11, 2004.

TABLE 8.3

Per Capita Annual Income and Age Dependency Ratio, by Region, 1994

Eastern	Per Capita Annual Income	Age Dependency Ratio (65+)	Welfare Funds (100 million yuan)
Shanghai	7555.89	18.01	161.5
Beijing	4417.85	11.96	88.3
Tianjin	3383.85	12.62	48.3
Jiangsu	2613.54	13.29	136.6
Guangdong	2450.21	12.14	153.8
Zhejiang	2443.99	12.52	80.5
Liaoning	2099.40	10.21	127.0
Hainan	1753.22	9.59	12.5
Shandong	1682.5	11.97	103.3
Fujian	1674.75	11.86	35.2
Hebei	1442.48	10.39	90.3
Guangxi	842.88	11.55	41.6
Regional Average	2696.71	12.18	89.9

Central	Per Capita Annual Income	Age Dependency Ratio (65+)	Welfare Funds (100 million yuan)
Heilongjiang	1541.01	6.93	85.9
Jilin	1456.39	9.09	46.6
Hubei	1341.40	10.39	70.4
Shaanxi	1186.92	10.12	38.8
Inner Mongolia	1112.49	7.69	38.1
Jiangxi	1106.78	10.20	34.6
Anhui	1047.83	11.69	52.9
Henan	1019.15	10.58	72.3
Hunan	977.06	11.34	74.4
Regional Average	1198.78	9.78	57.11

Western	Per Capita Annual Income	Age Dependency Ratio (65+)	Welfare Funds (100 million yuan)
Xinjiang	1456.63	7.72	44.5
Qinghai	1055.46	7.63	11.3
Gansu	1041.97	8.67	29.9
Ningxia	1020.06	6.13	8.3
Sichuan	985.39	11.91	128.4
Yunnan	942.46	9.59	53.7
Tibet	930.86	8.84	2.7
Shanxi	853.27	9.61	45.2
Guizhou	609.80	8.65	23.7
Regional Average	988.43	8.75	38.63

Source: Zhongguo Tongji Nianjian 1995 [China Statistical Yearbook 1995] (Beijing: Zhongguo tongji chubanshe, 1995).

unwilling to participate in the broader fund pooling because of unequal income levels and social policy expenses. In other words, the fact that other regions had lower-cost social policy expenses may be an inadequate offset for their much lower income levels.

My main argument regarding the unwillingness of provincial-level authorities in the eastern region to participate in an integrated scheme at the national level centers on the common knowledge among both central leaders and provincial authorities about why the goal was a national pension fund. In order to minimize its monetary contributions to the program, the government in Beijing searched for an alternative pool of funds available outside of its own budget. Existing labor and welfare funds in each locality were a perfect such source. The reform of the pension-related funding arrangement implied that any changes would take the existing system into account. For the Chinese central government, integration did not simply mean that the participants in different pooled funds would then submit their contributions to a newly-established unified pension fund pool. The new system called for the past contributions of insurers in local pension schemes to be transferred to the unified fund pool. By claiming existing resources, the central government maximized the redistributive effect of the integrated social insurance scheme. The strategy of transferring existing pooled funds from lower-level administrative units had been employed earlier when the CCP recommended a way for provincial authorities to "provincialize" the pension system and merge all city-, county-, and enterprise-level pooled funds. Therefore, the provincial authorities seemed to have a good idea of what would happen if scheme consolidation were to take place at the national level.

As shown in the columns on welfare funds in Table 8.3, the eastern region has the highest average amount of welfare-related reserves. Because of its highest age dependency ratio, the provinces in this region began to focus on solving the old-age security crisis before other regions. In the early 1980s, the central government transferred welfare-related responsibilities to the local governments as part of the package attached to the fiscal decentralization. Even though the local authorities had decision-making autonomy over the resources retained at the local levels, they had to fulfill the basic duties assigned to them by the central government. The Soviet-style political appointment evaluation system, a so-called *nomenklatura* system, remained under the auspices of the central state.[34]

34 John P. Burns, ed., *The Chinese Communist Party's Nomenklatura System: A Documentary Study of Party Control of Leadership Selection, 1979–1984* (Armonk, NY: M.E. Sharpe, 1989) and John P. Burns, "Strengthening Central CCP Control of Leadership Selection: The 1990 *Nomenklatura*," *China Quarterly*, no. 138 (June 1994): 458–91.

The protests by retirees against their SOEs have had a great impact, both politically and financially, on the local governments in the areas where the protests have taken place. The potential for social disorder alarmed the local authorities because it could endanger their careers. It then became the responsibility of the local governments to ensure that the delayed pension payments by the SOEs in their areas would not lead to public discontent that the central state might view as a source of regime instability. In addition, a tight-knit corporate-style relationship between the administrative authorities and the SOEs in their respective jurisdictions was common.[35] The following example is indicative of how these factors came together. As cited in Hurst and O'Brien, waves of protest in Shenyang, the capital of Liaoning province, over the halt of retirement benefits led municipal finance and labor departments to step in and provide a bailout of 240 million yuan.[36] This was because cities like Shenyang had sufficient funds to dispense and the central government hoped to merge all these existing funds into a national pool and use these resources to subsidize other provinces and regions. However, it is for this same reason that local authorities in the eastern provinces were reluctant to participate in a broader fund-pooling scheme, even though there was a greater share of the elderly in their administrative territories than the other regions.

The central state's inability to force the compliance of relevant actors helps explain why the CCP leaders adopted policies that deviated from an ideal social security program based on a socialization approach. The "eating in separate kitchen" policy left survival in the hands of the individual enterprise and the government body at each administrative level to fend for itself. Before the issuance of the 1990s unified regulations on the pension reform, some municipalities such as Shanghai and Beijing had already established a relatively sound system of pension fund pooling to redistribute risks and resources among the enterprises within their jurisdiction. As presented in Table 8.3, the amount of reserved welfare funds in these localities was significant. Although these provided a good model for the central state, it was constrained from further promoting integration of the scheme in the provinces. These municipalities feared that integration of the pension reforms would destabilize their respective systems. In addition, they had more

35 This kind of patron-client relationship also takes place in the rural areas; see Jean C. Oi, "Fiscal Reform and the Economic Foundations of Local State Corporatism in China," *World Politics* 45, no. 1 (October 1992): 99–126 and Jean C. Oi, *Rural China Takes Off: Institutional Foundations of Economic Reform* (Berkeley: University of California Press, 1999).

36 Hurst and O'Brien, "China's Contentious Pensioners," 349.

to gain from controlling the welfare funds exclusively on their own as they then could borrow the resources to fund public projects and make profitable investments that created economic growth and promoted social stability in their respective jurisdictions. Exclusive rights over the use of welfare funds simultaneously helped advance the local leaders' careers and boosted their incomes.[37]

The fiscal decentralization implemented during the early 1980s limited the central government's ability to integrate the pension system at the national level because of weak central control over the collection and administration of local financial resources. In the past, China did not have a centralized revenue collection system and Beijing relied on the local authorities to collect taxes and to hand over a portion to the central levels. Naturally, this created serious problems of leakage and misreporting.[38] When the central government decided to reform the national tax system in 1994, it had to create a separate agency to collect taxes for the center in order to avoid conflicts of interest with the localities. I argue that the Chinese central state could have treated the pension collection system in the same manner as it handled the tax reform. But it would have been unlikely that it could have appropriated the existing fund reserves, at least not in their entirety. Its lack of control over the social welfare funds, coupled with incomplete information about the amount of welfare funds that actually existed in the deposit accounts and the amount that had been used for investments, put the central state at a disadvantage vis-à-vis the local authorities. It is possible that had the central government decided to merge all locally administered welfare funds, the local authorities would have used up all their funds and turned in only a fraction of the actual amount. The CCP has already learned this lesson. In 1998, in an attempt to promote a provincially integrated pension scheme, the central government ordered large state corporations to turn in their occupational-based welfare funds, which they had administered since the early 1990s, to the provincial authorities where the enterprises were located. However, only 4 billion yuan, out of an estimated total of 14.7 billion yuan of occupational-based pension funds, ended up in the hands of the provincial authorities.[39]

37 Mark Selden and Laiyin You, "The Reform of Social Welfare in China," *World Development* 25, no. 10 (1997): 1957–68.

38 Christine P.W. Wong, "Central-Local Relations in an Era of Fiscal Decline: The Paradox of Fiscal Decentralization in China," *China Quarterly*, no. 128 (December 1991): 691–715.

39 Mark W. Frazier, "After Pension Reform: Navigating the 'Third Rail' in China," *Studies in Comparative International Development* 39, no. 2 (Summer 2004): 55-56.

The Politics of Health Insurance Reform in China

Despite comparable outcomes, the reform of China's health insurance system took on a separate life from pension reform. What distinguishes the health insurance system reform is that it did not pose political and fiscal threats to the Chinese state to the same degree as the old-age pension system. Unlike pension benefits that most disgruntled workers regarded as a core element in their social contract with the state, medical insurance was not perceived as such. The stark differences between the nature of health insurance provisions and pension provisions may help explain the differences in terms of workers' expectations. Workers can manage to pay for their own medical expenses as long as they are employed and receive incomes. Retirees, however, do not have such a luxury; their retired life depends entirely on the pension benefits they receive from the state. This idea conforms to the "social contract" concept that applies to most welfare rights subsistence claims. A survey conducted in Benxi, Datong, Chongqing, Shanghai, and Beijing shows that, "pensions take precedence over most other grievances because they are a symbolic recognition by the state and firm of an employee's years of devoted service as well as a vital source of support for those who are too old to work."[40] Even though I did not conduct a detailed survey of workers' attitudes, there is reason to believe that they do not consider health care as a part of their "social contract." Among the protests documented by scholars as well as by the Chinese authorities, there are no reports of demonstrations demanding that health insurance benefits be provided by the state.[41] This does not mean that workers do not hope to receive various kinds of additional welfare benefits, including health insurance; however, protesting for these types of welfare provisions, which the state does not consider as part of their subsistence claims, involves greater risk. There is a higher probability that the government will crack down on such protests and consider them to be "non-rightful resistance."[42]

From the perspective of the authorities, China's health insurance benefits are ranked low as subsistence rights due to their belief that the financial crisis in the system of medical provision was a result of over-consumption, corruption, and waste because of workers' use of free health services.[43] In

40 Hurst and O'Brien, "China's Contentious Pensioners," 350.

41 Hurst and O'Brien, "China's Contentious Pensioners," 346.

42 For cost-benefit analyses of the decision to protest, see, for example, the detailed study by Yungshun Cai, *The State and Laid-off Workers in Reform China: The Silence and Collective Action of the Retrenched* (London: Routledge, 2006).

43 Gu, "Market Transition and the Transformation of the Health Care System in Urban China," 197–215.

order to cope with the rising costs, the central government initiated a series of reform policies for medical enterprises that focused mainly on lowering costs, which otherwise would have been a financial burden on the state.
These reform policies included: 1) encouraging medical facilities to operate like private firms, 2) controlling in-budget medical expenses, and 3) developing a co-payment system whereby patients were required to share the
costs of medical expenditures. These reform policies required simultaneous
implementation in order to be effective in curbing overall expenditures in the
health sector. First, medical facilities that formerly were run under the central planning system were encouraged to become financially independent.
Under this decentralization policy, the state gradually scaled back its role
in funding medical facilities and personnel. Hospital revenue and salaries
increasingly relied on the costs of services and prescribed drugs. As SOEs
subsidized the medical expenditures of urban workers, the state faced yet
another challenge. These self-financing medical facilities had incentives to
provide excessive services and drugs in order to maximize their incomes. As
a result, the SOEs paid more for employees who received medical treatment.
Indirectly, this phenomenon affected government expenditures because SOE
losses tended to be underwritten by the state. Edward Gu estimates that
the proportion of health care expenditures paid by the enterprise-based free
health care system increased rapidly from about 3.5 percent of total government spending in the 1980s to about 10 percent in the mid-1990s.[44] To deal
with the problem of medical practitioners overcharging for services and prescriptions drugs, the central government issued a list of drugs that patients
were required to purchase on their own. According to a World Bank report,
out-of-pocket payments rose from 20 percent of the revenue in the health
sector in 1978 to 26 percent in 1986 and to 42 percent in 1993. In turn, health
care spending as a share of the government budget dropped from 32 percent
in 1986 to 14 percent in 1993.[45]

Beginning with the pilot reforms in 1994-98, the CCP decided to implement health insurance system reforms in the same way it had introduced
pension system reforms with a focus on capping the costs of the system.[46]
The outcome of the health insurance reform resembles that of the pension
reform both in terms of scheme consolidation and coverage extension; but

44 Gu, "Market Transition and the Transformation of the Health Care System," 206.

45 World Bank. *Financing Health Care: Issues and Options for China* (Washington,
DC, 1997).

46 To control the rising costs in the health care sector, the reform concurrently focused on three areas: hospitals and medical facilities, drugs and medication, and the
health insurance system. Author's interview, December 11, 2004.

the government placed a greater emphasis on lowering the costs of medical services. From the state's perspective, pension benefits are the responsibility of the state but health-related expenditures are the responsibility of the individual.[47] As a consequence, the new health insurance program provides basic medical expenses but the maximum reimbursement is limited to 40 percent of the patient's annual wage. On average, patients in China pay 60.6 percent of their total medical costs out of their own pockets. According to a survey conducted in Wuhan, an associate professor, who belongs to a group considered to have some of the most generous health insurance benefits, was responsible for 72 percent of his total medical expenses after he was admitted to a local hospital for ten nights of treatment for a broken leg.[48] Unlike the pension benefits, the central state rarely funds the medical insurance system, with the exception of limited subsidies to keep the prices of certain medications at a controlled level.[49]

Without imminent political and fiscal pressures, the CCP was not hard-pressed to increase the redistributive effect of the reform by further integrating the health insurance program and expanding it more broadly. In addition to the less threatening political and funding pressures, strong resistance from policy agents to consolidation of the health insurance schemes further explains why medical funds were pooled at lower administrative levels than pension funds. In the mid-1990s, health insurance schemes were arranged throughout the country based on the "two jiangs" model. At least 50 cities had reportedly set up health insurance programs.[50] Unlike pension programs where two major parties are involved, e.g., pension fund managers and pension benefit recipients, health insurance programs also involve medical providers. To make the system work, a business network needs to be established between those who provide the medical treatment and benefits and the program administrators. In China, the medical providers are mainly hospitals and medical facilities and the managers of the health insurance funds are the local authorities, both of whom constitute the insured as designated by the state.

47 Author's interview, December 20, 2004.
48 Author's interview, December 23, 2004.
49 Author's interview, December 16, 2004.
50 The "two Jiangs" model, two 1994–97 successful experimental schemes in Jiujiang of Jiangxi province, later became the basis for the unified guidelines for the reform of national health insurance. For details, see Hans J. Rosner, "China's Health Insurance System in Transformation: Preliminary Assessment and Policy Suggestions," *International Social Security Review* 57, no. 3: 65–90; Edward X. Gu, "Market Transition and the Transformation of the Healthcare System in Urban China," *Policy Studies* 22, no. 3–4 (September 2004): 197–215; and Jane Duckett, "State Collectivism and Worker Privilege: A Study of Urban Health Insurance Reform," *China Quarterly*, no. 177 (March 2004): 155–73.

In the case of China's health insurance reform, state agents, specifically those in the medical profession, covertly led a resistance against the reform. Public medical facilities have increasingly been run like private firms and their main revenue is now derived from providing services and drug prescriptions. At present, only 30-40 percent of doctors' salaries come from government coffers. It was in their interest, especially the interests of those in affluent areas, to oppose health insurance system reform because it threatened their incomes. From my interviews I discovered that the areas where health insurance schemes have been set up are quite healthy; the relatively high-income levels in those areas made such an arrangement possible.[51] Their vested interests in the existing arrangement obstructed any further consolidation beyond the county or city levels. Hospitals and related staff in these affluent areas did not want to participate in a broader integrated system for fear that sharing the risks with the poorer areas would make them worse off.[52]

The Transitional System

The first episode of the reform that relied mainly on fiscal decentralization widened the socio-economic gap and exacerbated the administrative capacity of the central government vis-à-vis the other actors. This resulted in limiting social security reform in the late 1990s, especially the pension reform. As a consequence, there were two major problems:

Empty accounts, the first sign of an unsustainable pension program, pose a serious challenge to the CCP party-state. The separate individual savings accounts are supposed to give the newly-added participants greater incentives not to evade the submission of premiums to the authorities. Although the regulations stipulating that these two accounts should remain separate and the individual savings accounts belong to the particular beneficiary, they did not prevent the use of individual accounts for current pension payments to retired workers. This practice resulted in widespread "empty" individual accounts (*kong zhanghu*). According to an estimate by the head of the MoLSS, in 2004 more than 190 billion yuan had been taken out of the individual retirement accounts to subsidize current pension payments.[53] Public concern about the "empty accounts raised central government awareness about local government abuses. To combat the problem,

---

51 Author's interview, November 17, 2004.

52 Author's interview, November 17, 2004.

53 Zhang Zhouji, "Guanyu Shehui Baozhang Tixi Jianshe Wenti" [On the Question of the Construction of a Social Security System], *Zhonggong Zhongyang Dangxiao Baogao Xuan* [Selections from Reports of the Central Party School of the Chinese Communist Party], no. 10 (May 2004): 1–11.

in 2000 the central government issued State Council Document No. 42 to provide guidelines to the provincial authorities. In essence, the document calls for the separate management of social pooling funds and individual accounts, thus social pooling funds would no longer be able to borrow from the individual accounts.[54] At the same time, the central government decided to carry out a trial of this newly revised policy in Liaoning province to test the waters. A preliminary study of Shenyang by the Social Security Research Office of Peking University in June 2003 indicated that the experiment to prevent cross-subsidization between social pooling funds and individual accounts thus far had been successful because of the large amount of financial support from the central and local treasuries. In 2002, financial subsidies totaled more than 900 million yuan.[55] From this study, it seems clear that for the central government to maintain the current level of pension subsidies, it cannot abandon the implicit borrowing from the individual accounts to fund the current pension payments unless either the central or the local governments are able to find alternative financial sources.

Because a national old-age pension system is yet to be established and the country currently relies on provincial-level pension fund pooling, there is no redistribution of resources between the well-performing provinces or regions and the poor-performing regions. This has created the problem of financial inadequacies in certain localities. Under these circumstances, the central government has had no choice but to subsidize these localities. Because the pension reform regulations are enforced nationwide, the Ministry of Finance has had to subsidize the nation's old-age pensions by more than 30 billion yuan per year,[56] and this amount seems to increase annually.[57] Based on information received by the MoLSS, only seven provinces or provincial-level municipalities all located in the eastern area of the country—Beijing, Shanghai, Guangdong, Zhejiang, Jiangsu, Shandong, and Fujian—did not receive any pension-related subsidies from the central government.[58] Since the pension reform began in the mid-1990s, the central government has already spent 50,000 million yuan on subsidies.[59]

54 Nelson Chow and Yuebin Xu, "Pension Reform in China," in Catherine Jones Finer, ed., *Social Policy Reform in China: Views from Home and Abroad* (Aldershot: Ashgate, 2003), 129–42.

55 Social Security Research Office, *Shenyangshi Yanglao Baoxian Gaige Shidian Qingkuang Kaocha Baogao* [A Preliminary Study of the Experiment in Pension System Reform in Shenyang City] (Beijing: Beijing daxue chubanshe, 2003).

56 Mark O'Neil, "Early Retirement Swells China Pension-fund Deficit to $33 Billion," *South China Morning Post,* June 25, 2001.

57 Author's interview, December 11, 2004.

58 Author's interview, December 11, 2004.

59 Author's interview, December 11, 2004.

The central government has recently become greatly concerned about its increased spending as well as about the incentives in place for provincial authorities to free-ride off the subsidies provided by the center. According to my interviews, although the State Council has decided to continue increasing central annual subsidies to the provinces for the next several years, the rate of growth of the subsidies should be slower than in the past. Also, the central government has decided to add a criterion that will raise the amount of subsidies based on an assessment of the provincial authorities' improvements to their own pension programs during the previous year. This adjustment is an attempt to encourage each local government, which formerly had depended on state subsidies, to improve its own funding collection system. Hopefully, this will lower the state's financial burden in the future.[60] In addition, the criteria for determining the amount of central subsidies have also changed. In previous years, the amount was calculated based on the income level of the respective province as well as the number of recipients. Foreseeing the continuation of pension subsidies to the poor provinces, in 2000 the central government set up the National Social Security Fund as a source of funding separate from the general state revenue, by selling state-owned assets.[61] In his chapter in this volume, Walter discusses how the state attempted to sell state shares on the market to fund this institution. Other financial means, such as issuing lotteries for welfare fund support, are also encouraged.

Conclusion

Four main points can be taken away from this chapter. First, to facilitate corporate restructuring in China, the country's firm-based social security system must be reformed. However, the outcome of the reform cannot be determined solely by complementing corporate governance. In fact, it will be determined by three additional factors: political pressure, fiscal austerity, and the administrative capacity of the state. Second, the struggles over budget allocations and fiscal responsibilities between the central and local authorities and among the local authorities have had the most salient impact on the outcome of the reform. There are also struggles between the various business sectors that over time have developed distinctive demographic and economic profiles, particularly between the public and private sectors. Third, the way the economic reforms were sequenced in China had an unintended negative impact on the deepening of the national social security system. This is not to say that the Chinese government made a terrible mistake.

---

60 Author's interview, December 11, 2004.

61 *Renmin Ribao* [People's Daily], September 25, 2000; Author's interview, December 11, 2004.

After all, we need to remember that this outcome should be weighed against other concerns of the state, especially when considering that in order to take off China's once-stagnant economy needed a big boost. Finally, the reform requires a transitional strategy. Financial resources must be subsidized by the central government at least, I would argue, until the socio-economic conditions in China are more equalized.

In some senses, the corporate-based social security system in China does not differ much from the systems in Japan or South Korea in terms of the institutional forms of social insurance. The latter two East Asian countries, despite different economic and political systems, also rely predominantly on corporate-based social security institutions.[62] Therefore, the success of corporate restructuring in all three countries hinges in part on the complementarities of their social security reforms. Based on this preliminary comparison, it is possible that we cannot explain the outcome of the reform based solely on the political system. I do not argue that the political system does not matter. However, its impact may be more subtle and indirect than is assumed and we may need to consider additional variables, such as the socio-economic profiles of the participants in the different corporate-based funds and the administrative control of the state over these funds.

62 For comparison, see the papers by Ito Peng on the social safety net in South Korea and by Sarah Ingmanson on the social safety net (pension) in Japan, prepared for the Conference on System Restructuring in East Asia, Stanford Center for East Asian Studies in collaboration with the Shorenstein Asia-Pacific Research Center, Stanford University, June 22–24, 2006.

9 Stock Markets and Corporate Reform

A PANDORA'S BOX OF UNINTENDED CONSEQUENCES

Carl E. Walter

China's stock markets were formally established in late 1990 when corporate restructuring was in its early stages. With unsecured private property rights and a government determined to maintain the primacy of the state-owned sector, their very existence unavoidably opened up a Pandora's Box of conflicts and problems that have grown in number and severity. Even worse, the operation of the markets over time came to reflect and deepen the rifts between levels of government and between major agencies in government as all sought access to the capital that could be provided by the stock markets. These divisions were manifested in business disputes over the ownership and disposal of state assets that inevitably led to political factionalism. By the beginning of the twenty-first century this struggle over capital was a key issue on the country's political agenda as China's politics became monetized.

This chapter argues that powerful business groups (*jituan*) formed around key government agencies[1] as the latter developed stakes in the stock markets. By the end of the 1990s these groups controlled massive amounts of capital and could easily hijack those parts of the government policy process that threatened their interests. Such actions set back critically needed stock market reforms. Equally important, because these institutions were intimately linked, these problems with the stock market further affected other policy

[1] The People's Bank of China (PBOC), China Securities Regulatory Commission (CSRC), Ministry of Finance (MOF), State Administration of State-owned Assets Commission (SASAC), and National Development and Reform Commission (NDRC), to name but a few.

areas necessary for effective corporate restructuring. This theme is evident in a close examination of what happened to the stock market during two events that took place during the 2001–5 period. The first was the collapse of the stock market in 2001 after the failure of a policy initiative that tried to use the stock market to help fund China's National Social Security Fund (NSSF). The second was the collapse of the market in an effort to transform the bankrupted Chinese securities industry in 2005.

Findings from this study will help shed light on whether the collapse of the market in 2001 and of the securities industry in 2005 were the result primarily of inadequate institutional infrastructure, i.e., institutional complementarity, or the result of other factors. The analysis shows how well-endowed political actors, all with significant central and local government connectivity, captured the markets and perverted their role in the economy. In this environment, a struggle arose between a group of reformists who sought a restructuring of the entire securities industry and an array of institutional market participants who sought to protect their own business interests. This ended with the defeat of the reformers and the restoration of the status quo, which continues until today. Neither have the stock markets been truly reformed, nor has the problem of inadequate funding for the NSSF been resolved.

I begin by first examining the reasons why stock markets became a necessary supplement to the banking system, both in terms of providing capital, but also as a means of corporate restructuring. This is important because it makes clear the mixed agendas that were in place from the start as the stock markets were created. A key point is that the state adopted stock markets to limit privatization rather than as a way to completely open the economy to market forces. Understanding these interests helps explain why the stock markets subsequently experienced so many problems that had little to do with the actual performance of the firms listed on the exchanges. This also makes sense of the two classes of shares—those that could be traded and those that were non-tradable. The issue of state shares, what they were, who actually owned them, and how they should interact with the tradable shares has deeply shaped the evolution of China's stock market to this day.

Why Did China Need Stock Markets?

Why would China's government in 1990 decide to open stock markets at a time when the very topic was inevitably an object of political and ideological contention? The Shanghai Exchange opened just eighteen months after the June 4 tragedy in the midst of a malicious debate about whether the reforms of the 1980s belonged to "Mr. Capitalism" or to "Mr. Socialism." China's Big Four banks provided the vast majority of capital to China's state-owned sector and to this day continue to dwarf the financing role of the stock and corporate debt markets. So the reason for establishing stock markets does not seem to have been related to political expediency or the capital requirements of the SOEs. Rather, the reason for establishing this capitalist market can be found in a debate about the sources of the dismal SOE performance in the 1980s.[2] China needed a more effective way to enforce financial discipline and achieve better enterprise performance. Banks had failed in this task.

Why Banks Could Not Change Corporate Performance

Banks and bank lending alone could not bring about changes in corporate behavior in China for three principal reasons. First, in spite of various reforms, banks continued as an administrative arm of the state that was incapable of enforcing financial discipline on firms. Second, banks were subject to local government intervention in directing bank lending. Third, even had the banks been run efficiently and professionally, bank lending by itself could not promote corporate reform.

The Framework of the Banking System. From 1979 to 1993 the government attempted to rebuild and strengthen the banking sector, first by moving away from the Soviet model, where banks were purely an administrative arm of the state, and second by attempting to insulate banks from local influence over lending decisions. The inflationary experiences of 1987–88 and 1992–95 when bank lending continued to be a major factor in driving inflation demonstrated all too well that these attempts had not worked (see Table 9.1).

In late 1993 the State Council announced the "Decision on Reform of the Financial System," marking an abrupt departure from the Soviet-style system. Based on this decision, in mid-1995 two new laws were put into effect—the "Central Bank Law" and the "Commercial Bank Law." These laws provided the foundation for a Western-style central bank and a system of state banks operating on a commercial basis. At the same time, three policy banks were created to assume the policy loans that had been

---

2 Wu Jinglian, *Dangdai Zhongguo Jingji Gaige* [Modern China's Economic Reforms] (Shanghai: Shanghai yuandong chubanshe, 2004), 142–43 and 74–75.

TABLE 9.1

Table 9.1 Inflation versus Bank Lending, 1981–1994

	Retail Price Percent Inflation	Total Bank Loans (RMB bn)	Percent Change YoY	Big 4 Percent of Total
1981	2.4	296	19.0	96.6
1982	1.9	330	12.0	96.4
1983	1.5	375	14.0	95.7
1984	2.8	512	37.0	93.2
1985	8.8	631	23.0	93.7
1986	6.0	840	33.0	90.4
1987	7.3	1,030	24.0	87.7
1988	18.5	1,222	19.0	86.3
1989	17.8	1,436	18.0	86.4
1990	21.0	1,768	23.0	85.8
1991	2.9	2,134	21.0	84.5
1992	5.4	2,632	23.0	82.1
1993	13.2	3,294	25.0	81.4
1994	21.7	4,081	24.0	81.0

Source: *Zhongguo Tongji Nianjian* [China Statistical Yearbook] (Beijing: Zhongguo tongji chubanshe, various years).

extended by existing banks. However, events during the remainder of the decade showed that this new structure was no better than the old.

In 1999, as a result of the Asian financial crisis (AFC), the four state banks—Bank of China (BOC), China Construction Bank (CCB), Industrial and Commercial Bank of China (ICBC), and Agricultural Bank of China (ABC)—were recapitalized by a RMB270 billion Ministry of Finance (MOF) bond issue. At the same time, a total of RMB1.6 trillion ($200 billion) of problem loans was identified and transferred to asset management companies (AMCs), also funded by the MOF through an additional injection of RMB40 billion, along with the People's Bank of China (PBOC), which provided some RMB1.6 billion in credit lines.[3] Despite these efforts to clean the bank books of problem loans, at the end of 2004 the four banks continued to have RMB1.7 trillion ($2.1 billion) in bad loans on their books, or 15.6 percent of their total loan portfolios, still an excessive level.[4] Independent

3 Li Liming and Zeng Renxiong, *1979–2006 Zhongguo Jinrong Da Biange* [The Great Transformation of China's Banking Sector 1979–2006] (Shanghai: Shanghai renmin chubanshe, 2007), ch. 3.

4 Wu Jinglian, *Dangdai Zhongguo Jingji Gaige*, 218. The fourth of the Big Four, the ABC, was still undergoing restructuring in 2009.

sources, however, estimated the total to be over RMB5.3 trillion ($500 billion) and a later report, which the PBOC forced the issuing firm to withdraw, concluded the total was RMB7.2 trillion ($900 billion).[5] The size of these figures can be seen as a reflection of the strength of local governments in directing loans. These losses, in effect, represented the amount of local budget deficits funded by bank lending.

Local Government Staffing Authority.   Since 1979 effective bank reform has been plagued by the weak supervisory function of the PBOC. For most of their history, the senior managers of the provincial PBOCs and state commercial bank branches were named by the local party committees. Even after 1995 when the banks were supposedly acting as for-profit economic actors, in reality banks at all local levels were still thoroughly co-opted by the local party in its drive for economic growth.[6] Some real change came as part of the post–Asian financial crisis banking system cleanup. On January 1, 1999 the PBOC adopted a regional system modeled after that of the U.S. Federal Reserve Bank.[7] At that time, the PBOC's organization departed from China's post-1949 administrative system, but there was no significant change in the organization of the commercial banks. So the commercial lending operations of the banking system continued to be vulnerable to political influence, as events clearly showed in the first half of 2009.

Capital Mobilization Limitations of Bank Lending.   Even without local government interference, there was an additional factor that limited the effect of bank lending: scale. Because banks had always been organized along the lines of the administrative hierarchy reaching to Beijing, their deposit base was geographically circumscribed. When the PBOC spun off the ICBC in 1984 it exited from normal banking operations, with the result that provincial bank

5 PricewaterhouseCoopers estimated RMB4.0 trillion in bad loans at the end of 2004; Standard & Poor's estimated RMB5.3 trillion for the same period; and most recently KPMG, in a similar report, estimated RMB7.2 trillion. An excerpt of the KPMG data is cited in Min Xu, "Resolution of Nonperforming Loans in China," Stern School of Business, New York University, 2008.

6 Wu Jinglian, *Dangdai Zhongguo Jingji Gaige*, 212. After the 1988 round of inflation, there was a flurry of measures to centralize the PBOC staffing decisions. For these measures, see Wu Xiaoling, *Zhongguo Jinrong Gaige Kaifang Dashiji* [Major Events in the Reform and Opening of China's Banking System] (Beijing: Zhongguo jinrong chubanshe, 2008), 170, 177, 179–80, 225.

7 State Council, "Guanyu Pizhuan Renmin Yinhang Shengji Jigou Gaige Shishi Fang'an De Tongzhi" [Notice on Comments on the Proposal to Implement Reform of the Provincial-level Organization of the People's Bank], October 17, 1998, in Wu Xiaoling, *Zhongguo Jinrong Gaige Kaifang Dashiji*, 470–71.

branches were increasingly forced to rely either on a slowly growing national inter-bank market and central budget grants, or on intra-provincial retail and SOE deposits.[8] Given the limitations on local funding resources, provincial governments were unable to finance large-scale enterprises without central government support. This helps explain why China's industrial landscape is populated by a myriad of small, uncompetitive enterprises, whether steel, automobiles, or consumer goods. Provincial governments simply could not mobilize significant amounts of capital.[9]

The National and International Character of Stock Markets

The chief capacity of a stock market is to mobilize large amounts of capital on behalf of a company selling what is, in effect, an option on its future growth, profitability, and competitiveness. But this was not what the Chinese government considered in the late 1980s and early 1990s as it thought about how to reform the SOEs. Still focused on the need to separate government influence from enterprise operations, the state was persuaded to permit stock markets, third-party investors, and a specialized securities market regulator to try SOE reform. In 1992, when Zhu Rongji approved the experiment with international listings in Hong Kong and beyond, the maturity and rigor of the regulatory environment was a major selling point.[10] The thought was that stricter regulatory reporting requirements along with independent financial audits and international investor pressures would reduce the moral hazard, increase transparency, and thus positively influence the listed SOEs[11] to improve their management and operating performance.

The attraction of stock markets for local levels of government was more practical and immediate. Stock markets opened the door for provincial governments to raise amounts of capital far beyond what the local banking system and budget could provide. From the very beginning, local governments

8 Nor were there debt markets that the local governments could access directly. Li Fei, *Zhongguo Jinrong Tongshi 1949–1996* [General History of China's Banking System 1949–1996] (Beijing: Zhongguo jinrong chubanshe, 6 vols., 2000), 6: 272–77.

9 See David Faure, *China and Capitalism: A History of Business Enterprise in Modern China* (Hong Kong: Hong Kong University Press, 2006). Faure argues that China's delayed modernization was partially a result of its historic inability to mobilize sufficiently large amounts of capital to enable its businesses to achieve economies of scale.

10 Carl E. Walter and Fraser J.T. Howie, *Privatizing China: Inside China's Stock Markets* (Singapore: Wiley, 2nd ed., 2006), 54–56.

11 Listed companies remained SOEs because only a minority interest was sold to investors and the state owner remained in absolute control. The listing experiment was most definitely not about privatization.

understandably have been the most active and aggressive proponents of China's stock markets.[12] At their inception in 1991 the Shanghai and Shenzhen markets, like the banking system, were geographically based. Each was limited to listing local companies and relied largely on local retail investors. This rapidly changed, however, and the Shanghai and Shenzhen exchanges soon became markets that mobilized capital on a national basis. The opening to international capital markets from 1993, two years after the domestic exchanges began operations, changed the game entirely by providing Chinese companies with access to nearly endless amounts of international capital. During the 1992–2005 period, Chinese SOEs raised US$240 billion in new capital from both the domestic and international markets. In short, since 1993 China's SOE reforms and enterprise restructurings have adopted the Western corporate form and have sought capital through the sale of shares.

But the acceptance of reform through corporate restructuring and stock market listings brought a host of other problems that embroiled state agencies in a struggle for control over a significant new source of wealth and power. Stock markets became a catalyst that forced the regime to solve problems of ownership, privatization, and regulatory control—all of which had significant social and political implications.

Opening Pandora's Box: Ownership, Shares, and Regulation

Stocks and markets did not just spring into existence in China with the approval of the central government. Over the course of the 1980s the demand for capital at the most basic levels and in remote areas of the economy had driven traditional forms of money-raising in this direction. However, no one could possibly have foreseen the implications of securities sold in villages for China's future economic development.[13] But once enterprises had been transformed into corporations with equity investment denominated in shares, it was a short step to raise capital by "selling" some of the shares.

12 For Zhu Rongji's reaction to discovering that Shanghai was "broke" after he was appointed mayor in 1988, see Wang An, *Guye nin shangzuo* (Stock Investor, Sit at the Head of the Table) (Beijing: Huayi chubanshe, 2000), 82ff.

13 The state's acknowledgement of such local financing is found in a brief sentence in a State Council policy that permits agriculture-related businesses to experiment with self-financing through the issuance of securities. See State Council, "Guanyu Fazhan Shedui Qiye Ruogan Wenti De Guiding" [Decision on Several Problems in the Development of Agricultural Brigade Enterprises], July 3, 1979, as cited in Xue Weihong, *Gupiao Yunzuo Falü Shiwu* [Legal Affairs of Share Operations] (Beijing: Zhongguo chengshi chubanshe, 2001), 4; and Wu Xiaoling, *Zhongguo Jinrong Gaige Kaifang Dashiji*, 18.

The capital-raising aspect of these markets was never a source of disagreement among China's political stakeholders. But to get at this capital, the state had to solve problems of ownership, privatization, and regulatory control—all of which had social and political implications. It was these issues that created fissures among the political stakeholders.

The Creation of Ownership Rights in SOEs

Creating and listing securities went far beyond marginal tinkering with SOE performance incentives. If investors were to buy stocks, enterprises were required to thoroughly restructure their operations and financial structures to bring them in line with profitable Western-style corporations.[14] This inevitably required a detailed, legally enforceable, and practically useful definition of ownership.[15] Under the existing Marxist system, enterprise ownership "by the whole people" was non-fungible, theoretical, and abstract. It was entirely unclear who owned a given asset other than some entity known as the "state" which acted as the agent of some other thing known as "the whole people." Systematic documentation showing what state agency had bought what equipment was virtually non-existent prior to the corporatization reforms.

The corporatization of SOEs created a legal box containing the company's operations and detailing ownership rights to its assets. A full audit provided a record of the value of the assets, as it did the source of the funds that enabled them to be acquired. Subtracting total liabilities from total assets yielded a net asset value (NAV), which then was denominated in shares valued at RMB1 each.

This specification of legal ownership and financial rights and obligations altered the relationship between the enterprise and the state.[16] The determination of which government agency or agencies had invested in the company and attributed to them marketable equity shares created the possibility of monetizing ownership by selling a fraction or all of the ownership of such assets. In contrast, an uncorporatized SOE could only be sold in pieces of machinery, buildings, or real estate. Failing incorporation as a company limited by shares, pieces of an enterprise's future operating value, by definition greater than the sum of its book value, could not be sold.

14 For a detailed discussion of how this was done, see Walter and Howie, *Privatizing China*, chs. 4 and 5.

15 For the tortuous path traveled by China's philosophical Marxists, see Tang Weibing, *Zhongguo Zhuangui Shiqi Suoyouzhi Jiegou Yanjin De Zhidu Fenxi* [Institutional Analysis of the Evolution of the Ownership Structure during China's Transitional Period] (Beijing: Jingji kexue chubanshe, 2004), ch. 4.

16 Walter and Howie, *Privatizing China*, 73ff.

It was not simply that government agencies now had outright legal ownership rights over the former SOEs—this was far too abstract.[17] In reality, it was the head of a SOE's parent group and certain senior government officials in supervisory agencies who were the true beneficiaries because, in fact, they controlled the new company's assets. As one company CEO said, "It doesn't matter who 'owns' the cash, it matters who gets to spend it."[18]

The creation of such transferable property rights inevitably prompted particularistic business interests to form within the state. These interests developed goals significantly different from those of the state.[19] In fact, the rapid adoption of SOE reform through listings owes much to the self-interested efforts of officials who could foresee the possibility for significant creation of individual wealth.

Non-tradable Shares and Market Distortions

But it was not the state's intent to make ownership of such wealth explicit: individuals could achieve wealth, but it would be at the state's discretion. This, then, is the key fault line in China's SOE reform effort and it is commonly known as the "Original Sin." The definition of this sin can be traced to China's first corporate law, the 1992 "Standard Opinion" (*guifan yijian*). The Opinion stipulated two classes of company shares, tradable (the listed A-shares) and non-tradable (the unlisted shares held by state agencies, also called state shares) that have come to distinguish China's markets. This distinction is critically relevant for understanding how and why an institution such as a stock market was adapted by the political economy in which it had been adopted. The non-tradable shares were not permitted to be sold on the stock market or, initially, even to be transferred among government agencies because the government well understood the temptations of those managing state assets and thus sought to prevent the sale of

17 Of course, there was plenty of supervision from above. See State Asset Management Bureau, "Qiye Guoyou Zichan Suoyouquan Jieding Zanxing Guiding" [Provisional Rules for the Definition of the Ownership Rights of State-owned Assets), June 17, 1991, in Jiang Ping, ed., *Jinrong Falü Fagui Quanshu* [Compendium of Banking Laws and Regulations] (Beijing: Zhongguo sanxia chubanshe, 3 vols., 1997), 2: 2243–46.

18 Author's conversation with a state enterprise chief executive officer, Anyang, Henan province, July 1996.

19 The true attraction of listing shares is in the fact that pricing reflects estimates of future earnings that, when translated into the share price, typically yields a multiple of the net asset value per share. Hence, when a new company is formed, its shares are worth an NAV of RMB1 per share; when it is listed, prices will be far in excess of this. It was, in short, seen as free money!

the state's shares and the consequent privatization of China's SOEs.[20] The Chinese government's support for stock markets has never been about explicit privatization.[21]

Not surprisingly, this bifurcated approach gave rise to significant market distortions by creating separate and independent markets for each of these two classes of shares. From the very start, therefore, the public A-share markets did not provide a price for companies as they do in the West. The markets valued only those shares actually trading on the market (the "float"), ignoring the existence of the non-tradable shares entirely. Not only were the markets distinct, each had a different regulator[22] and there were different share valuation methodologies for shares of the same company![23] Whereas A-shares could be publicly traded on the Shanghai Stock Market, as in New York or Hong Kong, the transfer of non-tradable shares required a complex and time-consuming administrative approval process. This division of regulatory responsibility became a problem.

Centralization of Regulatory Control and Central Support

Sooner or later Beijing needed to assume authority for the equity capital markets in China, otherwise their capital-raising potential probably never would have been achieved. But from the start it was reluctant. It approved the exchanges primarily to maintain social order that had become threatened by the "share fever" that had erupted in the late 1980s.[24] This cautious attitude continued through the mid-1990s, as evidenced by the first of three landmark *People's Daily* editorials by a "Special Correspondent" who warned against the "speculative nature" of the then-rampaging bull market.

20 Liu Hongru, perhaps the godfather of the stock markets, stated that there were three requirements for such reforms. These included: 1) to avoid privatization; 2) to avoid the loss of state assets; and 3) to guarantee the primacy of the state-owned economy. See Liu Hongru, *Tansuo Zhongguo Ziben Shichang Fazhan Zhilu* [Exploring the Road to the Development of China's Capital Markets] (Beijing: Zhongguo jinrong chubanshe, 2003), 29.

21 The strict meaning of "privatization" refers to the exit of the state as the controlling shareholder of a company and the assumption of ownership by non-state investors.

22 The CSRC regulated the A-share market and the State Asset Management Bureau (SAMB; later an entirely different entity, the SASAC, but with a similar role) regulated the non-tradable market shares.

23 See Walter and Howie, *Privatizing China*, ch. 8, for a full analysis of China's twisted valuation methodologies.

24 Li Zhangzhe, *Zhongyu Chenggong: Zhongguo Gushi Fazhan Baogao* [Success at Last: Report on the Development of China's Stock Markets] (Beijing: Shijie zhishi chubanshe, 2001), 120-28. Also see Walter and Howie, *Privatizing China*, 21–28.

But scandals forced Beijing's hand and by 1997 the two exchanges, as well as the influential *Shanghai Securities Daily*, had been taken over. Even so, through 1998 the central government continued to perceive the market as marginal in importance, but large in its disruptive potential—an arena in which largely local companies could raise money—and less as a positive force for change.

This attitude, however, was completely reversed in mid-1999. Throughout 1998 the markets stagnated in an aimless trading range following the outbreak of the Asian financial crisis. Then, suddenly, on May 19, 1999, the markets took off—catalyzed by an article in *Shanghai Securities Daily* describing the impact of the Internet on China.[25] This was followed by a series of stimulus policies approved by Zhu Rongji. Topping all this off, on June 15 the central government made formal its support for the emerging bull market, again acting through a "Special Correspondent" writing for a third time in the *People's Daily*. The editorial claimed that, given the "strength" of the economy, it was "natural" for the market to rise and it called on investors to "double" its value. And, as if this were not clear, the head of the CSRC said, "The daily jump in the stock markets since May 19 ... represents a major turning point in the development of China's stock markets." This marked the first time that the central government suspended its suspicion of the markets and aligned itself with local governments and market participants, not to mention the various market stakeholders owned by central government entities.[26]

In the midst of this raging bull market, China's first Securities Law went into effect on July 1, 1999, making the CSRC a ministerial-level entity.[27] The law authorized the commission to establish a national network along the same lines as the PBOC's regional offices: no longer would the CSRC lack sufficient resources. Then, with the party behind the markets, wholly in control of the two exchanges and the securities press and, even more importantly, with power of approval over listings and the establishment of licensing and supervision, the CSRC was the most powerful player in the industry. The central government, using the MOF, the PBOC, and the CSRC,

25 For more on the "519" incident, China's copy of the U.S. Internet bubble, see Walter and Howie, *Privatizing China*, 269-70; and A Kui, *Xuanhua Yu Saodong: Xin Zhongguo Gushi Ershi Nian* [Noise and Commotion: Twenty Years of New China's Stock Market] (Beijing: Zhongxin chubanshe, 2008), 200–204.

26 Yuan Jian, *Zhongguo Zhengquan Shichang Pipan* [Criticism of China's Securities Markets] (Beijing: Zhongguo shehui kexue chubanshe, 2004), 81–93.

27 Wang Lianzhou and Li Cheng, *Fengfeng Yuyu Zhengquan Fa* [The Difficulties and Hardships Surrounding the Securities Law] (Shanghai: Shanghai sanlian chubanshe, 2000).

was in a position to control access to major capital resources through the stock market. Central control, however, did not ensure the stable development of the markets.

The sections that follow examine two actions taken by state agents that involved the stock markets. Both were attempts at reform, but both ended causing harm to the markets. As such, these actions provide insights into how politics affected the development of China's stock markets.

Reform 1: The CSRC Uses the Stock Market to Fund Social Security, 2001

By the late 1990s Beijing had to find ways to fund social security reform. The country's aging demographics (see Table 9.2) and the increasing number of those who would suffer dislocation from corporate restructuring made the need urgent.

In 1999 the agency responsible for regulating China's stock markets, the CSRC, came up with a plan. On September 22, 1999, at the Fourth Plenum of the Fifteenth National Congress of the Chinese Communist Party, the CSRC received support for the principle underlying its proposal. The principle represented a watershed as the party for the first time conditionally approved selling some of its holdings of state shares in the SOEs.[28] The CSRC under its new chairman, Zhou Xiaochuan, used this principle to create a policy that would achieve two goals: 1) merge the tradable and non-tradable markets; and 2) provide a significant funding mechanism for social security reform. The plan was simple: sell a small proportion of the government's state shares to the public markets, with the proceeds to be used to fund the newly established NSSF (see Table 9.3).

In theory, the CSRC plan was quite modest and should have had minimum market impact. It called for a mere 10 percent of the total number of shares involved in a listing to be existing state shares.[29] Assume a company in its offering sold a number of shares equivalent to 25 percent of its post-offering total number of shares. The state-share portion of such an issue, therefore, would represent less than 2.5 percent of the company's total

28 The party decision states, "Under the premise of not impacting the state's controlling interest, appropriately reduce a part of the state's shares, with the capital to be used for the reform and development of state-owned enterprises." See Li Zhangzhe, *Zhongguo Gushi Fazhan Baogao 2001* [Report on the Development of China's Stock Markets 2001] (Beijing: Jixie gongye chubanshe, 2002), 80.

29 The other 90 percent would be new shares. Previously all IPOs and secondary placements relied only on the issuance of new shares.

TABLE 9.2

China's Aging Population, 1995-2050

	Population (bn)	0–14 years (mm)	15–64 years (mm)	65+ years (mm)
1995	1.21	327	808	76
2000	1.26	328	845	87
2010	1.35	293	956	104
2020	1.43	287	989	214
2030	1.48	278	989	214
2040	1.49	287	950	252
2050	1.47	211	962	300

Source: Asian Wall Street Journal, June 15–17, 2001, M1.

TABLE 9.3

Trends in NSSF Funding Sources, 2000–2007

(RMB bn)	2000	2001	2002	2003	2004	2005	2006	2007	Total
MOF	20	47.4	30.4	–	17.1	10.0	38.6	10.0	173.5
Sale of State Shares	–	12.2	8.8	0.4	4.7	8.3	11.4	12.5*	48.3
Lottery	–	–	2.4	4.5	6.1	4.6	7.4	8.3	33.3
Total	20	59.5	41.6	4.9	27.9	22.9	57.4	30.8	255.1

Source: "Quanguo Shebao Jijin Niandu Baogao" [National Social Security Fund Annual Report], 2000-2007.

Note: * Includes only RMB4.4 bn derived from listings or secondary offerings; for the first time, RMB8.1 bn came from over-the-counter transfers of state shares into the fund.

outstanding shares. Such a minimal amount of new shares introduced into the market should not have had any market impact on the company's valuation or on the market index; such has indeed been the case for all overseas listed companies.[30] Zhou Xiaochuan, CSRC chairman, said, "The direction of the policy to reduce state shareholdings is correct." Wang Lijun, vice minister of the MOF, said at an Asia Pacific Economic Conference (APEC) meeting, "Reducing the holdings of state shares by 10 percent really isn't very much. The reason for there being many different opinions now is that

30 Although this policy was, as will be discussed, quickly shelved for domestic share offerings, it has continued in effect until the present for international offerings, with no negative impact on share valuations. This is because international investment banks value a company based on its total number of shares, whereas until June 2001 the domestic market, as noted previously, ignored the existence of non-tradable shares. Chi-Chu Tschang, "Welfare Fund Still Gains from Share Sales," *South China Morning Post*, April 29, 2002.

most people do not understand its significance."[31] But the market vigorously disagreed with these senior voices of the government. Interests with a stake in the status quo saw such sales as a first step toward releasing a potential flood of new shares onto the market. The boundaries between the two classes of shares were becoming blurred.

Why some saw a threat can be gauged from the size of the state's holdings at the time. In 2000 the state held controlling stakes in the form of state shares in 963 different listed A-share companies (Shanghai 551, Shenzhen 412), representing about 65 percent of the total outstanding listed company shares.[32] If valued at A-share prices, the shares were worth US$252 billion, but at net asset value they were worth far less, only US$89 billion.[33] The NAV price, the basis for negotiated state-share transfers, is important because the government prohibits the sale of state-owned assets below the NAV in any market anywhere.[34] Consequently, transfers among state entities of such shares were routinely priced at small premiums to the NAV. The question being asked was whether the market could absorb the sale of state shares without negatively impacting its then current valuation levels.[35]

It happens that the year 2000 set a record for domestic issuances: the Shanghai and Shenzhen markets raised just over US$18 billion, or about 20 percent of the government's holdings valued at the NAV. Using this figure as a basis for reference, it is clear that unloading the state's huge position in the market would require a massive injection of fresh capital plus investor willingness to buy if then current trading values were to be maintained. But it was never the State Council's or the CSRC's intent to sell out the state's holdings entirely. The State Council in June 2001 made this quite clear: only

31 The quotes by Zhou and Wang can be found in *Caijing* [Finance], November 5, 2001, 56.

32 Wind Information, at www.wind.com.cn, accessed September 3, 2010. Wind is the preeminent Chinese company providing data on listed companies and stock markets, similar to Bloomberg in the United States.

33 The NAV per share is the product of accounting, not markets that look to future values. It is arrived at by a specialized asset appraisal company that values the total assets and liabilities of the company and subtracts the liabilities to arrive at a net figure per share. This approach does not value the ongoing character of the company, only its value at liquidation.

34 Prices below the NAV indicate that the state lost money in its investment. At the time of incorporation, the original investment in the new company is RMB1 per share, which represents its NAV per share.

35 More shares, less enterprise value per share. The introduction of many more shares into a relatively small market will dilute not only the value of the shares of specific companies, but that of the overall market as well.

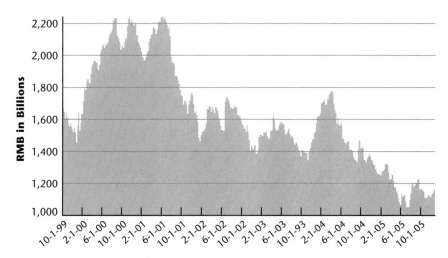

FIGURE 9.1 Shanghai Index Performance, 10/1/1999–10/1/2005
Source: Wind Information.

10 percent of all new share issues—domestic and overseas—were to consist of state shares that would be traded on the exchanges.[36]

Although seemingly modest, it is easy to see why the CSRC plan ended up having a huge impact on the stock market. On the Monday following the first IPO to incorporate state shares the markets began a six-day free fall, with Shanghai losing 5.3 percent on July 30 alone (see Figure 9.1). Six days later, Shanghai recorded a 9.8 percent drop, the biggest fall to date. During these two weeks Shanghai fell from 2233 to 1971, a 236-point drop. A panicked reaction set in among market participants as the indexes continued to dive when new IPOs continued. The head of the investment management department of the People's Insurance Company of China (PICC) stated ominously, "If the market falls to 1300, the securities companies, funds, the entire market will be completely bankrupt. The financial links between the securities companies and the banks will be broken and this will have an impact on bank funding and therefore lead to systemic risk in China's financial sector."[37] Reports circulated of runs on local brokerage offices. When the

36 By regulation, prior to 2001 publicly listed companies sold only new shares, not existing shares. Although both had the effect of diluting the holdings of the original shareholder(s), the sale of existing shares suggests that the state was selling out and privatizing the entity. The new 2001 regulation means that when a company offers shares to third-party investors, 90 percent of the total number of shares involved in the offering consists of new shares and 10 percent consists of existing shares.

37 Yuan Jian, *Zhongguo Zhengquan Shichang Pipan*, 149.

market broke through 1600 on October 22, the CSRC, on orders from the State Council, took responsibility for the debacle and announced a "temporary" halt to the sale of state shares on the domestic exchanges.[38] Intense securities industry lobbying plus government fear of widespread bankruptcies and social unrest had forced its hand.

During the period the policy was in effect, seventeen new domestic issues succeeded in raising just over RMB2.31 billion (US$279 million) for the NSSF. The failure of this policy to go forward struck a major blow to the growth of the NSSF, which was then forced to rely on MOF budget advances for the bulk of its funding (see Table 9.3). As a senior official from the NSSF and a proponent of the original policy stated in mid-2003, "The government can fix the social security program's lack of funding if it desires to do so."

Why did the CSRC's simple plan to sell a portion of state shares, a policy that had been implemented without a hitch in international markets, have such important social and political consequences in China's domestic markets? The answer requires a deeper examination of the evolution of China's markets and the politics that surrounded that evolution.

Revisiting Pandora's Box: Sources of the Stock Market Collapse, 2001–2005

The evolution of China's non-capitalist stock market and its institutions explains the following collapse of the markets and the failure of subsequent reforms. As one witness explained, "You can complain about the market's lack of liquidity, or about the repeated earnings announcement shocks, or about violations of regulations—all this is just because you invest based on foreign ideas. The profit in China's stock markets mainly comes from political easing (*zhengzhi kongjian*)."[39] The CSRC's modest policy to sell shares to fund the NSSF had come in the first bull market publicly supported by the central government. By raising the issue of selling non-tradable shares, it seemed to indicate that the government had changed its position on the market's basic founding principles. Major participants immediately headed for the doors. This can be seen in the extended debate that ensued over the future character of the stock market as well as the selling of state shares.[40]

---

38 Yuan Jian, *Zhongguo Zhengquan Shichang Pipan*, 148–51.

39 A Kui, *Xuanhua Yu Saodong*, 201. This is another way of stating that the moral hazard can be profitable.

40 See *Zhengquan Shichang* [Securities Market], November 29, 2003, 15–22, for a discussion among twenty fund managers regarding the definition of and solution for the share overhang.

Business Interest Groups Define Their Legal Rights

What market participants disagreed with emerged very clearly in public discussions. Market stakeholders wanted to ensure their rights in the event that the promises made by the State Council and the CSRC in 2001 and 2002, confirming the prohibition of the sale of state shares, were to be reversed. The debate, therefore, dealt only with the extent to which state shares should be sold and not, in fact, whether they would be sold.

There were two "official" positions with regard to selling state shares: the first, represented by the SASAC,[41] accepted a "reduction in holdings" (*guoyougu jianchi*); the second called for a "100 percent float" (*quan liutong*), the announced objective of the CSRC. SASAC's head, Li Rongrong, stated outright in public that state shares would "absolutely never fully float,"[42] by which he meant that the state would never sell out all its shares; this would have meant outright privatization. For a time these two slogans were confused, but, finally, in 2004 the CSRC developed a neutral (but awkward) term called "share segmentation" (*guquan fenzhi*).[43] The issue was then rephrased by the CSRC as "share segmentation reform" (*guquan fenzhi gaige*).

The debate then swiftly focused on actual ownership rights to state shares.[44] The fundamental point that emerged was that the central government, although it represented the interests of the "whole people," did not

41 The SASAC, established in March 2003, reported directly to the State Council. It was the agent for the central government to hold ownership of the 189 strategically most-important SOEs. See Walter and Howie, *Privatizing China*, 219–22.

42 Guo Fenglin, "Shangshi Gongsi Guoyougu Liutong Banfa Hui Shishi Chutai" [Introduction to Implementation of the Method for Floating Listed Company State Shares], February 6, 2004, at http://www.corplawinfo.ecupl.edu.cn/ArticleShow.asp?Article ID=2458, accessed September 28, 2010.

43 This term was designed to defuse the conflict between the SASAC and the CSRC. The latter's phrase, "full float," suggests that it supported all shares of all companies being traded on the market, i.e., privatization. Clearly the CSRC did not really mean for this to be taken literally. It simply meant that all the existing classes of shares should be legally tradable on the market. The SASAC, in contrast, felt that the term was rife with hints of full privatization and it preferred the phrase to mean a "reduction of non-tradable shares." This was, in fact, more accurate: the state did want to monetize a small portion of its holdings while still retaining control over the listed companies. "Share segmentation" reform better addresses the intents of all sides: to eliminate the existing segmented markets in which tradable and non-tradable shares traded separately and independently. See Walter and Howie, *Privatizing China*, ch. 8, for a full discussion of this problem.

44 Much of the following discussion is taken from Luo Peixin, "Quan Liutong Fang'an De Falü Jiexi" [Legal Explanation of the Full Float Proposal], *Zhongguo Zhengquan Qihuo* [Chinese Securities Futures], no. 3 (2004): 20–29.

have the right to decide unilaterally the disposition of "its" state shares. This argument, founded on the various laws that underpinned the corporatization effort, asserted that the ownership of non-tradable shares belonged to the actual investor in the shares.[45] For example, if the investor were a wholly state-owned parent or government agency contributing state funds and assets, then the state, that is the SASAC,[46] was the authoritative entity, and the particular agencies, for example, the enterprise groups, would be deemed as having agreed to whatever disposition the state had decided. The problem, however, was who "owned" the state funds and assets at the time of corporatization. As a part of the contract responsibility reforms of the 1980s, SOEs had been permitted to retain profits from sales above the plan quota. These monies, in part, had been reinvested in their businesses so that when part of their operations became corporatized, the SOEs typically contributed two types of assets: 1) those that had been funded by the state budget; and 2) those that the SOEs had used their own funds to acquire. The first gave rise to "state shares" and the second to "state legal person shares" (see Figure 9.2).[47] The argument stemmed from the fact that for listed state-owned enterprises, any decision of the state would have an impact on the allegedly private property rights of various types of investors, including the SOE group companies and A-share investors whose agreement would have to be sought. After all, a listed company had its own board of directors that was legally responsible to all shareholders. This defense of property rights took place without any law to define, much less protect, private property.

According to this reasoning, any decision to reduce state holdings in these kinds of companies exceeded the authority of the SASAC and even the State Council. Authorization could come only from the National People's Congress (NPC), which institutionally represents the "whole people," or all investor classes. To get around this awkward requirement in the case of the CSRC's original 2001 proposal, the State Council had drawn the intent of its original decree very broadly. But in the aftermath of that policy debacle, the central government's actions were restricted by the notion of property: it could not dispose of state shares as it saw fit. A further ramification followed: what about the rights over dividends paid by the listed company? Did these belong to the parent group, the SASAC, or the MOF? This particular

45 For a good discussion of this point, see *Caijing*, March 7, 2005, 40-41.

46 There are central and local SASAC entities; this example deals with centrally-owned enterprises under the central SASAC.

47 See Walter and Howie, *Privatizing China*, 75ff.

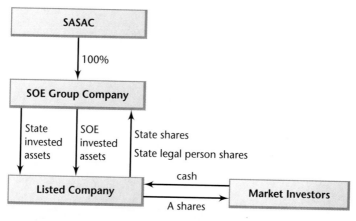

FIGURE 9.2 Investor Relations for a Central Government Listed Company
Source: Author.

question continued to be debated on technicalities up through 2008.[48] These were the terms of the debate, but from the start the real question hovering around its edges was whose rights were being defended? Who benefited?

The second key argument got to the heart of the issue. This held that even with NPC authorization, any proposal to sell state shares had to confront the contradiction between market practice and existing laws. Although the Company Law clearly specified that all shares of a given category should have the same rights and the same price when issued; in practice, over the years tradable and non-tradable shares de facto had become two different categories of shares[49] and China's markets had developed for nearly ten years based on the understanding that non-tradable shares would remain just that. This created, it was argued, a kind of contract between the two classes of shareholders. From this it followed that if holders of non-tradable shares wanted to sell their shares on the market, they would need to pay

48 Representative of the issues is Wang Changyong and Ling Huawei, "State Firms Targeted in Profit-dipping Plan," *Caijing*, May 8, 2007, at www.//English.caijing.com.cn/ 2007-05-08/100043065.html, accessed August 21, 2010. In late 2009 a breakthrough appeared to have been reached.

49 When state agencies or SOEs invested in a new corporatized company limited by shares, they received one share for every RMB1 worth of contributed net assets. But when private investors bought A-shares, they inevitably paid a multiple of the original NAV price. Hence the claim of the legalists that the Company Law had, in fact, been violated, since the same category of shares had been sold at different prices and private investor rights had been hurt from the very start of the market experiment!

some sort of "consideration" (*duijia*) to the owners of tradable shares since their action would dilute the value of listed shares. One of China's preeminent economists, Wu Jinglian, supported this idea saying that the government should compensate A-share investors for the losses that they would inevitably suffer.[50] Wu's call was chorused by securities companies and other institutional market participants[51] who, with significant holdings of tradable shares, stood to benefit handsomely from such a plan. Retail investors past or present strongly favored some form of compensation, knowing that they were the biggest losers of all, a point that no one was willing to dispute.

In short, this deliberately legalistic approach, advanced with strong securities industry support, fenced the central government into a passive role in any plan to resolve the non-tradable share problem. Framed using its own laws and lobbied hard by its own institutions and companies, the government would not necessarily be able to impose a solution for the two classes of investors unless it took the consuming time to manage the step of going through the people's congress. By establishing the concept of a contract between the two classes and requiring some form of compensation, institutional holders of tradable shares—fund management companies, securities firms, trust companies, and large SOEs—had positioned themselves to be the major beneficiaries of any future reform.[52] But this proved to be a Pyrrhic victory.

The CSRC Mobilizes NSSF Funds to Support the Market

The continuing publicity given to the debate over ownership probably doomed the CSRC's efforts to restore the markets to the pre-2001 levels. The specter of divided markets publicly acknowledged by the state simply would not go away.[53] But that does not mean that the regulator, from 2002 under a new chairman, Shang Fulin, did not pull out all the stops to get new investors and money into the stock market.

During these years a large number of ideas to prop up the markets were suggested and then dismissed, most for good reason. But there were some

50 Jinglian Wu, "An Alternate Proposal to Reduce State-owned Shares," *Caijing*, January 21, 2002. For other views of the compensation issue, see *Caijing*, March 7, 2005, 38-39.

51 For example, see "China's Xiangcai Mulls Special A-share Rights," *Dow Jones International News*, November 26, 2002. A local brokerage suggested the government should give A-shareholders "special rights," but failed to disclose a workable solution.

52 See Walter and Howie, *Privatizing China*, ch. 10, for an analysis of the "reform" that "solved" the segmentation problem.

53 For example, see *Shenzhen Tequ Bao* [Shenzhen SEZ Daily], December 17, 2003.

important openings designed to attract new capital that could, perhaps, reverse the falling indices. These initiatives included the establishment of a QFII (Qualified Foreign Institutional Investor) program on November 12, 2002, that allowed foreign investors direct access to A-shares[54] and a reversal on an old ban on foreigners buying state or legal-person shares in M&A transactions;[55] in the short run, neither of these measures would have a material impact on the market's structural problems.

In early 2003, the government decided to take direct action and invest in the market. The Ministry of Labor, the supervisory agency of the NSSF, stated that its NSSF fund would soon begin investments in A-shares, and on June 13 the NSSF took its first step into the market.[56] It should be noted that the markets continued to hit new lows over the course of 2003, but at year-end, 5.2 percent (RMB6.9 billion) of the NSSF's total investment portfolio consisted of A-shares. The markets continued their downward slide in 2004 and the NSSF continued to invest, announcing in March that its holding objective for A-shares was in the neighborhood of 25 percent of its total portfolio. As of year-end 2004, it had achieved only 11 percent, but even this represented investments of RMB18 billion ($2.2 billion).[57] Although the market had fallen 16.5 percent in 2004, the NSSF had increased its holdings of A-shares by a factor of three. These actions clearly support the conclusion that the state authorized the use of NSSF funds to help prop up the falling market.

Lest one think that this policy move was similar to the effort in 2001 to use state shares to fund the NSSF, let us look more carefully at these two actions. Under the discredited 2001 CSRC program the NSSF would have received cash from the sale of state shares. The central government via an IPO or share placement would have sold down a small portion of its SOE stakes in the market to third-party investors, receiving cash in return that

54 CSRC and PBOC, "Provisional Measures on Administration of Domestic Securities Investments of Qualified Foreign Institutional Investors (QFII)," November 5, 2002, at http://www.csrc.gov.cn/n575458/n4001948/n4002030/4064521.html, accessed September 4, 2010.

55 CSRC, MOF, and SETC, "Guanyu Waishang Zhuanrang Shangshi Gongsi Guoyougu He Farengu Youguan Wenti De Tongzhi" [Notice Regarding the Transfer to Foreign Investors of State-owned Shares and Legal-Person Shares of Listed Companies], *Zhongguo Zhengquan Bao*, November 4, 2002.

56 Zhao Xiaojian, "Shebao Jijin Rushi Fengbo" [NSSF Enters the Market Turmoil], *Caijing*, February 20, 2003, 40-42.

57 Ren Bo, "China Seeks to Finance the Social Security Fund," *Caijing*, September 19, 2005, at http://english.caijing.com.cn/2005-09-19/100043024.html, accessed August 21, 2010.

the NSSF would have invested as it saw fit. But now the NSSF was being "allowed" by the government to invest in and, most certainly, hold a portfolio of A-shares in a sharply declining market. The government's intent with the NSSF purchase of shares was to remove A-shares from the market and thereby to prop up the market index. In other words, now the market was shrinking—fewer shares were being traded—while, in contrast, the slow addition of state-share sales under the 2001 policy would have expanded the market and, over time, diminished the difference between the tradable and non-tradable shares.[58]

By 2004 the government took a further step to support the market. On top of directing the NSSF efforts, it put its own reputation officially on the line and this time there was no "Special Correspondent." On February 2, 2004, the State Council for the first time since 1992 publicly committed to support development of capital markets by issuing what became known as the "Nine Articles."[59] The articles represented a confirmation by the government and the Communist Party of the markets' important role and called for a host of new policies and reforms, including the opening of the securities industry to foreign investment.

The articles proved to be a fountainhead of specific incentives designed to drive higher the market index. For example, in August the CSRC called a "temporary" halt to all IPOs, in October the PBOC permitted securities firms to issue short-term commercial notes[60] and the CSRC and CIRC opened the A-share markets directly to insurance companies. This was not all: in early November the CSRC, MOF, PBOC, and CBRC introduced a fund that would repay small investor losses due to securities fraud incurred prior to September 30, 2004.[61] Finally, the following month the CSRC issued

58 See Walter and Howie, *Privatizing China*, ch. 10, 219–39.

59 State Council, "Guanyu Tuijin Ziben Shichang Gaige Kaifang He Wending Fazhan De Ruogan Yijian" [Several Opinions on Promoting the Reform and Opening and Stable Development of the Capital Market], February 2, 2004, *Zhongguo Zhengquan Bao*, February 3, 2004, 1.

60 This opening of the inter-bank market by Zhou Xiaochuan's PBOC to cash-strapped SOEs five years later proved to be the most important capital market initiative of the new century. In 2009 corporate fixed income debt issuance in China had already exceeded the level of a similar market in Japan, whereas Shang's CSRC had halted all IPOs due to the still weak stock markets. The halting of IPOs is contained in CSRC, "Guanyu Shouci Gongkai Faxing Gupiao Shixing Xunjia Zhidu" [On the First Implementation of the Price-seeking Mechanism for IPOs], August 2, 2004, at http://www.csrc. gov.cn/pub/newsite/fxb/gzdt/200701/t20070108_69301.htm, accessed October 29, 2010.

61 MOF, PBOC, CSRC, and CBRC, "Geren Zaiquan Ji Kehu Zhengquan Jiaoyi Jiesuan Zijin Shougou Yijian" [Opinion on the Acquisition of Individual Debt and Client Transaction Settlement Funds], November 5, 2004, at http://news.xinhuanet.com/

a "provisional" regulation actually permitting A-share investors to vote on issues with a material impact on company performance.[62] This represented almost unprecedented encouragement of shareholder activism.

In the end, few, if any, of the government efforts had a positive impact on the markets. Accompanied by a huge media barrage, the market jumped 5 percent in the week after the government announcement in February, but then fell back and continued to fall, dropping nearly 14 percent by the end of June. The market fell another 10 percent from its June level, ending the year down over 29 percent. In spite of the CSRC's heroic efforts, retail investors exited the market altogether. Just prior to the market collapse, best estimates suggested there were really only three million active retail investors;[63] by the end of 2005 nearly 64 percent of the existing 70 million open accounts held no securities at all.[64] The withdrawal of active retail investors who saw no upside in the political fight is a major reason why the markets failed to rise for so long. Because securities companies primarily relied on brokerage fees for the bulk of their profits, this was also a major factor in the industry's collapse.

By year-end 2004, it was clear that the CSRC's orchestrated efforts to restore the status quo by all major government ministries including the State Council were not going to revive the market. (As a participant commented, this was a traditional strategy often used in China of "dragging everyone else down to save yourself." At this point in time, two years into Shang Fulin's term as chairman, the CSRC was perceived as a weak, ineffective organization.)

---

zhengfu/2004-11/05/content_2179451.htm, accessed September 28, 2010; and CSRC et al., "Zhengquan Touzizhe Baohu Jijin Guanli Banfa" [Method for the Management of the Securities Investor Protection Fund], June 30, 2005, in CSRC, ed., *Zhonghua Renmin Gongheguo Zhengquan Qihuo Fagui Huibian 2005* [Compilation of PRC Securities and Commodities Laws and Regulations 2005] (Beijing: Falü chubanshe, 2005), 1:5862. The central government, through the PBOC, took full responsibility for repaying small investors, ratcheting up the moral hazard yet another level.

62 These material issues included secondary convertible bond and rights offerings, major restructurings, debt for equity swaps, and overseas listings of important subsidiaries. See CSRC, "Guanyu Jiachang Shehui Gongzhonggu Gudong Quanyi Baohu De Ruogan Guiding" [Several Decrees on Strengthening Protection of the Shareholder Rights of Society and the Public], December 8, 2004, at http://news.xinhuanet.com/fortune/2004-12/08/content_2307095.htm, accessed September 28, 2010 – as if the public actually owned these shares.

63 For analysis see Walter and Howie, *Privatizing China*, 142ff; see also Hu Shuli, "Ruoshi Qunti Yingdang Yuanli Gupiao Shichang" [The Disadvantaged Masses Should Stay Away From the Stock Market], *Caijing*, October 2002.

64 *Jingji Guancha Bao* [Economic Observer], January 2, 2006, 18.

The Securities Industry Collapses

The harm done to China's stock market by the debate over who owns state shares spread to the securities industry. As late as the first half of 2003, China's securities companies as a whole had been profitable due to brokerage fees.[65] Sounds of complaints, warnings of imminent disaster,[66] and criticism of the CSRC[67] had driven away retail brokerage business and with it the securities companies' major source of cash flow. Rumors of huge losses by Southern Securities began to circulate and by November were revealed as true by *Caijing* magazine.[68] Southern was perhaps the largest player in the markets at the time. It was reported to have over RMB10 billion in illegal guaranteed return contracts and RMB8.3 billion committed to proprietary trading, as against registered capital of RMB3.5 billion. Where did this huge amount of money invested in guaranteed returns come from? The CSRC's official mouthpiece, *China Securities Daily,* on September 12, 2001, stated that some 172 listed companies had placed a total of RMB21.7 billion with securities companies, to be managed on a guaranteed return basis.[69] In 2001 industry estimates of the total exposure of all securities companies to such contracts was RMB150 billion,[70] nearly twice as much as the total industry capital of RMB76.5 billion at year-end 2000.

The same report stated that total industry funds committed to proprietary trading was RMB50 billion.[71] For Southern alone, an incomplete

65 The industry broke even for the full year in 2003. *Jingji Guancha Bao*, August 18, 2003, 16.

66 *Jingji Guancha Bao*, August 18, 2003, 14.

67 Zhu Qiwen, "Make or Break Choice for Regulator," *China Daily*, September 15, 2003, 34.

68 Xia Bin, "Zhongguo 'Simu Jijin Baogao'" [Report on China's Private Funds], *Caijing*, July 2001, 69; and Li Qing, "Shei Tiao Nangang Zhengquan Kulong?" [Who Filled Up Southern Securities Liabilities?], *Caijing*, November 5, 2003, 47, and 52 for a copy of Southern's FY2002 balance sheet.

69 *Caijing*, November 5, 2001, 66.

70 *Caijing*, November 5, 2001, 66.

71 "Proprietary trading" refers to a company using its own capital to invest and trade in securities and other products. "Exposure" means that the industry had entered into RMB150 billion of guaranteed return contracts, i.e., it had guaranteed the principal of these contracts plus a fixed return. The securities company then bought a portfolio of shares. As the market tanked, the value of these shares tanked. If the market declined 10 percent, then the nominal loss at that point would have been RMB15 billion. If the securities company did not liquidate the portfolio at that market level, losses would have increased as the market continued down. Most firms expected a turnaround that never came. Since they guaranteed the invested principal and return, the securities companies' contract losses grew, eventually wiping out their capital.

estimation of its proprietary trading exposure showed the company to be among the top ten shareholders in twenty-eight listed companies, whose market value had declined 25 percent or RMB467 million in value between June and October 2001.[72] So it was not surprising that on January 2, 2004, the industry giant was closed, groaning under nearly US$4 billion in debt owed to investors and various other entities, including banks and the central securities settlement company. Southern was revealed as simply the tip of the iceberg as the number of other illiquid securities companies that collapsed increased during the remainder of 2004 and accelerated in 2005.

Southern's sister companies had market exposures of a similar magnitude and fared little better. For example, bankrupt Huaxia Securities was later taken over and dismembered, and Guotai Junan received a huge dollop of cash from the PBOC in 2005. China Development Trust, one of the major market players, and owned directly by the MOF, was finally closed by the PBOC in 2002, with RMB7 billion in debt. Jinxin Trust and Investment, another major player that had survived, was closed in October 2004, following massive losses totaling just over RMB4 billion from its proprietary trading activities alone. It had been owned by the famously bankrupted D'Long Group. In 2004, overall industry losses mounted; it was reported that for 57 of the then 130 securities companies losses totaled RMB680 million.[73] By the end of 2005, losses in the entire industry had reached RMB19.2 billion ($2.5 billion). These figures most certainly underestimate the actual extent of the industry's problems; there has never been a thorough and professional audit of their financial books.

Although many of these companies were technically illiquid and a few had been closed by 2005, they had not yet lost their political power. Corporate bankruptcy in China, especially in the financial sector, is a rare thing. But where could the securities companies look for new capital and who was going to "pick up the bill" (*maidan*) for the enormous small-investor losses? Local governments were not about to commit new money. At the central level, the CSRC had no money, and the MOF's national budget that required approval by the people's congress had no such funds approved. One doubts if the NDRC had even considered such funds in its Big Book. In its role as the central bank only the PBOC could serve as the lender of last resort and the PBOC was ready with a plan.

72 *Caijing*, November 5, 2001, 63.
73 *Jingji Guancha Bao*, May 23, 2005, 14. Reliable financial statements for most of the medium-sized and smaller companies may not have existed; because they were not "public" companies, their shareholders may not have required formal audited statements—as incredible as that may seem.

Reform 2: PBOC Seeks to Transform
the Securities Industry, 2005

So the man who at the CSRC had developed a policy that could have helped resolve both the divided stock market and the underfunded NSSF was five years later at the head of the PBOC. He was faced with cleaning up a mess the interest groups had blamed him for in the first place. His personal involvement and sponsorship of a new policy that would have opened the markets to meaningful foreign participation inevitably led to conflict with a CSRC-led by a man with deep industry ties. This dispute shed light over the entire world inside of the central bank that was normally obscure to public eyes: the Financial Stability Bureau, a shadowy company called China SAFE Investments Ltd., commonly referred to as Huijin, as well as other murky but important entities.

Huijin had been established on December 6, 2003, as a wholly-owned PBOC investment company with capital of RMB372.5 billion sourced directly from the government's foreign exchange reserves held by the State Administration for Foreign Exchange (SAFE), also a department of the PBOC.[74] At first, its role was clear: to serve as the state's agent to recapitalize the Bank of China ($22.5 billion), Bank of Communications ($3 billion), ICBC ($15 billion), and CCB ($22.5 billion). During the process of the latter's restructuring, however, the PBOC split the CCB's designated $22.5 billion of new capital into two pieces. One half remained in Huijin but the other was injected by Huijin as capital into a new organization called China Jianyin Investments Ltd. (China Jianyin) formed in September 2004 to hold the CCB's noncommercial banking assets.[75] Then, as the securities industry crisis worsened during 2004, Zhou Xiaochuan, PBOC governor, considered using both Huijin and China Jianyin to stabilize illiquid securities companies under the aegis of maintaining financial stability. After all, the industry was screaming "systemic risk" to get what it wanted; why should the PBOC not use the same excuse to attempt industry reform? By mid-year 2005 events had deteriorated, but the PBOC had a plan to address the crisis faced by the securities industry.[76]

---

74 These reserves were transferred from the SAFE. Huijin had ten directors, four from the SAFE, two from the PBOC, three from the MOF, and one from the CSRC who later joined the PBOC. *Caijing*, October 4, 2004, 58; *Jingji Guancha Bao*, May 23, 2005, 10.

75 This was done as part of the CCB's restructuring into a commercial bank. See *Jingji Guancha Bao*, August 29, 2005, 10 and May 23, 2005, 10.

76 Xie Ping, "Jinkuai Jianli Touzi Baohu Jijin" [Quickly Establish a Fund to Protect Investments], *Zhongguo Zhengquan Bao*, October 18, 2004. Xie Ping was chairman of Huijin and former head of the PBOC Financial Stability Bureau.

TABLE 9.4

Total Estimated Cost of "Financial Stability" to the PBOC

Time Period	Amount (RMB bn)	Use
1997–2002	141.1	Re-lending to closed trust companies, city cooperatives, and rural agricultural cooperatives to repay individual and certain external debts
1998	604.1	Re-lending to the 4 AMCs for the first round of acquisition of bank non-performing loans
From 2002	30.0	Re-lending to 11 closed securities companies to repay retail investor debt
2003 and 2005	60.0	Huijin recapitalizes BOC, CCB, and ICBC
2004–2005	1,223.6	Re-lending to Cinda and 3 other AMCs for the second round of acquisition of bank NPLs
2005	60.0	To resolve systemic risks of securities companies
2005	10.0	Re-lending to the Investor Protection Fund
Total	2,128.8	
USD equivalent (bn)	266.1	

Sources: *Jingji Guancha Bao*, November 14, 2005, 3; *Caijing*, July 25, 2005, 67.

On June 12, the market dropped below 1000 points for the first time in eight years, causing broad panic in the CSRC and State Council. This provided an opening and the PBOC announced through Huijin it would provide a RMB6.5 billion re-lending facility to two major securities firms, Shenyin Wanguo and Guotai Junan.[77] Historically, the PBOC had simply provided loans of last resort to various parts of a broken financial sector as "coffin money"; it had extended many loans but little was ever repaid (see Tables 9.4 and 9.5).[78] Indeed, like bank loans, recipients saw such re-lending simply as a reallocation of state monies between its right and left pockets: where was the obligation to repay and to whom? Such thinking, at least in the mind of the PBOC team, did not accord with China's new market-based reform.

So why did the PBOC decide to alleviate the liquidity problems of two historically disreputable[79] firms rather than bury them? Before this question

77 *Jingji Guancha Bao*, August 8, 2005, 13 and June 13, 2005, 9, which describe the panic in the government when the market broke through 1000 points; and *Caijing*, July 25, 2005, 60–64.

78 *Caijing*, June 27, 2005, 46–47; also see *Caijing*, July 25, 2005, 67–68, for the story of how the PBOC has been continuously stiffed by its borrowers.

79 As noted, Shenyin Wanguo was a product of the 1995 bond futures scandal, whereas Guotai Junan was the product of the collapse of Junan Securities following its chairman's attempt to steal ownership of the company! Walter and Howie, *Privatizing China*, 154.

TABLE 9.5

Security Company Debt and PBOC Small Investor Repayments, 2004–2005

Legend:

A. Misappropriated deposits and certificates of deposit sold to retail investors.

B. Loss-making guaranteed return contracts for institutional and retail investors.

C. Cash losses from sale of government bonds in repo transactions.

D. Misappropriation of client bond portfolios to raise cash through repo.

E. Overdrawn securities settlement accounts at Central Settlement Company.

F. Defaulted financing provided by banks and others.

G. Losses of proprietary trading position in equities.

(in RMB bn) Name	A	B	C	D	E	F	G	Total	PBOC Funding
Southern	8.4	–	–	–	1.2	12.8	7.8	30.2	8.4
Minfa	2.1	–	7.1	0.66	1.1	10.4	–	21.4	2.1
Hantang	1.7	3.0	–	0.84	0.96	–	–	6.5	2.0
Deheng	1.8	8.2	–	7.4	–	·	–	17.4	5.0
Hengxin	0.2	–	–	2.28	0.1	3.5	–	6.1	1.85
Zhongfu	–	0.89	0.38	–	–	0.2	–	1.5	0.42
Liaoning	4.1	–	–	–	–	–	–	4.1	4.2
Xinhua	–	1.4	–	–	–	–	–	–	1.4
Galaxy*	–	–	–	–	–	–	–	–	5.5
Huaxia*	1.6	3.4	–	–	–	–	–	5.0	5.0
Guotai Junan*	–	–	–	–	–	–	–	–	2.5
Shenyin Wanguo*	–	–	–	–	–	–	–	–	4.0
Dapeng	1.8	–	–	.6	.2	–	–	2.6	1.8
Southwest**	–	–	–	–	–	–	–	–	2.0
Minzu*	–	–	–	–	–	–	–	–	0.5
Hua'an**	–	–	–	–	–	–	–	–	0.6
Xiangcai**	–	–	–	–	–	–	–	–	1.5
Totals	21.7	16.89	7.5	11.8	3.6	26.9	7.8	94.9	48.8

Sources: Caijing, July 25, 2005, 68 for Xinhua, Hantang; 62 for Huaxia; *Caijing,* July 27, 2005, 46, for Galaxy; *Jingji Guancha Bao,* August 30, 2005, 18 for Guangdong, 4 for Kunlun, and 22 for Minzu, Southwest, and Hua'an; September 5, 2005, 9 for Xiangcai; and August 8, 2005, 13 for Shenyin Wanguo and Guotai Junan; all others are official sources.

Notes: *PBOC acting through Huijin injected these amounts as capital; **China Jianyin Investment.

could even be posed, in early July the PBOC suddenly added direct equity injections to the idea of loans. In speeches by Zhou and a senior vice governor, the PBOC's new strategy was described as, "using market forces to reorganize key securities companies."[80] With this it became clear that Zhou Xiaochuan intended to use Huijin and China Jianyin to take over major portions of the securities industry as the first step in a so-called "market-based

80 See *Caijing,* July 25, 2005, 62; and *Jingji Guancha Bao,* September 12, 2005, 9.

solution." Instead of paying for coffins, the PBOC and its agents would assume direct control over key securities companies by injecting equity capital, with the aim of reorganizing them so that they could later be sold and recoup at least some of the funds.[81] At this point, the central bank viewed only ten of the existing 130 securities companies as sufficiently important to rescue. In addition to Shenyin and Guotai, the others included Galaxy, Huaxia, Beijing, Xiangcai, Hua'an, Tiantong, Zhongguo Keji, and Zhongfu. All had been major players before the crisis.

Observers commented that by taking equity the PBOC was putting itself in the position of a cash machine for these bankrupt companies.[82] This comment was entirely disingenuous: the PBOC had always been the ATM for failure in the financial sector, as Table 9.5 clearly shows. This time around the PBOC's real motivation was obvious. As an unnamed (but nevertheless well-known) official in its Financial Stability Bureau said, "What's going on now is that the PBOC comes up with the money to deal with the troubled securities companies and no one is willing to repay it. At least this way we get an equity interest." He also was being disingenuous: the more important reason was to gain control over a process that under the CSRC had been going nowhere and with PBOC control would come reform of the securities industry.[83]

The PBOC's intent became clearer as the list of target invested firms expanded and China Jianyin began to invest as well. A division of labor emerged as Huijin invested primarily in major central government-owned entities (the banks and Galaxy Securities), whereas China Jianyin invested in medium-sized companies such as Beijing and Hua'an Securities (see Figure 9.3). Under this arrangement, the CSRC confirmed which firms were to receive aid and the AMCs were entrusted to carry out the restructuring of bankrupt companies on behalf of the new owner, the PBOC. As an official at Minzu Securities commented in September 2005, "The CSRC may sponsor a securities company but all the money is from the PBOC and following its restructuring, all the controlling shareholders will be under the PBOC's banner. Hereafter, all good securities companies will be under the true control of the PBOC."[84]

81 A vice chairman of Huijin, however, stated that Huijin would not become the SASAC of the financial sector. *Jingji Guancha Bao*, May 23, 2005, 10.

82 An editorial in *Quanqiu Caijing Guancha* [Global Business Observer], June 20, 2005, 2, vigorously argued against the PBOC's justification, saying that the bank's lender-of-last-resort role should only be exercised in the event of systemic risk and that bankrupt securities firms should either be acquired by other investors or simply closed.

83 This strategy continues to this day, as seen in China's bond markets. Faced with a non-reformist bureaucratic adversary, the CSRC and the NDRC, the PBOC leveraged the inter-bank market by creating new, previously unplanned, corporate fixed-income securities.

84 *Jingji Guancha Bao*, September 12, 2005, 9.

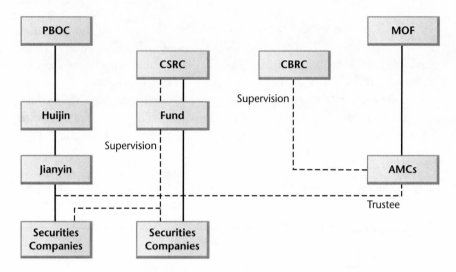

FIGURE 9.3 Institutional Approach to Failed Securities Companies
Source: Author.

What then of the proposed Investor Protection Fund[85] and the CSRC's position as industry and market regulator? Huijin and China Jianyin seemed to control, and even to be spending, the capital that would otherwise have financed the fund, leaving the CSRC out in the cold. In fact, the idea of such a fund was stillborn as none of the ministries involved—MOF, PBOC, CSRC, and CBRC—could agree on how much money would go into it or its source. As a result, no regulations governing the fund or its use appeared.[86] In the absence of an agreement, the PBOC unilaterally acted and acted swiftly, based broadly on the authority given to it by the November 2004 "Opinion" on the repayment of small investor losses.[87] Table 9.5 shows the extent and type of fraudulent financial losses incurred by seventeen securities companies, for which the PBOC provided equity and debt financing

85 The fund would have involved the PBOC by providing the money to establish the fund and the fund would have re-lent funds to the bankrupt securities companies to repay the defrauded retail investors. In other words, the PBOC would not have been repaid.

86 *Caijing*, July 25, 2005, 61.

87 The loophole is in PBOC, MOF, CBRC, CSRC, "Geren Zhaiquan Ji Kehu Zhengquan Jiaoyi Jiesuan Jijin Shougou Yijian" [Opinion on the Purchase of Individual Debt and Client Securities Transactions Settlement Fund], November 5, 2004. Article 6 states, "The purchase of client settlement funds-related debt will first be done by re-lending from the PBOC. The repayment of this re-lending will then come first from funds recovered from the liquidation of the bankrupt financial organizations in which the regulators participate and any remainder will be repaid from a securities investor-protection repayment fund to be set up afterwards," *Jingji Guancha Bao*, February 20, 2006, 18.

totaling RMB49 billion in 2004-5. These funds were used to repay the losses of retail investors totaling about RMB50 billion (columns A, B, and D); institutional investors received nothing under this program.[88]

From the transfer of brokerage licensing power from the PBOC to the CSRC in 1998, to its elevation to ministry status in 1999, and then under the strong leadership of Zhou Xiaochuan from 2000 to 2002, the CSRC had aggressively pursued cases of fraud and market reform. In early 2002, following Zhou's departure for the central bank, the CSRC's reformist momentum seemed to go with him. With its overseas trained and experienced staff gone, the "new" CSRC scrambled for four years as it pulled out all stops at the industry's behest to restore the market's status quo. As Huijin's outspoken director Xie Ping stated, "As soon as the market index falls, regulation becomes lax and this is not appropriate."[89] So, in the absence of CSRC action and with the indecisiveness of other parts of the state, by mid-2005 the PBOC was quickly taking over ownership of a major part of the securities industry.

Although Zhou Xiaochuan may have been facing a problem created by a failed policy initiative, he and his team were still reformist and most certainly not in the industry's pocket. In the eyes of the central bank, the securities industry was not yet strategic to the country's economy—such importance was reserved for the banks. Nonetheless, it was critical for the country's future to promote the healthy and proper development of true capital markets in order to diversify risk away from the banks. Now the PBOC and Zhou Xiaochuan would have a turn at accomplishing what had never been done before: fix the industry.

Business Interests Fight Again for the Status Quo

It is one thing to take over troubled securities companies and another to manage them, but the PBOC did not intend to become the SASAC of the financial industry.[90] The central bank intended to restructure the firms it

---

88 This is at best a partial list compiled from official and public sources; there may be a few smaller securities companies not included here. In general, however, this table represents the vast bulk of the PBOC's financial assistance. Retail investors were compensated for up to 100 percent of their losses up to RMB100,000 and 90 percent of their losses over RMB100,000.

89 For a profile of the highly idiosyncratic director, see Jamil Anderlini, "Firm Hand Steers Vehicle of Financial Reform," *South China Morning Post*, February 6, 2006.

90 The PBOC viewed the SASAC as a failed structure. In the case of the banks, Huijin acts as the state's representative to hold equity stakes and is represented on the board of directors. Bank senior management, however, is appointed by the party acting through the Ministry of Personnel. In the case of the securities companies, the story is a bit more complicated. See *Jingji Guancha Bao*, May 23, 2005, 10.

had invested in, close down and liquidate non-securities–related assets, and then sell the restructured new firms to other healthy securities companies. The sales would have the direct benefit of partially recovering the bank's capital investment and loans. China Jianyin's acquisition of the 74 broker-age offices of Southern Securities and their use to establish a new company is an example of this strategy, as is China Jianyin's joint venture with Citic Securities (Citic Jianyin Securities), formed on the ruins of the old Huaxia.[91]

This initiative, however, would not drive the transformation of the in-dustry as a whole. Knowing this, the PBOC had in mind an even more far-reaching plan: open the industry's door directly to foreign investment banks. This would have two benefits: it would bring in new money rather than re-cycling the state's own money, and foreign-controlled firms would over time catalyze industry and market change. At the start of 2005 there were a number of foreign banks exploring entry into the domestic market, largely on the terms of the highly unattractive CSRC 2002 regulation.[92] Zhou had played an important role in facilitating the formation of Goldman Sachs' so-called "joint venture" securities company in 2003. Goldman's JV repre-sented the first significant breach in the protectionist wall surrounding the industry. In private discussions in late 2004, the PBOC offered a 51 percent controlling stake in Liaoning Securities to a handful of foreign banks, one of which won the opportunity and, sponsored by the PBOC, submitted an application to the State Council early in the summer of 2005.

The CSRC caught wind of this and began working with a second for-eign bank in order to develop an alternative to the PBOC. This particu-lar bank, prior to the PBOC bidding, had been working with Mayor Wang Qishan and the city of Beijing to restructure one of its broken securities firms, Beijing Securities. The CSRC was unwilling to give this bank outright economic control, but it made a verbal promise that it could have unchal-lenged management control even with a minority stake.[93] The CSRC, deeply aligned with industry interests, was adamantly opposed to opening the in-dustry to any form of foreign control, but it had to have a plan to coun-ter the PBOC plan. Both applications were formally submitted to the State

---

91 *Jingji Guancha Bao*, July 18, 2005, 9. Huaxia was such a mess that it was dismem-bered and entered into bankruptcy proceedings.

92 This regulation requires a foreign bank to work with a local securities company to establish a JV investment banking operation. The JV can only underwrite and it is excluded from proprietary trading and brokering activities. These profitable businesses remain with the JV's Chinese investor; the maximum stake the foreign bank can hold in the JV is 33 percent.

93 See "Fixing Broken Brokers," *The Economist*, February 9, 2006.

Council for approval at the end of the summer. By late September it seemed that the PBOC's vision would prove successful.[94]

Of course, the CSRC opposed the PBOC's view and regarded the securities industry as strategic. Given these differing views, staff in the two organizations were not even speaking to each other at this point and there remained and remains to this day deep personal animus. Unfortunately, however, the PBOC's actions on a variety of fronts that year did not go unchallenged by other powerful political actors. In August, the director of the NDRC publicly criticized the PBOC for infringing on the territory of other ministries, including the MOF (and, of course, himself).[95] He had reason: the PBOC in May had announced the creation of a short-term bond market for corporations that soon became very active. This was a sphere of NDRC control—except for the less than one year market that the PBOC had claimed.[96] And the MOF had not been happy at all: the PBOC through Huijin now owned three of the four major commercial banks that the MOF had previously controlled. The PBOC was taking actions that would concentrate huge chunks of the banking and securities industry, replacing the MOF as the state's principal holder of financial assets.[97] This fact became public when the press compared the PBOC's equity holdings in the financial sector with the SASAC's holdings in industry.[98] There was also the CBRC that claimed jurisdiction over China Jianyin and the MOF that directly owned the asset management companies, which acted as trustee over many of the bankrupt securities firms. The political environment grew ugly and Zhou Xiaochuan came under unprecedented personal attack in the Hong Kong press.[99]

94 *Jingji Guancha Bao*, October 3-10, 2005, 14.

95 *Market News International*, August 15, 2005; at about the same time a small newspaper in Hong Kong published an article severely criticizing Zhou Xiaochuan; see Richard McGregor, "Ominous Undertones of an Attack on Reform," *Financial Times*, February 27, 2006.

96 In fact, through 1999 the PBOC and NDRC together had overseen the enterprise bond market. The AFC, however, had led to many corporate bond defaults, resulting in the PBOC handing over the entire product to the NDRC. But under the new governor, Zhou Xiaochuan, the corporate debt market was seen as a way to provide capital when the stock markets remained closed and commercial paper was introduced.

97 *Caijing*, June 27, 2005, 46.

98 At this point, the PBOC, SASAC, and MOF all held substantial financial assets, according to *Jingji Guancha Bao*, December 12, 2005, 1 and 5. The SASAC's SOEs were investors in a large number of non-bank financial institutions and the PBOC had three state banks and innumerable security companies, leaving the MOF in a much less prestigious position.

99 Su Meice, "Zhongguo Xuyao Yige Wenzhongde Yanghang Hangzhang" [China Needs a Serious Central Bank Governor], *Chengbao* (Hong Kong), January 4, 2006. This article was clearly sourced by a mainland author.

During the summer months this bureaucratic struggle mounted, forcing the State Council to adjudicate during the October National Day holidays. On September 28, the quiet establishment of China Securities Investor Protection Fund Limited perhaps signified which way the winds were blowing.[100] Immediately after the holidays it became clear that the PBOC and its subsidiaries had lost the battle and that its efforts to open the market to foreign banks in a straightforward manner were deferred in favor of the CSRC model. The CSRC promptly went back on its word given in the Beijing Securities case and negotiated tooth and nail with the foreign bank to limit its management control rights.[101] It was not until 2007 that the restructured Beijing Securities, now called UBS Securities, was actually able to begin business operations.

Making things worse, following the CCB's successful IPO in Hong Kong in late October 2005, a vicious political debate broke out opposing foreign investment in the financial sector and even challenging the entire direction that China's reform process had taken.[102] This was capped by Premier Wen Jiabao's comments at the annual Central Economic Work Conference in early December when he declared the financial sector "critical to national security" and called for the maintenance of outright control. Against this background, it was riskless for the CSRC to state that the securities market was closed to foreign investment until it had been cleaned up, perhaps in two years' time.[103] Chairman Shang Fulin relayed to foreign visitors innumerable times the following little homily, "Until the living room is thoroughly swept clean, we won't invite any guests to visit."

100 *Caijing*, October 3, 2005, 69. This was a CSRC-subordinated entity that would manage the Investor Protection Fund.

101 The deal received CSRC approval in early fall 2006 and opened for operations over a year later after difficult and costly negotiations.

102 See Richard McGregor, "A Fierce Battle Hobbles China's March to the Market," *Financial Times*, February 27, 2006, at http://www.ft.com/cms/s/d4004660-a7c4-11da -85bc-0000779e2340,Authorised=false.html?_i_location=http%3A%2F%2Fwww.ft .com%2Fcms%2Fs%2F1%2Fd4004660-a7c4-11da-85bc-0000779e2340.html&_i_referer =http%3A%2F%2Feconomistsview.typepad.com%2Feconomistsview%2F2006%2F02 %2Feconomic_reform.html, accessed September 4, 2010. This occasioned many articles; see the section dedicated to defending reform in *Jingji Guancha Bao*, December 19, 2005, 37ff.

103 *Jingji Guancha Bao*, December 5, 2005, 15. Under tremendous pressure, the CSRC shortly thereafter changed its tactics and said that the doors were not really closed. But it was just being polite, the doors were closed. See *Diyi Caijing Ribao* [China Business News], January 23, 2006, B1. The loose coalition of leftists, conservatives, and old Marxists who opposed foreign participation in the reforms of the financial sector became known as "Boxers."

In November the CSRC's Investor Protection Fund suddenly came to life and in January 2006 it made its first disbursement—a total of RMB1.2 billion to Guangdong Securities and five other smaller firms.[104] It seemed that moving forward into 2006, the CSRC would seek to use its Investor Protection Fund to restructure and sell selected securities firms and that the PBOC would now be back in its old coffin money business.[105] How much remained of the originally discussed RMB68 billion was uncertain as the PBOC had already lent or injected nearly RMB50 billion in capital. Rumor had it that the CSRC had received only RMB10 billion by the end of 2005.[106] Then early in 2006 the PBOC announced that it would provide new funding only in cases specifically approved by the State Council. Given the nature of such approvals, in practice this meant no more money was available: the CSRC would have to find another way to revive the industry by its declared deadline of October 31, 2006.[107] At the same time, China Jianyin also ran out of funds: the CBRC would not permit it to issue bonds as the PBOC had originally planned. The pace of securities company takeovers slowed down dramatically and then stopped altogether. From all this it was clear that China's securities industry and its interest groups had survived their greatest crisis intact and without fundamental change.

Conclusion

What do our findings have to say about corporate restructuring and reform? The lesson seems clear. China has most of the institutions in place that support capital market development—exchanges, Western-style corporations, clearing houses, securities and mutual fund companies, industry

104 *Jingji Guancha Bao*, January 16, 2006, 23.

105 The CSRC idea of restructuring the industry did not differ from the PBOC's: restructure firms, make them healthy, and sell them off at a high premium to foreign banks. The new regulation allows foreign banks to buy up to 24.99 percent of a listed Chinese securities company; at recent valuations this would involve more than US$3 billion. Therefore, on the surface the market is open, but the reality is that no one will pay such an inflated price.

106 For this figure, see *Caijing*, July 25, 2005, 67. In early March 2006, Zhou Xiaochuan counterattacked, stating at a press conference during the National People's Congress that any further bailouts and expenditure of PBOC funds would require State Council approval; see Guo Fenglin, "Zhou Xiaochuan: Wenti Quanshang Qiuzhu Xu Jing Guowuyuan Pizhun" [Assistance to Troubled Securities Firms Requires State Council Approval], March 8, 2006, at http://finance.sina.com.cn/stock/y/20060308/13012401133.shtml, accessed October 29, 2010.

107 In fact, with no funds of its own, the CSRC forced existing investors in troubled firms to come up with recapitalization plans or lose their licenses and be shut down.

associations, bankers, regulators, accountants, asset appraisers, and a host of policies, regulations, and operating procedures. There are supporting institutions, but the country's adaptation of the Western capital market model is superficial. The problem is not the lack of institutions but the character of the institutions as they operate in China's political economy. This chapter has shown that all aspects of the capital markets remain owned by some agency of the state. Moral hazard remains rife throughout the economy and government. Until these "Chinese characteristics" are removed and strong and independent institutions that underpin functioning stock markets are established, truly internationally competitive Chinese companies and banks will remain a chimera.

Over a decade of economic reform had created the foundation for China's stock markets, but events demonstrated time and again that the struggle over ownership of assets—in fact, the privatization of state assets—was the future that could not be given a name and if named could not be spoken out loud. This inability to address the most basic aspect of economic life is the source of China's corporate restructuring problems. In the transition between the amorphous ownership of a so-called centrally planned economy to that of a market system, private individuals have been aggressively stripping the state of assets under the guise of the state itself.[108]

Corporatization and listing by its most fundamental definition—selling ownership interests in a corporation—place the entirety of the securities industry at the very heart of this reality. The government's effort to avoid this issue—the creation of non-tradable shares and the sale of only new shares—did not work. The government was kidding itself that this prevented the sale of those assets that it had originally invested in and owned. Many market and government entities understood this full well and sought to increase and protect their own interests in the guise of the state. This created confusion, distorted the market mechanism, weakened institutions like the CSRC, and had negative policy consequences both for market and social development. To this extent, China is lacking the proper institutions that would give clarity to the functioning of a stock market.

At the same time, however, the actions of the PBOC in 2005, like those of the CSRC in 2001, can be seen as an instance when part of the state, in each case organizations under the same person and set of subordinates, attempted to make use of and strengthen those institutions to drive forward reform of the economy. The restructuring and sale of bankrupt

---

108 The most outrageous example of the privatization of major state assets by a senior official is that of Shandong Power (Luneng). See Li Qiyan, "Shui de Luneng?" [Whose Shandong Power?], *Caijing*, January 8, 2007, 2ff.

securities companies could have helped recover the banks' original invest-ment; a broader securities market reform could have aided in the creation of true capital markets and made possible the funding of social security and other important state policy initiatives. The contrast in policies, actions, and objectives, both personal and institutional, between the CSRC under Zhou Xiaochuan and the same agency under Shang Fulin, clearly illustrate why Chinese call their country's system of government "rule by persons" (renzhi).

During his Southern Tour in January 1992 Deng Xiaoping was asked about his support for the stock market experiments of the 1980s. His reply provided the basic political support reformers needed to push forward enter-prise reform through the markets. He said:

> Are such things as securities and stock markets good or not? Are they dangerous? Do these things exist only in capitalist systems or can socialist ones use them too? It is permitted to try them out, but it must be done with determination. If they work out, if they are tried out for a year or two and work out right, then we will open up. If they are mistakes, then just correct them or close the markets. If they are closed, they can be closed quickly or they can be closed slowly, or we can leave a little bit of a tail.[109]

Over fifteen years later there is no doubt but that China has experi-mented with stock markets in a "determined" fashion and that these mar-kets have set in motion a process that ultimately may completely change the character of the country's economy. As for corporate restructuring, the lesson seems to be more uncertain. The findings in this chapter question the role markets can play when they remain subject to capture by the state and/or its agents.

109 *Deng Xiaoping wenxuan* [Selected Works of Deng Xiaoping] (Beijing: Renmin chubanshe, 1993), 3: 373.

10 Spin-offs and Corporate Governance

LISTED FIRMS IN CHINA'S STOCK MARKETS

Lu Zheng and Byung-Soo Kim

The purpose of this chapter is to examine the relationship between listed firms and their state-controlled parents in China's domestic stock markets. We argue that largely due to a concentrated share structure, many state-controlled listed firms are used by their parent groups to extract capital from the stock market. Our research reveals that capital is transferred from listed firms to their unlisted parents through a variety of related-party transactions. We utilize an institutional framework to understand the problems of the ineffective corporate governance associated with China's stock markets.

This study makes three important contributions to the existing literature. First, we open the "black box" of Chinese public firms to examine how and the extent to which they are constructed and utilized as cash cows for their parent corporations. Second, we contribute to the corporate governance literature by focusing on dominant shareholders, as opposed to the conventional focus in the literature on the top managers.[1] We contend that many premises of the existing literature on corporate governance, such as dispersed ownership and takeover markets, do not fit the reality of China's stock markets. Therefore, the fundamental problem in corporate governance of China's public companies has less to do with aligning managers' interests to shareholder value than to controlling and balancing the power of the parent groups, the controlling shareholders of most listed

---

1 Adolf A. Berle and Gardiner C. Means, *The Modern Corporation and Private Property* (New York: Macmillan, 1932).

firms. Third, we argue that by synthesizing the concept of institutional complementarities[2] and the sociological definition of institutions,[3] we will have a better understanding of institutional changes in general and China's transition to a market economy in particular.

Introduction

By year-end 2007, over 1,500 firms had made initial public offerings (IPOs) in the Shanghai and Shenzhen stock exchanges. One of the main objectives of establishing the stock markets was to provide a new financing channel to fund thirsty state-owned enterprises (SOEs). Thus, the selection process for the IPOs purposely favored the SOEs, whereas it discriminated against privately-owned or foreign-owned firms. Therefore, it is not surprising that the majority (around 1,200) of the listed firms were former SOEs.

As Walter argues in this volume and elsewhere, to ensure that the state retains control over listed firms, publicly-traded former SOEs are governed by a state-dominated share structure, meaning that the majority of the shares are held by the state, either directly through its government agencies or indirectly through state-owned companies. In a typical SOE-turned-listed firm, only about one-third of the total shares are issued to the public (called "individual person shares") and are freely traded on the exchanges. The other two-thirds, including state shares and legal-person shares, are not tradable on the stock exchanges. The state shares reflect the state assets injected into the firm in its previous operations; various state-controlled institutions (SOEs or government agencies) hold state shares on behalf of the ultimate owner, the state.[4] Legal-person shares represent a complex and mixed category. They are issued to domestic institutions, such as stock companies, non-bank financial institutions, and state and non-state firms.

2 Bruno Amable, "Institutional Complementarity and Diversity of Social Systems of Innovation and Production," *Review of International Political Economy* 7, no. 4 (December 2000): 645–87; Peter A. Hall and David Soskice, eds., *Varieties of Capitalism: The Institutional Foundations of Comparative Advantage* (New York: Oxford University Press, 2001).

3 Richard W. Scott, *Institutions and Organizations* (Thousand Oaks, CA: Sage Publications, 2nd ed., 2001).

4 After the creation of the State-owned Assets Supervision and Administration Commission (SASAC) in March 2003, central and local SASACs took control of the state shares.

TABLE 10.1

State-controlled Listed Companies, as of 2001

Categories	Number	Percentage
State-owned enterprises	668	58.9
Government agencies	102	9.0
State-controlled unlisted firms	114	10.0
State-controlled listed firms	30	2.6
State-owned academic institutions	13	1.1
Total state-controlled companies	927	81.6
Total non-state-controlled companies	209	18.4

Source: Guy S. Liu and Pei Sun, "The Class of Shareholdings and Its Impacts on Corporate Performance: A Case of State Shareholding Composition in Chinese Public Corporations," *Corporate Governance* 13, no. 1 (January 2005): 46–59, based on FY2001 data.

State-controlled Listed Firms

Given the preset share structure, listed firms are largely controlled by local governments and parent business groups that hold state shares and/or legal-person shares. According to one study,[5] the state, including the SOEs, the SASAC, and other government agencies, is the ultimate controlling shareholder of 81.6 percent of all listed firms. Among these 81.6 percent, 58.9 percent are controlled by SOEs (see Table 10.1). This clearly reveals that the majority of listed firms are ultimately controlled by SOEs or other government agencies.

Analysis of the ownership structure of listed firms over time, however, indicates a gradual and steady decline in the proportion of state-controlled listed firms. Based on data compiled by the China Center for Economic Research (CCER) at Peking University, we found the figure decreased from about 84 percent in 1998 to 76 percent in 2007 (see Figure 10.1).[6] These numbers suggest that the controlling shareholding of some listed companies has been transferred from the state to private parties. Nevertheless,

5 The study is based on all listed companies at the end of 2001. See Guy S. Liu and Pei Sun, "The Class of Shareholdings and Its Impacts on Corporate Performance: A Case of State Shareholding Composition in Chinese Public Corporations," *Corporate Governance* 13, no. 1 (January 2005): 46–59.

6 This figure does not include the companies listed on the Medium and Small Enterprise Board of the Shenzhen Stock Exchange. The board was established in 2004 to provide a platform for smaller-sized companies. By 2007, among the 216 companies listed on this board, 152 were controlled by private parties.

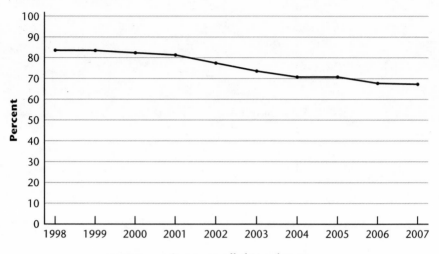

FIGURE 10.1 State-controlled Listed Firms as a
Proportion of All Listed Firms, 1998–2007
Source: CCER database (2008).

about two-thirds of the companies listed on China's stock markets are still under the grip of SOEs or, to a lesser extent, other state agencies.

Related-party Transactions

The state-dominated share structure and the prevalence of listed spin-offs from the SOE parent group provide fertile ground for what is known as *related-party transactions*, referring particularly to business transactions between a major shareholder and the company. In many cases, such related-party transactions may be normal and legal when they fulfill underlying economic needs of the company. However, the special relationship between the involved parties may create potential conflicts of interest, which may potentially result in actions that benefit the parties involved rather than the shareholders. Even in a developed market like that in the United States, where all public companies are required to disclose all transactions with related parties, a series of scandals relating to this problem have been disclosed. For instance, related-party transactions with "special-purpose entities" were used to help Enron disguise its troubled financial position.[7] In the current financial crisis, "structured investment vehicles," which were set up by big banks to trade U.S. subprime mortgage-backed bonds and collateralized

7 Simon Deakin and Suzanne J. Konzelmann, "Learning from Enron," *Corporate Governance* 12, no. 2 (April 2004): 134–42.

debt obligations, played a key role in dragging the global financial market to the verge of collapse.[8]

Similar corporate scandals have frequently occurred in China's stock markets. During the ten-year period from 1993 to 2003, 200 of 1,200 listed firms were apprehended for malfeasance.[9] Violations include asset appropriations, illegal guarantees for bank loans, non-disclosure of information, and false financial statements. Such violations were often committed through related-party transactions between listed firms and their SOE parents. These irregularities distorted market information and dampened investor confidence. In light of the above problems, we attempt to understand and explicate the origin and nature of the relationship between listed firms and their SOE parents. We will attempt to answer the following two questions: (1) how is this ownership structure manifested in related-party transactions? and (2) what is the reason for the failure of current corporate governance mechanisms?

The remainder of this chapter consists of four parts. We first discuss why SOEs adopt the spin-off tactic, pointing out that SOEs spin off subsidiaries primarily to list them rather than to use them as a way to increase efficiency. Second, we examine the corporate governance mechanisms of listed firms. Third, we analyze related-party transactions between listed companies and their parent SOEs. We identify a pattern by which many listed firms and their parent groups manipulate the system to benefit the dominant shareholders at the cost of the minority shareholders. In the conclusion, we link the empirical findings to a theoretical discussion on institutional complementarities and institutional change.

Listed Firms as Artificial Spin-offs

The Shanghai and Shenzhen stock markets are magnets for financially troubled enterprises. By gaining access to the emerging equity markets in China, an average listed firm will raise approximately RMB869 million (around US$104.7 million) in investment capital.[10] As Walter's chapter in this volume argues, such huge rewards create strong incentives for SOEs to rush onto the IPO playing-field. Although tens of thousands of SOEs desire

8 Gillian Tett, Paul J. Davies, and Norma Cohen, "Structured Investment Vehicles' Role in Crisis," *Financial Times*, August 12, 2007.

9 Zhang Yi and Guang Ma, "Law, Corporate Governance, and Corporate Scandal in a Transition Economy," Guanghua School of Management, Working Paper, Peking University, 2005.

10 Stephen Green, "The Privatization Two-Step at China's Listed Firms," in Stephen Green and Guy S. Liu, eds., *Exit the Dragon? Privatization and State Control in China* (Malden, MA: Blackwell, 2005).

to go public, fewer than 1,600 firms have been lucky enough to join this club since the establishment of China's stock markets. The majority of listed firms are located in the coastal provinces, reflecting the regional disparities in China's economic development. For example, corporations in ten provinces (or provincial-level municipalities), such as Guangdong, Shanghai, Zhejiang, and Jiangsu, accounted for almost 65 percent of all IPOs from 1991 to 2007, leaving the other twenty-plus economically less-developed provinces with fewer opportunities to raise capital from the stock market (see Table 10.2). In terms of industries, as of 2007 more than half of the listed firms were in manufacturing. Modern industries, such as IT and banking and finance, constituted less than 10 percent of all listed firms (see Table 10.3).

A closer look at the listing process further reveals the characteristics shared by the lucky firms. According to the stated requirements, any share-holding limited-liability company with equity capital of over RMB50 million (around US$8.7 million) is eligible for listing if it has been profitable during the previous three years. However, this statement reveals little about the actual process. The regulations allow applicant firms that were formerly part of an SOE to claim assumed profit figures in previous years as if they were independent from the parent. Thus, many listed firms are established as spin-offs of large SOEs specifically for the purpose of meeting the IPO financial criteria. In many cases, an SOE initially identifies which parts of the SOE are productive and which parts are not. The SOE then carves out the productive parts and repackages them as an independent child company

TABLE 10.2

Provincial Distribution of
Approved IPOs, 1991–2007

Province	Number	Percentage
Guangdong	205	12.5
Shanghai	158	9.6
Zhejiang	124	7.5
Jiangsu	119	7.2
Beijing	106	6.4
Shandong	96	5.8
Sichuan	73	4.4
Hubei	64	3.9
Liaoning	60	3.6
Fujian	59	3.6
Other 21 Provinces	583	35.4
Total	1,647	100.0

Source: CCER database (2008).

TABLE 10.3

*Industrial Distribution of
Listed Companies, as of 2007*

Industrial Sector	Number	Percentage
Agriculture	39	2.5
Mining	33	2.1
Manufacturing	893	57.8
Energy and Water	64	4.1
Construction	34	2.2
Transport	69	4.5
IT	96	6.2
Wholesale and Retail	92	6.0
Banking and Finance	27	1.8
Real Estate	64	4.1
Social Services	46	3.0
Media	14	0.9
Conglomerates	74	4.8
Total	1,545	100.0

Source: CCER database (2008).

for listing. Meanwhile, the SOE is often restructured into a business group that controls the listed child company along with other unlisted companies. This process, known as "packaging" (*baozhuang*), explains why most listed firms in China are legally independent subsidiaries of the large SOEs. The SOE parents adopt the spin-off practice primarily to meet the stated financial performance criteria and to boost their child firm's chances of being selected for an IPO. This allows the large SOEs to move forward with change without forcing an immediate radical transformation.[11]

In addition to lacking a reliable track record, listed spin-offs also lack clear boundaries with their SOE parents. As Tenev and his collaborators note,

> Listing and parent companies are often in the same business sector and may compete with each other, have business transactions with each other, or share resources and functions. In some cases, the listed company may depend on the rest of the group for distributing products or supplying raw materials. Senior managers often work for both the listed and unlisted parts of the group. This type of interdependence between listed companies and their parent firms creates fertile ground for agency problems.[12]

11 Jean C. Oi, "Patterns of Corporate Restructuring in China: Political Constraints on Privatization," *China Journal*, no. 53 (January 2005): 115–36.

12 Stoyan Tenev and Chunlin Zhang, with Loup Brefort, *Corporate Governance and Enterprise Reform in China: Building the Institution of Modern Markets* (Washington, DC: International Finance Corporation, 2002).

This type of spin-off in China contrasts sharply with those in other market economies, where parent companies usually spin off subsidiaries in unrelated industries in order to streamline operations.[13] As a result, parents and spin-off companies do not usually have overlapping businesses. For example, in 1999 Hewlett Packard (HP) spun off Agilent, its semiconductor test and measurement unit, thus allowing HP to focus on its core computer and printer businesses.[14]

In contrast, the dominant role of SOE parents, by virtue of their controlling shareholding position, constitutes a constant challenge to the listed firm. Instead of operating in a way to maximize returns for *all* shareholders, listed firms in China are often hijacked by the controlling SOE parent to advance its own interests over those of the minority shareholders. To make things worse, safeguards that are supposed to prevent such hijackings, such as an effective corporate-governance regime, are not yet functioning.

Corporate Governance in China's Listed Firms

In a broad sense, corporate governance consists of "the whole set of legal, cultural, and institutional arrangements that determine what publicly traded corporations can do, who controls them, how that control is exercised, and how the risks and returns from the activities they undertake are allocated."[15] An ideal view of corporate governance holds that corporate structures, state corporate law and securities markets, should serve to enhance shareholder value for all shareholders, both large and small. A key to achieving this goal is to keep the company's top management, or the large shareholders, from enriching their own pockets at the expense of the widely dispersed minority shareholders.

It has been argued that corporate governance also requires an appropriate balance between the economic goals of the organization and social responsibility. Although an organization pursues its own economic goals, it is bounded by "communal goals" as well as "business ethics."[16] In other

---

13 Gerald F. Davis, Kristina A. Diekmann, and Catherine H. Tinsley, "The Decline and Fall of the Conglomerate Firm in the 1980s: The Deinstitutionalization of an Organizational Form," *American Sociological Review* 59, no. 4 (August 1994): 547–70.

14 David P. Hamilton, "Investors are Expected to Cheer HP's Agilent IPO," *Wall Street Journal* (Eastern Edition), November 18, 1999, B12.

15 Margaret M. Blair, *Ownership and Control: Rethinking Corporate Governance for the Twenty-First Century* (Washington, DC: Brookings Institute, 1995).

16 Ingrid Bonn and Josie Fisher, "Corporate Governance and Business Ethics: Insights from the Strategic Planning Experience," *Corporate Governance* 13, no. 6 (November 2005): 730–38.

words, the fundamental concept of corporate governance is based on an alignment among "the interests of individuals, corporations, and society."[17]

As complex and systematic as it should be, corporate governance adopted by public firms worldwide typically consists of a set of monitoring mechanisms to align the managers' interests with those of the shareholders. In the following, we examine two internal mechanisms, share structure and the board of directors, and two external mechanisms, market takeover and the legal system.

Share Structure

The share structure refers to the identities of the firm's shareholders as well as the size of their shares. Shareholders exert control over the firm by virtue of the percentage of shares that they possess. Developed markets, as in the United States and the United Kingdom, have large numbers of publicly traded firms, most of which are relatively widely held. In the United States, the largest shareholder on average controls 22.8 percent of the total shares. The level of share concentration in the UK is lower; the largest shareholder controls 14.0 percent of the total shares.[18] Compared to their counterparts in the advanced market economies, Chinese listed firms tend to have a higher level of share concentration. Our analysis, based on CCER data, shows that as of 2007 the largest shareholders in China's listed companies controlled on average 36 percent of all shares. Such a phenomenon, however, is not unique to Chinese public companies. Outside of the United States and the United Kingdom, the proportion of shares owned by the largest shareholders in several Western countries in 2007 was actually even higher than that in China; it was a staggering 82.2 percent in Austria, 59.7 percent in Germany, and 56 percent in France.[19] But what makes China different is not the rate of share concentration, but the identity of the controlling shareholders.

Many researchers have noted that German and Japanese markets feature not only more concentrated share structures, but also that the banks play a greater role in the equity markets. Financial institutions are the most important shareholders in Japan.[20] Also, German banks have the right to vote the proxies of many individual shareholders, which gives them greater voting

17 Bonn and Fisher, "Corporate Governance and Business Ethics."

18 Asian Development Bank, *Country Studies under RETA* (Manila, 1999); Robert Tricker, "Corporate Governance and the Challenges Ahead," *Corporate Governance International* 2, no. 2 (1999): 64-81.

19 Tricker, "Corporate Governance and the Challenges Ahead."

20 Stephen D. Prowse, "The Structure of Corporate Ownership in Japan," *Journal of Finance* 47, no. 3 (July 1992): 1121-40.

power than their ownership share would indicate.[21] In this regard, some researchers call Germany and Japan bank-centered economies, in contrast to the market-centered economies in the United States and the United Kingdom.

One important characteristic of China's stock markets, compared to their U.S. counterparts, is the lack of substantive ownership by institutional investors, whose ascent to corporate ownership has played an important role in encouraging management to maximize shareholder value.[22] The dominant shareholder in China is still the state or its agents. We argue that the dominant role of state ownership in Chinese public firms has compromised corporate governance in many ways.

The state has a variety of political and economic goals and therefore is often motivated by factors other than to increase the share value of a listed firm. Such intervening motivations include maintaining full employment, funding pensions and medical insurance, and providing housing and social services, all of which may conflict with cutting costs or improving efficiency.[23] In addition, state ownership often imposes non-market assessment criteria on the top managers of listed firms.[24] Since many top managers aspire to be promoted to high-level government positions and to advance their careers, the priorities of state owners have an undue influence on the managers' business decisions. To illustrate, local governments generally have an incentive to encourage firms under their jurisdiction to pile up investment and therefore churn out more taxes. This expansionist strategy may increase output and taxes, but it does not necessarily increase efficiency and profits. Han and Oi's study of Chinese corporations finds that restructured enterprises tend to pay higher taxes than they did before restructuring.[25] They attribute this increase to be one of the

21   Julian R. Franks and Colin Mayer, "Ownership and Control of German Corporations," *Review of Financial Statistics* 14, no. 4 (2001): 943-77.

22   Michael Useem, *Investor Capitalism: How Money Managers Are Changing the Face of Corporate America* (New York: Basic Books, 1996).

23   Janos Kornai, *Economics of Shortage* (Amsterdam: North-Holland, 1980) and Janos Kornai, *The Socialist System: The Political Economy of Communism* (Princeton, NJ: Princeton University Press, 1992); Andrew G. Walder, "Factory and Manager in an Era of Reform," *China Quarterly*, no. 118 (June 1989): 242–64; and Andrew G. Walder, "Property Rights and Stratification in Socialist Redistributive Economies," *American Sociological Review* 57, no. 4 (August 1992): 524–39.

24   Andrew G. Walder, "Career Mobility and the Communist Political Order," *American Sociological Review* 60, no. 3 (June 1995): 309-28; Andrew G. Walder, Bobai Li, and Donald J. Treiman, "Politics and Life Chances in a State Socialist Regime: Dual Career Paths into the Urban Chinese Elite, 1949-1996," *American Sociological Review* 65, no. 2 (April 2000): 191–209.

25   Han Chaohua and Dai Muzhen [Jean Oi], "Zhongguo Minyinghua De Caizheng Dongyin" [Fiscal Motivation for Property-Rights Restructurings of Public Enterprises in China], *Jingji Yanjiu* [Economic Research], no. 2 (2008): 56–82.

most important fiscal incentives for local governments to privatize public firms.[26] This implies many potential conflicts of interest between the incentives of management and managerial fiduciary responsibilities to shareholders.

In addition to local governments, SOE parent groups assert more influential control over their listed companies. Such groups often directly control a listed firm by either owning the controlling share or acting on behalf of the local government that owns the controlling share. Although a parent group as a whole has its own agendas and goals, top managers are often simultaneously in charge of both the parent group and the listed company. In many cases, as the listed firm was formerly the core asset of the parent group, the two entities also tend to be in the same industry. Business transactions between the two therefore are often unavoidable. A substantial part of the related-party transactions are actually used by the parent group to transfer capital or profits from the listed firm. To the extent that the interests of the parent group diverge from those of the other owners of the company, the minority shareholders in particular, the latter's rights and interests are overridden and sacrificed. Typical shenanigans that the parent groups engage in will be discussed in detail below.

Besides parent groups, other shareholders include managers, institutional investors, and individual shareholders. Management equity holding, which is widely embraced in Western public companies, has not shown traction in SOE-turned-listed firms. As a matter of fact, our analysis of the CCER data shows that among all state-controlled public companies in China, about two-fifths of the top management do not own a single stock in the company they run. In other companies where top managers do own some shares, it is a miniscule 0.4 percent.[27] This is in stark contrast to privatization in Russia

---

26 It is worth noting that increased tax revenue does not necessarily result from increased efficiency or profitability. It can be imposed or induced by local governments to achieve their own political and economic goals. Several managers interviewed for this study noted that they sometimes overstate their earnings to meet the profit and tax targets set by the local governments. The interviews were conducted by the first author in Shanghai in 2004 and in Hebei province in 2005.

27 This statistic does not rule out the possibility that managers may buy company stock from the secondary market using the names of family members or others. We should also note that this finding differs from those in Oi, "Patterns of Corporate Restructuring in China" and Han and Dai [Oi], "Zhongguo Minyinghua De Caizheng Dongyin." Size matters in terms of MBOs. Listed firms and other firms in Oi's 2000 survey belong to a different league of firms. An average listed firm is worth more than RMB10 billion, although there is a huge variation among them. Therefore, managers owning large chunks of shares or MBOs are less likely when the size and value of the company increase. Second, the qualifier in this statistic is "among all state-controlled public companies," thus it does not include the 250-300 listed firms that are already privatized.

in the early 1990s when most large state-owned enterprises ended up in the private pockets of incumbent directors.[28] Although Russia's radical regime change provided greater opportunities for "insider privatization" of concentrated state assets, in China ownership by managers of large public firms has been highly restricted.[29]

Institutional investors, owned either by other government agencies or SOEs, do not yet behave differently from their government or SOE owners. In 2002 a Qualified Foreign Institutional Investor (QFII) system was instituted as a bold move to open the stock market to foreign institutional investors; however, the Chinese government allows a QFII to hold only a maximum of 10 percent of a single company's shares. All QFIIs together are not permitted to control more than 20 percent of the shares of a listed firm. Partly due to these strict regulations, as of year-end 2006 total QFII funds accounted for less than 1 percent of the US$1 million market value of China's stock markets.[30] In terms of individual investors, although the number of individual trading accounts surpassed 100 million in 2007,[31] a classic "free rider" problem still persists. The widely dispersed ownership provides little or no incentive for individuals to spend time and effort monitoring managers or coordinating activities to influence decision-making within the firms. To summarize, neither institutional nor individual investors play an active or effective role in governing listed firms.

Boards of Directors

The board of directors, in performing their fiduciary duty to maximize shareholder value, has formal authority for hiring, monitoring, and firing management. Yet, in practice, a typical Chinese board works quite differently from its idealized role. Board members are often recommended by top managers who act on behalf of state owners. Moreover, it is not uncommon for the CEO also to be the chairman of the board. According to one study, almost 70 percent of all directors in a sample of listed firms were nominated

28 Michael McFaul, "State Power, Institutional Change, and the Politics of Privatization in Russia," *World Politics* 47, no. 2 (January 1995): 210–43.

29 Andrew G. Walder, "Elite Opportunity in Transitional Economies," *American Sociological Review* 68, no. 6 (2003): 899-916.

30 Zhang Xudong, "Zhongguo Hege Jingwai Jigou Touzizhe Zi'e Du Yi Po 90 Yi Meiyuan" [QFII Fund Surpassing US$9 Billion], Xinhua News Agency, January 1, 2007, at http://finance.people.com.cn/GB/1037/5239954.html, accessed August 20, 2010.

31 CSRC (China Securities Regulatory Commission), *Zhongguo Zhengquan Qihuo Tongji Nianjian 2007* [China Securities and Futures Statistical Yearbook 2007] (Beijing: Zhongguo tongji chubanshe, 2007).

and selected by the top managers, who in turn held about half of the seats on the board of directors.[32] Another study reveals that in more than 20 percent of the listed firms, the same person holds the position of chairman and CEO.[33] These figures imply that those who are to be monitored are part of the monitoring body. In contrast, it is common international practice for a special committee to nominate the directors. The open nomination process seeks to replace the former practice whereby the chairman "rang up a couple of old friends" to sit on the board. Under this new regime, the search for directors in the most reputable companies is carried out by outside head-hunters, and candidates are interviewed by non-executive directors as well as by the chairman or the CEO.[34] Although adopting a board nominating committee cannot entirely eliminate the effect of an "old boy network," it makes the entire process more transparent. Evidence from other societies shows that board nominating committees help increase board diversity and independence.[35]

In China there have been calls for more seats to be reserved for outside or independent directors in the hope that they can monitor management teams more effectively. In 2003, the China Securities Regulatory Commission (CSRC) took measures to strengthen the independence of boards by increasing the number of independent directors. The new regulations require that at least one-third of the members of the board consist of independent directors, and the board must include at least one accounting professional. To indicate pro forma compliance with the new rules, the CEOs or chairmen can invite their friends as independent directors. Comments by an independent director who is a full-time university professor suggest how these relationships affect their work on the board. This independent director noted that the CEO of the listed company, a friend of his since college, constantly reminded him how he had received his position and therefore how he should vote. The professor confessed that he never disagreed with the CEO at board meetings and never spent enough time carefully reading reports or proposals

32 Tenev and Zhang, with Brefort, *Corporate Governance and Enterprise Reform in China*.

33 Zhong Jiyin, "Shei Shi Zhongguo Shangshi Gongsi Zhenzheng De Laoban?" [Who Are the Real Bosses in Chinese Listed Firms], *Zhongguo Zhengquan Bao* [China Securities News], January 31, 2002.

34 Keith Gay, "A Boardroom Revolution? The Impact of the Cadbury Nexus on the Work of Non-executive Directors of FTSE 350 Companies," *Corporate Governance* 9, no. 3 (July 2001): 152–64.

35 Winfried Ruigrok et al., "The Determinants and Effects of Board Nomination Committees," *Journal of Management and Governance* 10, no. 2 (June 2006): 119–48.

that were being discussed. However, by attending four board meetings each year and signing some papers, he received a compensation package almost equal to his annual salary as a professor.[36] This example sheds light on how the independent director system may deviate from its original objectives.[37] No wonder that Zhang and Ma's study on corporate malfeasance in Chinese listed firms finds no evidence that independent directors help to deter corporate malfeasance.[38] Similar phenomena have also been found in studies on public firms in the United States.[39]

Furthermore, the functions of the board are not carried out by specialized committees, but are more likely to be dominated by directors appointed by the controlling shareholders. A survey by the Shanghai Stock Exchange shows that only 5.4 percent of the companies had already established specialized committees (e.g., compensation, finance, or nomination committees) to ensure that the board functioned properly, and only 14 percent had plans to set up such committees. Moreover, the board is often overrepresented by the controlling shareholders (again, in most cases the SOEs). For an average firm in the sample, the largest shareholder accounts for 47 percent of all shares but controls more than half of the board seats. Similarly, in this sample the percentage of shares held by the three largest shareholders averages 59 percent; however, they appoint 79 percent of the directors.[40] Such arrangements provide fertile ground for "insider control."

Takeover Markets

A takeover is an external corporate governance mechanism utilized when outside parties seek control of a listed firm. It provides an exit strategy for poor-performing firms. At the macro level, the replacement of troubled firms by new players eliminates inefficient players in the market. At the micro level,

36 The first author's interview with an independent board director (E2) in Beijing in 2004.

37 In China's listed firms, there is a supervisory board along with the board of directors. The role of the former is more decorative than that of the latter. It is no more than a rubber-stamp to reconfirm decisions already taken by the top managers and the board of directors.

38 Zhang and Ma, "Law, Corporate Governance, and Corporate Scandal in a Transition Economy."

39 Benjamin E. Hermalin and Michael S. Weisbach, "Boards of Directors as an Endogenously Determined Institution: A Survey of the Economic Literature," *Economic Policy Review* 9, no. 1 (2003): 7–26.

40 Tenev and Zhang, with Brefort, *Corporate Governance and Enterprise Reform in China.*

a takeover benefits shareholders because changes in the control of targeted firms always come with a premium. The mere threat of changing controlling power may provide the top managers of targeted firms with incentives to perform better, which would help defend against hostile takeovers by increasing the firm's equity value. Research on active takeover markets in the United States finds that poorly performing firms are more likely to be the targets of takeovers. The top managers of these firms in turn are likely to be fired after the takeover.[41]

In China's stock markets, a highly concentrated share structure raises the bar for acquiring a majority of shares. Since only a fraction of the shares are tradable, even if one party were to buy all the tradable shares, that party may still not have enough shares to ensure control. Nevertheless, in recent years, there have been several hundred takeovers whereby the listed firms have become privately-controlled. This is largely due to a recent development in China's stock markets that permits private investors to buy legal-person shares from state-affiliated entities, which on average own roughly one-third of the shares in the listed companies. It is estimated that by the end of 2002, 200 to 250 state-controlled listed firms had become privately-controlled through transfers of legal-person shares.[42] A more recent estimate suggests that by the end of 2005, private individuals controlled 26 percent (about 360 firms) of all listed firms on China's stock markets.[43] Because the CSRC since 2005 has carried out a share structure reform to release non-tradable shares, a greater supply of tradable shares is now available. This offers a potential for the growth of takeover markets, primarily driven by private firms that seek a presence in the stock market.

Changes at the level of the organizational populations usually proceed through two different mechanisms. One mechanism is adaptation by the existing players; the other is replacement of the existing organizations by new organizations.[44] Many private enterprises have played an active role in the takeover market by becoming new owners of listed firms. One reason for this is that private firms have been discriminated against from going public. Therefore, purchasing a controlling share of a listed firm provides

41 Bengt Holmstrom and Steven N. Kaplan, "Corporate Governance and Merger Activity in the United States: Making Sense of the 1980s and 1990s," *Journal of Economic Perspectives* 15, no. 2 (Spring 2001): 121–44.

42 Green, "The Privatization Two-Step at China's Listed Firms."

43 Carl E. Walter and Fraser J.T. Howie, *Privatizing China: Inside China's Stock Markets* (Singapore: John Wiley, 2nd ed., 2006).

44 Glenn R. Carroll and Michael T. Hannan, *The Demography of Corporations and Industries* (Princeton, NJ: Princeton University Press, 2000).

a back door to becoming listed. Once a private firm acquires a listed firm and makes it profitable, the new firm can apply to issue more shares in the following year. As an illustration, in 2002 the privately-owned Shanghai Zhonglu Group, a bowling equipment manufacturer, purchased 54 percent of the shares of the bankrupt Shanghai Yongjiu, which once had been a renowned bicycle maker. After controlling the listed firm, Shanghai Zhonglu shifted its own profitable assets and businesses to the listed "shell" and turned it around to regain market and investor confidence.[45]

However, not all private takeovers lead to increased market efficiency; some private investors buy controlling shares to manipulate stock prices in order to collect windfall profits. One well-known case is the buyout of Zhongke Chuangye in 1999. The mastermind behind the buyout was private businessman Lu Liang, who mobilized RMB540 million and engaged in price manipulation of the company's stock. The game unfolded as Mr. Lu had masterfully crafted it. Due to the sudden increase in demand created by Mr. Lu, the price of a share jumped from RMB17 to RMB84 in a matter of several months, but then plummeted to RMB6 within one year immediately after Lu and his collaborators cashed out hundreds of millions RMB worth of stocks at the peak of the scam. Lu is still at large even though many of his fellow conspirators have been sentenced.[46]

Legal System

Early research on corporate governance largely ignored the legal system as an important external mechanism for corporate governance. This is primarily due to the fact that most research was country-specific. Evidence from a single country provides little scope for studying the effects of the legal system because all firms in a single country are subject to the same legal regime.[47] In a pioneering yet still rare effort to take the legal system into consideration, La Porta et al.[48] argue that the extent to which a country's laws protect investor rights and the extent to which those laws are enforced are the most basic determinants of how corporate finance and corporate

45 The first author's interview with an official at the Shanghai Stock Exchange in 2005.

46 Hu Shuli, Li Qiaoning, and Li Qing, "Zhuangjia Lu Liang" [The Market Manipulator Lu Liang], *Caijing*, February 5, 2001, 19-31. The first author's interview with a CSRC official (C5) in Beijing in 2005.

47 Michael C. Jensen, "The Modern Industrial Revolution, Exit, and the Failure of Internal Control Systems," *Journal of Finance* 4, no. 3 (December 1993): 831–80.

48 Rafael La Porta et al., "Law and Finance," *Journal of Political Economy* 106, no. 6 (December 1998): 1113–55.

governance evolve in that country. Based on a sample of 49 countries, they found significant differences across countries in terms of investor protection. Specifically, countries with low investor protection tended to have highly concentrated ownership patterns and less active public equity markets. La Porta et al. categorized the 49 countries into four groups: common law countries, French civil law countries, German civil law countries, and Scandinavian civil law countries. They found that the laws in common law countries provide the highest degree of protection for shareholders, whereas the laws in French civil law countries provide the least protection. Enforcement of laws is stronger in the German and Scandinavian law countries than in the common law countries; the weakest enforcement was observed in French civil law countries. In addition, related studies show that strong economic growth requires developed financial markets and that strong investor protection is necessary if strong financial markets are to develop.[49]

The securities laws governing China's stock markets have been strongly influenced by the American common law model. The major regulatory body overseeing China's financial market is the CSRC, which was elevated to full ministerial status in 1998 (see Walter's chapter in this volume). The CSRC enjoys a wide range of administrative and judicial powers, and it has standardized many rigorous procedures, ranging from disclosure requirements and accounting standards to guidelines on mergers and acquisitions. The CSRC has also cooperated with the courts to crack down on corporate misconduct. In December 2000, the Chengdu Intermediate Court found Hongguang Industries guilty of fraud. This ruling was the first court judgment against a listed company. The convicted company was fined RMB1 million for fabricating financial data for its IPO. The responsible managers were sentenced to up to three years.[50] In August 2001 the Ministry of Finance (MOF) took punitive action against sixteen listed firms and their forty-two accounting personnel, as well as thirteen accounting firms and twenty-one individual accountants. In September 2001, the MOF filed a lawsuit against auditors involved in fabricating financial figures for the Yinguangxia firm in order to achieve a listing. In January 2002, the Supreme Court issued a ruling allowing private investors to sue companies whose illegal activity is caught by the CSRC. In November 2002, the Sichuan Intermediate Court

49 For example, Raghuram G. Rajan and Luigi Zingales, "Financial Dependence and Growth," *American Economic Review* 88, no. 3 (June 1998): 559–86.

50 Xin Hong, "Zhongguo Zhengquan Minshi Jiufen Diyi'an Hongguang An Dachen Tiaojie Xieyi" [The No. 1 Civil Suit in China's Stock Market, the Hongguang Case, is Settled], *Fazhi Ribao* [Legal Daily], February 21, 2003.

ruled in favor of eleven individual investors against Chengdu Hongguang. This was the first court ruling in a lawsuit filed by minority shareholders. Despite its legal significance, the eleven individuals were compensated a total of RMB220,000, which barely covered their expenses during the four-year lawsuit.[51] Unfortunately, the outcome sent a signal to minority shareholders that it is costly and time-consuming to go after the big corporations.

Although the above landmark cases indicate some important improvements in the CSRC and the court's legal functions against fraudulent behavior, turning "law in the books" into "law in practice" remains a demanding task for the regulator of the stock market. Many well-written regulations are neither rigorously enforced nor able to deter transgressions. For example, since 2000 the CSRC has restricted listed firms from providing bank loan guarantees for parent groups. However, the practice remains prevalent. The CSRC often finds itself short of the necessary manpower and resources to conduct investigations. For most of the 1990s, the CSRC was a central-level agency without a local presence. Provincial governments established their own securities offices responsible for selecting listing candidates and for supervising local brokerages. As part of the staff of the provincial governments, these offices were not under the control of the CSRC and tended to align their interests with those of the provincial governments. Without local cooperation, the CSRC was ineffective in exerting its authority at local levels. The standoff did not end until 1999 when the State Council authorized the CSRC to take over the functions of all provincial securities offices.

Despite the consolidation of regulatory power, the CSRC still faces a shortage of manpower. As a whole, the CSRC has about 1,800 personnel, including in the Beijing headquarters and the thirty-six regional offices. The department responsible for monitoring listed companies is only one among two dozen departments. Furthermore, unlike its U.S. counterpart, the Securities and Exchange Commission, the CSRC has no right to block or freeze the bank accounts of firms under investigation, which makes those firms less likely to cooperate. Moreover, the CSRC can impose only nominal punishment on violating firms or their CEOs. Such punishments range from warnings and public denouncements to fines of up to RMB300,000. In interviews CSRC officials revealed that CEOs in some firms are praised as boardroom heroes. Despite their misdeeds, some are even promoted to higher-level positions.[52] Not only does the CSRC lack the necessary resources to dig up more hard evidence in order to bring these cases to court,

51 The first author's interview with CSRC official (C5) in Beijing in 2005.
52 The first author's interviews with CSRC official (C5) and CSRC official (C6) in Beijing in 2005.

but also the punitive options at its disposal are not severe enough to deter corporate misconduct.

Corporate governance mechanisms, including internal mechanisms such as the share structure and the board of directors and external mechanisms such as the takeover market and the legal system, have not played a sufficient and effective role in ensuring proper corporate governance and in protecting shareholder interests. It is no wonder that related-party transactions have not been scrutinized or curbed under such a weak governance regime.

Related-party Transactions

In this section, we discuss different types of related-party transactions that Chinese listed firms often utilize to transfer capital between parent groups and listed firms, concealing or disguising their real financial motivations. Related-party transactions between listed companies and parent groups are common in China's stock markets. Our analysis of the related-party transaction dataset compiled by the CCER finds that in 2006 more than 90 percent of the listed firms engaged in related-party transactions. These transactions fell into four main types: (1) asset transactions, (2) capital finance, (3) guaranteed bank loans, and (4) transfer pricing.

Types of Related Transactions

Asset transactions involve the sale of physical assets or shares between listed companies and the parent group. This is a common way for listed firms to produce fake profits. To illustrate, in 1999 Ningbo Zhongbai (now renamed Gongda Shouchuang) reported non-operating revenue accounting for 60 percent of its annual profits. A closer look finds that this revenue came from an asset swap with its parent group, the Capital Group. The parent group exchanged part of its highly profitable real estate in Beijing for much less valuable property, located in Ningbo, owned by the listed child company.[53] The transaction in question was seemingly beneficial to the shareholders since the listed company received higher-value assets. But it was more of a trick to cook the profit figures in order to look good and to be able to issue additional shares at a higher price. In such an instance, both the shareholders and the public were cheated.

Current regulations on information disclosures of such related-party transactions do not require listing market prices for the assets being transferred.

53 Zuo Min and Bo Hu, "Woguo Shangshi Gongsi Guanlian Jiaoyi Xingwei Yanjiu" [Research on Related-Party Transactions of Listed Firms in China], *Jingji Wenti* [Economic Problems], no. 11 (2001): 27–28.

There is no way for outsiders who have the interest and time to read through the numerous quarterly, semi-annual, or annual reports by the listed firms to judge from the simple descriptions of the assets in the transaction whether it is a fair transaction. Such dubious related-party transactions are only exposed either by investigative media or by courts when the firms are investigated for more outrageous misconduct.

Capital finance relates to capital transfers between listed firms and their parent groups. Most commonly, parent groups borrow funds from listed firms without specific terms for repayment. In one instance, in 1999 Power28 (Huoli Erba), then a household name in China for laundry detergent, shocked the stock market by listing a RMB200 million loss in its mid-term financial report, versus a RMB47 million profit the previous year. Where did the RMB200 million in losses come from? It was revealed that most of it was a RMB130 million debt write-off owed by the parent group. On top of the debt being exempt, the parent group borrowed an additional RMB113 million from the listed child. Even worse, the parent group had no cash or assets to pay off these debts. This eventually buried the listed child in a financial quagmire. In 2000, facing the prospect of bankruptcy, the listed company was finally taken over by another company under arrangements by the city government.[54]

Guaranteed bank loans are another popular way to enrich parent groups. Parent groups usually use a listed firm as a guarantor to borrow money from the banks. For example, in 2000 the real estate firm Shanghai Lujiazui guaranteed bank loans totaling RMB2.1 billion for other entities. Among the guaranteed bank loans, RMB1.8 billion went to the parent group. Although loan guarantees do not create problems if the parent group repays the loan, a default by the parent shifts liability to the listed child.[55] The example of Monkey King (Houwang) illustrates the problems of loan guarantees. Since 1997, Houwang had provided RMB890 million in loans to its parent group and had guaranteed another RMB244 million in bank loans. When the parent group went bankrupt in 2000, the child company was left with a huge debt burden that finally caused the listed company to face the same fate as its parent.[56]

Transfer pricing refers to the practice of selling services or products at artificial prices between listed firms and parent groups. For instance, in order

54 The first author's interview with CSRC official (C5) in Beijing in 2005.

55 The first author's interview with executive (E3) in Shanghai in 2005.

56 Wu Xiaoqiu, "Dangqian Zhongguo Ziben Shichang Zhenglun De Ruogan Wenti" [Several Controversial Issues in China's Capital Markets], *Jingji Daokan* [Economic Herald], no. 3 (2001): 1–6.

to show paper profits, since its IPO in 1994 the listed steel-maker Gongyi Gufen had been selling steel products to its parent group at a price 15 percent higher than the market price. This made the child company look good in its financial reports, and it helped to boost its share price. After the parent group was acquired by another business group in 2000, the event took an interesting turn when the listed company began to yield to the need of the new parent by selling it products at a price that was about 14 percent lower than market price. The main reason was that the new parent had its own core business listed on the stock market.[57] Because priority was given to the listed child of the new owner, the parent group exploited the adopted child.

The literature on transfer pricing in other societies shows that this practice is widely used to avoid taxation.[58] The similarity between China and its Western counterparts is that in the end transfer pricing benefits the controlling shareholders.[59] However, our examination of another listed firm finds yet another variation in price transferring. The transaction is not conducted within the business group but instead with a third party. Products are sold to a private company owned by management at a below-market price. In the end, management, rather than the parent group, pockets the profits. Ding's study[60] on the asset stripping of SOEs in China nicely characterizes this phenomenon as "one manager, two businesses." Under such a setup, a manager makes vast sums of money for his secretly owned private business while he does business with, and in most cases at the expense of, the SOE of which he is in charge.[61]

There are various reasons why parent groups and child companies engage in related-party transactions. Which side benefits from a particular transaction depends on the specific circumstances in which the transaction is conducted. The following are typical situations where the child company benefits from such transactions. The first goes back to the packaging stage

---

57 Hu Ruyin, Ti Liu, and Danian Situ, *Zhongguo Shangshi Gongsi Chengbai Zhizheng Yanjiu* [Case Studies on Chinese Listed Companies] (Shanghai: Fudan daxue chubanshe, 2003). Also from the first author's interview with CSRC official (C2) in Chongqing in 2005.

58 Harry Grubert and John Mutti, "Taxes, Tariffs and Transfer Pricing in Multinational Corporate Decision Making," *Review of Economics and Statistics* 73, no. 2 (May 1991): 285–93.

59 Simon Johnson et al., "Tunneling," *American Economic Review* 90, no. 2 (May 2000): 22–27.

60 X.L. Ding, "The Illicit Asset Stripping of Chinese State Firms," *China Journal*, no. 43 (January 2000): 1-28.

61 Some mid-level managers in a listed firm believe the ultimate purpose for setting up a private company is for a future management buyout. The executives whom the first author interviewed in this firm refuted such speculation.

before the listing. In order to meet the listing requirements, a series of related-party transactions may be required to package the child company at the expense of the other non-listed parts of the parent. The second situation occurs when the listed child attempts to meet the requirements to issue secondary offerings (i.e., selling new shares). The CSRC stipulates that listed firms with an average return on net assets (RONA) that is above 10 percent during the previous three years are eligible to sell new shares to raise extra capital. As both listed companies and parent groups do not want to miss such an opportunity, related-party transactions offer a convenient solution to manipulate the profits of the listed firms. A third possible situation, although less frequent, is to save a listed firm from de-listing. The regulations stipulate that listed companies that fail to show a profit over three consecutive years should be de-listed. Since being a public firm is a highly sought-after opportunity, parent groups and/or local governments exhaust every possible effort to prevent any de-listing. Under such circumstances, life-saving capital is transferred to the listed firms through related-party transactions. A final motivation to engage in related-party transactions is to take advantage of the preferential policies that are only granted to listed companies. For example, listed companies in the high-tech industries are subject to a 15 percent income tax rate, whereas their parent groups are subject to an ordinary tax rate of 25 percent. This provides the parent groups with incentives to transfer assets to the listed firms for tax purposes, which is totally legal by law.[62]

Although child companies benefit from related-party transactions in the above specified occasions, a more dominant theme is that parent groups use such transactions with a reversed flow of revenue for their own benefit at the expense of the other minority shareholders. The next sub-section spells out the details.

Deciphering the Game

Why do listed firms sometimes benefit from related-party transactions whereas parent groups make sacrifices? Why are there other transactions with benefits flowing in the opposite direction to the parent group? This puzzle can be disentangled by examining the rules of the game. The game begins by the parent groups taking productive assets to form a child company for a public listing. The fundamental motivation of the parent group is to raise capital from the stock market by selling shares to investors. There

62 A parallel example is that many American corporations register in "tax havens," such as the British Virgin Islands or Bermuda.

are many other tangible and intangible benefits associated with listed-firm status, such as enjoying higher prestige, tax breaks from the localities, and easier access to bank loans. After the IPO, the parent groups reap benefits through a series of related-party transactions. In the case of Power 28, the proceeds from the child company's IPO in 1996 totaled about RMB200 million, whereas in the three-year period after the company's IPO, the parent group borrowed RMB243 million from the listed child, more than the amount raised from the IPO.[63] The cases of Lujiazui and Monkey King are similar.

To keep the "cash cow" (i.e., the listed firm) alive and therefore to sustain capital accumulation from the stock market over time, parent groups must be willing to engage in sacrifice from time to time by engaging in other rounds of related-party transactions to make the listed firms appear healthy and profitable, at least on paper. In Ningbo Zhongbai's case, the parent group headquartered in Beijing traded its own profitable Beijing commercial office building for less valuable real estate in Ningbo that was owned by the listed company to add to the assets of the listed child in the annual financial report.[64] Gongyi Gufen's former parent group was willing to buy Gongyi's steel products at a price 15 percent higher than Gongyi's other customers paid.[65] The purpose again was to make the listed company appear more profitable.

After the equity market injects cash into the listed firm, a new round of related-party transactions are in order. But this time the money is channeled to the parent group. Although assets and capital flow back and forth between the listed firms and the parent groups, the parent groups tend to make sure that ultimately they have a positive net gain. As long as the flow of related-party transactions continues, a listed firm is a financing vehicle for the parent group to raise capital from investors or bank loans. However, the downfall of both Power 28 and Monkey King are reminders that not every parent group can keep the game going forever. When parent groups excessively exploit the "cash cow" or their own businesses fail, they can actually push their listed child into deep financial trouble or even bankruptcy.

Institutional Complementarities and Institutional Change

Thus far, we have illustrated that the majority of Chinese public firms are spin-offs of large SOEs, which hold controlling shares and exert great control over the former. Treating listed firms more or less as their cash cows,

63 Wu Xiaoqiu, "Dangqian Zhongguo Ziben Shichang Zhenglun De Ruogan Wenti."
64 Zuo Min and Bo Hu, "Woguo Shangshi Gongsi Guanlian Jiaoyi Xingwei Yanjiu."
65 Hu Ruyin, Ti Liu, and Danian Situ, *Zhongguo Shangshi Gongsi Chengbai Shizheng Yanjiu.*

large SOEs utilize various artificial related-party transactions to transfer capital and assets between the listed firms and the parent groups at the expense of the interests of the minority shareholders. We argue that this prevailing theme among Chinese public firms is only possible due to the failure of current corporate governance mechanisms to provide checks and balances over the controlling shareholders. Yet, a broader question remains: How should institutions be developed in order to have effective corporate governance? We approach this question in three ways.

What Institutions Does China Need in Order for Public Firms to be Accountable and for the Stock Market to Function Well?

Let us recall Polanyi's insight that markets do not create institutions so much as institutions create markets.[66] A coherent and predictable administrative and regulatory structure is necessary to enforce that market participants play by the rules. The history of stock markets in the United Kingdom and the United States shows that redressing imperfections through institution-building is a prerequisite for developing markets. The British stock markets were severely deficient until the Gladstone Committee's recommendations led to a major change in company law in 1844.[67] In the United States, the creation of the Securities Exchange Commission in 1934 was intended to address misleading information and fraudulent companies.[68] Even today, the Securities Exchange Commission is looking for a way to maintain an appropriate balance that ensures market integrity while at the same time promotes an entrepreneurial spirit and innovation.

In this sense, although China has come a long way in building up its stock markets, many supporting institutions still need to be developed. For example, the CSRC does not yet provide a robust supervisory regime with clear and transparent rules; institutional investors, both domestic and international, are not allowed to play a significant role in bringing a diversified and balanced ownership structure; financial institutions do not provide objective and independent financial information, analysis, or research. The list goes on. China can learn a great deal from the experiences of other developed markets. However, the question remains: Can the solution to the problems of China's public firms and stock markets be reduced to mimicking the

66 Karl Polanyi, *The Great Transformation* (Boston: Beacon Press, 1957).

67 David F. Hawkins, *Corporate Financial Disclosure, 1900–1933: A Study of Management Inertia Within a Rapidly Changing Environment* (New York: Garland, 1986).

68 Joel Seligman, *The Transformation of Wall Street: A History of the Securities and Exchange Commission and Modern Corporate Finance* (Boston: Northeastern University Press, rev. ed., 1995).

best practices observed in other parts of the world? The answer depends on whether or not such imported institutions can work together.

How Do Institutions Work?

Research on institutional complementarities originated in studies that attempted to understand the institutional diversity between the United States and Germany and other continental European countries.[69] For example, an accommodating monetary policy and flexible labor markets are considered complementary in the United States, whereas a monetary regime by a conservative central bank is seen as complementary in the rigid labor markets of continental Europe. The idea of institutional complementarities also provides the theoretical underpinnings for the "big-bang" approach. Some neoliberal economists argue that partial reforms compromise their intended positive effects and cause disorganization in the economy; therefore, reformers need to simultaneously implement all constituent elements of a market economy in a comprehensive way.[70] When the big-bang approach resulted in economic catastrophe in Russia and other Eastern European countries,[71] neoliberals attributed the failure to incomplete implementation of neoliberal policies by the local elites.[72] Admittedly, there is some truth to this line of reasoning with respect to how institutions work together. However, it fails to capture that even within a single institution different elements can affect the way the institution as a whole functions.

Institutions are more than rules or regulatory systems. According to DiMaggio and Powell[73] and Scott,[74] institutions consist of three types of elements that provide stability and meaning to social behavior. The first type is regulatory elements, which are associated with the laws and regulations enforced by the political institutions. The second type is normative elements, often manifested as professional ethics and norms in certain occupations

69 For example, Amable, "Institutional Complementarity"; Hall and Soskice, eds., *Varieties of Capitalism*.

70 For example, David Lipton et al., "Creating a Market Economy in Eastern Europe: The Case of Poland," *Brookings Papers on Economic Activity* 1 (1990): 75-147.

71 For example, Lawrence King, "Shock Privatization: The Effect of Rapid Large-Scale Privatization on Enterprise Restructuring," *Politics and Society* 31, no. 1 (March 2003): 3-30.

72 For example, Andres Aslund et al., "How to Stabilize: Lessons from Post-Communist Countries," *Brookings Papers on Economic Activity* 1 (1996): 217-313.

73 Paul J. DiMaggio and Walter W. Powell, "The Iron Cage Revisited: Institutional Isomorphism and Collective Rationality in Organizational Fields," *American Sociological Review* 48, no. 2 (April 1983):147-60.

74 Scott, *Institutions and Organizations*.

and professions. The last type is cultural-cognitive elements, which are associated with general beliefs or things that are taken-for-granted. Such a sociological understanding of institutions contrasts with that in economics or political science,[75] which tends to view institutions as systems of rules or governance systems while ignoring their normative and cultural-cognitive elements. In most institutions, all three of these elements are present and interact.

We now can better understand how institutions work by bringing together the concept of institutional complementarities and the sociological conceptualization of institutions. In relatively stable societal settings where the status quo is maintained, the three elements are compatible and mutually reinforcing. However, in transitional social settings, tensions and inconsistencies among these elements may emerge such that the elements no longer work together. In general, institutional regulatory elements are more visible, and more readily designed and altered, whereas normative and culture-cognitive elements tend to be more durable.

For instance, executives in China's listed firms are aware that sometimes they cross the line when engaging in related-party transactions between the listed firm and affiliated firms of the same parent group. Nevertheless, they believe it is their obligation to help "brothers" when they are in need. In interviews, they constantly bring this up to justify their use of related-party transactions.[76] In such cases, regulatory and normative elements guiding the behavior of management are at odds with one another. Previous research on institutional complementarities focuses only on interactions *among* institutions and it pays little attention to interactions among the different elements *within* the institutions.

How Can Institutional Changes be Possible?

It is generally easier to change the regulatory parts of institutions than the normative and cultural-cognitive parts. The deeper the elements are nested in people's mentality or in the society's belief system, the more difficult it is to change them. Although the pace of change for various types of institutional elements differs, evidence suggests that in many cases inconsistencies among the institutional elements are the impetus for institutional change. Changes, however small, in the behavior of China's CEOs seem to be a case in point.

75 E.g., Douglass North, *Institutions, Institutional Change and Economic Performance* (Cambridge: Cambridge University Press, 1990).

76 The first author's interviews with executives at several listed firms during 2002–5.

Institutional changes occur when the institutional logics—the belief systems and related practices that dominate—shift.[77] Echoing Stark's observation that citizens from the transitional Eastern European societies experienced parallel and contradictory logics,[78] we argue that social actors in China face the same situation daily. As the institutionalization of China's stock markets is well underway, former SOEs that are listed are now subject to different rules imposed by the financial market. Although assets and capital were often transferred from one part of an SOE to another, this formerly common and acceptable practice is no longer legal for a SOE parent when dealing with its listed company because of infringement of the interests of minority shareholders. If we consider SOE parent groups and the regulatory CSRC as two forces competing to guide the stock market, they are actually driven by conflicting institutional logics: one from a planned economy and the other from a market economy. How this competition plays out decides whether state dominance or market mechanisms gain an upper hand. Under enhanced regulations and monitoring by the CSRC in recent years, it has become more difficult for listed firms to cook the books to cover up fund transfers without being caught. Meanwhile, listed firms facing the possibility of being de-listed or taken over are beginning to be more concerned about their own survival and are adjusting their behavior accordingly.

In order to win out, the new institutional logics should provide incentives for social actors to adopt the new rules of the market economy and to abandon many taken-for-granted old rules prevalent in the planned economy. Although many anomalies in China's stock markets relate to the prevailing institutional logics from an earlier time, the new logics are beginning to gain momentum. One executive shared his anxiety in dealing with the media after his firm was listed. Before the IPO, he never expected that managerial decisions and the company's operations would be so closely scrutinized by the media. Now he constantly worries about the impact on the firm's public image when something negative is reported.[79] A CSRC official compared the ST label[80] attached to listed firms that incurred losses in the previous year as a "hall of shame." He pointed out that many CEOs perceive it as a personal

77 Scott, *Institutions and Organizations.*

78 David Stark, "Recombinant Property in East European Capitalism," *American Journal of Sociology* 101, no. 4 (January 1996): 993–1027.

79 The first author's interview with Executive (E2) in Hebei province in 2005.

80 ST stands for "special treatment," a label attached to a listed firm that reports a negative profit figure for the previous fiscal year. "*ST" stands for firms with two consecutive years of reports of negative profits. According to CSRC regulations, firms with three years of reports of negative profits should be de-listed from the stock exchanges.

stigma. They therefore work hard to have the label removed as quickly as possible.[81] In another instance, as the ownership of listed firms diversifies, some listed firms learn to use the status of being a public firm as a counter-measure to administrative interventions. One executive of a listed company proudly noted that he could finally say "no" to the local government. When he was asked to inflate output figures so that the locality could report higher GDP growth, his reply was that it is illegal for a public company to do this.[82] In these cases, social actors are receiving cues from or drawing on different institutional elements that reflect competing logics during a time of institutional change.

In conclusion, we argue that to understand institutional change, the framework of institutional complementarities falls short by focusing on the comparability and interactions *among* institutions. The full picture is not complete unless we also pay attention to the interactions among different elements *within* institutions as well as their underlying institutional logics. Such a synthesized framework for understanding institutional change, we believe, will not only shed light on the evolution of Chinese corporations and stock markets, but can also be applied to studies of other subjects in China's broader social and economic transformation.

81 The first author's interview with CSRC official (C5) in Beijing in 2005.
82 The first author's interview with Executive (E3) in Shanghai in 2004.

Bibliography

Appleton, Simon et al. "Labor Retrenchment in China: Determinants and Consequences," pp. 19–42, in Li Shi and Hiroshi Sato, eds., *Unemployment, Inequality and Poverty in Urban China*. London: Routledge, 2006.

Bienen, Henry and John Waterbury. "The Political Economy of Privatization in
Developing Countries," *World Development* 17, no. 5 (May 1989): 617–32.

Blecher, Marc. "Hegemony and Workers' Politics in China," *China Quarterly*, no.
170 (June 2002): 283–303.

Booth, Charles D. "Drafting Bankruptcy Laws in Socialist Market Economies:
Recent Developments in China and Vietnam," *Columbia Journal of Asian Law*
18, no.1 (Fall 2004): 94–147.

Brødsgaard, Kjeld Erik. "Institutional Reform and the Bianzhi System in China,"
China Quarterly, no. 170 (2002): 361–86.

Buckley, Peter J., Jeremy Clegg, and Chengqi Wang. "The Relationship Between
Inward Foreign Direct Investment and the Performance of Domestically-owned
Chinese Manufacturing Industry," *Multinational Business Review* 12, no. 3
(Winter 2004): 23–40.

Cai, Yongshun. "Power Structure and Regime Resilience: Contentious Politics in
China," *British Journal of Political Science* 38, no. 3 (July 2008): 411–32.

Cai, Yongshun. "Relaxing the Constraints from Above: Politics of Privatising Public
Enterprises in China," *Asian Journal of Political Science* 10, no. 2 (December
2002): 94–121.

Cai, Yongshun. "The Resistance of Chinese Laid-off Workers in the Reform
Period," *China Quarterly*, no. 170 (June 2002): 327–44.

Cai, Yongshun. *State and Laid-off Workers in Reform China: The Silence and Collective Action of the Retrenched*. London: Routledge, 2006.

Cao, Yuanzheng, Yingyi Qian, and Barry R. Weingast. "From Federalism, Chinese
Style to Privatization, Chinese Style," *Economics of Transition* 7, no. 1 (1999):
103–31.

Chen, Feng. "Industrial Restructuring and Workers' Resistance in China," *Modern China* 29, no. 2 (April 2003): 237–62.

Chen, Feng. "Subsistence Crises, Managerial Corruption and Labour Protests in China," *China Journal*, no. 44 (July 2000): 41–63.

Chen Jinsheng. *Quntixing Shijian Yanjiu Baogao* [Research Report on Instances of Collective Action]. Beijing: Qunzhong chubanshe, 2004.

Chow, Nelson and Yuebin Xu. "Pension Reform in China," pp. 129–42, in Catherine Jones Finer, ed., *Social Policy Reform in China: Views from Home and Abroad*. Aldershot: Ashgate, 2003.

Clarke, Donald, Peter Murrell, and Susan H. Whiting. "The Role of Law in China's Economic Development," pp. 375–428, in Loren Brandt and Thomas Rawski, eds., *China's Great Economic Transformation*. New York: Cambridge University Press, 2008.

Cook, Sarah and Margaret Maurer-Fazio, eds. *The Workers' State Meets the Market: Labour in China's Transition*. London: Frank Cass, 1999.

Croll, Elisabeth. "Social Welfare Reform: Trends and Tensions," *China Quarterly*, no. 159 (September 1999): 684–99.

Ding, X.L. "The Illicit Asset Stripping of Chinese State Firms," *China Journal*, no. 43 (January 2000): 1–28.

Duckett, Jane. "State Collectivism and Worker Privilege: A Study of Urban Health Insurance Reform," *China Quarterly*, no. 177 (March 2004): 155–73.

Esping-Andersen, Gøsta. *The Three Worlds of Welfare Capitalism*. Princeton, NJ: Princeton University Press, 1990.

Fan, Gang and Wing Thye Woo. "The Parallel Partial Progression (PPP) Approach to Institutional Transformation in Transition Economies: Optimize Economic Coherence, Not Policy Sequence," *Modern China* 35, no. 4 (July 2009): 352–69.

Faure, David. *China and Capitalism: A History of Business Enterprise in Modern China*. Hong Kong: Hong Kong University Press, 2006.

Gallagher, Mary Elizabeth. *Contagious Capitalism: Globalization and the Politics of Labor in China*. Princeton, NJ: Princeton University Press, 2005.

Garnaut, Ross et al. *China's Ownership Transformation: Process, Outcomes, Prospects*. Washington, DC: World Bank, 2005.

Gold, Thomas B. et al., eds. *Laid-Off Workers in a Workers' State: Unemployment with Chinese Characteristics*. New York: Palgrave Macmillan, 2009.

Green, Stephen and Guy S. Liu, eds. *Exit the Dragon? Privatization and State Control in China*. London: Blackwell, 2005.

Gu, Edward X. "Dismantling the Chinese Mini-Welfare State? Marketization and the Politics of Institutional Transformation, 1979–1999," *Communist and Post Communist Studies* 34, no. 1 (2001): 91–111.

Gu, Edward X. "Foreign Direct Investment and the Restructuring of Chinese State-Owned Enterprises (1992–1995): A New Institutionalist Perspective," *China Information* 12, no. 3 (Winter 1997–98): 46–71.

Gu, Edward X. "Market Transition and the Transformation of the Health Care System in Urban China," *Policy Studies* 22, nos. 3–4 (September 2001): 197–215.

Guan, Xinping. "China's Social Policy: Reform and Development in the Context of Marketization and Globalization," pp. 231–56, in Huck-ju Kwon, ed., *Transforming the Developmental Welfare State in East Asia.* New York: Palgrave, 2005.

Guowuyuan Bangongting Mishuju, Zhongyang Jigou Bianzhi Weiyuanhui Bangongshi Zonghesi [State Council Secretariat Office and Central Bianzhi Committee Office]. *Zhongyang Zhengfu Zuzhi Jigou 1994* [Central Government Organizational Structure 1994]. Beijing: Zhongguo fazhan chubanshe, 1994.

Guowuyuan Bangongting Mishuju, Zhongyang Jigou Bianzhi Weiyuanhui Bangongshi Zonghesi [State Council Secretariat Office and Central Bianzhi Committee Office]. *Zhongyang Zhengfu Zuzhi Jigou 1998* [Central Government Organizational Structure 1998]. Beijing: Gaige chubanshe, 1998.

Guthrie, Doug. *Dragon in a Three-Piece Suit: The Emergence of Capitalism in China.* Princeton, NJ: Princeton University Press, 1999.

Hall, Peter A. and David Soskice, eds. *Varieties of Capitalism: The Institutional Foundations of Comparative Advantage.* Oxford: Oxford University Press, 2001.

Han Chaohua and Dai Muzhen [Jean Oi]. "Zhongguo Minyinghua De Caizheng Dongyin" [Fiscal Motivation for Property-Rights Restructurings of Public Enterprises in China], *Jingji Yanjiu* [Economic Research], no. 2 (2008): 56–82.

Heilmann, Sebastian. "Policy Experimentation in China's Rise," *Studies in Comparative International Development* 43, no.1 (March 2008): 1–26.

Howell, Jude. *China Opens its Doors: The Politics of Economic Transition.* Boulder, CO: Lynne Rienner, 1993.

Hu Ruyin, Ti Liu, and Danian Situ. *Zhongguo Shangshi Gongsi Chengbai Zhizheng Yanjiu* [Case Studies on Chinese Listed Companies]. Shanghai: Fudan daxue chubanshe, 2003.

Huang, Yasheng. "Ownership Biases and FDI in China: Evidence from Two Provinces," paper presented at the China's Rise conference, Tuck School of Business, Dartmouth College, Hanover, NH, May 13–14, 2006.

Huang, Yasheng. *Selling China: Foreign Direct Investment During the Reform Era.* New York: Cambridge University Press, 2003.

Hurst, William. *The Chinese Worker After Socialism.* New York: Cambridge University Press, 2009.

Hurst, William. "Understanding Contentious Collective Action by Chinese Laid-Off Workers: The Importance of Regional Political Economy," *Studies in Comparative International Development* 39, no. 2 (2004): 94–120.

Hurst, William and Kevin J. O'Brien. "China's Contentious Pensioners," *China Quarterly*, no. 170 (June 2002): 345–60.

Jefferson, Gary H. et al. "Ownership, Productivity Change, and Financial Performance in Chinese Industry," *Journal of Comparative Economics* 28, no. 4 (December 2000): 786–813.

Jian Xie. *Wenzhou Minying Jingji Yanjiu: Touguo Minying* [Research on Wenzhou's Private Economy: Penetrating the Private Sector]. Beijing: Zhonghua gongshang lianhe chubanshe, 2000.

Jowell, Roger. *Trying It Out: The Role of "Pilots" in Policy-Making*. London: Government Chief Social Researcher's Office, 2003.

Jung, Joo-Youn. "Retreat of the State? Restructuring the Chinese Bureaucracies in the Era of Economic Globalization," *China Review* 8, no. 1 (Spring 2008): 105–25.

Lau, Lawrence J., Yingyi Qian, and Gérard Roland. "Reform Without Losers: An Interpretation of China's Dual-Track Approach to Transition," *Journal of Political Economy* 108, no. 1 (February 2001): 120–43.

Lee, Ching Kwan. "From the Specter of Mao to the Spirit of the Law: Labor Insurgency in China," *Theory and Society* 31, no. 2 (April 2002): 189–228.

Li, Hongbin. "Government's Budget Constraint, Competition, and Privatization: Evidence from China's Rural Industry," *Journal of Comparative Economics* 31, no. 3 (2003): 486–502.

Li, Shaomin, Shuhe Li, and Weiying Zhang. "The Road to Capitalism: Competition and Institutional Change in China," *Journal of Comparative Economics* 28, no. 2 (2000): 269–92.

Li Zhangzhe. *Zhongyu Chenggong: Zhongguo Gushi Fazhan Baogao* [Success at Last: Report on the Development of China's Stock Markets]. Beijing: Shijie zhishi chubanshe, 2001.

Lin Bai, Gong Mu, and Zhang Gang, eds. *Wenzhou Moshi De Lilun Tansuo* [Theoretical Investigations of the Wenzhou Model]. Nanning: Guangxi renmin chubanshe, 1987.

Lin, Justin Yifu. "Guoqi Zhengce Fudan Taizhong Siyouhua Bushi Gaige Fangxiang" [The Burdens SOEs Shoulder Are Too Heavy: Privatization is Not the Solution], January 12, 2005, at http://business.sohu.com/20050112/n223903598.shtml, accessed May 19, 2010.

Liu, Guy S. and Pei Sun. "The Class of Shareholdings and Its Impacts on Corporate Performance: A Case of State Shareholding Composition in Chinese Public Corporations," *Corporate Governance* 13, no. 1 (January 2005): 46–59.

Liu, Guy S., Pei Sun, and Wing Thye Woo. "The Political Economy of Chinese-Style Privatization: Motives and Constraints," *World Development* 34, no. 12 (2006): 2016–33.

Liu Hongru. *Tansuo Zhongguo Ziben Shichang Fazhan Zhilu* [Exploring the Road to the Development of China's Capital Markets]. Beijing: Zhongguo jinrong chubanshe, 2003.

Liu Zhao, Wang Songqian, and Huang Zhanfeng. "Lun Gonggong Guanli Shidian Zhong De 'Shidian Fangfa'" [On the "Pilot Method" in Public Management Practice], *Dongbei Daxue* [Journal of Northeastern University], no. 4 (2006): 281–82.

Ma Jinlong, "Guanyu Wenzhoushi Guoying He Geti, Siying Qiye Waibu Huanjing De Bijiao Yanjiu" [Comparative Studies on the External Environment of State-owned Enterprises, Individual Businesses, and Private Enterprises in Wenzhou], *Jingji Gongzuozhe Xuexi Ziliao* [Study Materials for Economic Work] (1991).

Ma Jinlong. "Wenzhou Jingji Gaige De Lishi, Xianzhuang He Qianjing" [The History, Current Situation, and Prospects for Wenzhou's Economic Reforms], *Jishu Jingji Yu Guanli Yanjiu* [Technology, Economy, and Management Studies], no. 3 (1996): 15–18.

Ma, Shu-Yun. "Foreign Participation in China's Privatization," *Communist Economies and Economic Transformation* 8, no. 4 (December 1996): 529–48.

Manion, Melanie. *Corruption by Design: Building Clean Government in Mainland China and Hong Kong.* Cambridge, MA: Harvard University Press, 2004.

Mann, Jim. *Beijing Jeep: A Case Study of Western Business in China.* Boulder, CO: Westview, updated ed., 1997.

McDermott, Gerald A. "Institutional Change and Firm Creation in East-Central Europe: An Embedded Politics Approach," *Comparative Political Studies* 37, no. 2 (2004): 188–217.

Montinola, Gabriella, Yingyi Qian, and Barry Weingast. "Federalism, Chinese Style: The Political Basis for Economic Success in China," *World Politics* 48, no. 1 (October 1995): 50–81.

Naughton, Barry. *The Chinese Economy: Transitions and Growth.* Cambridge, MA: MIT Press, 2007.

Naughton, Barry. *Growing Out of the Plan: Chinese Economic Reform, 1978–1993.* New York: Cambridge University Press, 1996.

Naughton, Barry. "Implications of the State Monopoly over Industry and Its Relaxation," *Modern China* 18, no. 1 (January 1992): 14–41.

Naughton, Barry. "SOE Policy: Profiting the SASAC Way," *China Economic Quarterly* 12, no. 2 (June 2008): 19–26.

Nolan, Peter. *China and the Global Economy: National Champions, Industrial Policy and the Big Business Revolution.* New York: Palgrave, 2001.

Nolan, Peter and Fureng Dong, eds. *Market Forces in China: Competition and Small Business—The Wenzhou Debate.* London: Zed Books, 1989.

O'Brien, Kevin J. "Rightful Resistance," *World Politics* 49, no. 1 (1996): 31–55.

Oi, Jean C. "Fiscal Reform and the Economic Foundations of Local State Corporatism in China," *World Politics* 45, no. 1 (October 1992): 99–126.

Oi, Jean C. "Patterns of Corporate Restructuring in China: Political Constraints on Privatization," *China Journal*, no. 53 (January 2005): 115–36.

Oi, Jean C. "Political Crosscurrents in China's Corporate Restructuring," pp. 5–25, in Jean C. Oi, Scott Rozelle, and Xueguang Zhou, eds., *Growing Pains: Tensions and Opportunity in China's Transformation.* Stanford: Walter H. Shorenstein Asia-Pacific Research Center, Stanford University, 2010.

Oi, Jean C. *Rural China Takes Off: Institutional Foundations of Economic Reform.* Berkeley: University of California Press, 1999.

Pan Xining. "Gaige Shidian Chengbai Bian" [Debating the Success and Failure of Experimental Points for Reform], *Fazhan* (Development), no. 2 (1995): 26–29.

Park, Jung-Dong. *The Special Economic Zones of China and their Impact on its Economic Development.* Westport, CT: Praeger, 1997.

Parris, Kristen. "Local Initiative and National Reform: The Wenzhou Model of Development," *China Quarterly*, no. 134 (June 1993): 242–53.

Qian, Yingyi. "How Reform Worked in China," pp. 297–333, in Dani Rodrik, ed., *In Search of Prosperity: Analytic Narratives on Economic Growth*. Princeton, NJ: Princeton University Press, 2003.

Rawski, Thomas G. "Implications of China's Reform Experience," *China Quarterly*, no. 144 (December 1995): 1150–73.

Rosner, Hans J. "China's Health Insurance System in Transformation: Preliminary Assessment and Policy Suggestions," *International Social Security Review* 57, no. 3: 65–90.

Sachs, Jeffrey et al. "Structural Factors in the Economic Reforms of China, Eastern Europe and the Former Soviet Union," *Economic Policy* 9, no. 18 (April 1994): 102–45.

Sachs, Jeffrey D. and Wing Thye Woo. "Understanding China's Economic Performance," NBER Working Paper, no. 5935 (February 1997).

Sargeson, Sally and Jian Zhang. "Reassessing the Role of the Local State: A Case Study of Local Government Interventions in Property Rights Reform in a Hangzhou District," *China Journal*, no. 42 (July 1999): 77–99.

Selden, Mark and Laiyin You. "The Reform of Social Welfare in China," *World Development* 25, no. 10 (1997): 1957–68.

Shleifer, Andrei and Robert W. Vishny. "A Survey of Corporate Governance," *Journal of Finance* 52, no. 2 (June 1997): 737–83.

Solinger, Dorothy J. "Labour Market Reform and the Plight of the Laid-off Proletariat," *China Quarterly*, no. 170 (June 2002): 405–32.

Steinfeld, Edward S. *Forging Reform in China: The Fate of State-Owned Industry*. New York: Cambridge University Press, 1998.

Steinfeld, Edward S. "Moving Beyond Transition in China: Financial Reform and the Political Economy of Declining Growth," *Comparative Politics* 34, no. 4 (July 2002): 379–98.

Streek, Wolfgang and Kathleen Thelen, eds. *Beyond Continuity: Institutional Change in Advanced Political Economies*. Oxford: Oxford University Press, 2005.

Tang Weibing. *Zhongguo Zhuangui Shiqi Suoyouzhi Jiegou Yanjin De Zhidu Fenxi* [Institutional Analysis of the Evolution of the Ownership Structure in China's Transitional Period]. Beijing: Jingji kexue chubanshe, 2004.

Tenev, Stoyan and Chunlin Zhang, with Loup Brefort. *Corporate Governance and Enterprise Reform in China: Building the Institution of Modern Markets*. Washington, DC: International Finance Corporation, 2002.

Thun, Eric. *Changing Lanes in China: Foreign Direct Investment, Local Governments, and Auto Sector Development*. New York: Cambridge University Press, 2006.

Tian Guoqiang. "Guoyou Qiye Gufenzhi Gaige He Zhongguo Zhidu De Pingwen Zhuanxing" [Shareholding Reform of State-owned Enterprises and the Stable Institutional Transition in China], *Dangdai Zhongguo Yanjiu* [Modern China Studies], no. 2 (1998): 73–86.

Tian, Guoqiang. "A Theory of Ownership Arrangements and Smooth Transition to a Free Market Economy," *Journal of Institutional and Theoretical Economics* 157, no. 3 (2001): 380–412.

Tsai, Kellee S. *Back-Alley Banking: Private Entrepreneurs in China*. Ithaca, NY: Cornell University Press, 2002.

Walder, Andrew G. "Career Mobility and the Communist Political Order," *American Sociological Review* 60, no. 3 (June 1995): 309–28.

Walder, Andrew G. *Communist Neo-traditionalism: Work and Authority in Chinese Industry*. Berkeley: University of California Press, 1986.

Walder, Andrew G. "Elite Opportunity in Transitional Economies," *American Sociological Review* 68, no. 6 (December 2003): 899–916.

Walder, Andrew G. "Factory and Manager in an Era of Reform," *China Quarterly*, no. 118 (June 1989): 242–64.

Walder, Andrew G. "Property Rights and Stratification in Socialist Redistributive Economies," *American Sociological Review* 57, no. 4 (August 1992): 524–39.

Walder, Andrew G. and Jean C. Oi, eds. *Property Rights and Economic Reform in China*. Stanford: Stanford University Press, 1999.

Walter, Carl E. and Fraser J.T. Howie. *Privatizing China: Inside China's Stock Markets*. Singapore: Wiley, 2nd ed., 2006.

Wang Lianzhou and Li Cheng. *Fengfeng Yuyu Zhengquan Fa* [The Difficulties and Hardships Surrounding the Securities Law]. Shanghai: Shanghai sanlian chubanshe, 2000.

Wank, David L. *Commodifying Communism: Business, Trust, and Politics in a Chinese City*. New York: Cambridge University Press, 1999.

Wedeman, Andrew. "The Intensification of Corruption in China," *China Quarterly*, no. 180 (December 2004): 895–921.

Weller, Robert P. and Jiansheng Li. "From State-Owned Enterprise to Joint Venture: A Case Study of the Crisis in Urban Social Services," *China Journal*, no. 43 (January 2000): 83–99.

White, Gordon. "Social Security Reforms in China: Towards an East Asian Model?" pp. 175–97, in Roger Goodman, Gordon White, and Huck-ju Kwon, eds., *The East Asian Welfare Model: Welfare Orientalism and the State*. New York: Routledge, 1998.

Whiting, Susan H. *Power and Wealth in Rural China: The Political Economy of Institutional Change*. New York: Cambridge University Press, 2001.

Wong, Christine P.W. "Central-Local Relations in an Era of Fiscal Decline: The Paradox of Fiscal Decentralization in China," *China Quarterly*, no. 128 (December 1991): 691–715.

Woo, Wing Thye. "The Real Reasons for China's Growth," *China Journal*, no. 41 (January 1999): 115–37.

Woodard, Kim and Anita Qingli Wang. "Acquisitions in China: A View of the Field," *China Business Review* 31, no. 6 (November/December 2004): 34–38.

Wu Jinglian. *Dangdai Zhongguo Jingji Gaige* [Modern China's Economic Reforms]. Shanghai: Shanghai yuandong chubanshe, 2004.

Wu, Jinglian. *Understanding and Interpreting Chinese Economic Reform*. Mason, OH: Thomson, 2005.

Yang, Dali. *Beyond Beijing: Liberalization and the Regions in China*. New York: Routledge, 1997.

Yang, Dali L. *Remaking the Chinese Leviathan: Market Transition and the Politics of Governance in China*. Stanford: Stanford University Press, 2004.

Yang Yiyong et al. *Gongping Yu Xiaolü* [Equality and Efficiency]. Beijing: Jinri Zhongguo chubanshe, 1997.

Yu Shizhang, ed. *Wenzhou Gaige Moshi Yanxin Yingxiang* [New Reflections on Wenzhou's Reform Model].Wenzhou: Zhonggong Wenzhou shiwei xuanchuangu, 1989.

Yuan Enzhen, ed. *Wenzhou Moshi Yu Fuyu Zhilu* [The Wenzhou Model and the Road Toward Affluence]. Shanghai: Shanghai shehui kexueyuan chubanshe, 1987.

Yuan Jian. *Zhongguo Zhengquan Shichang Pipan* [Criticism of China's Securities Markets]. Beijing: Zhongguo shehui kexue chubanshe, 2004.

Yusuf, Shahid, Kaoru Nabeshima, and Dwight H. Perkins. *Under New Ownership: Privatizing China's State-Owned Enterprises*. Stanford: Stanford University Press, 2006.

Zeng, Jin. "Performing Privatization—The Restructuring of Small and Medium Public Enterprises in China," Ph.D. diss., Johns Hopkins University, 2007.

Zhang, Xianchu and Charles D. Booth. "Chinese Bankruptcy Law in an Emerging Market Economy: The Shenzhen Experience," *Columbia Journal of Asian Law* 15, no.1 (Fall 2001): 1–32.

Zhang Zhouji, "Guanyu Shehui Baozhang Tixi Jianshe Wenti" [On the Question of the Construction of a Social Security System], *Zhonggong Zhongyang Dangxiao Baogao Xuan* [Selections from Reports of the Central Party School of the Chinese Communist Party], no. 10 (May 2004): 1–11.

Zheng, Yongnian. *Globalization and State Transformation in China*. New York: Cambridge University Press, 2004.

Zuo Min and Bo Hu. "Woguo Shangshi Gongsi Guanlian Jiaoyi Xingwei Yanjiu" [Research on Related-Party Transactions of Listed Firms in China], *Jingji Wenti* [Economic Problems], no. 11 (2001): 27–28.

Zweig, David. *Internationalizing China: Domestic Interests and Global Linkages*. Ithaca, NY: Cornell University Press, 2002.

Index

RECENT PUBLICATIONS OF THE WALTER H. SHORENSTEIN ASIA-PACIFIC RESEARCH CENTER

BOOKS (distributed by the Brookings Institution Press)

Karen Eggleston and Shripad Tuljapurkar, eds. *Aging Asia: The Economic and Social Implications of Rapid Demographic Change in China, Japan and South Korea.* Stanford, CA: Walter H. Shorenstein Asia-Pacific Research Center, 2010.

Rafiq Dossani, Daniel C. Sneider, and Vikram Sood, eds. *Does South Asia Exist? Prospects for Regional Integration.* Stanford, CA: Walter H. Shorenstein Asia-Pacific Research Center, 2010.

Jean C. Oi, Scott Rozelle, and Xueguang Zhou. *Growing Pains: Tensions and Opportunity in China's Transition.* Stanford, CA: Walter H. Shorenstein Asia-Pacific Research Center, 2010.

Karen Eggleston, ed. *Prescribing Cultures and Pharmaceutical Policy in the Asia-Pacific.* Stanford, CA: Walter H. Shorenstein Asia-Pacific Research Center, 2009.

Donald A. L. Macintyre, Daniel C. Sneider, and Gi-Wook Shin, eds. *First Drafts of Korea: The U.S. Media and Perceptions of the Last Cold War Frontier.* Stanford, CA: Walter H. Shorenstein Asia-Pacific Research Center, 2009.

Steven Reed, Kenneth Mori McElwain, and Kay Shimizu, eds. *Political Change in Japan: Electoral Behavior, Party Realignment, and the Koizumi Reforms.* Stanford, CA: Walter H. Shorenstein Asia-Pacific Research Center, 2009.

Donald K. Emmerson. *Hard Choices: Security, Democracy, and Regionalism in Southeast Asia.* Stanford, CA: Walter H. Shorenstein Asia-Pacific Research Center, 2008.

Henry S. Rowen, Marguerite Gong Hancock, and William F. Miller, eds. *Greater China's Quest for Innovation.* Stanford, CA: Walter H. Shorenstein Asia-Pacific Research Center, 2008.

Gi-Wook Shin and Daniel C. Sneider, eds. *Cross Currents: Regionalism and Nationalism in Northeast Asia.* Stanford, CA: Walter H. Shorenstein Asia-Pacific Research Center, 2007.

Stella R. Quah, ed. *Crisis Preparedness: Asia and the Global Governance of Epidemics*. Stanford, CA: Walter H. Shorenstein Asia-Pacific Research Center, 2007.

Philip W. Yun and Gi-Wook Shin, eds. *North Korea: 2005 and Beyond*. Stanford, CA: Walter H. Shorenstein Asia-Pacific Research Center, 2006.

Jongryn Mo and Daniel I. Okimoto, eds. *From Crisis to Opportunity: Financial Globalization and East Asian Capitalism*. Stanford, CA: Walter H. Shorenstein Asia-Pacific Research Center, 2006.

Michael H. Armacost and Daniel I. Okimoto, eds. *The Future of America's Alliances in Northeast Asia*. Stanford, CA: Walter H. Shorenstein Asia-Pacific Research Center, 2004.

Henry S. Rowen and Sangmok Suh, eds. *To the Brink of Peace: New Challenges in Inter-Korean Economic Cooperation and Integration*. Stanford, CA: Walter H. Shorenstein Asia-Pacific Research Center, 2001.

STUDIES OF THE WALTER H. SHORENSTEIN ASIA-PACIFIC RESEARCH CENTER
(published with Stanford University Press)

Yongshun Cai. *Collective Resistance in China: Why Popular Protests Succeed or Fail*. Stanford, CA: Stanford University Press, 2010.

Gi-Wook Shin. *One Alliance, Two Lenses: U.S.-Korea Relations in a New Era*. Stanford, CA: Stanford University Press, 2010.

Jean Oi and Nara Dillon, eds. *At the Crossroads of Empires: Middlemen, Social Networks, and State-building in Republican Shanghai*. Stanford, CA: Stanford University Press, 2007.

Henry S. Rowen, Marguerite Gong Hancock, and William F. Miller, eds. *Making IT: The Rise of Asia in High Tech*. Stanford, CA: Stanford University Press, 2006.

Gi-Wook Shin. *Ethnic Nationalism in Korea: Genealogy, Politics, and Legacy*. Stanford, CA: Stanford University Press, 2006.

Andrew Walder, Joseph Esherick, and Paul Pickowicz, eds. *The Chinese Cultural Revolution as History*. Stanford, CA: Stanford University Press, 2006.

Rafiq Dossani and Henry S. Rowen, eds. *Prospects for Peace in South Asia*. Stanford, CA: Stanford University Press, 2005.